AF842339

THE RIGHT TO THE CONTINUOUS IMPROVEMENT OF LIVING CONDITIONS

What does the right to the continuous improvement of living conditions in Article 11(1) of the International Covenant on Economic, Social and Cultural Rights really mean and how can it contribute to social change? The book explores how this underdeveloped right can have valuable application in response to global problems of poverty, inequality and climate destruction, through an in-depth consideration of its meaning.

The book seeks to interpret and give meaning to the right as a legal standard, giving it practical value for those whose living conditions are inadequate. It locates the right within broader philosophical and political debates, whilst also assessing the challenges to its realisation. It also explores how the right relates to human rights more generally and considers its application to issues of gender, care and the rights of Indigenous peoples. The contributors deeply probe the meaning of 'living conditions', suggesting that these are something more than the basic rights to housing, water, food and clothing. The chapters provide a range of doctrinal, historical and philosophical engagements through grounded analysis and imaginative interpretation.

With a foreword by Professor Sandra Liebenberg (former Member of the UN Committee on Economic, Social and Cultural Rights), the book includes chapters from renowned and emerging scholars working across disciplines from around the world.

Oñati International Series in Law and Society

A SERIES PUBLISHED FOR THE OÑATI INSTITUTE FOR THE SOCIOLOGY OF LAW

Recent titles in this series

Criminologies of the Military: Militarism, National Security and Justice
Edited by Andrew Goldsmith and Ben Wadham

Law and the Precarious Home: Socio Legal Perspectives on the Home in Insecure Times
Edited by Helen Carr, Brendan Edgeworth and Caroline Hunter

Collective Bargaining and Collective Action: Labour Agency and Governance in the 21st Century?
Edited by Julia López López

Fundamental Rights and Legal Consequences of Criminal Conviction
Edited Sonja Meijer, Harry Annison and Ailbhe O'Loughlin

Digital Family Justice: From Alternative Dispute Resolution to Online Dispute Resolution?
Edited by Mavis Maclean and Bregje Dijksterhuis

The Legacies of Institutionalisation: Disability, Law and Policy in the 'Deinstitutionalised' Community
Edited by Claire Spivakovsky, Linda Steele and Penelope Weller

Gender and Careers in the Legal Academy
Edited by Ulrike Schultz, Gisela Shaw, Margaret Thornton and Rosemary Auchmuty

Contesting Austerity: A Socio-Legal Inquiry
Edited by Anuscheh Farahat and Xabier Arzoz

The Right to the Continuous Improvement of Living Conditions: Responding to Complex Global Challenges
Edited by Jessie Hohmann and Beth Goldblatt

For the complete list of titles in this series, see 'Oñati International Series in Law and Society' link at www.bloomsburyprofessional.com/uk/series/onati-international-series-in-law-and-society

The Right to the Continuous Improvement of Living Conditions

Responding to Complex Global Challenges

Edited by
Jessie Hohmann and Beth Goldblatt

Oñati International Series in Law and Society

A SERIES PUBLISHED FOR THE OÑATI INSTITUTE FOR THE SOCIOLOGY OF LAW

•HART•

OXFORD • LONDON • NEW YORK • NEW DELHI • SYDNEY

HART PUBLISHING

Bloomsbury Publishing Plc

Kemp House, Chawley Park, Cumnor Hill, Oxford, OX2 9PH, UK

1385 Broadway, New York, NY 10018, USA

29 Earlsfort Terrace, Dublin 2, Ireland

First published in Great Britain 2021

A catalogue record for this book is available from the British Library.

Library of Congress Cataloging-in-Publication data

Names: Hohmann, Jessie, editor. | Goldblatt, Beth, editor.

Title: The right to the continuous improvement of living conditions : responding to complex global challenges / edited by Jessie Hohmann and Beth Goldblatt.

Description: Oxford, UK ; New York, NY : Hart Publishing, an imprint of Bloomsbury Publishing, 2021. | Series: Oñati international series in law and society | Includes bibliographical references and index.

Identifiers: LCCN 2021033266 (print) | LCCN 2021033267 (ebook) | ISBN 9781509947836 (hardback) | ISBN 9781509947874 (paperback) | ISBN 9781509947850 (pdf) | ISBN 9781509947843 (Epub)

Subjects: LCSH: Human rights. | International law and human rights. | Social rights. | International Covenant on Economic, Social, and Cultural Rights (1966 December 16) | Economic rights. | Cultural policy.

Classification: LCC KZ1266 .R54 2021 (print) | LCC KZ1266 (ebook) | DDC 341.4/8—dc23

LC record available at https://lccn.loc.gov/2021033266

LC ebook record available at https://lccn.loc.gov/2021033267

ISBN: HB: 978-1-50994-783-6
ePDF: 978-1-50994-785-0
ePub: 978-1-50994-784-3

Typeset by Compuscript Ltd, Shannon

Foreword

WHAT CONSTITUTES A good life and how should it be pursued? This profound question is particularly salient as we confront the multiple crises of climate change and environmental destruction, burgeoning inequality and the havoc wreaked by the Covid pandemic on human livelihoods, social systems and well-being. But does human rights law and practice offer any answers or ways to approach this question, or is it best posed in other epistemological domains?

Within international human rights law, the right that comes closest to the concerns raised by this question, is the right of everyone to the 'continuous improvement of living conditions' (CILC) in Article 11 of the International Covenant on Economic, Social and Cultural Rights (ICESCR). The right to CILC is nestled alongside the right to an adequate standard of living, including adequate food, clothing, housing and, through interpretative derivation, the right to water.

This right has the potential to expand the horizons of economic, social and cultural rights beyond individual rights to encompass the broader frame of the conditions of life necessary for human flourishing. Despite this potential, it has been sorely neglected in the practice of the Committee on Economic, Social and Cultural Rights and in scholarship generally.

This important collection of essays travels a considerable distance to remedy this neglect. The authors traverse the history and nature of the right, its relationship with other rights and doctrinal concepts both within and beyond the ICESCR, its potential role in poverty reduction, and its relationship with concepts of a good life in Indigenous knowledge systems, feminist theory and children's rights. A number of essays offer searing critiques of the threats posed by contemporary neoliberal economic policies to human well-being, agency, and ability to sustain caring and supportive communal relationships. Questions are posed regarding the limits of the notion of 'continuous improvement' in the light of the finite and strained ecological resources of our planet and our responsibility to future generations. The potential and limitations of existing modalities for realising the right, such as the duty of international assistance and cooperation and the Sustainable Development Goals, are explored.

The book skilfully interweaves utopian visions of what the right could be whilst simultaneously uncovering strategic pathways for its advancement. This is the first scholarly work devoted to the exploration of the right to CILC. The editors and authors have succeeded brilliantly in demonstrating the untapped potential of human rights law to offer answers to the question posed at the outset. For this, they deserve our gratitude and congratulations.

Sandra Liebenberg
Distinguished Professor and H.F. Oppenheimer Chair in Human Rights Law, Stellenbosch University
Former Vice-Chair, UN Committee on Economic, Social and Cultural Rights

Acknowledgements

We began this project hoping to bring together innovative social and economic rights scholars to develop the underexplored right to the continuous improvement of living conditions at a workshop at the International Institute for the Sociology of Law in Oñati, Spain in June 2020. Like so many other events, the workshop had to be cancelled due to the Covid-19 pandemic; however, our work continued remotely. We wish to thank the Institute for its generous support for the planned workshop. We also thank the editors of the Oñati International Series in Law and Society, published by Hart, for including this book in the series despite the fact that the workshop never took place as envisaged. We are so grateful to our authors for their willingness to continue with this project during the many challenges of 2020 and for their participation in the virtual mini-conference held in place of the workshop across so many time zones. We owe special thanks to Professor Sandra Liebenberg. Professor Liebenberg kindly wrote the Foreword and contributed so generously by reading every chapter closely and providing feedback to all of us at the conference. We are enormously grateful to her for her expertise and commitment to this project. We acknowledge the support of the Faculty of Law at the University of Technology Sydney for research assistance. Jessie was the recipient of an Independent Social Research Foundation Early Career Fellowship in 2017–18. This research time facilitated the preliminary research on the topic, as well as the initial collaboration with Beth. We also wish to thank Rosie Mearns and the team at Hart for their professionalism and enthusiasm for this book. We are grateful to our families for their love, care and support.

The editors' research and writing of this book took place on the Lands of the Bidjigal and Gadigal Peoples of the Eora Nation and on the lands of the Dharawal People, whose sovereignty was never ceded. We pay our respects to their elders past, present, and emerging. We also know that many of our contributors are situated on Indigenous lands, and we acknowledge those Peoples, and pay our respects to them.

Contents

Notes on Contributors

Juan Pablo Bohoslavsky was the United Nations Independent Expert on Debt and Human Rights from 2014 to 2020. He previously worked at UNCTAD and as a consultant for the OHCHR, ECLAC and the Argentine State. He co-edited *Pinochet's Economic Accomplices: An Unequal Country by Force* (Lexington 2020) with K Fernández and S Smart, and *Sovereign Debt Crises: What have we Learned?* (CUP 2017) with K Raffer.

Meghan Campbell is a Senior Lecturer at the University of Birmingham and the Deputy Director of the Oxford Human Rights Hub. Her monograph *Women, Poverty, Equality* (Hart 2018) explores how the Committee on the Elimination of Discrimination against Women (CEDAW) can redress women's poverty.

Francisco Cantamutto is Associate Researcher at the National Council of Scientific and Technical Research (CONICET), based in the Southern Institute of Economic and Social Research (IIESS) of the National University of the South (UNS), Argentina. He is also Assistant Professor of Principles of Economics at the same University. He is a member of the Critical Economics Society (SEC), and part of the editorial board of its journal, Cuadernos de Economía Crítica (CEC). He specialises in political disputes on the development patterns in contemporary Latin America, particularly in Argentina.

Ruth Fletcher is a Senior Lecturer at the School of Law, Queen Mary University of London. She has published widely in the fields of socio-legal studies, feminist theory and health law, with a particular focus on law and reproduction. She is an editor of the journal *Feminist Legal Studies* and co-editor of *ReValuing Care in Theory, Law and Policy* with Rosie Harding and Chris Beasley (Routledge 2017).

Sandra Fredman is Professor of the Laws of the British Commonwealth and the USA at the University of Oxford. She is a Fellow of the British Academy and Queen's Council (honoris causa). She has published widely and has numerous peer reviewed publications in the fields of gender equality, labour law and human rights. Her books include *Comparative Human Rights* (OUP 2018); *Human Rights Transformed* (OUP 2008); *Discrimination Law* 2nd edn (OUP 2011); and *Women and the Law* (OUP 1997)

Beth Goldblatt is Professor in the Faculty of Law at the University of Technology Sydney, Australia and Visiting Professor of the School of Law at the University of the Witwatersrand, South Africa. Her work focuses on equality, human rights and feminist theory. She is the author of *Developing the Right to Social Security – A Gender Perspective* (Routledge 2015) and co-editor of *Women's Rights to*

Social Security and Social Protection with Lucie Lamarche (Hart 2014) and *Women's Social and Economic Rights – Developments in South Africa* with Kirsty McLean (Juta 2011).

Luke D Graham is a Lecturer in Law at Coventry University, UK. His Economic and Social Research Council funded PhD, undertaken at Lancaster University, applied an economic, social and cultural rights framework to destitution in the UK. A monograph based on this thesis titled *International Human Rights Law and Destitution: An Economic, Social and Cultural Rights Perspective* is under contract with the Routledge Research Series in Human Rights and is expected for publication in 2022.

Jeffery G Hewitt is mixed-descent Cree and an Assistant Professor at Osgoode Hall Law School, York University, Canada. His research interests include Indigenous legal orders and governance, constitutional law, and visual legal studies. Jeffery holds an LLB and LLM from Osgoode Hall Law School and was called to the Bar in Ontario in 1998. Jeffery is past-President of the Indigenous Bar Association of Canada and served on various boards, including most recently the National Theatre School of Canada.

Jessie Hohmann is Associate Professor in the Faculty of Law, University of Technology Sydney. She is an acknowledged expert on the right to housing in international law, and her publications include *The Right to Housing: Law, Concepts, Possibilities* (Hart 2013). Her research also engages with the material culture, objects and materiality of international law, and with Indigenous Peoples and international law.

Lucie Lamarche is a professor at the Faculty of Political Science and Law at Université du Québec à Montréal (UQAM), Canada. She teaches social protection, labour law, women's rights and human rights. She privileges approaches that combine both international and domestic perspectives. She is a member of the Royal Society of Canada and an administrator of the Québec Civil Rights and Liberties Association.

Naomi Lott is a Research Fellow in Law, Survivor Support and Children's Rights at the Rights Lab, University of Nottingham, UK. Her PhD research, funded by the Economic and Social Research Council and undertaken at the University of Nottingham, provided an in-depth examination of the child's right to play.

Isaac de Paz González is Research Professor of the Faculty of Law at the Autonomous University of Baja California, México. He is the author of *The Social Rights Jurisprudence in the Inter-American Court of Human Rights: Shadow and Light in International Human Rights* (Edward Elgar 2018). His research interests are social and Indigenous rights in Latin American constitutional courts and within the Inter-American system.

Sigrun I Skogly is Professor of Human Rights Law at Lancaster University, UK, and member of the Centre for International Law and Human Rights at Lancaster University Law School. She has worked extensively in the area of international human rights law obligations, particularly related to States' extra-territorial human rights obligations. She is the author of books and articles in this field, including *The Human Rights Obligations of the World Bank and the International Monetary Fund* (Cavendish 2001), and *Beyond National Borders: States' Human Rights Obligations in International Cooperation* (Intersentia 2006).

1

Introduction

Situating the Right to Continuous Improvement of Living Conditions and Considering its Interpretations and Applications

JESSIE HOHMANN AND BETH GOLDBLATT

I. INTRODUCTION

THIS BOOK EXPLORES the meaning, implications, and possibilities of the right to continuous improvement of living conditions, contained in Article 11(1) of the International Covenant on Economic, Social and Cultural Rights (ICESCR).[1] We ask how the right can be unpacked, interpreted, and applied to respond to complex problems of poverty, inequality, environmental destruction and injustice. As we worked on the chapters, we watched as the unfolding Covid-19 pandemic not only took millions of lives, but worsened poverty and increased joblessness for millions around the world.[2] It has exposed health, housing, educational and many other inequalities, and deepened imbalances between countries of the global North and South in their capacity to weather economic crises and support their citizens.[3] At the same time, the

[1] International Covenant on Economic, Social and Cultural Rights, 16 December 1996, 993 UNTS 3.

[2] UNCESCR, 'Statement on the coronavirus disease (COVID-19) pandemic and economic, social and cultural rights' (17 April 2020) UN Doc E/C.12/2020/1.

[3] C Bambra et al, 'The Covid-19 Pandemic and Health Inequalities' (2020) 74 *Journal of Epidemiology and Community Health* 964; S Nanda, 'Inequalities and Covid-19' in JM Ryan (ed), *Covid-19: Volumes I and II* (Routledge 2020) 109.

bigger existential threat caused by human damage to the climate looms large in its present and future impacts.[4]

What might the right to continuous improvement of living conditions mean in such a context? How should it be understood on a theoretical and philosophical level? And how should it be translated into actual social change? In a world of unsustainable, yet vastly unequal, production and consumption, the right to the continuous improvement of living conditions can seem both naively and dangerously rapacious. At the same time, considering and seeking to embed this right into human rights in a way that responds meaningfully to these problems offers a potential break from a never-ending economic growth model to more sustainable ideas of what it means to be human.

We can use the right to continuous improvement of living conditions as a lens to focus attention both on this marginalised right, and on a number of questions that underlie its content, scope and potential for realisation. Examining the right gives us new ways in which to move beyond polarised debates in human rights. This is particularly the case for debates on whether human rights have anything to offer on questions of economic equality and distributive justice, and whether economic, social and cultural rights are concerned only with minimum standards, or with human flourishing. Considering the right forces us to examine a number of pressing and fundamental socio-legal questions – from why we have lost or turned away from utopian projects in international law, to issues of distributive justice, to fundamental issues of what constitutes a good life and a just international order. To address such questions, we need radical new ways of thinking about old problems, institutions and arrangements, which draw on the grounded and socially embedded work of scholars.

This collection is thus both a practical project with tangible application in developing the content of the right toward its realisation, and an imaginative project that involves critical exploration of what this right means for our understanding of human rights as a broader goal.

In this introductory chapter we situate the right, and the discussions it prompts, both within human rights scholarship, and within international and regional human rights instruments. Following this contextualisation, we draw together some key themes that emerge from the chapters in the collection that seek to recover the right from its largely forgotten status. These themes provide shape to this interpretive project and prompt important future research agendas on the right to continuous improvement of living conditions. We address the following: First, the question of how to interpret this right going forward, within the context of the ICESCR, human rights as a whole, and the wider architecture of international ordering such as through the international

[4] United Nations Human Rights Council, 'Human rights and climate change' (12 July 2019) A/HRC/RES/41/21; N Islam and J Winkel, 'Climate Change and Social Inequality', UN Department of Economic and Social Affairs (DESA 2017) Working Papers, No 152.

financial institutions. Second, we draw out the complex issue of resources. This involves both a fine-grained look at the measurement of poverty, for instance, and a wider discussion of the pressing need to reconsider the current global economic system, in which the structural injustice of human rights violation unfolds. A third theme is the need to define 'living conditions' and consider how an expansive meaning informs the right. A final theme we draw out is direction, trajectory and (forward) movement in human rights realisation, and its relation to recovering the right to continuous improvement of living conditions' radical potential in human rights thought and practice. The right invites us to re-consider questions of the history, current interpretations and critical understandings of human rights, and their (utopian) futures. We conclude with some suggested future directions for work on this important right.

II. SITUATING THE RIGHT

Article 11(1) enshrines a right to an adequate standard of living in the following terms:

> The States Parties to the Present Covenant recognize the right of everyone to an adequate standard of living for himself and his family, including adequate food, clothing and housing, *and to the continuous improvement of living conditions*. The States Parties will take appropriate steps to ensure the realization of this right, recognizing to this effect the essential importance of international co-operation based on free consent. (Emphasis added)

Article 11(1) has been interpreted as an umbrella for a number of separate rights. In particular, food and housing have received significant attention,[5]

[5] On the right to food see CESCR, 'General Comment No. 12: The Right to Adequate Food (Art. 11)' (12 May 1999) UN Doc E/C.12/1999/5; Food and Agriculture Organization of the United Nations (ed), *The Right to Food in Theory and Practice* (FAO 1998); B Saul, D Kinley and J Mowbray, *The International Covenant on Economic, Social and Cultural Rights: Commentary, Cases, and Materials* (OUP 2004) 867–923; OHCHR, Special Rapporteur on the Right to Food <https://www.ohchr.org/EN/Issues/Food/Pages/FoodIndex.aspx> accessed 16 March 2021. On the right to housing see CESCR, 'General Comment No. 4: The Right to Adequate Housing (Art. 11(1) of the Covenant)' (13 December 1991) UN Doc E/1992/23; CESCR, 'General Comment No. 7: The Right to Adequate Housing (Art. 11.1): Forced Evictions', UN Doc E/1998/22; OHCHR, Special Rapporteur on Adequate Housing as a Component of the Right to an Adequate Standard of Living, and on the Right to Non-discrimination in this context, <https://www.ohchr.org/en/issues/housing/pages/housingindex.aspx> accessed 16 March 2021; J Hohmann, *The Right to Housing: Law, Concepts, Possibilities* (Hart 2013). Although the right to clothing has received little attention from the CESCR or other UN actors, there has been some engagement with it: S James, *A Forgotten Right? The Right to Clothing in the Universal Declaration of Human Rights*, (2008), <http://citeseerx.ist.psu.edu/viewdoc/download?doi=10.1.1.615.860&rep=rep1&type=pdf#page=14> accessed 7 February 2020; A Shahvisi, E Meskele and G Davey, *A Human Right to Shoes? Establishing Rights and Duties in the Prevention and Treatment of Podoconiosis* (2018) 20 *Health and Human Rights Journal* 53; Saul, Mowbray and Kinley, ibid 924–27.

as has an implied right to water and sanitation.[6] The final sentence of the right elaborates State obligations for realising the right, including the necessity of action taken in concert, beyond national borders. However, the last clause of the first sentence – the right to the continuous improvement of living conditions – has been largely ignored. It has not yet received extensive or substantive scholarly engagement, or been fleshed out by the relevant human rights bodies, despite otherwise exponential growth in the scholarship and practice on economic and social rights.

A. Consideration of the Right within Human Rights Scholarship

Explicit academic and scholarly attention to the right has been limited to date. This is the case across the leading texts, many of which should be otherwise commended for their rigorous interpretation and analysis of Article 11. For example, a leading Commentary on the ICESCR mentions the right only in a few sentences, and does not engage at all with its content, scope or meaning.[7] Recent handbooks have not picked up the right for analysis.[8] Books specifically on economic, social and cultural rights also fail to engage in a sustained way with this clause,[9] and more general textbooks on human rights have overlooked it.[10] Even those authors who focus specifically on the right to an adequate standard of living, doing much to advance understanding of Article 11, regularly omit any consideration of the right to continuous improvement of living conditions. For example, Eide, a leading expert on the right to an adequate standard of living,

[6] See eg CESCR, 'General Comment No. 15: The Right to Water (Arts. 11 and 12 of the Covenant)' (20 January 2003) UN Doc E/C.12/2002/11; M Langford and AFS Russell (eds), *The Human Right to Water: Theory, Practice and Prospects* (CUP 2017); I Winkler, *The Human Right to Water: Significance, Legal Status and Implications for Water Allocation* (Hart 2012); N Singh (ed), *The Human Right to Water: From Concept to Reality* (Springer 2016); S Takele Bulto, *The Extraterritorial Application of the Human Right to Water in Africa* (CUP 2014).

[7] Saul, Kinley and Mowbray (n 5) 862–63.

[8] See J Dugard et al (eds), *Research Handbook on Economic, Social and Cultural Rights as Human Rights* (Elgar 2020); C Binder et al (eds), *Research Handbook on International Law and Social Rights* (Elgar 2020).

[9] See eg M Ssenyonjo, *Economic, Social and Cultural Rights in International Law* 2nd edn (Hart 2016); K Young (ed), *The Future of Economic and Social Rights* (CUP 2019); P O'Connell, *Vindicating Socio-Economic Rights: International Standards and Comparative Experiences* (Routledge 2012); G MacNaughton and D Frey (eds), *Economic and Social Rights in a Neoliberal World* (CUP 2018); J Wills, *Contesting World Order? Socioeconomic Rights and Global Justice Movements* (CUP 2017).

[10] Neither Steiner and Alston's ground-breaking *International Human Rights in Context* nor its successor, engage with the right, although Alston served as the Chair of the CESCR during the years of its most explicit engagement with the right. See HJ Steiner and P Alston, *International Human Rights in Context* (OUP 1996) and P Alston and R Goodman, *International Human Rights* (OUP 2012). It is also omitted from de Schutter's exacting texts. See O de Schutter, *International Human Rights Law: Cases, Materials and Commentary* (CUP 2010); O de Schutter, *International Human Rights Law: Cases, Materials and Commentary* 2nd edn (CUP 2014).

has not referred to the right as a substantive head of Article 11 in his work.[11] Moreover, a number of important works on the link between human rights and development, a logical area in which to initiate a discussion, particularly given the definition of development as 'the right of all peoples and individuals to the constant improvement of their well-being'[12] – do not engage with the right.[13]

There are important, if limited, exceptions to this neglect. Craven, an early commentator on the ICESCR, includes discussion of the drafting history of the clause in his authoritative text,[14] and Haugen includes a short, but specific, analysis, concluding that continuous improvement of living conditions is only an element of the right to an adequate standard of living, rather than a substantive right like food, clothing or housing.[15] Haugen's analysis is based on the grammar of the clause, read in conjunction with the fact that the right 'has never appeared in the literature as a substantive human right'.[16] Salomon engages with the right in critiquing minimalist approaches to economic, social and cultural rights.[17] And the previous United Nations Independent Expert on Foreign Debt and Human Rights began to engage with the right in the context of mass consumption, and the failure of exponential economic growth to fulfil human rights, in 2019.[18]

An important contribution considering the meaning of the right has also been made by Löfquist.[19] In a 2011 article on climate change, justice and the

[11] A Eide, 'Adequate Standard of Living' in D Moeckli, S Shah and S Sivakumaran (eds), *International Human Rights Law* 2nd edn (OUP 2014) 195, 195 (writing '[t]his chapter considers the right to an adequate standard of living and its components, namely, the rights to food, housing and health').

[12] UNHRC, *Right to Development: Report of the High-level Task Force on the Implementation of the Right to Development on its Sixth Session*, UN Doc A/ HRC/15/WG.2/TF/2/Add.2, Annex, Implementation of the Right to Development: Attributes, Criteria, Sub-criteria and Indicators, 8 (8 March 2010).

[13] See eg P Alston and M Robinson (eds), *Human Rights and Development: Towards Mutual Reinforcement* (OUP 2005). Vanderbogaerde argues that all elements of a right to development are already present in international human rights. While invoking the definition of the High-level Task Force (n 12), he makes no reference to the right to continuous improvement under ICESCR, and only passing reference to the right to an adequate standard of living. All discussion of improvement is seen through the lens of Article 2(1)'s obligation of progressive realisation. See A Vanderbogaerde, 'The Right to Development in International Human Rights Law: A Call for its Dissolution' (2013) 21 *Netherlands Quarterly of Human Rights* 187, 197.

[14] M Craven, *The International Covenant on Economic, Social and Cultural Rights: A Perspective on its Development* (OUP 1995) 94–95.

[15] HM Haugen *The Right to Food and the TRIPS Agreement: With A Particular Emphasis on Developing Countries' Measures for Food Production and Distribution* (Brill 2007) 122–23.

[16] ibid 122.

[17] M Salomon, 'Why Should it Matter that Others Have More? Poverty, Inequality, and the Potential of International Human Rights Law' (2011) 37 *Review of International Studies* 2137.

[18] See UNOHCHR, End of Mission Statement by the Independent Expert on the Effects of Foreign Debt and other Related International Financial Obligations of States on the Full Enjoyment of all Human Rights, Particularly Economic, Social and Cultural Rights, Juan Pablo Bohoslavsky, on his Visit to Bolivia (6–15 May 2019) <https://www.ohchr.org/EN/NewsEvents/Pages/DisplayNews.aspx?NewsID=24607&LangID=E> accessed 16 March 2021.

[19] L Löfquist, 'Climate Change, Justice and the Right to Development' (2011) 7(3) *Journal of Global Ethics* 251.

right to development, he situated the central aspect of the right to development (drawing from the Preamble of the Declaration on the Right to Development) as a 'comprehensive economic, social, cultural and political process, which aims at the constant improvement of the well-being of the entire population and of all individuals'.[20] Although Löfquist makes only passing reference to ICESCR Article 11(1), concentrating instead on continuous improvement in the definition of the right to development, he proceeds to make a careful and close analysis of a right to continuous improvement of living conditions in a world of finite resources.[21] Even if, Löfquist argues, the right to continuous improvement of living conditions can be achieved sustainably – through for example an interpretation that focuses on well-being, rather than material standards (which he argues it can), there still remains a problem. This is the issue of who the right holder is: everyone, only some below a certain threshold, or no one? Löfquist seeks to find a solution to this issue that protects the universality of human rights, while at the same time giving extra weight to the needs of the poorest.[22] For Löfquist, there is no adequate solution to this problem in ethical and analytical terms: all three categories of rights-holder are, for him, problematic. He thus concludes that the Covenant, and the Declaration on the Right to Development, overreach in setting out such a right:

> There is no need to claim that we have a right to an ever-increasing improvement. It is enough to claim that every person should have a right to reach a certain minimum level of well-being; an idea that is more in line with the Declaration from 1948, which stresses that we only have a right to an adequate standard of living.[23]

While Löfquist's analysis rejects the right to continuous improvement of living conditions, it nevertheless provides one of the most explicit analyses of the right in scholarship to date.[24]

Given that the references to, and analyses of, the right to continuous improvement of living conditions can only be characterised as embryonic, the chapters in this collection significantly expand our understanding of the right, and its implications and importance.

B. The Centrality of the Right to the Human Rights Project

Despite the general neglect of the right to continuous improvement of living conditions, the twinned projects of improved standards of living and human

[20] UNGA Res 41/128 (4 December 1986), preamble.

[21] Löfquist is primarily concerned with the issue of energy use and its effects on climate change in this respect. However, his analysis has broader relevance to the question of finite resources and environmental degradation.

[22] Löfquist (n 19) 255–56.

[23] ibid 259.

[24] The argument also relates in important ways to broader debates about minimum core obligations and progressive realisation of ICESCR rights, as discussed in a number of chapters in this volume. See discussion below.

rights lie at the heart of the post-war UN project. While the right to continuous improvement of living conditions has become a marginal right, continuous improvement of living conditions was not a marginal concern in twentieth century international law. The presumption that a main goal for States was to continuously improve living conditions through, or by the realisation of, rights was a familiar one for international organisations and institutions. In fact, the right to continuous improvement of living conditions was axiomatic to a broader, social justice-regarding, international framework, as a close reading of a number of international and regional instruments shows.

i. International Instruments

To begin with, the link between human rights and better standards of living is explicit in both the Universal Declaration of Human Rights and in the United Nations Charter.[25]

A main aim of the United Nations is set out in the first preambular paragraph of its Charter, which opens: 'We the peoples of the United Nations, determined … to promote social progress and better standards of life in larger freedom.'[26] Article 55, on International Economic and Social Cooperation, is phrased:

> With a view to the creation of conditions of stability and well-being which are necessary for peaceful and friendly relations among nations based on respect for the principle of equal rights and self-determination of peoples, the United Nations shall promote:
>
> a. higher standards of living, full employment, and conditions of economic and social progress and development;
> b. solutions of international economic, social, health, and related problems; and international cultural and educational cooperation; and
> c. universal respect for, and observance of, human rights and fundamental freedoms for all without distinction as to race, sex, language, or religion.[27]

The Universal Declaration of Human Rights' (UDHR) 5th preambular paragraph, referring back to the UN Charter, states that:

> Whereas the peoples of the United Nations have in the Charter reaffirmed their faith in fundamental human rights, in the dignity and worth of the human person and in the equal rights of men and women and have determined to promote social progress and better standards of life in larger freedom.[28]

These foundational documents of the post-war international order are clearly premised on a mutually reinforcing relationship between better standards of living and human rights.

[25] UN, Charter of the United Nations, 24 October 1945, 1 UNTS XVI.
[26] ibid preamble.
[27] ibid Art 55.
[28] Universal Declaration of Human Rights (adopted 10 December 1948) UNGA Res 217 A(III), preamble.

A number of other international legal instruments also reflect this. For example, the Declaration of Philadelphia, concerning the aims and purposes of the International Labour Organization[29] (ILO) is similarly based on an underpinning assumption of continuous improvement of living conditions twinned with rights. One such framing is in Article III(e), which reads:

> III The Conference recognizes the solemn obligation of the International Labour Organization to further among the nations of the world programmes which will achieve:
>
> (e) the effective recognition of the right to collective bargaining, the cooperation of management and labour in the continuous improvement of productive efficiency, and the collaboration of workers and employers in the preparation and application of social and economic measures[30]

This theme remains current in the work of the ILO. The 2008 ILO Declaration on Social Justice for a Fair Globalization, for example, makes similar links between improvement of living conditions, social justice and fundamental rights,[31] though neither the Declaration of Philadelphia nor the 2008 Declaration on Social Justice use the term 'human rights'.

The United Nations General Assembly has also generated a number of important declarations which interlace improved living conditions and rights. For example, the Declaration on the Right to Social Progress and Development of 1969:[32]

> Social progress and development shall aim at the continuous raising of the material and spiritual standards of living of all members of society, with respect for and in compliance with human rights and fundamental freedoms, through the attainment of the following main goals:
>
> Art 10 … (c) The elimination of poverty; the assurance of a steady improvement in levels of living and of a just and equitable distribution of income.[33]

The 1986 Declaration on the Right to Development is also an important expression of the link between human rights and better standards of living, articulated strongly in a number of the preambular paragraphs, as well as infusing the text as a whole.[34] Here, development – in the sense of better living conditions – is sutured to human rights enjoyment and fulfilment. Indeed Saul, Kinley and Mowbray write, that, if not a central objective, then at least one intended consequence of the Declaration was to 'enhance the means, methods

[29] International Labour Organization, Declaration concerning the aims and purposes of the International Labour Organization (Declaration of Philadelphia), 10 May 1944.

[30] ibid Art III(e).

[31] ILO, Declaration on Social Justice for a Fair Globalization, 10 June 2008.

[32] UNGA Res 2542 (XXIV) 11 December 1969.

[33] ibid.

[34] (n 20) See eg Arts 1, 2, 3, 6, 8, 10.

and magnitude of international development assistance and cooperation in the realization of economic, social and cultural rights'.[35]

UN-led efforts to implement a right to development continue, and in 2010 the High Level Task Force on the Implementation of the Right to Development expressed the 'core norm' of the right to development as 'the right of all peoples and individuals to the constant improvement of their well-being and to a national and global enabling environment conducive to just, equitable, participatory and human-centered development respectful of all human rights'.[36] The definition of development contained in this document is 'the right of all peoples and individuals to the constant improvement of their well-being'.[37]

There are also links in international trade regimes. For example, the Marrakesh Agreement preamble lists 'raising standards of living' as an objective of economic activity under the WTO,[38] and one commentator has noted, in discussing the right to food and the WTO rules on agriculture, that a right to continuous improvement of living conditions 'could contribute to the harmonious interpretation of the trade and international human rights regimes'.[39]

Focusing specifically on the ICESCR, in addition to Article 11(1) a number of Articles contemplate material improvement as the foundation for realising a right. Art 11(2) on the right to be free from hunger is premised on State obligations to:

> 11(2)(a) improve methods of production, conservation and distribution of food by making full use of technical and scientific knowledge, by disseminating knowledge of nutrition and by developing or reforming agrarian systems in such a way as to achieve the most efficient development and utilization of natural resources.[40]

The right to the highest attainable standard of health also requires '[t]he improvement of all aspects of environmental and industrial hygiene',[41] while the right to education must be underpinned by an adequate standard of living for teachers: 'the material conditions of teaching staff shall be continuously improved'.[42]

[35] Saul, Kinley and Mowbray (n 5) 140.
[36] A/HRC/15/WG.2/TF/2/Add.2 (n 12) Annex at 8.
[37] ibid.
[38] Marrakesh Agreement Establishing the World Trade Organization, 15 April 1994, 1867 UNTS 154, preamble.
[39] R Ferguson, *The Right to Food and the World Trade Organization Rules on Agriculture* (Brill 2018) 118.
[40] ICESCR (n 1) Art 11(2)(a).
[41] ibid Art 12(2)(b).
[42] ibid Art 13(2)(e).

ii. Regional Legal Instruments

At the regional level, in the American Declaration on the Rights and Duties of Man[43] there is an explicit link between improvement of living conditions and rights within the right to education, which aims to 'prepare [a person] to attain a decent life, and to raise his standard of living, and to be a useful member of society'.[44] In addition, the right to 'betterment' of whole peoples was a common right in Latin American constitutions, informing the inclusion of social and economic rights in the UDHR.[45]

This is also true of the European Social Charter of 1961.[46] The preamble notes one of the aims of the Council of Europe:

> is the achievement of greater unity between its members for the purpose of safeguarding and realising the ideals and principles which are their common heritage and of facilitating their economic and social progress, in particular by the maintenance and further realisation of human rights and fundamental freedoms[47]

Here, economic and social progress will be secured by the realisation of human rights. The preamble also notes that States Parties are 'resolved to make every effort in common to improve the standard of living'.[48] These preambular paragraphs are repeated in the 1996 Revision to the Treaty.[49] The Preamble to the African Charter on Human and Peoples'. Rights reaffirms a pledge 'to achieve a better life for the peoples of Africa',[50] and the Phnom Penh Statement on the Adoption of the ASEAN Human Rights Declaration acknowledges the role of the ASEAN Intergovernmental Commission on Human Rights 'as a vehicle for progressive social development and justice, the full realization of human dignity and the attainment of a higher quality of life for ASEAN peoples'.[51] The ASEAN Human Rights Declaration, however, does not include a right that explicitly requires improvement, though it includes a right to development and a progressive obligations clause.[52] Finally, the Arab Charter on Human Rights,[53] adopted

[43] Inter-American Commission on Human Rights, American Declaration on the Rights and Duties of Man, 2 May 1948.

[44] ibid Art XII.

[45] See eg U Davy 'How Human Rights Shape Social Citizenship: On Citizenship and the Understanding of Economic and Social Rights' (2014) 13 *Washington University Global Studies Law Review* 201, 221.

[46] Council of Europe, European Social Charter, preamble, 18 October 1961, ETS No 035.

[47] ibid.

[48] ibid.

[49] Council of Europe, European Social Charter (Revised) preamble 5 March 1996, ETS No 163.

[50] Organization of African Unity, African Charter on Human and Peoples' Right (Banjul Charter) preamble 27 June 1981, CAB/LEG/67/3 rev 5, 21 ILM 58 (1982).

[51] Association of Southeast Asian Nations, ASEAN Human Rights Declaration and Phnom Penh Statement on the Adoption of the ASEAN Human Rights Declaration (February 2013) at 13, <https://www.asean.org/storage/images/ASEAN_RTK_2014/6_AHRD_Booklet.pdf> accessed 16 March 2021.

[52] Association of Southeast Asian Nations, ASEAN Human Rights Declaration, 18 November 2012, Arts 35–37 (right to development); Art 33 (obligations for economic, social and cultural rights).

[53] League of Arab States, Arab Charter on Human Rights, 15 September 1994.

in 2004, while self-consciously distinguishing itself from the UN Covenants and other regional sources, also opens in Article 1(1):

> Article 1 The present Charter seeks, within the context of the national identity of the Arab States and their sense of belonging to a common civilization, to achieve the following aims:
>
> 1. To place human rights at the centre of the key national concerns of Arab States, making them lofty and fundamental ideals that shape the will of the individual in Arab States and enable him to improve his life in accordance with noble human values.

Considering these legal sources, we can see that some frame better standards of living as necessary underpinnings for the realisation of rights. Conversely, some express the purpose of human rights as enabling a better life. Some see human rights and improved standards of living as *inherently* intertwined.

Continuous improvement of living conditions and the equitable distribution of the world's resources are, therefore, 'part of a much larger post-1945 international effort to situate the eradication of material deprivation within a process of human-centered development'.[54] A *right* to continuous improvement is certainly the most explicit link between human rights and improvement of living conditions, making this a right itself, but it is a small – if important – further step when viewed within this broader context.

Having established that the right to continuous improvement of living conditions is an integral right to the human rights project, while also a neglected one in the interpretative literature, in the next section we draw out four central themes that emerge from the chapters in this collection. These advance the project of giving meaning to the right to continuous improvement of living conditions, and point to a research agenda moving forward.

III. ORGANISING THEMES AND EMERGING IDEAS

A. Interpreting the Right

Pressing questions of interpretation face us in understanding the right to continuous improvement of living conditions since it has received only marginal attention to date. Fletcher's chapter (chapter thirteen) is a call to recognise and support this imaginative work. She reminds us that the work of imagining and actualising what rights might be is socially necessary labour, 'because rights struggle is one of the life-making activities that is routinely denigrated and devalued by the legal and other arrangements of our world'.[55]

[54] Salomon (n 17) 2152.
[55] Fletcher, chapter thirteen in this volume.

The *travaux préparatoires* provide some guidance on States Parties' understanding of the right at the time of drafting, as Hohmann (chapter two) shows, noting that the original emphasis for what ultimately became Article 11(1) was a right to continuous improvement of living conditions, rather than a list of social goods which are now usually foregrounded. Nevertheless, Hohmann notes, the delegates raised a number of interpretative issues which remain unanswered, such as who the rights holder is, and from what baseline improvement should be measured. Graham's chapter (chapter four) delves into both questions in interrogating the relationship between the right and poverty.

There are also important questions about the relationship between the right to continuous improvement of living conditions and other rights, both in the ICESCR and beyond it. Regarding the ICESCR, further work is needed to consider the relationship among the rights in Article 11: an adequate standard of living; food, clothing, housing; and the right to continuous improvement of living conditions, as Lott discusses (chapter seven); and the requirement of international cooperation, critically examined by Campbell (chapter three). The right prompts reflection on other ICESCR rights, too: rights to social security (discussed by Lamarche, chapter six), just and favourable conditions of work (discussed by Goldblatt, chapter eleven) as well as rights to health, education and culture, for example.

The right to continuous improvement of living conditions can help us to understand other rights. Lott (chapter seven) brings the right into dialogue with the also often forgotten right to play in the Convention on the Rights of the Child,[56] using her analysis of both rights to argue against a minimum 'set' of rights which are more important than others. De Paz González (chapter nine) sets out how the right might enrich the Inter-American Court's jurisprudence on social rights, economic equality and the 'vida digna', while Hewitt (chapter ten) brings into focus the potential of the right to critique the Canadian State's approach to its treaties with First Nations peoples. Skogly (chapter eight) questions, meanwhile, the relationship between the right to continuous improvement of living conditions, and the rights of future generations, asking whether it is 'a circle impossible to square'.

Returning to ICESCR, it will be important in advancing our understanding of the right to continuous improvement of living conditions to consider how the right might relate to other interpretive doctrines (of both rights and obligations) developed by the Committee on Economic, Social and Cultural Rights (CESCR). These include the concepts of minimum core obligations, progressive realisation, retrogression and interpretations of the maximum use of available resources. There are important synergies and tensions between the ICESCR's main 'obligations' clause, Article 2(1), and a right to continuous improvement of living conditions, and these are deserving of further attention.

[56] UN Convention on the Rights of the Child (adopted 20 November 1989, entered into force 2 September 1990) UNTS 1577, 3.

The lack of clarity around the meaning of the right to continuous improvement of living conditions may have been a factor in the amnesia around it, as Lott argues in chapter seven, and will certainly hamper efforts towards realisation. For this reason, as Lott suggests, the work of the CESCR, scholars and others in providing interpretive or conceptual clarity is vital to the right's recovery into the human rights corpus.

B. Resources: How the Right Challenges the Economic System

A second central theme in the volume is how to interpret and realise the right to continuous improvement of living conditions in the context of poverty, extreme inequality within and between countries, and the resource limits of the earth. In chapter four Skogly makes it clear that by focusing on provision of resources at the levels and in the ways we currently understand these is unsustainable and in fact harmful for future generations. This dilemma requires an acknowledgment that rights' realisation must be informed by a long view of resource use.

Chapter five by Bohoslavsky and Cantamutto provides a devastating examination of how financial capitalism leads to continuous and growing indebtedness that essentially leads to deterioration rather than improvement of living conditions for the majority of the world's population. Increasing financialisation and commodification of services that should be provided by the State has severe implications for the realisation of human rights. The right to continuous improvement of living conditions requires public rather than private resourcing of the means to a better life, and a sharing of responsibility for this resourcing by society rather than further burdening the individual. The impact of reduced State provision due to privatisation, financial crisis and austerity has deepened poverty and the stresses that accompany it across the global North and South.

Graham in chapter four suggests that addressing poverty must be central to the right to continuous improvement of living conditions but this does not result in a minimalistic or unambitious understanding of the radical capacity of human rights to transform structural inequality. He argues that the right requires that poverty be overcome, but that the meaning of poverty must be understood as relative in a given society and may change over time and place. This conception of poverty eradication is also premised on the idea of development as requiring a wider, rights-informed conception of human need that goes well beyond a simple response to income deprivation. Meeting the broader need for 'resources, capabilities, choices, security and power'[57] leads to societies that are fairer and better for all. This value-informed conception of rights-based development is echoed by Fredman in chapter twelve, critiquing

[57] Graham, chapter four in this volume.

the quantitative and insufficiently nuanced measurement built into some of the targets in the Sustainable Development Goals. The right to continuous improvement of living conditions offers a richer understanding of resourcing, informed by the underlying values of the human rights project that can be socially transformative.

In chapter six, Lamarche suggests that the right to continuous improvement of living conditions can operate as a 'meta right' to inform the interpretation of other social rights in the Covenant. Her discussion of the right to social security, informed in this way, leads to a stronger and fuller right. It should be used to oppose retrogressive tax credit policies that have emerged in Canada that undermine social protection, leading to deterioration rather than improvement of living conditions. She suggests that the CESCR is adopting this broader reading of the right in its response to Canada.

These and other contributions in the volume point to the significant potential of the right to continuous improvement of living conditions in tackling key resource questions facing our world.

C. Definitional Questions: What are 'Living Conditions'?

The limited consideration of the meaning of the right to continuous improvement of living conditions and its open-textured nature make it ripe for definitional interrogation and imaginative interpretation. While there are many questions about the idea of 'continuous improvement' as it relates to time frame and notions of perpetual betterment (as discussed below), it is important to consider what is meant by the living conditions the right seeks to improve. A number of the chapters in the volume refuse to assume that living conditions are purely material or reducible to money, bricks, taps or nutrients.

Skogly argues in chapter eight for a focus on aspects of living conditions such as culture, nature, art, social interactions, rest and leisure, to name but a few. We also need to rethink our idea of resources and our use of them within the planetary boundaries – these less tangible goods must inform the meaning and application of the right to the continuous improvement of living conditions.

Understanding what is meant by 'living' in interpreting 'living conditions' requires a window into the private world of home and community. It is here where care occurs, often profoundly shaped by gender, and where society is reproduced both biologically and socially. In chapter eleven Goldblatt explores how a social reproduction lens offers insight into an interpretation of the right that sees opportunities for improved ways of living where caring activities are shared better and where unpaid work is recognised and valued. Showing how the focus on social reproduction might disrupt fast, linear, and extractivist readings, in chapter thirteen Fletcher raises questions about continuity and timeliness in the right.

In chapter ten, Hewitt powerfully demonstrates that repairing the ongoing damage of colonisation on the lives of Indigenous Peoples must be central to the human rights project. The impact on the lives of Canada's First Nations is evidenced not only in their lack of access to adequate housing, water and employment, but is experienced in the bodies and psyches of women and girls facing systemic violence and children removed from family and community. Indigenous Peoples draw on their own philosophies, laws, traditions and world views of what constitutes a good 'living', often informed by love, care of children and sustainability. Opening the interpretation of the right to continuous improvement of living conditions to such conceptions promises a richer meaning for this and other human rights. It may also orient the right towards reparation for historical harms and acknowledgment of Indigenous self-determination and fairer sharing of resources.

Further chapters develop arguments based on the underlying values informing the right. In chapter twelve, Fredman argues that the right to continuous improvement of living conditions requires attention to the values of positive freedom, substantive equality and social solidarity in exploring whether improvements are being made. The values behind the right to continuous improvement of living conditions are also foregrounded by de Paz González in chapter nine on the jurisprudence of the Inter-American Court of Human Rights on the subject of 'vida digna' or a life lived with dignity. This jurisprudence, emerging from cases concerning Indigenous communities and other vulnerable groups facing discrimination and deprivation, gives attention to environmental issues, spiritual and cultural concerns, alongside issues of health care, housing and land.

All of these approaches to interpreting 'living conditions' force a rethink about what it is we value and, as the next theme shows, how this changes over time.

D. The Question of Direction, Trajectory and (Forward) Movement; and the Right's Radical Potential in Human Rights Thought and Practice

The assumption of progress or movement toward something better is at the very least inherent in all human rights instruments, motivates countless human rights activists, advocates and scholars, and infuses the international machinery underpinning the international legal order.[58] The chapters in this volume demonstrate

[58] See eg MO Hudson, *Progress in International Organization* (Stanford University Press 1932); R Miller and R Bratspies (eds), *Progress in International Law* (Martinus Nijhoff 2008). See also the much more ambivalent sources on this question: T Skouteris, 'The Idea of Progress' in A Orford, F Hoffmann and M Clark (eds), *The Oxford Handbook on the Theory of International Law* (OUP 2016); K Young, 'Waiting for Rights: Progressive Realization and Lost Time' in K Young (ed), *The Future of Economic and Social Rights* (CUP 2019) 654; S Hopgood, *The Endtimes of Human Rights* (Cornell University Press 2015).

that the right to continuous improvement of living conditions offers important new perspectives on and resources for understanding the meaning of progress, helping to contextualise other forward looking provisions, as well as interpret them within the broader debates of what is meant by improved living conditions and an adequate standard of living.

At the same time, it cannot be denied that the right to continuous improvement of living conditions raises prospects that are not easy to resolve in human rights terms. For example, can it really be said that there is no human rights ceiling? Are all people – including 'the one per cent' – entitled to continuously improving living conditions? In this case, what is the threshold for a violation of the right to continuous improvement of living conditions, as Graham asks in chapter four? Or when might the obligation for cooperation in ensuring the right be triggered, as Campbell considers in chapter three? There are related conundrums about whether infinite human rights can have (legal) meaning, and how they can be squared with a finite planet and with the rights of future generations, as Skogly articulates in chapter eight.

These chapters demonstrate how questions of trajectory, progress and movement in human rights realisation are already present and are deeply important, if complex questions.

However, the right also opens up questions of a different order. For example, new avenues for considering human rights' temporality and timeliness.[59] This possibility is taken up by Fletcher in chapter thirteen, which engages questions of law and time, the nature of continuity and linear progress, and those time-consuming activities seldom 'captured' in law's accounting of time, for the purposes of building a dialogue between 'rights labourers'.

The right's always-future orientation points to the need for continual reflection. It invites us to see human rights not directed at a fixed end point, but as a part of an ongoing process of social, political and economic conversation (and/or contestation). These questions of improvement and progress point to the utopian potential of the right to continuous improvement of living conditions. A radical reading of the right suggest that there are always better ways of negotiating the tensions between individuals and the State, among individuals, and among States.

IV. UNANSWERED QUESTIONS AND FUTURE RESEARCH AGENDAS

The chapters in this collection are aimed at provoking thought about the possibilities of this under-explored right. They do not claim to be comprehensive

[59] See eg Young (n 58); K McNeilly, 'The Temporal Ontology of the Human Rights Council's Universal Periodic Review' (2021) 21 *Human Rights Law Review*; K McNeilly and B Warwick, *The Times and Temporalities of International Human Rights Law* (forthcoming Hart). See more generally on law and time E Grabham and S Beynon-Jones (eds), *Law and Time* (Routledge 2018).

in their interpretations – in fact human rights interpretations, like the right itself, are a continuous project. It is our hope that, in time, the collection of papers here will be complemented by further research in a number of important areas.

First, while the book raises important questions about the environmental limits of continuous growth, further attention needs to be given to the particular effects of climate change and its implications for rights' realisation. Related to this, the ontological focus on the human as the subject of rights rather than our interdependent location within the ecological system, requires a reorientation of our understanding of living conditions and what it means for these to improve.

Second, the book has given some attention to certain groups such as women, Indigenous Peoples and children. However, the perspectives of other vulnerable groups such as people with disabilities, refugees or older persons might bring new insights into the meaning of the right.

A third avenue for further research is the regional and national human rights applications of the right to continuous improvement of living conditions in the ICESCR or rights closely resembling it at other levels. Likewise, while the collection has been situated in some countries (such as Canada) or regionally (such as the Americas), there would be value in hearing from grounded engagements in other parts of the world and reflections on the right from other cultures and belief systems. While the book has touched on the relationship between the right to continuous improvement of living conditions and other social and economic rights such as social security and work, further engagement with rights to housing, health, education and others will bring new depth to the right. This would be particularly valuable given the complex challenges arising from the impact of the Covid-19 pandemic across the world. Finally, the work we have done here is not academic alone, but is aimed at informing human rights practice. We would very much encourage further work showing how the right can and is being engaged in advocacy to address injustice and create a better world.

The profound hope, by the authors of this collection, is that the excitement informing our project to excavate and illuminate this neglected right, will be infectious in generating new insights into its meaning and potential applications.

2

Sources for a Nascent Interpretation of the Right to Continuous Improvement of Living Conditions

The *Travaux Préparatoires* and the Work of the CESCR

JESSIE HOHMANN

I. INTRODUCTION

IN THIS CHAPTER, I turn my attention to the largely ignored right to continuous improvement of living conditions in Article 11(1) of the International Covenant on Economic, Social and Cultural Rights (ICESCR).[1] I argue that it deserves more attention and interpretation than it has so far received. The right is important, as it prompts us to reconsider the meaning of Article 11(1), and the debates over the scope and content of economic, social and cultural rights as a whole. Recovering the right can help reassess the ICESCR rights' potential contributions to human flourishing, respond to human rights minimalism, and offer radical re-framings of what count as continuous improvement in living conditions. I focus in this chapter on the *travaux préparatoires* of the international bill of rights, and the approach of the Committee on Economic, Social and Cultural Rights (CESCR) to this right. In doing so, I seek to uncover a nascent interpretation of the right, and suggest how it can be further elaborated to respond to pressing global problems.

[1] International Covenant on Economic, Social and Cultural Rights, 16 December 1996, 993 UNTS 3. I am grateful to the Independent Social Research Foundation for funding me as an early career fellow during the initial research for this chapter. Beth Goldblatt, Sandra Liebenberg, Naomi Lott, Sigrun Skogly and Ben TC Warwick provided rigorous and thoughtful comments on the draft, and Professor Skogly generously shared research materials. I also thank the participants at the ESRAN-UKI work in progress workshop in November 2018 for discussion in the very early stages, those at the Expert Seminar on 'Steps to Adequate Housing' organised by Nico Moons at Antwerp in March 2017 where the ideas for this chapter were first raised, and the other contributors to this volume. Any errors remain my own.

Article 11(1) refers to a number of social goods, which have been interpreted as separate rights, while the umbrella concept of an adequate standard of living often remains in the background.[2] Of the enumerated rights, food and housing have received significant attention,[3] while the Covid-19 pandemic has highlighted the importance of the previously little-remarked right to clothing, particularly with respect to personal protective equipment (PPE).[4] A right to water and sanitation have also been implied into the Article.[5] The second sentence in Article 11(1) elaborates State obligations, including of assistance and cooperation beyond borders.[6] However, the last clause of the first sentence in Article 11(1) – 'the right to the continuous improvement of living conditions' – has rarely been treated as a stand-alone right, and when mentioned, its normative content and its implications have been little discussed.[7]

However, the right to continuous improvement of living conditions offers something qualitatively different to, and not merely an aggregate

[2] The importance of the adequate standard of living as an overarching concept infuses, though is implicit, in much of the CESCR's work. See eg *Calero v Ecuador* (views adopted 26 March 2018) UN Doc E/C.12/63/D/10/2015.

[3] On the right to food see eg UNCESCR, 'General Comment No. 12 The Right to Adequate Food (Art. 11)' (12 May 1999) UN Doc E/C.12/1999/5; Food and Agriculture Organization of the United Nations, *The Right to Food in Theory and Practice* (UNFAO 1998); B Saul, D Kinley and J Mowbray (eds), *The International Covenant on Economic, Social and Cultural Rights: Commentary, Cases, and Materials* (OUP 2014) 867–923; UNHRC Special Rapporteur, 'Special Rapporteur on the Right to Food' <www.ohchr.org/EN/Issues/Food/Pages/FoodIndex.aspx>. On the right to housing see eg UNCESCR 'General Comment No. 4: The Right to Adequate Housing (Art. 11(1) of the Covenant)' (13 December 1991) UN Doc E/1992/23; UNCESCR, 'General Comment No. 7: The Right to Adequate Housing (Art. 11.1): Forced Evictions' (20 May 1997) UN Doc E/1998/22; OHCHR Special Rapporteur, 'Special Rapporteur on adequate housing as a component of the right to an adequate standard of living, and on the right to non-discrimination in this context' <www.ohchr.org/en/issues/housing/pages/housingindex.aspx>; J Hohmann, *The Right to Housing: Law, Concepts, Possibilities* (Hart Publishing 2013).

[4] See UNCESCR, 'Statement on the coronavirus disease (COVID-19) pandemic and economic, social and cultural rights' (17 April 2020) UN Doc E/C.12/2020/1 para 13; L Graham, 'The Right to Clothing and Personal Protective Equipment in the Context of COVID-19' (2021) *The International Journal of Human Rights* (forthcoming); S James, *A Forgotten Right? The Right to Clothing in the Universal Declaration of Human Rights* (Activating Human Rights and Peace Conference 2008) <http://citeseerx.ist.psu.edu/viewdoc/download?doi=10.1.1.615.860&rep=rep1&type=pdf#page=14>; A Shahvisi, E Meskele and G Davey, 'A Human Right to Shoes? Establishing Rights and Duties in the Prevention and Treatment of Podoconiosis' (2018) 20 *Health and Human Rights Journal* 53; Saul et al (n 3) 924–27.

[5] See eg UNCESCR 'General Comment No. 15: The Right to Water (Arts. 11 and 12 of the Covenant)' (20 January 2003) UN Doc E/C.12/2002/11; M Langford and A Russell (eds), *The Human Right to Water: Theory, Practice and Prospects* (Cambridge University Press 2017); I Winkler, *The Human Right to Water: Significance, Legal Status and Implications for Water Allocation* (Hart 2012); N Singh (ed), *The Human Right to Water: From Concept to Reality* (Springer 2016); TS Bulto, *The Extraterritorial Application of the Human Right to Water in Africa* (Cambridge University Press 2014).

[6] See further Campbell, chapter three in this volume.

[7] The scant literature explicitly mentioning this right is discussed in the introduction to this volume.

of, rights to housing, water, food and clothing and the broader right to an adequate standard of living. It captures something different and irreducible to those separate rights, and illuminates the gaps between them, as well as how they relate to one another. It might help us value and care for things, concepts or ways of living that are not captured in any of these substantive categories, but are still precious or necessary to a good existence and an adequate standard of living.

Discussion about the role of rights in a good or decent life is a longstanding one, but focusing on this question through the right to continuous improvement of living conditions has the capacity to move us beyond a tired debate. It prompts reconsideration of what the improvement of living conditions would – or could – look like in the face of global challenges such as poverty, inequality within and across states, and environmental degradation. It has the potential to counter the reductionism of global soft targets, such as the Sustainable Development Goals,[8] and the reactive and minimalist responses that economic and social rights have been accused of generating.[9]

In the next section I draw on primary and secondary legal sources in international law, and analyse the nascent interpretation of the right to continuous improvement of living conditions found in them, beginning with an analysis of the *travaux préparatoires* of the international human rights covenants. I then examine the work of the CESCR through: its Concluding Observations on State reports, as well as the States reports themselves; its General Comments; its Reporting Guidelines; and its Open Letters and Occasional Statements. The final section concludes with a call for further research and serious engagement with the right to continuous improvement of living conditions, in order to harness the potential of this forgotten right in rethinking what improved living conditions might look like in light of our pressing global challenges.

In drawing out this nascent interpretation of the right, I begin to flesh out what such a right might mean, and how it might be understood on a theoretical, practical and philosophical level. The analysis contributes a preliminary proposal for how to interpret the right in a way that rejects growing inequality, unsustainable impacts on the planet, and narrow metrics of what constitutes a better life; and provides a foundation for further research on this right.

[8] See Fredman, chapter twelve in this volume; see also S Fukuda-Parr and D McNeill, 'Knowledge and Politics in Setting and Measuring the SDGs: Introduction to Special Issue' (2019) 10(S1) *Global Policy* 5, 10–13; D De La Rosa Reyes, 'The Sustainable Development Goals and the Dangers of Policy Reductionism' (2017) 8(1) *International Journal of Policy Studies* 23.

[9] See eg A Nolan, 'Not Fit for Purpose? Human Rights in Times of Financial and Economic Crisis' (2015) 4 *European Human Rights Law Review* 360, 369; M Salomon, 'Why Should it Matter that Others Have More? Poverty, Inequality, and the Potential of International Human Rights Law' (2011) 37 *Review of International Legal Studies* 2137; KH Ragnarsson, 'Humanising not Transformative? The UN Committee on Economic, Social and Cultural Rights and Economic Inequality in OECD Countries 2008-19' (2020) 8(2) *London Review of International Law* 261; S Moyn, *Not Enough: Human Rights in an Unequal World* (Belknap 2018).

II. SOURCES FOR INTERPRETING THE RIGHT IN INTERNATIONAL LAW

A. Drafting History – The *Travaux Préparatoires*

On 2 May 1951, at the United Nations 222nd meeting of the Seventh Session of the Commission on Human Rights, the United States' delegate introduced a proposed article to the International Covenant on Human Rights:

> The States Parties to this Covenant recognize the right of everyone to improved standards of living including adequate housing.[10]

In its embryonic form, the right that eventually became ICESCR Article 11(1) was a right to improved living conditions, expressed as requiring adequate housing. It was the Yugoslavian delegate who introduced the word 'continuous' to the debate. He favoured a provision with two elements: the recognition of the 'right to a standard of living worthy of man',[11] and 'the need for continuous improvement in that respect'.[12] He reasoned that including the words 'to the continuous improvement of living conditions' would result in a 'dynamic' article.[13]

After a number of further proposals, the chair put the issue to a vote. It was adopted six votes in favour, five against, and seven abstentions.[14] The phrase 'and to the continuous improvement of living conditions' was included in the right to an adequate standard of living by the narrowest of margins, although when the whole text of the provision was voted, fourteen voted in favour, none against, and four abstained on:

> The State parties to this Covenant recognize that everyone has the right to an adequate standard of living and the continuous improvement of living conditions.[15]

This initial draft invites us to see the impetus for Article 11(1) afresh: as concerned *at its core* with improved standards of living for everyone, as a right. This reverses the current emphasis, which is on Article 11 as a list of social goods. However, delegates raised a number of important questions for understanding both the right, and State obligations for realising it. These questions, discussed below, still remain relevant to our interpretation and understanding of the right.

[10] UN ECOSOC, 'Draft International Covenant on Human Rights and Measures for Implementation: Revised Proposal on Provisions Concerning Women and Children' (30 April 1951) UN Doc E/CN.4/582 in ECOSOC 'Commission on Human Rights, 7th Session: Summary Record of the 222nd Meeting' (8 June 1951) UN Doc E/CN.4/SR.222, 16.

[11] E/CN.4/SR.222, ibid, 20.

[12] ibid.

[13] ECOSOC, 'Commission on Human Rights Seventh Session: Summary Records of the 223rd Meeting' (13 June 1951) UN Doc E/CN.4/SR.223, 2.

[14] ibid 8.

[15] ibid.

i. The Base Line: From What is Improvement Measured?

First, delegates queried the base line from which improvement would be measured. The Guatemalan delegate objected to the inclusion of the word '*meilleur*' ('better') in the French text of the US proposal because of the comparative implications: he noted that it 'would be necessary to specify what was to be used as the basis for comparison'.[16] The US delegate responded that 'by "improved standards of living" she meant standards better than those obtaining at the present time'.[17] The response seems obtuse: the Guatemalan delegate in fact raised a question in which were couched a number of issues that still remain unanswered: *whose* living standards, *where*, should be taken as the floor from which continuous improvement be calculated as a universal right?

The Uruguayan delegate also expressed discomfort with pegging the right to existing living standards, and preferred an 'entirely neutral' assertion such as to the right to an adequate standard of living.[18] Chile's thought there were 'so many widely differing standards in the world that it was difficult to say which of them everyone should have the right to enjoy', and that the aim 'should be to improve living conditions in accordance with the economic capabilities of each state'.[19] These questions still motivate pressing debates over the role of socio-economic rights in responding to aspects of injustice and inequality both within and beyond State borders.[20] The ongoing nature of these debates give us further impetus to understand what the right means, and how it can meaningfully be interpreted in light of global injustices.

ii. Who is the Subject of the Right?

A second question concerns who the rights holder is. The UK delegate pointed out that 'everyone' would not necessarily be an appropriate category, given that a minority of people in the world already enjoyed an adequate 'if not an excessively high' standard of living.[21] She suggested the Covenant follow the wording in Art 25(1) of the Universal Declaration of Human Rights (UDHR), which lacks a clause on improvement or forward progress.[22]

[16] E/CN.4/SR.222 (n 10) 17.

[17] ibid.

[18] ibid. This, however, ignores the contextual and evolutionary nature of the concept of adequacy, as the Greek delegate noted. See E/CN.4/SR.223 (n 13) 8.

[19] E/CN.4/SR.222 (n 10) 19.

[20] See eg S Marks, *Human Rights and the Bottom Billion* (2009) 1 *European Human Rights Law Review* 37; Salomon (n 9); T Pogge *World Poverty and Human Rights* (Polity 2008); J Dehm 'Highlighting Inequalities in the Histories of Human Rights: Contestations over Justice, Needs and Rights in the 1970s' (2018) 31 *Leiden Journal of International Law* 871; J Linarelli, M Salomon and M Sornarajah, *The Misery of International Law: Confrontations with Injustice in the Global Economy* (OUP 2018).

[21] E/CN.4/SR.222 (n 10) 17.

[22] ibid. See Universal Declaration of Human Rights Art 25(1) (adopted 10 December 1948) GA Resolution 217 A(III).

Later, at the General Assembly's 1957 discussions of the Third Committee, the Belgian Representative raised a similar objection, arguing that 'the primary aim should be to improve the living conditions of the most under-privileged; persons outside that category could hardly claim, at the current stage, to have a right to continuous improvement of their living conditions'.[23] However, he continued, he could accept the article as framed, since the Covenant looked to the 'very long-term',[24] picturing a future world in which the right would be universally applicable.

The more limited reading – a right to continuous improvement of living conditions only for the most deprived – was not endorsed in either forum. But that does not resolve the issue of whether the right should apply only to those falling below a certain minimum standard of living, particularly in the short term, and in light of the obligations set out in Article 2(1) of ICESCR.[25] A minimal approach would have the advantage of providing a social protection floor,[26] an understanding underpinning the CESCR's current 'minimum core' approach to violations. It also has the potential to concentrate resources where needed most in the short term, and to redress the worst deprivations in a profoundly unequal world. But a minimal understanding also introduces limitations: is it sufficient, for example, as Margot Salomon asks, that a minimum standards approach be the basis for compliance, such that 'a marginally tolerable life nonetheless passes the human rights test'?[27]

On a plain text reading the right applies to *everyone*. This introduces issues of its own, also related to questions of the base line, raised above. Can it be just that people who already enjoy social goods are entitled to *more*, when millions are living in hunger, are homeless, suffer from disease, or are exploited in dangerous and unhealthy livelihoods? As Löfquist asks, do the rich have the right to continuous improvement of living conditions, too?[28] These are pressing questions, but rather than being insurmountable problems, they open up opportunities for rethinking what count as better living conditions.[29] For example, considering

[23] UNGA, Third Committee 'Official Records' (28 January 1957) 11th Session (A/C.3/SR.743) 309, 8.

[24] ibid.

[25] See further Graham, chapter four in this volume.

[26] See ILO, 'Social Protection Floor for a Fair and Inclusive Globalization: Report of the Advisory Group chaired by Michelle Bachelet,' (October 2011) <http://www.oit.org/wcmsp5/groups/public/---dgreports/---dcomm/---publ/documents/article/wcms_166486.pdf>; ILO, 'World Social Protection Report 2017-19: Universal Social Protection to Achieve the Sustainable Development Goals' (2017) <https://www.ilo.org/wcmsp5/groups/public/---dgreports/---dcomm/---publ/documents/publication/wcms_604882.pdf>; T Kotkas, I Leijten and F Pennings (eds), *Specifying and Securing a Social Minimum in the Battle against Poverty* (Hart Publishing 2019).

[27] Salomon (n 9) 2143.

[28] L Löfquist, 'Climate Change, Justice and the Right to Development' (2011) 7(3) *Journal of Global Ethics* 251; see also MJ Dennis and DP Stewart, 'Justiciability of Economic, Social and Cultural Rights: Should There Be an International Complaints Mechanism to Adjudicate the Rights to Food, Water, Housing and Health?' (2004) 98 *American Journal of International Law* 462, 221.

[29] For a careful interpretation of the concepts 'living' and 'conditions' in Article 11(1) of ICESCR see Goldblatt, chapter eleven in this volume.

living conditions that move beyond unsustainable practices of accumulation and consumption, thinking about the ecological parameters for a good life, engaging Indigenous world views, and harnessing ideas of how neighbourly, inclusive or conducive to happiness our modes of living are.[30] These ways of thinking can guide us in reimagining not only the right, but the broader global order within which it sits.

iii. Right versus Obligation

While a right might apply to each individual, State obligations may be different for differently situated people. So, while the right to continuous improvement of living conditions may be held by every person, it may be the case, as Haugen notes, that obligations arising from it 'must be observed particularly with regard to the most vulnerable'.[31] This raises questions of the relationship between a right to continuous improvement of living conditions and the obligation of progressive realisation in Article 2(1). The *travaux* clearly demonstrate that the right to continuous improvement in Article 11(1) is distinct from the question of obligations in Article 2(1). When the Human Rights Commission met in 1951–52 to consider the inclusion of provisions relating to the implementation of (and limitations to) economic and social rights, the concepts of the obligations to take steps; to use all available resources; and to progressively realise, were considered as separate to the issue of the continuous improvement of living conditions as a substantive right.[32] Alston and Quinn write: '[a]fter considerable debate in the Commission on Human Rights' (where a single human rights Covenant was being drafted) 'the view that prevailed was that, in addition to

[30] See eg J Mander and V Tauli-Corpuz, *Paradigm Wars: Indigenous Peoples' Resistance to Globalisation* (Sierra Club 2006); J Cavanagh and J Mander, *Alternatives to Economic Globalization: A Better World is Possible* (Berrett-Koehler Publishers 2002); A Escobar, 'Encountering Development: the Making and Unmaking of the Third World' 2nd edn (Princeton University Press 2002) vii–viii; R Patel and J Moore, *A History of the World in Seven Cheap Things: A Guide to Capitalism, Nature, and the Future of the Planet* (University of California Press 2018) 202–12; UNOHCHR, End of Mission Statement by the Independent Expert on the Effects of Foreign Debt and other Related International Financial Obligations of States on the Full Enjoyment of all Human Rights, Particularly Economic, Social and Cultural Rights, Juan Pablo Bohoslavsky, on his Visit to Bolivia (6–15 May 2019) <https://www.ohchr.org/EN/NewsEvents/Pages/DisplayNews.aspx?NewsID=24607&LangID=E>; UNGA, 'Resolution adopted by the General Assembly on 28 June 2012 International Day of Happiness' (28 June 2012) A/Res/66/281; J Nedelsky and T Malleson, *A Care Manifesto: (Part)Time for all* (OUP 2021) (forthcoming); A Stewart, *Gender, Law and Justice in a Global Market* (CUP 2012); J Helliwell, R Layard and J Sachs, *World Happiness Report 2018* (2018) <https://worldhappiness.report/ed/2018/>.

[31] HM Haugen, *The Right to Food and the TRIPS Agreement: With a Particular Emphasis on Developing Countries' Measures for Food Production and Distribution* (Brill 2007) 123.

[32] ECOSOC Commission on Human Rights, 'Summary Record of the 236th Meeting' (10 May 1951) 7th Session UN Doc E/CN.4/SR.236. See also P Alston and G Quinn, 'the Nature and Scope of States Parties' Obligations under the International Covenant on Economic, Social and Cultural Rights' (1987) 9(2) *Human Rights Quarterly* 156 generally, and in particular Annex 1 on the drafting history of Art 2(1), 223–29.

specific obligations attaching to each particular right, the draft Covenant should also contain an "umbrella" article imposing a general obligation that would apply to all of the economic, social, and cultural rights'.[33] While the *travaux* thus distinguish the obligation of progressive realisation in Article 2(1) from the scope of the right to continuous improvement of living conditions in the Covenant, the drafting history does demonstrate the closely intertwined nature of these rights and the obligations arising from them.[34] In fact, there are both synergies and tensions between a right to continuous improvement of living conditions and the obligations set out in Art 2(1). During later debates before the Third Committee it appeared generally accepted, as voiced by the Saudi delegate, that 'the idea of a continuous improvement of living conditions was entirely consistent with the principle of progressive realization of economic and social rights'.[35] This has generally been accepted,[36] however, the relationship between a *right* to continuous improvement of living conditions, and an *obligation* of progressive realisation, including the discrete sub-obligations (to take steps; to use maximum available resources; to avoid retrogression; and to employ economic and technical cooperation), are deserving of further attention.

iv. Continuous Improvement: What are the End Points of the Right?

A further complicating factor concerns the nature of *continuous* improvement. The Chilean delegate to the Commission on Human Rights 7th Session noted that long-term economic plans in some States might cause a drop in living conditions in the short term, and away from the overall improvement of living conditions 'if not of contemporary workers, at least of their children'.[37] The Iranian delegate speaking before the General Assembly Third Committee in 1957, also noted barriers to continuous improvement, for instance restrictions on the right to property, and the progressive taxation of income.[38] This raises issues of permissible State policies in light of a right to the continuous improvement

[33] Alston and Quinn, ibid, Annex 1, 223.

[34] See eg ECOSOC, Commission on Human Rights, '7th Session: Summary Record of the 612th Meeting' (5 May 1951) UN Doc E/CN.4/612, as amended by ECOSOC, Commission on Human Rights, '7th Session: Summary Record of the 615th Meeting' (8 May 1951) UN Doc E/CN.4/615.

[35] UNGA, Third Committee 739th Meeting (23 January 1957) 11th Session UN Doc A/C.3/SR.739, 293, 6.

[36] See eg M Craven, 'The International Covenant on Economic, Social and Cultural Rights: A Perspective on its Development (OUP 1995) 294; P Bailey, 'The Right to an Adequate Standard of Living: New Issues for Australian Law' (1997) 4 *Australian Journal of Human Rights* 14, 16. But see O De Schutter, 'Introduction' in O De Schutter (ed), *Economic, Social and Culture Rights as Human Rights* (Edward Elgar 2013) for a careful analysis of the intersections between different obligations to progress under ICESCR, and the right to an adequate standard of living (although without explicit reference to the right to continuous improvement of living conditions).

[37] E/CN.4/SR.222 (n 10) 19. The comment suggests that there is an important intergenerational facet to the right to continuous improvement of living conditions, as further discussed by Skogly, chapter eight in this volume.

[38] UNGA, Third Committee, 739th Meeting (24 January 1957) UN Doc A/C.3/SR.741, 1.

of living conditions that remain relevant both with respect to Article 11 and Article 2(1).

These questions point, first, to the close relationship between development policy, the right to development, and the right to continuous improvement of living conditions. The right to development can be defined as 'the right of all peoples and individuals to the constant improvement of their well-being'.[39] The United Nations' High Level Task Force on the Implementation of the Right to Development has also expressed this as the 'core norm' of the right.[40]

Second, and more fundamentally, they direct us to enquire into the end-points of human rights. When, if ever, is a human right to continuous improvement of living conditions fulfilled? What are the consequences of the answer in a finite world? These problems shrink, though do not disappear, if we understand improvement of living conditions as not primarily economic, or even material, in nature.[41] A better understanding of what an adequate standard of living entails might rest not on increased income or material goods for all, though these might be necessary for the fulfilment of the right for many. The measurement of a standard of living might actually mean less in some contexts: fewer working hours, in fairly paid and dignified work, shared more equally; increased time for care; more leisure time or family time.[42] It might rest on a fuller understanding of social reproduction and its role in the adequate standard of living, and fuller acknowledgement of it.[43] These as yet unresolved questions point both to practical issues of interpretation, and to the power of the right to continuous improvement of living conditions to engage our thinking in creative and productive ways.

B. The Right to Continuous Improvement of Living Conditions in the Work of the CESCR

The CESCR's work on the right to continuous improvement of living conditions can only be characterised as underdeveloped. We can, however, find some

[39] Declaration of the Right to Development (adopted 4 December 1986) UN Doc A/RES/41/128, Preamble. See also OHCHR, 'Right to Development: Report of the high-level task force on the implementation of the right to development on its sixth session – Right to development criteria and operational sub-criteria' (8 March 2010) 6th Session UN Doc A/HRC/15/WG.2/TF/2/Add.2 Annex, 8.

[40] ibid.

[41] See eg Löfquist (n 28) 253–54.

[42] See, on part-time work and the value of unpaid contributions to the community, Nedelsky and Malleson (n 30); on basic income as a response to precarious and poorly regulated work and growing inequality see Philip Alston, 'Report of the Special Rapporteur on extreme poverty and human rights' (22 March 2017) UN Doc A/HRC/35/26, 5–6.

[43] See eg Goldblatt, chapter eleven in this volume; Stewart (n 30); B Goldblatt and L Lamarche (eds), *Women's rights to Social Security and Social Protection* (Hart Publishing 2014); I Bakker and R Silvev (eds), *Beyond States and Markets: the Challenges of Social Reproduction* (Routledge 2012).

clues to the Committee's nascent interpretation in its reporting guidelines; concluding observations on State reports; General Comments; and in interpretive statements and open letters issued by it from time to time. As yet, the Committee has not dealt with the substance of the right in any of its individual complaints.[44]

i. Reporting Guidelines

The core reporting guidelines for ICESCR are contained in Part IV of the Covenant. In addition to outlining the process of reporting, Part IV refers to the progressive realisation of rights, and to measuring or assessing States' progress in fulfilling them, without explicit attention to specific Covenant rights.[45] General Comment No 1 of 1989 concerned Reporting by States Parties and fleshed out the bare bones of Part IV.[46] In it are a number of references to the obligation of progressive realisation in the Covenant, but no explicit attention to a right to continuous improvement of living conditions. However, in 1991, the CESCR clarified its reporting guidelines.[47] The 1991 guidelines take the form of a list of questions that States should answer in their reports. These questions ask for a comparative picture over time,[48] and here the Committee explicitly addresses continuous improvement of living conditions, asking States to:

> 1(a) Please supply information on the current standard of living in your population, in respect of both the aggregate and different socio-economic, cultural, and other groups within the society. How has the standard of living changed over time (e.g., compared with 10 years ago and 5 years ago) with regard to these different groups? Has there been a continuous improvement of living conditions for the entire population or for what groups?[49]

The Guidelines also asks for information on the per capita GNP of the poorest 40 per cent of the population; the existence of a poverty line, and the basis for it; and the country's Physical Quality of Life index.[50] While paragraph 1(a) suggests a right to continuous improvement for all, the questions that follow suggest that rights of the poorest members of society are of particular concern,

[44] As at 6 January 2021.

[45] See, ICESCR (n 1), Arts 16(1), 17(2), 21, 22.

[46] CESCR, 'General Comment No.1: Reporting by States Parties' (27 July 1981) UN Doc E/1989/22.

[47] CESCR, 'Revised Guidelines Regarding the Form and Contents of Reports to be Submitted by States Parties under Articles 16 and 17 of the International Covenant on Economic, Social and Cultural Rights' (17 June 1991) UN Doc E/C.12/1991/1.

[48] See ibid, asking for 'calendar and time-related bench-marks for measuring your achievements in this regard' at paras 3(b), 4, 6(a) and 6(b).

[49] ibid 11. Measurement within a specific window of time does not reveal rising (or falling) living standards beyond that frame, and hence this question provides limited insight into continuous improvement of living conditions as a normative statement of right, or as materially experienced beyond that window. With thanks to Ben TC Warwick for discussion on this point.

[50] ibid 12.

reflecting an earlier Commission on Human Rights Recommendation of 1987 to that effect.[51]

Harmonised revised guidelines on State reporting were adopted in 2009,[52] replacing the 1991 guidelines. Under the revised guidelines, States are asked to report specifically on the right to continuous improvement of living conditions:

> 42. Indicate whether the State party has defined a national poverty line and on what basis it is calculated. In the absence of a poverty line, what mechanisms are used for measuring and monitoring the incidence and depth of poverty?
>
> 43. Indicate:
>
> (a) Whether the State party has adopted a national action plan or strategy to combat poverty that fully integrates economic, social and cultural rights and whether specific mechanisms and procedures are in place to monitor the implementation of the plan or strategy and evaluate the progress achieved in effectively combating poverty; and
>
> (b) Targeted policies and programmes to combat poverty, including among women and children, and the economic and social exclusion of individuals and families belonging to the disadvantaged and marginalized groups, in particular ethnic minorities, indigenous peoples and those living in rural and deprived urban areas.[53]

These 2009 guidelines appear to reflect a change from overall development policy as a driver of improved living conditions as a right,[54] to a right that is a response to poverty, and a greater focus on minimal standards, rather than on overall human development or flourishing. This shift had an impact on the understanding of all Covenant rights, and State obligations for them, as discussed further below.

Currently, the Committee is transitioning to the Simplified Reporting Procedure and Predictable Review Calendar (SRP/PRC) in anticipation of the 2020 Treaty Body Strengthening process.[55] This will result in an informal updating and adjustment of reporting guidelines, including potential streamlining of the List of Issues across State reports. As the List of Issues now provides the

[51] Commission on Human Rights, Res 1987/20 (1999) UN Doc E/CN.4/1999/167, 12th preambular paragraph. See also P Alston and B Simma, 'First Session of the UN Committee on Economic, Social and Cultural Rights' (1987) 81 *American Journal of International Law* 747, 753.

[52] International Human Rights Instruments, 'Compilation of Guidelines on the Form and Content of Reports to be Submitted by States Parties to the International Human Rights Treaties' (3 June 2009) UN Doc HRI/GEN/2/Rev.6.

[53] ibid paras 42–43.

[54] See eg the discussion of the relationship between the right to development and the right to continuous improvement of living conditions in J Hohmann, 'The Forgotten Right to Continuous Improvement of Living Conditions in Article 11(1) of the International Covenant on Economic, Social and Cultural Rights: Seeking the Roots of the Right in International Law' (2020) working paper, available at <http://dx.doi.org/10.2139/ssrn.3668638>, part B.

[55] See UNGA, 'Implementation of Human Rights Instruments: Note by the Secretary General' (30 July 2019) UN Doc A/74/256 Annex I, Annex II.

dominant frame for the Committee's engagement with States' periodic reports, the revised process may enable new approaches by the Committee to reporting, to obligations, and to the Covenant rights, including the right to continuous improvement of living conditions.

ii. Concluding Observations and the Reporting Process

States' periodic reports can give us an indication of international law through State practice and *opinio juris*, though whether State reports reflect with any accuracy the situation on the ground is questionable.[56] The Committee's concluding observations, meanwhile, demonstrate its concerns with States Parties' compliance, as well as its position on what the Covenant requires of states.

Prior to the establishment of the CESCR in 1985,[57] State reports were considered by ECOSOC. These early concluding observations point to States' understanding that they should demonstrate continued improvement in living standards, not only with respect to the enumerated heads of Article 11, but more generally. For example, in 1980, the observer for the Byelorussian Soviet Socialist Republic stated that, due to the State's economic and cultural programmes 'the material well-being, education, culture and intellectual and moral life of the working people were improving every year'.[58] In the same record, the observer for Romania noted that 'systematic creation of new jobs, particularly for young people and women, was a basic component of Romania's economic and social policy and of the policy of continually raising the standard of living of the entire population'.[59] The records of the 1982 session of the Working Group on the Implementation of the ICESCR reveal similar assumptions on the part of States reporting.[60] The representative of Barbados, for example, stated that policy for the previous 20 years had been 'to make economic, social and cultural development a continuous process' and aim towards 'removing the welfare aspect of development and to providing guarantees that its citizens would enjoy the right

[56] E Tars, 'Who Knows What Lurks in the Hearts of Human Rights Violators – The Shadow (Reporter) Knows – Human Rights Shadow Reporting: A Strategic Tool for Domestic Justice' (2009) 42 *Clearinghouse Review* 475, 476–77 (discussing the 'very rosy picture' presented by a number of US State reports). See also ECOSOC, 'NGO Participation in Activities of the Committee on Economic, Social and Cultural Rights' (12 May 1993) UN Doc E.C./12/1993/WP.14.

[57] OHCHR, 'Review of the Composition, Organization and Administrative Arrangements of the Sessional Working Group of Governmental Experts on the Implementation of the International Covenant on Economic, Social and Cultural Rights' (28 May 1985) UN Doc E/Res.1985/17.

[58] ECOSOC, 'Sessional Working Group on the Implementation of the International Covenant on Economic, Social and Cultural Rights, Summary Record of the 16th Meeting' (28 April 1980) UN Doc E/1980/WG.1/SR.16, 1.

[59] ibid para 20, 24.

[60] ECOSOC, Sessional Working Group on the Implementation of the International Covenant on Economic, Social and Cultural Rights, 'Summary Record of the 3rd Meeting' (12 April 1982) UN Doc E/1982/WG.1/SR.3.

to a better quality of life'.[61] The Italian delegation, while stressing that Italy was 'in full compliance'[62] with the Covenant 'within the limits of its available resources'[63] also noted that in coming to compliance 'the process had been continuous and progressive'.[64] Interestingly, despite the delegation's statement of full compliance, it also admitted the need for further action to improve the situation of economic rights.[65]

It is unclear whether States reporting considered they were answering the Covenant's progressive realisation obligations (though this is implicit at least in the Italian report), or were explicitly engaging with a right to continuous improvement of living conditions, or how they might have understood these to interrelate. There are clearly synergies between the right to continuous improvement of living conditions, and the obligations in Article 2(1).

State reports in the 1980s provided a baseline. After the first reporting cycle the overall focus is on whether the State has demonstrated improved protection of rights. Thus, concluding observations generally follow a pattern, showing concern where living conditions have fallen, praising States for demonstrating improvements, and, in either case, urging states to improve the situation further, with a particular focus on those who are vulnerable or marginalised.[66]

Similarly, trends in the way States have reported can be identified. Ulrike Davy, engaging empirically with the CESCR's work on the right to an adequate standard of living using a comprehensive database of State reports up to the year 2011, provides a useful mapping.[67] In the early decades, she finds, Latin

[61] ibid 2, 14.
[62] ibid 37.
[63] ibid 45, 37.
[64] ibid 41.
[65] ibid 42.
[66] See eg ECOSOC 'Report of the Committee on Economic, Social and Cultural Rights on its Tenth and Eleventh Sessions' (1994) UN Doc E/1995/22-E/C.12/1994/20 and Corr 1, 82 (Uruguay), 94 (Romania), 194–95 (Gambia), 274 and 280 (UK), 104 (Morocco); ECOSOC, 'Report of the Committee on Economic, Social and Cultural Rights on its Twelfth and Thirteenth Sessions' (1995) UN Doc E/1996/22 E/C.12/1995/18, 99 (Portugal), 108 (Philippines); ECOSOC, 'Report of the Committee on Economic, Social and Cultural Rights on its Eighteenth and Nineteenth Sessions' (1998) UN Doc E/1999/22 E/C.12/1998/26, 146 (Poland), 86 (Sri Lanka); CESCR, 'Consideration of reports submitted by States parties under articles 16 and 17 of the Covenant, Concluding observations of the Committee on Economic, Social and Cultural Rights: Zambia' (23 June 2005) UN Doc E/C.12/1/Add.106; CESCR, 'Consideration of reports submitted by States parties under articles 16 and 17 of the Covenant' (31 May 2012) UN Doc E/C.12/NZL/CO/3 (New Zealand); CESCR, 'Concluding observations on the fourth periodic report of Iraq' (27 October 2015) UN Doc E/C.12/IRQ/CO/4; CESCR, 'Concluding observations on the sixth periodic report of the United Kingdom of Great Britain and Northern Ireland' (14 July 2016) UN Doc E/C.12/GBR/CO/6 (14 July 2016); CESCR, 'Concluding Observations on the sixth periodic report of the Netherlands' (6 July 2017) UN Doc E/C.12/EST/CO/3. See also the analysis of concluding observations by AR Chapman and B Carbonetti, 'Human Rights Protections for Vulnerable and Disadvantaged Groups: The Contributions of the UN Committee on Economic, Social and Cultural Rights' (2011) 33 *Human Rights Quarterly* 682, 732 (noting this pattern).
[67] U Davy, 'Social Citizenship Going International: Changes in the Reading of UN Sponsored Economic and Social Rights' (2013) 22 *International Journal of Social Welfare* S1, S15.

American States paid the most attention to overall development trends, and to the need for improvement, readily admitting the need for better standards of living among their populations; while Eastern European States also interpreted Article 11 as requiring a persistent policy of economic development based on State planning and agrarian reform.[68] However, Eastern European governments tended to deny their population were not already enjoying an adequate standard of living.[69] OECD States, in Davy's analysis, 'never mentioned "development" as a policy goal. As a last resort, the adequate standard of living … was to be secured through state-financed cash benefits.'[70] There was little attention, with the exception of Latin American States, to the unevenness in living standards, and those left behind by economic development.[71] Davy's analysis demonstrates that the focus in State reports on overall development or improvement waned,[72] in favour of a focus on poverty, socio-economic inequalities, and cash transfers as a policy to mitigate vulnerability.[73] This shift occurred around the time of the CESCR's new reporting guidelines, themselves occurring alongside an increased focus on 'development with a human face' and world poverty.[74]

One way to read this shift is to see it as reflecting States' new focus on the *individual* nature of the right to an adequate standard of living.[75] A second is to read it as a less robust approach to continuous improvement of living conditions, focusing not on flourishing, but on minimums for the most vulnerable – an approach that the Committee has since been criticised for.[76] Certainly, the 2009 guidelines explicitly altered what the Committee expected States to report on, moving from a wider developmental emphasis to focus attention on the poor or disadvantaged. The shift may also represent similar concerns expressed differently: work by Ben TC Warwick demonstrates an *increase* in the Committee's attention to *obligations* of progressive realisation, and overall use of 'progress based language' from the 2007 financial crisis onwards,[77] though the phrase 'continuous improvement' rarely appears after the end of the 1990s.

[68] ibid S25.
[69] ibid.
[70] ibid S26.
[71] ibid.
[72] ibid S27 (Davy notes that there were only four references to economic development or socialist planning in the 175 reports submitted between 2000 and 2009).
[73] ibid S26–S27.
[74] See eg J Perelman, 'Human Rights, Investment and the Rights-ification of Development' in KG Young (ed), *The Future of Economic and Social Rights* (CUP 2019) 438; Davy (n 67); S Hickey and D Mitlin (eds), *Rights-Based Approaches to Development: Exploring the Potential and Pitfalls* (Kumarian Press 2009); P Uvin 'From the Right to Development to the Rights-Based Approach: How "Human Rights" Entered Development' (2007) 17 *Development in Practice* (2007); P Alston and M Robinson, *Human Rights and Development: Towards Mutual Reinforcement* (OUP 2005); UNDP *Human Development Report 1990: Concept and Measurement of Human Development* (UNDP 1990); Amartya Sen's influential *Development as Freedom* (OUP 1999) is also notable in this shift.
[75] This is Davy's thesis: see Davy (n 67) s28.
[76] See eg Salomon (n 9).
[77] See BT Warwick, 'A Hierarchy of Comfort? The CESCR's Approach to the 2008 Economic Crisis' in G MacNaughton and D Frey (eds), *Economic and Social Rights in A Neoliberal World* (CUP 2018) 134–35.

In the current reporting process the Committee's List of Issues takes centre stage in framing State reports. Questions of improved standards feature strongly in the Lists of Issues, demonstrating that the CESCR remains attentive to better standards of living through rights compliance over time.[78] While Lists of Issues often focus on poverty and on the most marginalised groups, these questions can be understood as at least implicitly interrogating the State Party's approach to what a good, decent or adequate standard of living is. There is room for the Committee to make this facet of both rights and obligations more explicit in future, including through renewed attention to the right to continuous improvement of living conditions itself.

Overall, however, if improvement and progress remain the ethos that infuses the concluding observations and the questions framed in the Lists of Issues, a *right* to continuous improvement of living conditions still remains ambiguous in these sources.

iii. General Comments

The CESCR has addressed the right to continuous improvement of living conditions in a number of General Comments, although there is no Comment dedicated specifically to it.

After its first General Comment, which addressed reporting,[79] in 1990 General Comment No 2 on International Technical Assistance Measures tackled the problem of the adverse impact of debt and structural adjustment on the enjoyment of Covenant rights.[80] In what can be interpreted as an early capitulation to a minimal approach, the Committee noted that 'adjustment programmes will often be unavoidable and that these will frequently involve a major element of austerity. Under such circumstances, however, endeavours to protect the most basic economic, social and cultural rights become more, rather than less, urgent.'[81] This General Comment would have been a welcome place for the Committee to expand on continuous improvement of living conditions as a right, and while the Committee noted the need for 'adjustment with a human face', or 'the human dimension of development',[82] it did not engage with the right per se, despite the potential here for exploring the relationship between development policy, individual rights and improved standards of living. In General Comment No 3 on the Nature of States Parties Obligations,[83] the

[78] See eg CESCR, 'List of issues in relation to the initial report of South Africa' (13 October 2017) UN Doc E/C.12/ZAF/Q/1.

[79] E/1989/22 (n 46).

[80] CESCR, 'General Comment No. 2: International technical assistance measures (Art. 22 of the Covenant)' (2 February 1990) UN Doc E/1990/23, see particularly 9.

[81] ibid.

[82] ibid.

[83] CESCR 'General Comment No. 3: The Nature of States Parties' Obligations (Art. 2, Para. 1, of the Covenant)' (14 December 1990) UN Doc E/1991/23.

Committee made note of the Declaration on the Right to Development,[84] but there is no engagement with a right to continuous improvement under ICESCR itself. This, again, appears to be a missed opportunity, particularly given the rich potential overlap and normative relationship between the right to continuous improvement of living conditions, obligations of progressive realisation in Article 2(1), and international cooperation and assistance in Article 11.

However, in General Comment No 4 on the Right to Housing,[85] the Committee explicitly mentions the right to continuous improvement, as follows:

> Policies and legislation should … not be designed to benefit already advantaged social groups at the expense of others. The Committee is aware that external factors can affect *the right to a continuous improvement of living conditions*, and that in many States parties overall living conditions declined during the 1980s. However as noted by the Committee in its general comment No 2 … despite externally caused problems, the obligations under the Covenant continue to apply and are perhaps even more pertinent during times of economic contraction. It would thus appear to the Committee that a general decline in living and housing conditions, directly attributable to policy and legislative decisions by States parties, and in the absence of accompanying compensatory measures, would be inconsistent with the obligations under the Covenant.[86]

This statement clearly indicates that the Committee treats the continuous improvement of living conditions as a *right*. In addition, it goes some distance to repair the lack of attention to the right in the two earlier General Comments on international technical assistance, and on States Parties' obligations. As welcome as this statement is, the Committee did not further flesh out the right here. In fact it was not until 1999 that the Committee mentioned the right again in a General Comment.

In that year, General Comment No 12, on the right to adequate food lists the right to continuous improvement of living conditions as one of the key components of Article 11(1), though it does not further engage with it.[87] A number of other General Comments, however, when referring to the rights under Article 11, do not mention a right to continuous improvement of living conditions. This is true for example, of General Comment No 15 on Water.[88] While the right to water is implied from Article 11, there is no reference in discussion of Article 11 to continuous improvement of living conditions. This is also the case in General Comment No 6, on the rights of older persons.[89] General Comment

[84] ibid 14. See also Hohmann (n 54) 15–16.
[85] E/1992/23 (n 3).
[86] ibid para 11, emphasis added.
[87] E/C.12/1999/5 (n 3).
[88] E/C.12/2002/11 (n 5).
[89] CESCR, 'General Comment No. 6: The Economic, Social and Cultural Rights of Older Persons' (8 December 1995) UN Doc E/1996/22.

No 6 refers to Article 11 and to the 1991 United Nations Principles for Older Persons, which references the rights of older persons to an adequate standard of living[90] but in discussing Article 11, there is no reference to continuous improvement.[91]

In listing the rights that Article 11(1) is composed of, the Committee has often not listed continuous improvement of living conditions.[92] Indeed, General Comments No 17 to No 22 (produced between 2006 and 2016) make no reference to improvement of any kind. However 2016's General Comment No 23, on just and favourable conditions of work, marked a return to the language of improvement.[93] This General Comment adds to the Committee's approach to improvement, explicitly invoking decent conditions (and the relevance of international cooperation and assistance), albeit decent working, rather than living, conditions.[94] It does not, however, add to our understanding of the Committee's approach to the right to continuous improvement of living conditions, beyond pointing to the intersections between international action, decent work, and an adequate standard of living.

We find a fuller exploration of improvement of living conditions in General Comment No 25 on science and economic, social and cultural rights.[95] Here, the Committee engages with progress and improvement on multiple levels. The first of these is prompted by the phrasing of Article 15 itself, which refers in 15(1)(b) to 'the right to enjoy the benefits of scientific progress and its applications', explicitly referencing forward movement in scientific endeavour and knowledge. On a second and more promising level for an understanding of the right to continuous improvement of living conditions, the General Comment recognises social goods inherent in scientific endeavour. In interpreting the term 'benefits', the Committee notes:

> The term 'benefits' refers first to the material results of the applications of scientific research, such as vaccinations, fertilizers, technological instruments and the like. Secondly, benefits refer to the scientific knowledge and information directly deriving from scientific activity, as science provides benefits through the development

[90] UNGA Res 46/91 (16 December 1991).

[91] E/1996/22 (n 89) 32.

[92] See eg CESCR, 'General Comment No. 16: The Equal Right of Men and Women to the Enjoyment of All Economic, Social and Cultural Rights (Art. 3 of the Covenant)' (11 August 2005) UN Doc E/C.12/2005/4. The most recent example is CESCR, 'Statement on the Pledge to "Leave no-one Behind:" The International Covenant on Economic, Social and Cultural Rights and the 2030 Agenda for Sustainable Development' (8 March 2019) UN Doc E/N.12/2019/1, 5.

[93] CESCR, 'General Comment No. 23 (2016) on the right to just and favourable conditions of work (Article 7 of the International Covenant on Economic, Social and Cultural Rights)' (27 April 2016) UN Doc E/C.12/GC/23 paras 50 and 51.

[94] See Goldblatt, chapter eleven in this volume, on the distinction between working and living conditions.

[95] CESCR, 'General Comment No. 25 (2020) on science and economic, social and cultural rights (article 15(1)(b), (2), (3), and (4) of the International Covenant on Economic, Social and Cultural Rights' (30 April 2020) UN Doc E/C.12/GC/25.

> and dissemination of the knowledge itself. Lastly, benefits refer also to the role of science in forming critical and responsible citizens who are able to participate fully in a democratic society.[96]

This points to the Committee's understanding that the enjoyment of rights in the Covenant is not only material. Their realisation, and their enjoyment, also hinges on social and political conditions, capacity for critical thought, and reflection on what makes a good or decent life. While so much attention to economic, social and cultural rights is captured by their monetary costs, the Committee's statement that 'to enjoy the benefits of scientific progress' should not be interpreted as 'restricted to the material benefits or products of scientific advancement, but include the development of the critical mind and faculties associated with doing science'[97] is a welcome reminder that the realisation of economic, social and cultural rights is not merely a question of State expenditure. It serves to refocus attention on human flourishing and its conditions beyond economic minimums.

iv. Statements and Open Letters

A final relevant aspect of the CESCR's work is the statements and open letters it issues from time to time, often in reaction to particular events, global challenges or specific rights-impacting situations. None of these deal with the right to continuous improvement of living conditions specifically, but many demonstrate the Committee's engagement with broadly related issues. Most prominently, this includes the Committee's efforts to ensure that the rights under ICESCR are not violated through retrogression, especially in the context of economic crisis, globalisation, debt or structural adjustment.

Beginning in 1998, the CESCR dealt explicitly with the negative impact of globalisation, international trade and the work of the international financial institutions on the enjoyment of economic, social and cultural rights. The Committee's Statement following its Day of Discussion on Globalization and its Impacts on the Enjoyment of Economic, Social and Cultural Rights[98] strongly conveys that 'globalization risks downgrading the central place accorded to human rights by the Charter of the United Nations in general and the International Bill of Human Rights in particular. This is especially the case in relation to economic, social and cultural rights.'[99] The records of the Day of Discussion capture both the then Chair of the Committee's disappointment that 'the international trade and financial institutions had never referred in their work to the Covenant, or the obligations thereunder assumed by the

[96] ibid para 8.
[97] ibid para 10.
[98] E/1999/22 E/C.12/1998/26 (n 66) Ch V.
[99] ibid Ch VI, 3.

Governments with which they were dealing',[100] and his strong opinion that 'the monitoring and enjoyment of [Covenant] rights could not be left exclusively to a committee of 18 experts with no mandate for monitoring the development of international financial markets, with no capacity for technical analysis and with diminishing secretariat support'.[101]

The CESCR's Statement on Human Rights and Development of 15 May 1998 is similarly strongly worded on the need to include the realisation of economic, social and cultural rights within development activities. The statement opens:

> The Committee considers that development activities which do not contribute to respect for human rights, either directly or indirectly, are not worthy of the name. It therefore welcomes the commitment of the Secretary-General to ensure that human rights, including economic, social and cultural rights, are part of the mainstream of all United Nations activities.[102]

In the same statement, the Committee recommends that the guidelines for the United Nations Development Assistance Fund should be reformed to include specific reference to the ICESCR as part of the essential framework; and to require States to establish specific benchmarks against which to measure their performance in promoting realisation of these rights.[103] These statements show that the Committee was, in the early years, at pains to contest the marginalisation of economic and social rights within the UN system, and its impact on the realisation of better standards of living and human rights enjoyment.

The emphasis on economic, social and cultural rights and their importance for development then appears to have dropped away, but from the time of the 'Global Financial Crisis' in the latter 2000s, the Committee turned its attention again to the impacts of austerity and financial adjustment. A number of statements, especially in 2007[104] and 2012,[105] exhorted States to take economic, social and cultural rights into account in their response to financial crises or other economic downturns, but these statements focused on preventing retrogressive measures or backwards steps, rather than improvement.

In 2016, the Committee issued a statement on public debt, austerity measures and the Covenant, which revives the Committee's concern with global structural inequality and the detrimental impacts it often has on economic and social rights.[106] While offering detailed guidance to borrowers and lenders on their human rights obligations, it also re-articulates the link between the realisation

[100] ibid 441.
[101] ibid 442.
[102] ibid 'A: Human Rights and Development' 94 at 1.
[103] ibid 'B: United Nations reform and the UNDAF process' 95 at 3–4.
[104] CESCR, 'An evaluation of the obligation to take steps to the "maximum of available resources" under an optional protocol to the covenant' UN Doc E/C.12/2007/1, 54.
[105] CESCR, 'Letter' (16 May 2012) UN Doc CESCR/48th/SP/MAB/SW.
[106] CESCR, 'Public debt, austerity measures and the International Covenant on Economic, Social and Cultural Rights' (22 July 2016) UN Doc E/C.12/2016/1.

of human rights, and the broader purposes of the UN organs. Urging international financial institutions to take their obligations seriously, the Committee states:

> as specialized agencies of the United Nations, IMF and IBRD are obligated to act in accordance with the principles of the Charter of the United Nations, which sets the realization of human rights and fundamental freedoms as one of the purposes of the Organization, to be achieved in particular through international economic and social cooperation.[107]

This links to the CESCR's earlier focus on human rights as part of a broader developmental agenda, discussed above with regard to the Concluding Observations: a focus that was sidelined as the Committee reacted to austerity policies, and their negative impacts on rights enjoyment. Glimmers of a more proactive agenda for rights realisation are emerging in the Committee's recent work, with its 2020 statement on the Covid-19 pandemic and economic, social and cultural rights closing with the following:

> the Committee calls upon all States parties to ensure that the extraordinary mobilization of resources to address the COVID-19 pandemic provides the impetus for long-term resource mobilization towards the full and equal enjoyment of the economic, social and cultural rights enshrined in the Covenant. In so doing, they will lay the foundation for achieving the ideal enshrined in the Universal Declaration of Human Rights of achieving a world of free human beings enjoying 'freedom from fear and want' …[108]

A proactive and clearly articulated vision of how ICESCR rights can provide a foundation for a better global order could involve a more robust interpretation of the right to continuous improvement of living conditions by the CESCR in future.

v. Conclusion on the Approach of the CESCR to the Right to Continuous Improvement of Living Conditions

What can we draw from the Committee's underdeveloped conception of the right to continuous improvement of living conditions? There are three important strands.

First, the Committee appears to have treated the right to continuous improvement of living conditions as a substantive right. This is clear particularly in General Comment No 4, of 1991,[109] which states that the Committee 'is aware that external factors can affect the right to a continuous improvement of living conditions'.[110] The reporting Guidelines of 1991 and 2009 also indicate that the

[107] ibid 8.
[108] E/C.12/2020/1 (n 4) para 25.
[109] E/1992/23 (n 3).
[110] ibid para 11.

Committee expects States to report on it, even though State reports themselves do not make a distinction between (and may even conflate) the right with obligations under Article 2. There is no evidence of conflation by the Committee in this manner, though certainly the relationship between right and obligation remains underexplored.

Second, the Committee has been inconsistent in its approach to the right to continuous improvement of living conditions as distinct to, rather than as descriptive of, the right to an adequate standard of living more broadly. Only in a few General Comments does the Committee mention it when it lists the rights that make up Article 11. And it has often not engaged with it even in those General Comments that address another Covenant right that requires material improvement, such as the right to food.[111] Between 2006 and 2016, the Committee's General Comments make no mention of improvement of any kind, even though empirical work suggests an increased incidence of 'progress based' language in the Committee's Concluding Observations, General Statements and Open Letters between 2007 and 2015.[112] This progressive language has not occurred in tandem with an explanation or consideration of the right to continuous improvement of living conditions in Article 11, even if the ethos of forward movement remains very strong in the Covenant, and in the work of the Committee, in part due to the centrality of Article 2(1).

Third, that a right to continuous improvement of living conditions has undergone a long period of hibernation, from which it may now be stirring, can tell us something about the CESCR's work and its priorities. The CESCR has, as its early chair Philip Alston lamented, been hampered by lack of support and funding to tackle serious, complex and pressing global challenges, which often require technical expertise in areas well beyond human rights per se.[113] Perhaps for this reason, the Committee has tended to react to world events rather than setting pro-active agendas for human-rights based flourishing through improved standards of living. The serious increase in inequality and materially precarity for so many may explain the Committee's focus on preventing retrogressive steps. However, there is little to suggest in the Committee's work the potential that a right to continuous improvement of living conditions may hold in moving beyond human rights minimalism and reactiveness.

The CESCR could mobilise the right to shift the terrain on which economic, social and cultural rights debates unfold, for example following the lead of the former United Nations independent expert on the effects of foreign debt and human rights, Juan Pablo Bohoslavsky. Bohoslavsky has discussed the right to continuous improvement of living conditions in the context of mass

[111] See also CESCR, 'General Comment No. 14: The Right to the Highest Attainable Standard of Health (Art. 12 of the Covenant)' (11 August 2000) UN Doc E/C.12/2000/4, 15.
[112] See Warwick (n 77).
[113] E/1999/22 E/C.12/1998/26 (n 66) para 442.

consumption and economic growth, noting at the conclusion to his visit to Bolivia in May 2019:

> While economic growth has brought many benefits to the population, I do see the need for deep reflection on rising tensions among different values and goals – mass consumption and the concept of living well; property and collective rights, solidarity and individualism propelled by the market economy; and extractivism and the protection of Pachamama [mother earth]. … [T]he Government has an obligation to progressively realize economic, social and cultural rights of people within its territory, including the rights of everyone to an adequate standard of living and 'the continuous improvement of living conditions'. These rights cannot be reduced to exponential economic growth and mass consumption of goods and services.[114]

Resuscitating the right to continuous improvement of living conditions might offer new avenues for the CESCR to move forward in addressing these pressing global challenges.

III. CONCLUSION: TOWARD A RIGHT TO THE CONTINUOUS IMPROVEMENT OF LIVING CONDITIONS

The right to continuous improvement of living conditions has not yet received extensive or substantive scholarly engagement, or been fleshed out by the relevant human rights bodies: it appears largely forgotten. This sits at odds with the otherwise exponential growth in the scholarship and practice on economic and social rights over the last few decades. At the same time, within many social, protest, and human rights movements lies a demand to take seriously a right to something more, or something better, for everyone. We need radical new ways of thinking about old problems, institutions, and arrangements. The right to continuous improvement of living conditions might offer new avenues, or help us to see these difficult problems in new ways.

Much remains to be done in order to fully flesh out what such a right might mean. Undertaking this work is crucial to translating the right into actual social change. In a world where inequality is growing, and we are confronted by our unsustainable impacts on the planet, the right to continuous improvement of living conditions can seem both naively and dangerously rapacious. At the same time, considering and seeking to embed this right into human rights in a way that responds meaningfully to these problems offers a potential break from a never-ending economic growth model to more sustainable ideas of what it means to be human, and may be more timely now than ever.

[114] End of Mission Statement by the Independent Expert on the Effects of Foreign Debt (n 30) 15. See also Bohoslavsky and Cantamutto, chapter five in this volume.

3

Cooperating to Continuously Improve

MEGHAN CAMPBELL

I. INTRODUCTION

THE OBLIGATION TO continuously improve living conditions does not stop at territorial borders. Woven throughout Article 11 of the International Covenant on Economic, Social and Cultural Rights (ICESCR)[1] is an obligation of international cooperation. This cross-border obligation is made explicit twice in the right to an adequate standard of living. Article 11(1) recognises the importance of international cooperation to the realisation of the right and Article 11(2) requires States to take measures through international cooperation to guarantee the fundamental right of everyone to be free from hunger. There is an unspoken assumption in the text that cooperation is an essential ingredient to realising the right to continuous improvement of living conditions. Despite the centrality of international cooperation to Article 11, its role in continuously improving living conditions has been largely ignored. In part, this is due to the pull of the obligation of international assistance and cooperation in Article 2(1) of ICESCR and to the enduring controversy around the idea that human rights obligations are not circumscribed by territorial boundaries.[2] Saul, Kinley and Mowbray observe 'that in terms of a legal obligation in the Covenant' to cooperate to continuously improve living conditions 'the Committee … talk[s] mainly in hope rather than expectation'.[3] In the last five years, however, the Committee on Economic, Social and Cultural Rights (CESCR) has been building a body of jurisprudence on international cooperation, moving this obligation from hopeful aspiration to concrete reality. This chapter analyses the jurisprudential developments by CESCR on the duty of international cooperation and considers how these relate to the right

[1] (Adopted 16 December 1966, entry into force 3 January 1976) 993 UNTS 3.

[2] M Langford, F Coomans and F Gomez Isa, 'Extra-Territorial Duties in International Law' in M Langford et al (eds), *Global Justice, State Duties: The Extraterritorial Scope of ESCR in International Law* (CUP 2013).

[3] B Saul, D Kinley and J Mowbray (eds), *ICESCR: Commentary, Cases and Materials* (OUP 2014) 967.

to continuous improvement of living conditions. It evaluates the clarity that CESCR has brought to this cooperative obligation and diagnoses where blind spots remain in relation to the right. Understanding the practice of CESCR can provide crucial insights and open up new lines of inquiry into the theory and practice of cross-border human rights obligations.

This chapter proceeds as follows. Section II analyses the textual base for cooperation in ICESCR and briefly sketches the continued uncertainties around this duty. Section III turns to assess how CESCR is engaging with these uncertainties and developing a duty of cooperation under ICESCR by mapping how CESCR is monitoring States in respect of their obligation to cooperate to improve living conditions in Article 11. It also expands the scope of analysis by mapping CESCR's approach to the other cooperative obligations threaded through ICESCR as CESCR rarely differentiates between cooperation in different obligations. This provides greater clarity on how CESCR is answering conceptually difficult questions on the development of a duty of cooperation.

The analysis in Section III illuminates unseen patterns in the evolution of international cooperation. First, CESCR is seeking to build legitimacy for holding States to account for cooperation and, second, it is taking tentative steps to put in place criteria for determining when a State has a duty to cooperate. Unlike much of the academic discourse, CESCR is also considering the circumstances when a State is required to seek cooperation. Third, the majority of CESCR's focus has been towards developing the normative content of cooperation. Its attention to this aspect of cooperation, however, is skewed. CESCR disproportionately focuses on the cooperative measures a State can take to ensure that business and trade operating across borders upholds human rights. It only gives passing engagement to other facets of cooperation, largely ignoring the facets articulated in Article 11. An even more glaring absence is that CESCR does not frame cooperation as a necessary component for improving living conditions. The chapter concludes (Section IV) by considering where CESCR can further engage with cooperation in Article 11 of ICESCR.

II. THE CONTENTIOUS DUTY TO COOPERATE IN ICESCR

Cooperation is arguably the fulcrum of Article 11. It holds in full:

> 1. The States Parties to the present Covenant recognize the right of everyone to an adequate standard of living for himself and his family, including adequate food, clothing and housing, and to the continuous improvement of living conditions. The States Parties will take appropriate steps to ensure the realization of this right, recognizing to this effect the essential importance of ***international co-operation*** based on free consent.

> 2. The States Parties to the present Covenant, recognizing the fundamental right of everyone to be free from hunger, shall take, individually and through ***international co-operation***, the measures, including specific programmes, which are needed:
>
> (a) To improve methods of production, conservation and distribution of food by making full use of technical and scientific knowledge, by ***disseminating knowledge*** of the principles of nutrition and by developing or reforming agrarian systems in such a way as to achieve the most efficient development and utilization of natural resources;
>
> (b) Taking into account the problems of both food-importing and food-exporting countries, to ensure an ***equitable distribution of world food*** supplies in relation to need.

International cooperation is a vital ingredient to an adequate standard of living and to the right to continuous improvement of living conditions. It is a component of the right to be free from hunger. Cooperation is implicit in the dissemination of scientific and technical knowledge on food production and nutrition. The equitable distribution of food between importing and exporting States is also premised on coordination and cooperation. There is a strong textual basis to hold States to account for cooperation to continuously improve living conditions, particularly in respect to the right to food.

There are two further cooperative elements in ICESCR. Article 2(1) requires:

> Each State Party … undertakes to take steps, individually and through ***international assistance and co-operation***, especially economic and technical, to the maximum of its available resources, with a view to achieving progressively the full realization of the rights recognized in the … Covenant …

And Article 15(4) requires:

> The States Parties to the present Covenant recognize the benefits to be derived from the encouragement and development of ***international contacts and co-operation*** in the scientific and cultural fields.

Despite these explicit textual commitments, the cooperative obligation is both controversial and notoriously under-theorised. After combing through the *travaux preparatories*, Alston and Quinn concluded that it is difficult to sustain 'the argument that the commitment to international cooperation can be accurately characterized as a legally binding obligation upon a particular State to provide any particular form of assistance'.[4] In the intervening years, greater attention has been paid to cooperation, but at this stage, there are more questions than answers.[5] The aim here is not to give a full accounting of the

[4] P Alston and G Quinn, 'The Nature and Scope of States Parties Obligations Under ICESCR' (1987) 9 *Human Rights Quarterly* 156, 191.

[5] T Karimova, 'The Nature and Meaning of "International Assistance and Cooperation" under ICESCR' in E Riedel, G Giacca and C Golay (eds), *Economic, Social and Cultural Rights in International Law* (OUP 2014).

theoretical and practical challenges to fully implementing a duty of cooperation. Instead the chapter briefly outlines four of the key questions that illuminate the larger debates on a duty of cooperation, before turning to the practice of CESCR to understand and critique its current approach to cooperation, particularly cooperation to continuously improve living conditions.

The first question concerns whether there is a legal obligation to cooperate. As Alston and Quinn demonstrate there was initial resistance. While there is ample evidence of States embracing cooperation in a series of UN Declarations and Frameworks[6] and strong arguments in favour of a legal duty,[7] there is also ample evidence of States continuing to resist a human rights obligation to cooperate.[8] There remain questions on the legitimacy of a legal duty to fulfil socio-economic rights across borders that CESCR must and, as evidenced below, does address.

Second, perhaps the greatest challenge is in delineating when must a State provide cooperation and when must a State seek cooperation. There are competing theories based on the power and influence of the State, causation, historical relationships and the inability to fully protect socio-economic rights.[9] The difficulty in identifying principled triggering criteria lead Alston to conclude, in 2005, that at best the duty of international cooperation is 'a generic one that attaches to the undifferentiated international community'.[10] In CESCR's monitoring work it has had an opportunity to develop triggering criteria, arguably slowly evolving beyond this undifferentiated obligation.

Third, in popular discourse, international cooperation is invariably equated with the transfer of financial resources. However, beyond the transfer of economic resources, there are questions around what measures a State must undertake to discharge the cooperative obligations. There are convincing arguments that a wide range of measures are needed to meet the cooperative obligation under Article 2(1), although any measures that have resource implications remain highly controversial.[11] The academic discourse, however, has not yet fully unpacked the cooperative measures specifically engaged under Article 11.

[6] ibid; W Vandenhole, 'Towards a Division of Labour for Sustainable Development: Extraterritorial Human Rights Obligations' in M Kaltenborn, M Krajewski and H Kuhn (eds), *Sustainable Development Goals and Human Rights* (Springer 2020).

[7] O de Schutter, 'The International Dimensions of the Right to Development' (2018) UN Doc A/HRC/WG.2/19/CRP.1.

[8] A Vandenbogaerde and W Vandenhole, 'OP-ICESCR: An Ex-Ante Assessment of its Effectiveness in Light of the Drafting Process' (2010) 10(2) *Human Rights Law Review* 207.

[9] S Skogly, 'Causality and Extraterritorial Human Rights Obligations' in M Langford et al (eds), *Global Justice State Duties* (CUP 2013).

[10] P Alston, 'Ships Passing in the Night: The Current State of Human Rights and Development Debate Seen Through the Lens of the MDGs' (2005) 27(3) *Human Rights Quarterly* 755.

[11] M Sepulveda Carmona, 'The Obligations of "International Assistance and Cooperation": Under ICESCR' (2009) 13(1) *The International Journal of Human Rights* 86; The Maastricht Principles on Extraterritorial Obligations <https://www.etoconsortium.org/nc/en/main-navigation/library/maastricht-principles/?tx_drblob_pi1%5BdownloadUid%5D=23> accessed 9 July 2020.

In theory, a wide range of cooperative measures is needed to realise the right to continuous improvement as it speaks to cooperating through disseminating scientific knowledge on food production and in coordinating the global distribution of food. And the question explored below is whether CESCR has filled this gap and pinned down the normative content of cooperation under Article 11.

And a fourth and largely overlooked question is how the obligation to cooperate rooted in different socio-economic obligations may develop in different ways. Little attention has been paid to whether cooperation means the same in Articles 2(1) (maximising available resources), 11 (continuous improvement) and 15(4) (cultural rights). With these questions in mind, the chapter now turns to CESCR's practice of monitoring States in light of their duty to cooperate.

III. THE PRACTICE OF MONITORING COOPERATION

Since 2015, CESCR has been building up a body of jurisprudence on cooperating that has begun to delineate the contours of the obligation. This section maps CESCR's current practice of monitoring States' obligations to undertake international assistance and cooperation. Specifically, it examines the Concluding Observations, Statements, Open Letters and General Comments from the 54th Session in February 2015 to the 67th Session in March 2020. This is deliberately not a comprehensive assessment but zones in on the Committee's contemporary practice so as to have a detailed assessment that reveals current, previously unseen trends. There was no relevant material under the Optional Protocol to ICESCR.[12]

There are some intriguing insights that emerge from this mapping analysis. First, although the duty of international cooperation is threaded throughout multiple obligations in ICESCR, in practice CESCR rarely distinguishes between cooperation under Article 2(1), 11 and 15(4). The predominant practice is to refer to cooperation as a facet of the obligation to maximise the available resources under Article 2(1). Cooperation is infrequently connected to continuously improving living conditions or to an adequate standard of living. The lack of attention to the different requirements of cooperation in the text has an impact, as CESCR rarely encourages States to cooperate in relation to food, clothing, or housing. Implicitly, the aspects of cooperation CESCR homes in on under Article 2(1) will have positive spillover effects on Article 11, but there is room for further engagement with the different permutations of cooperation in ICESCR. Second, the most well-developed facet of the duty of cooperation is in relation to business and human rights. Amongst other things, CESCR routinely requires host and home States to regulate the practices of multinational corporations

[12] A/RES/63/117.

to uphold rights and requires States to ensure trade agreements are based on human rights. There is a rich academic discourse on business and human rights suggesting that CESCR has tapped into this momentum and echoes its insights.[13] Perhaps more cynically, it may also spring from a desire to preserve its position as the foremost instrument on socio-economic rights and negate the need for a treaty to address the relationship between socio-economic rights and business.[14] Comparatively, other aspects of cooperation are not developed to anywhere near the same degree.

This section proceeds as follows: (i) it begins by analysing CESCR's arguments for the legitimacy of cooperation; (ii) it evaluates the criteria CESCR has developed for activating the obligation to cooperate; and (iii) it concludes by exploring the different types of cooperation CESCR is advocating. Threaded throughout this assessment is an evaluation of CESCR's approach to the different permutations of cooperation under Article 11, Article 2(1) and Article 15(4). Due to the intertwining of these Articles, this chapter evaluates both 'cooperation' and 'assistance', although some have argued they are conceptually distinct.[15] The pertinent questions that arise from this mapping exercise are then explored in the Conclusion.

A. Legitimacy of Cooperation

The duty of cooperation is controversial. States, particularly in the Global North, deny any legal obligation to cooperate across borders and frame acts of cooperation as altruistic largesse.[16] In beginning to operationalise the duty of cooperation, CESCR must provide persuasive arguments to justify a legal duty to cooperate. This is particularly important for CESCR, as its outputs are not legally binding, and it must rely on the strength of its reasoning to 'enforce' its recommendations. Although CESCR has not released a General Comment on international cooperation and assistance, it has been dedicating notable space to developing this obligation in the General Comments released in the last five years. The General Comments serve overlapping functions and one of those functions is to justify evolutions in the UN human rights system.[17]

[13] S Deva and D Bilchitz (eds), *Building a Treaty on Business and Human Rights* (CUP 2017).

[14] Similar debates have arisen in relation to the Convention on the Elimination of All Forms of Discrimination against Women and the need for a treaty on gender-based violence. See R McQuigg, 'The CEDAW Committee and Gender-Based Violence Against Women' (2017) 6 *International Human Rights Law Review* 263.

[15] M Craven, 'The International Covenant on Economic, Social and Cultural Rights' in R Hanski and M Suksi (eds), *An Introduction to the International Protection of Human Rights* (2nd edn Abo Akademi University 1999) 108.

[16] Open Ended Working Group on Optional Protocol to ICESCR, 'Report of the Working Group' (2005) E/CN.4/2005/52 para 76.

[17] H Keller and L Grover, 'General Comments of the HRC and Their Legitimacy' in H Keller and G Ulfstein (eds), *UN Human Rights Treaty Bodies* (CUP 2012).

Across the UN treaty bodies, General Comments that contribute to the evolution of international human rights law follow a pattern.[18] They begin by justifying the need for the evolution: for example, that gender-based violence is endemic or water is vital for human dignity. The General Comment then proceeds to explain the legal basis in the treaty for the evolution and situates the evolution 'within broader trends in international law'.[19] CESCR generally follows this pattern when analysing international cooperation and assistance in conjunction with other substantive socio-economic rights.

Cooperation is needed to realise socio-economic rights. At various points, CESCR describes international cooperation and assistance as a 'key element', 'crucial' and 'essential'.[20] For instance, CESCR explains that without cooperation States Parties will lack the resources or capacity to fulfil sexual and reproductive health rights.[21] CESCR has added texture on the need for cooperation. First, the unique and starkly transnational nature of Covid-19 has emphasised the essentialness of international assistance and cooperation. CESCR correctly observes that 'pandemics are a crucial example of the needs for … cooperation … viruses and other pathogens do not respect borders'.[22] The inability of one State acting on its own to address the global and devastating nature of Covid-19 requires 'stronger commitments from States to international cooperation'.[23] The failure to address Covid-19 in developing countries will affect and impact on developed countries. Global interdependence requires cooperative efforts to fully protect socio-economic rights. While CESCR has used Covid-19 as a prism to discuss the need for cooperation to tackle to challenges to socio-economic rights that are inherently cross-border in nature, these insights can be extended to similar types of challenges such as climate change.

Second, in General Comment No 25 on science, CESCR notes the 'existence of deep international disparities among countries'.[24] To correct this disparity, in the context of science CESCR encourages 'developed states to contribute to the development of science and technology in developing countries' through overseas development aid, promoting collaboration across geographic borders and stemming the effects of the 'brain drain'.[25] Third, along with anchoring cooperation in the need generated by cross-border challenges and global disparities

[18] The CEDAW Committee, 'General Recommendation No. 19 on violence against women' (1992) CEDAW/C/GC/19 para 1; CESCR, 'General Comment No. 15 on the right to water' (2002) E/C.12/2002/11 para 1.

[19] M Campbell, *Women, Poverty, Equality: The Role of CEDAW* (Hart 2018) 215.

[20] CESCR, 'General Comment No. 22 on the right to sexual and reproductive health' (2016) E/C.12/GC/22 para 50; CESCR, 'General Comment No. 25 on science' (2020) E/C.12/GC/25 para 79.

[21] 'General Comment No. 22' (n 20) para 50; CESCR, 'Social Protection Floors: An essential element of the right to social security and the Sustainable Development Goals' (2015) E/C.12/2015/1.

[22] CESCR, 'Statement on the COVID-19 pandemic' (2020) E/C.12/2020/1 para 23.

[23] ibid.

[24] 'General Comment No. 25' (n 20) para 79.

[25] ibid para 79.

the rationale for cooperation is rooted in the realities of technology. CESCR explains that 'international cooperation should be enhanced as technologies need global regulations in order to be effectively managed'.[26] The scope, prevalence and power of technologies requires global cooperation. Without it, there is a risk of fragmented national regulations which could create governance gaps and 'perpetuate technological divides and economic disparities'.[27] Cooperation among States is needed because of global inequalities and failing to cooperate can entrench these gaps, thus the reasons CESCR provides for cooperation are linked together. At this stage, while CESCR is only giving passing acknowledgment to the complexities underpinning the disparities among States,[28] it could more fully engage with the magnitude of the need for cooperation. Fully unearthing the roots of global gaps and stressing the cross-border nature of human rights obstacles can act as a diagnostic tool and provide greater clarity on the role of cooperation in fulfilling socio-economic rights. Teasing out the reasons why international cooperation and assistance is required could also, in theory, build greater legitimacy and support among stakeholders for a legal duty of cooperation.

In contrast to earlier questions on whether there is a legal obligation to cooperate, CESCR holds that cooperation is not only needed to respond to cross-border challenges and global disparities, but it is a legal, as opposed to moral, obligation. CESCR provides a textual analysis by drawing an inverse inference from Article 14. States are only required to provide primary education within their jurisdictions; thus, the absence of any reference to jurisdictional limits in the remaining socio-economic rights obligations means ICESCR is not constrained by territorial borders.[29] To buttress this reading, CESCR also refers to the duty of cooperation in Articles 2(1) and 15(4).[30] It explains that it would be contradictory to allow a State to remain passive to the status of human rights in other States under Article 2(1).[31] Surprisingly, there is no reference in the latest General Comments to the role of cooperation in the right to continuous improvement of living conditions under Article 11. This is a missed opportunity to stress the centrality of a legal duty to cooperate in ICESCR.

Beyond the text of the treaty, CESCR references cooperation in other international legal instruments. This implicitly legitimates the obligation to cooperate and justifies CESCR's increased focus on this duty. It refers to the UN Charter, the International Court of Justice, the UN Special Rapporteur on extreme poverty and human rights, and customary international law.[32] In drawing on

[26] ibid para 74.
[27] ibid.
[28] J Linarelli, M Salomon and M Sornarajah, *The Misery of International Law* (OUP 2018).
[29] CESCR, 'General Comment No. 24 on business activities' (2017) E/C.12/GC/24 para 27.
[30] 'General Comment No. 25' (n 20) para 77.
[31] 'General Comment No. 24' (n 29) para 27.
[32] ibid.

these other sources, CESCR is employing techniques common among UN treaty bodies to legitimise international cooperation and assistance. There are odd omissions, as CESCR makes no reference to cooperation in the remaining core UN treaties[33] or Sustainable Development Goal 17, which calls for a global partnership to 'strengthen domestic resource mobilization including through international support to developing countries'.[34] At this stage CESCR has only begun to lay the foundation for a more in-depth engagement with the obligation of international cooperation.

B. Triggering the Obligation

In theory, a duty of cooperation, like many human rights, including the duty to continuously improve living conditions, could be so broad as to be a meaningless utopian goal. Crafting principled and practical triggering criteria for cooperation has bedevilled academic discourse.[35] CESCR is beginning to develop criteria to place boundaries on the obligation to cooperate. The criteria, however, are currently vague.

CESCR is considering triggering criteria for both sides of the cooperation equation. CESCR calls on States to maximise available resources through international cooperation[36] and urges them to seek cooperation 'when facing considerable difficulties in achieving progressive realisation'.[37] This statement is in the same paragraph where CESCR discusses the need to avoid deliberately retrogressive measures, suggesting that cooperation is a bulwark against retrogression.[38] In another place in the same General Comment, CESCR explains that 'when a State … is not in a position to meet its obligation' under ICESCR, 'it must seek international assistance''[39] This is a slightly broader requirement as it is not only failing to make forward progress that triggers the obligation, but the failure to realise the core obligation or any stagnation in the full enjoyment of socio-economic rights that activates the obligation to seek cooperation. If the obligation to seek cooperation hinges on the failure to fully realise socio-economic rights, then every State in the world would have to seek cooperation.

[33] Articles 4, 17(b), 22, 24(4), 45 of the Convention of the Rights of the Child (adopted 20 November 1989, entry into force 2 September 1990) 1577 UNTS 3; Articles 2, 32, 37 and 38 of Convention on the Rights of Persons with Disabilities A/RES/61/106.

[34] 'Sustainable Development Goal 17-Target 17.1' <https://sustainabledevelopment.un.org/sdg17> accessed 23 June 2020.

[35] W Vandenhole and W Benedek, 'Extraterritorial Human Rights Obligations and North-South Divide' in Malcolm Langford et al (eds), *Global Justice, State Duties: The Extraterritorial Scope of ESCR in International Law* (CUP 2013).

[36] 'General Comment No. 22' (n 20) para 50.

[37] CESCR, 'General Comment No. 23 on the right to just and favourable conditions of work' (2016) E/C.12/GC/23 para 52.

[38] ibid.

[39] ibid para 67.

While this might be attractive, as it accords formal equal treatment to all States, it fails to account for the global disparities that, as CESCR explains, anchors the need for cooperation. This overly broad formulation fails to provide concrete guidance on when a State has a legal obligation to seek cooperation. This makes it temptingly easy for States to continue to dismiss this duty as a rhetorical utopian dream. Furthermore, the triggering criteria have been developed in relation to Article 2(1) and mobilising resources, not in relation to the right to continuous improvement. In some ways, tying cooperation to failure to fully realise continuous improvement is potentially even more conceptually confusing as there is a lack of conceptual clarity on whether continuous improvement has a ceiling or upper limit.[40] It is difficult to unpack the triggering criteria for cooperating to continuously improve as the right itself is conceptually murky.

On the other side of the equation, States 'in a position to do so' must provide cooperation.[41] There has been a minimal engagement with what it means to be 'in a position' to provide cooperation. States must respond to requests for cooperation in good faith. CESCR also alludes to the availability of resources when providing cooperation and explains that 'economically developed States have a special responsibility for assisting developing countries'.[42] This seems to imply that the special responsibility is realised through the transfer of economic resources. In practice, CESCR sees the special responsibility to cooperate as not purely a function of the availability of economic resources but also of power, leverage and clout. States are obligated to cooperate when 'they are in a position to influence' business actors not to undermine human rights in other States.[43] CESCR illustrates this capacity to cooperate by influencing the corporation to pay taxes in other States. A State is also 'in a position' to provide cooperation if it has knowledge or can reasonably foresee a risk that a business will harm socio-economic rights in other States. The well documented risks in the extractive industry mean the State has a due diligence obligation to oversee mining and oil development projects operating beyond the State borders.[44] CESCR is working to refine the criteria to provide cooperation and is seeking to develop triggering conditions that are not exclusively tied to the availability of economic resources.

C. Facets of Cooperation

CESCR has devoted most of its energies towards developing the normative content of cooperation. This can be in the form of vague reminders to the State

[40] See Lott, chapter seven in this volume, and Skogly, chapter eight in this volume.
[41] 'General Comment No. 23' (n 37) para 66; 'General Comment No. 22' (n 20) para 50.
[42] ibid para 50; 'General Comment No. 23' (n 37) para 67.
[43] 'General Comment No. 24' (n 29) para 37.
[44] ibid para 32, fn 81.

to cooperate to realise socio-economic rights[45] or more specifically to strengthen cooperation on certain issues such as sex tourism, the Rohingya refugee crisis or the Sustainable Development Goals.[46] CESCR provides overarching guiding principles on the implementation of international cooperation. States must respond to requests for cooperation by providing economic and technical assistance.[47] Cooperation must be sustainable, culturally appropriate and uphold human rights standards, although CESCR does not expand on these standards.[48] It further explains that the transfer of knowledge and technology is a tool to maximise the available resources to fulfil socio-economic rights under Article 2(1).[49] Noticeably, there is no reference to economic, technological or knowledgeable cooperation in furthering Article 11. Although the cooperation it advocates for under Article 2(1) can have a positive knock-on effect on living conditions, CESCR for all intents and purposes appears to have forgotten about the cooperative obligation under Article 11. The transfer of economic or technical resources is rarely earmarked for improving food production, water or housing conditions. This subsection critically evaluates the different facets of cooperation advocated for by CESCR.

i. International Organisations

To begin with, CESCR consistently advocates that States cooperate with the other actors in the international human rights system. There are three methods of cooperation: (i) ratifying an international (and occasionally regional) instrument; (ii) collaborating with different branches of the UN; and (iii) influencing international organisations to strengthen socio-economic rights.

CESCR has a repeated pattern of encouraging States to adopt various International Labor Organization (ILO) Conventions, but only erratically recommends adoption of other human rights instruments. It consistently encourages States to domesticate ILO Conventions and Recommendations on social protection, collective bargaining, freedom of association, informal work and Indigenous peoples.[50] There are only isolated recommendations to adopt other ILO Conventions such as on minimum wage, domestic workers and forced labour.[51] There are only a handful of examples of CESCR encouraging States to

[45] CESCR, 'CO: Gambia' (2015) E/C.12/GMB/CO/1 para 31.

[46] CESCR, 'CO: Thailand' (2015) E/C.12/THA/CO/1-2; para 25(c); CESCR, 'CO: Bangladesh' (2018) E/C.12/BGD/CO/1 para 28; CESCR, 'CO: Costa Rica' E/C.12/CRI/CO/5 para 67.

[47] 'General Comment No. 23' (n 37) para 66.

[48] ibid para 67.

[49] ibid.

[50] CESCR, 'CO: Australia' (2017) E/C.12/AUG/CO/5 para 30; CESCR, 'CO: Canada' (2016) E/C.12/ para 20(e); CESCR, 'CO: Burkina Faso' (2016) E/C.12/BFA/CO/1 para 22; 'CO: Gambia' (n 45) para 19.

[51] CESCR, 'CO: Mexico' (2018) E/C.12/MEX/CO/5-6 para 33(d); CESCR, 'CO: South Korea' (2017) E/C.12/KOR/CO/4 para 37; CESCR, 'CO: North Macedonia' (2016) E/C.12/MKD/CO/2-4 para 32.

adopt UN treaties or soft law instruments, such as the UN Declaration on the Rights of Indigenous People[52] and World Health Organization standards.[53] The one outlier to this trend is that CESCR routinely advocates that States adopt the UN Food and Agriculture Organization Voluntary Guidelines on National Food Security.[54] Although there are a wealth of regional human rights agreements, CESCR only encourages relevant States to adopt the Istanbul Convention on Preventing and Combating Violence Against Women and Domestic Violence.[55]

CESCR strongly advocates that States seek guidance from international organisations. There are also trends to this aspect of cooperation. There are numerous instances where CESCR encourages States to collaborate with the Office of the High Commissioner of Human Rights (OHCHR).[56] It recommends that States seek OHCHR technical guidance on implementing CESCR's recommendations, in reducing maternal morbidity and mortality, and in developing human rights indicators.[57] There are a few examples of CESCR encouraging States to cooperate with the UN High Commissioner on Refugees, UNESCO and the ILO.[58] There are only a handful of occurrences of CESCR encouraging cooperation with the UN Special Mandate holders.[59] There are only three cases of CESCR recommending that the State cooperate with a regional human rights regime. It encourages Kenya to implement the African Commission decision on *Endorois* and that Namibia and Angola re-instate the right of access of natural and legal persons to the new protocol on the Southern African Development Community Tribunal.[60]

Through international cooperation, CESCR is seeking to integrate human rights within the work of international organisations, particularly financial organisations (IFIs), such as the International Monetary Fund (IMF). CESCR emphasises that States 'participating in decisions as members of international organizations cannot ignore their human rights obligations'.[61] It goes so far as

[52] 'CO: Canada' (n 50) para 20(d); CESCR, 'CO: Honduras' (2016) E/C.12/HND/CO/2 para 12(b); CESCR, 'CO: Philippines' (2016) E/C.12/PHL/CO/5-6 para 14(a); CESCR, 'CO: Guyana' (2015) E/C.12/GUY/CO/2-4 para 15.

[53] CESCR, 'CO: Uruguay' (2017) E/C.12/URY/CO/5 paras 39, 49; 'CO: Costa Rica' (n 46) para 45.

[54] CESCR, 'CO: UK' (2016) E/C.12/GBR/CO/6 para 54.

[55] CESCR, 'CO: Slovakia' (2017) E/C.12/SVK/CO/3 para 28; 'CO: North Macedonia' (n 51) para 40.

[56] 'CO: Gambia' (n 45) para 31; CESCR, 'CO: Sudan' (2015) E/C.12/SDN/CO/2 para 59.

[57] CESCR, 'CO: Namibia' (2016) E/C.12/NAM/CO/1 para 79; 'CO: Burkina Faso' (n 50) para 45; CESCR, 'CO: Dominican Republic' (2016) E/C.12/DOM/CO/4 para 60(b); 'CO: Sudan' (n 56) para 58; CESCR, 'CO: Morocco' (2015) E/C.12/MAR/CO/4 para 52.

[58] CESCR, 'CO: Ecuador' (2019) E/C.12/ECU/CO/4 para 60(a); 'CO: Thailand' (n 46) para 16; CESCR, 'CO: Greece' (2015) E/C.12/GRC/CO/2 para 11–para 12; 'General Comment No. 23' (n 37) para 68; CESCR, 'CO: Angola' (2016) E/C.12/AGO/CO/4-5 para 38.

[59] 'CO: Namibia' (n 57) para 16(c); 'CO: Mexico' (n 51) para 11; CESCR, 'Public Debt and Austerity Measures' (2016) E/C.12/2016/1 para 11.

[60] CESCR, 'CO: Kenya' (2016) E/C.12/KEN/CO/2-5 paras 15–6; 'CO: Namibia' (n 57) paras 8–9; 'CO: Angola' (n 58) paras 11–12.

[61] 'General Comment No. 25' (n 20) para 83; 'General Comment No. 23' (n 37) para 71; 'Public Debt and Austerity' (n 59) para 9.

to hold that States would be in violation of ICESCR if States 'were to delegate power to IMF or other agencies and allowed such powers to be exercised without ensuring that they do not infringe on human rights'.[62] Through their influence within the organisation and their voting power, States should ensure the international organisations uphold socio-economic rights.[63] Cooperating through influencing international organisations applies also to financial instruments such as lending policies, credit agreements and fiscal adjustment.[64] Cooperating via international organisations connects to the power-influence component of the triggering criteria to provide cooperation. For instance, CESCR regrets that Germany has not used 'its great leverage' to ensure that the IMF loan conditionalities 'do not result in unjustified retrogression' in socio-economic rights by borrowing States.[65] CESCR recommends that Germany use its position to influence high-level policy and ensure that IFIs undertake human rights impact assessment to loan provisions.[66]

There are also obligations on the States receiving support from IFIs. Lebanon is encouraged to dialogue with the IMF on debt servicing and to develop a legal framework to ensure transparency and accountability in loan negotiating and debt management.[67] However, the CESCR's guidance is not always sufficiently attentive to the different abilities of States and IFI to negotiate terms of financial support. CESCR warns that borrowing Sates should ensure that any financial assistance should not include conditions that 'unreasonably reduce its ability' to implement ICESCR.[68] These recommendations, however, arguably ignore the power imbalances between States and IFIs, and borrowing States may have limited ability to ensure loans are designed to fulfil socio-economic rights. In 2020, when reviewing IMF-imposed conditions on Ukraine, CESCR appears to have recognised these imbalances and it only requires the State to conduct a human rights impact assessment on the fiscal consolidation programme.[69] This is also one of the exceptionally rare incidents where CESCR has adopted an intersectional perspective to cooperation, expressing concern that IMF policies disproportionately affect 'women living in poverty or [people] in rural areas'.[70] Although CESCR rarely frames these discussions in terms of 'continuously improving', mainstreaming human rights into high level international and domestic law and policy could improve living conditions. In the future, CESCR could make more explicit how the right to continuous improvement of living

[62] 'Public Debt and Austerity' (n 59) para 9.
[63] ibid.
[64] 'General Comment No. 23' (n 37) para 71.
[65] CESCR, 'CO: Germany' (2018) E/C.12/DEU/CO/6 paras 16–17.
[66] ibid.
[67] CESCR, 'CO: Lebanon' (2016) E/C.12/LBN/CO/2 para 13; 'CO: Sudan' (n 56) para 18.
[68] 'Public Debt and Austerity' (n 59) para 4; CESCR, 'CO: Ireland' (2015) E/C.12/IRL/CO/3 para 35.
[69] CESCR, 'CO: Ukraine' (2020) E/C.12/UKR/CO/7 paras 4–5.
[70] ibid.

conditions requires an enabling legal framework and respect for the international human rights system.

ii. Cooperation between States

Along with cooperating with international organisations, CESCR encourages cooperation between States. This is a crucial step forward as it more clearly delineates the identity of the duty bearer and addresses the critique that the duty of cooperation is held in a generic manner by the international community. CESCR has yet to pinpoint that State Y must legally assist State X. Instead, it more obliquely encourages States to cooperate with regional neighbours; however, this is still a higher degree of clarity than previously articulated. Italy should seek cooperation from other Member States in the EU to protect the socio-economic rights of migrants.[71] Thailand is advised to engage with 'countries in the region' to address the Rohingya refugee crisis. Beyond the rights of migrants, CESCR recommends that Iraq seek cooperative agreements with neighbouring States to ensure fair use of the river courses within its territories.[72] In response to Covid-19, CESCR is also encouraging stronger cooperation between States. It encourages States to share research, medical equipment and supplies; to coordinate action to reduce economic and social impacts; and work together in pursuing recovery efforts.[73] CESCR also provides examples of non-cooperation, such as imposing limits on the export of medical equipment, or unilateral border measures or economic sanctions that hinder the flow of health equipment and staple foods.[74]

iii. Business and Human Rights

CESCR has an increasingly sophisticated approach to cooperation, relying heavily on the typology of duties (respect, protect and fulfil), to regulate businesses to protect human rights across territorial boundaries.

When a State owns, controls or subsidises an enterprise acting in another State it accrues obligations to respect human rights beyond its geographic territory.[75] The obligation of respect flows through the supply chain of the State-controlled enterprise and requires the State to mitigate risks of violations of ICESCR by subcontractors etc.[76] The home-State should not actively undermine the working conditions in host-States.[77] If the home-State has a stronger

[71] CESCR, 'CO: Italy' (2015) E/C.12/ITA/CO/5 para 19.
[72] CESCR, 'CO: Iraq' (2015) E/C.12/IRQ/CO/4 para 52.
[73] 'Statement on the COVID-19 pandemic' (n 22).
[74] ibid paras 20–22.
[75] 'General Comment No. 23' (n 37) para 69.
[76] 'CO: South Korea' (n 51) para 18(a).
[77] 'General Comment No. 23' (n 37) para 69.

legislative framework than the host-State, it must maintain the higher labour standards from the home-State when operating within the host-State, as far as practicable.[78] CESCR does stress that the obligation to protect human rights through international cooperation cannot infringe the sovereignty or diminish the obligations of the host-State.[79] At the same time, it explicitly hopes the home-State regulation of working conditions of businesses operating beyond its borders will act as a 'boot-strap' for improving labour regulation in the host-State.[80]

In negotiating bilateral, multilateral and regional trade, tax, investment or financial agreements States must respect human rights across borders. These types of agreement must not restrict the ability of any State to implement socio-economic rights, and human rights must be given weight and directly referred to in these agreements.[81] In the context of scientific progress, States must ensure when negotiating international agreements or adopting domestic laws on intellectual property that 'traditional knowledge is protected, contributions to scientific knowledge are … credited and that intellectual property regimes foster the enjoyment' of rights.[82] This is an acknowledgement that in cooperating via international agreements there is a requirement to approach scientific practice from an Indigenous perspective. Investor-State dispute settlement procedures must not create obstacles to the realisation of ICESCR.[83]

Home-States also have a due diligence cooperative obligation to protect individuals in host States through legislative and administrative measures from violations of human rights by business domiciled within the home-State.[84] Again, as further illumination of the special responsibility on developed States, the obligation to protect is particularly pronounced for States with an advanced labour law architecture.[85] CESCR has begun to flesh out 'legislative and administrative measures' from the perspective of both home- and host-States.[86] Home-States should investigate violations of rights,[87] formally monitor businesses,[88] strengthen embassies in host-States;[89] remedy violations[90] and facilitate communication between law enforcement in home- and host-States.[91]

[78] ibid.
[79] General Comment No. 24' (n 29) para 25.
[80] ibid para 70.
[81] ibid para 72.
[82] 'General Comment No 25' (n 20) para 83.
[83] 'CO: Canada' (n 50) para 16; CESCR, 'CO: France' (2016) E/C.12/FRA/CO/4 para 10(c).
[84] 'General Comment No. 23' (n 37) para 70; 'General Comment No. 24' (n 29) para 28; 'CO: Thailand' (n. 46) para 12; CESCR, 'CO: Sweden' (2016) E/C.12/SWE/CO/6 para 12; CESCR, 'CO: Chile' (2015) E/C.12/CHL/CO/4 para 11.
[85] 'General Comment No. 23' (n 37) para 70.
[86] 'CO: Germany' (n 65) paras 7–8; 'CO: Mexico' (n 51) paras 11–12.
[87] 'CO: Canada' (n 50) para 16; 'CO: Australia' (n 50) para 14(d).
[88] CESCR, 'CO: Netherlands' (2017) E/C.12/NLD/CO/6 para 12(a).
[89] ibid.
[90] CESCR, 'CO: Kazakhstan' (2019) E/C.12/KAZ/CO/2 para 18(c).
[91] 'General Comment No. 24' (n 29) para 34.

Home-States are routinely criticised for not having a national action plan for regulating companies acting overseas.[92] A home-State should also use its soft power to incentivise corporations domiciled within the home-State to protect human rights abroad through the public provision of contracts, loans, grants and subsidies.[93] CESCR has zoned in on due diligence obligations in relation to specific industries. The Netherlands was criticised for failing to protect Indigenous peoples in Peru from environmental damage and is encouraged to 'expedite an overhaul of the oil refinery industry in Curaçao' to prevent pollution.[94] This is rare evidence of CESCR exploring the linkages between cooperation, business, intersectional equality and the environment. There are also due diligence obligations on host-States. For example, CESCR encourages Uganda to address illicit financial flows by addressing transfer pricing by foreign investors and is urged to protect local farmers from the adverse effects of leasing land to foreign investors.[95] Senegal should strengthen its domestic control over fishing by foreign companies through the 'cooperation of the international community'.[96]

CESCR consistently advocates that home- and host-States undertake human rights impact assessments before proceeding with any economic enterprise.[97] Germany is encouraged to conduct human rights impact assessments on the 'overall impact of agricultural exports on developing countries in order to [comply] with its Covenant obligations on international assistance and cooperation' and ensure that food exports to developing countries do not threaten the local farming sector.[98] Kenya, through its role in the East African Community, should ensure that negotiations with the EU are not undertaken without both a human rights assessment and consultation process with farmers, fishers and healthcare providers to identify potential negative impacts on socio-economic rights.[99] CESCR recommends that no farmland be ceded to investors until Sudan completes a full human rights impact assessment.[100] Although these recommendations are not explicitly anchored in Article 11, these cross-border impact assessments are being directed towards food production and export which is a component of continuously improving living conditions under Article 11.

CESCR also encourages cross-border impact assessments in other fields of life. Switzerland and Kazakhstan are encouraged to conduct 'human rights

[92] CESCR, 'CO: Denmark' (2019) E/C.12/DNK/CO/6 para 19; CESCR, 'CO: Russia' (2017) E/C.12/RUS/CO/6 para 12.

[93] 'General Comment No. 24' (n 29) para 31; 'CO: South Korea' (n 51) para 18(c).

[94] 'CO: Netherlands' (n 88) paras 11, 12(d).

[95] CESCR, 'CO: Uganda' (2015) E/C.12/UGA/CO/1 paras 11, 31; 'CO: Sudan' (n 56) para 11.

[96] CESCR, 'CO: Senegal' (2019) E/C.12/SEN/CO/3 para 29(b).

[97] CESCR, 'CO: Norway' (2020) E/C.12/NOR/CO/6 para 9.

[98] 'CO: Germany' (n 65) para 13.

[99] 'CO: Kenya' (n 60) para 13.

[100] 'CO: Sudan' (n 56) paras 11–12.

and environmental impact assessments before entering into' investment, trade or licensing agreements.[101] CESCR is critical of France, as EU trade agreements do not devote sufficient attention to socio-economic rights in other countries.[102] This is a further indication, as discussed in more detail above, that CESCR is holding States, particularly powerful States, to account for their role in international organisation. While the focus on cross-border human rights implications of trade is a step forward, it may also signal the potential thinness of international cooperating via human rights impact assessments. CESCR only recommends that the State conduct the assessment – a procedural obligation – and there is almost never a follow-up recommendation to modify behaviour based on the outcome of the assessment – a substantive obligation. There is an unstated assumption that States will make the necessary modifications in light of the assessment. The connection between procedural obligations and substantive outcomes is far from settled. Questions on the transformative potential of cross-border impact assessment echoes debates on the value of meaningful engagement in realising socio-economic rights or of the legal obligation to have due regard to equality in public decision making.[103] An arguably stronger approach can be seen in relation to the UK. After recommending that the UK conduct an impact assessment on the arms trade, CESCR urges the State to refuse or suspend a 'license where there is a risk that arms could be used to violate' human rights.[104]

iv. Migrant Workers

The rights of migrant workers are ripe for international cooperation.[105] CESCR almost exclusively deals with this aspect of cooperation from the perspective of the State of origin, although noting that 'when confronted by large flows of migrants … some States face a heavier burden than others'.[106] In the last five years, CESCR has not consistently encouraged States of employment or transit to cooperate to protect migrants' socio-economic rights.[107] In General Comment No 23 on just and fair working conditions, there is passing reference to cooperation to protect migrant workers: States must protect their nationals working

[101] 'CO: Kazakhstan' (n 90) para 18(e); CESCR, 'CO: Switzerland' (2019) E/C.12/CHE/CO/4 para 14.

[102] 'CO: France' (n 83) paras 9–10.

[103] S Wilson and J Dugard, 'Constitutional Jurisprudence: The First and Second Waves' in M Langford et al (eds), *Socio-Economic Rights in South Africa* (CUP 2014); S Fredman, 'The Public Sector Equality Duty' (2011) 40 *Industrial Law Journal* 405.

[104] 'CO: UK' (n 54) para 12(c).

[105] Article 33, 64, 65(b), 67 of Convention on the Protection of the Rights of All Migrant Workers and Members of Their Families A/RES/45/15; CEDAW Committee, 'General Recommendation No 28 on women migrant workers' (2008) CEDAW/C/GC/28.

[106] CESCR, 'The Duties of States Towards Refugees and Migrants' (2017) E/C.12/2017/1 para 18.

[107] CESCR, 'CO: Mauritius' (2019) E/C.12/MUS/CO/5 para 33(e) and CESCR, 'CO: Israel' (2019) E/C.12/ISR/CO/4 para 29(c) are exceptions.

abroad through international cooperation.[108] The favoured measure for protection is through bilateral agreements to provide for labour, social and pension protection.[109] States of origin should strengthen consular support services in States of employment;[110] support migrant workers returning to the State of origin;[111] and strengthen the regulation of recruitment agencies.[112] In a few instances, CESCR is attentive to the intersectional dimensions to cooperation in relation to migrant workers. Tajikistan should integrate a gender perspective into its labour migration policies;[113] Kenya and Bangladesh should review existing bilateral agreements in relation to women migrant domestic workers;[114] and Kyrgyzstan should take all efforts 'to ensure that the spouses and children of Kyrgyz migrant workers obtain adequate residence permits in the country of employment'.[115]

v. Budget, Debt and Tax

There is only a small body of jurisprudence on cooperating via domestic economic and financial legislation and policy. Bohoslavsky and Cantamutto's chapter in this collection considers this aspect of cooperation and its role in continuous improvement in greater detail.[116] CESCR makes brief mentions of foreign debt, and some of its discussion on debt is through the lens of cooperating via international organisations, discussed above.[117] It does caution that lending States should not coerce other States into violating the ICESCR.[118] As best practice guidance it requires lending (and borrowing) States to conduct a human rights impact assessment prior to providing financial assistance.[119]

The primary focus is on global tax abuse. On the side of developed States, the UK is criticised for having financial secrecy law and permissive rules on corporate tax which negatively affect the ability of other States to mobilise resources for socio-economic rights.[120] CESCR urges States to ensure that fiscal policy is 'adequate, progressive and socially equitable' to increase the available resources and to intensify efforts to address global tax abuse, particularly by corporations and high-net-worth individuals.[121] On the developing States' side, South Africa

[108] 'General Comment' No 23 (n 37) para 73.
[109] CESCR, 'CO: Tajikistan' (2015) E/C.12/TJK/CO/2-3 para 22(c); CESCR, 'CO: Moldova' (2019) E/C.12/MDA/CO/3 para 29(c).
[110] 'CO: Tajikistan' (n 109) para 22(b).
[111] 'CO: Moldova' (n 109) para 29.
[112] 'CO: Bangladesh' (n 46) para 39(b).
[113] 'CO: Tajikistan' (n 109) para 22(e).
[114] 'CO: Bangladesh' (n 46) para 39(d); 'CO: Kenya' (n 60) para 34.
[115] CESCR, 'CO: Kyrgyzstan' (2015) E/C.12/KGZ/CO/2-3 para 13.
[116] See Bohoslavsky and Cantamutto, chapter five in this volume.
[117] 'CO: Tajikistan' (n 109) para 11; 'CO: Lebanon' (n 67) paras 12–13.
[118] 'Public Debt and Austerity Measures' (n 59) para 5.
[119] ibid para 5.
[120] 'CO: UK' (n 54) para 16.
[121] ibid para 17; 'CO: Switzerland' (n 101) para 13.

should combat tax avoidance by corporations by seeking cooperation with the home-State of the corporation.[122] CESCR is concerned that Mauritius' low rate of tax on direct investment will encourage a race to the bottom in the region.[123] Understandably this has been linked to Article 2(1) and resource mobilisation, but it has potential positive spillover in generating additional resources for the right to continuous improvement of living conditions.

vi. Overseas Development Aid

The transfer of economic resources from one State to another – overseas development aid (ODA) – is perhaps the quintessential and most controversial facet of cooperation. CESCR is holding States to account for a human rights obligation to provide and seek ODA. CESCR regrets that ODA levels are below the internationally agreed commitment to 0.7 per cent of gross national income.[124] Its recommendations, perhaps unsurprisingly given the resistance to a legal obligation on ODA, are tepid. CESCR only encourages these States to 'accelerate the increase of the level of its [ODA], with 0.7 per cent benchmark'.[125] This reflects Vandenhole's argument that the obligation to cooperate via the transfer of economic resources is subject to progressive realisation.[126] There are also obligations to seek ODA.[127] When reviewing Capo Verde, CESCR notes that financial support from international cooperation has diminished and urges the State to 'continue to seek assistance from relevant international organizations and development agencies'.[128]

CESCR is also exploring more of the nuances of ODA. It must be implemented in a manner that upholds socio-economic rights. For instance, it calls on receiving States to enhance the transparency of the receipt, management and spending of ODA.[129] Donor States must not exclude particular services from ODA funding.[130] This implicitly addresses the 'Global Gag Rule', that is, the prohibition, instated under US Republican governments, of providing ODA to organisations that promote, provide or even give information on abortion.[131] ODA should not push receiving States into privatising health care.[132] Essentially,

[122] CESCR, 'Concluding Observations: South Africa' (2018) E/C.12/ZAF/CO/1 para 17(d).
[123] 'CO: Mauritius' (n 107) paras 13–14.
[124] 'CO: South Korea' (n 51) para 20; 'General Comment No 22' (n 20) para 50.
[125] ibid.
[126] Vandenhole, 'Towards a Division' (n 6).
[127] CESCR, 'CO: Guinea' (2020) E/C.12/GIN/CO/1 para 13.
[128] CESCR, 'CO: Capo Verde (2018) E/C.12/CPV/CO/1 paras 12–13.
[129] CESCR, 'CO: Central African Republic' (2018) E/C.12/CAF/CO/1 para 16(b); 'CO: Tajikistan' (n 109) [11]; 'CO: South Korea' (n 51) para 21.
[130] 'General Comment No. 22' (n 20) paras 41, 52.
[131] A Starrs, 'The Trump Global Gag Rule: An Attack on US Family Planning and Global Health Aid' (2017) 389 (10068) *Lancet* 485.
[132] 'General Comment No. 22' (n 20) para 52.

ODA should not be used to promote beliefs or ideologies that can jeopardise the realisation of socio-economic rights. Along with sexual and reproductive health, CESCR recommends that donor States contribute to the funding of science in recipient States.[133] The cooperation on enhancing the ability of recipient States to pursue beneficial scientific progress could link to cooperation to continuously improve living conditions.

CESCR is critical of the fact that the implementation of ODA is perpetuating rights violations. The UK is criticised for financially supporting private actors in education 'which may have contributed to undermining the quality of free public education and created segregation and discrimination among pupils and students'.[134] France is taken to task by CESCR for failing to ensure that ODA does not perpetuate environmental or social harm.[135] CESCR is also critical of States receiving ODA. It is concerned that Cameroon has no measures to protect rights through development projects.[136] There is a strong intersectional analysis, as CESCR is worried that these projects are undermining the traditional lifestyles of Indigenous peoples. The critique of Cameroon is also one of the exceptional occurrences where CESCR makes explicit the relevance of Article 11 to ODA. To uphold human rights through ODA, donor and receiving States must undertake impact assessments, including consultation with Indigenous peoples, prior to any ODA project.[137] These are procedural obligations, akin to impact assessments for business and human rights, and raise similar questions on the transformative potential of assessments and consultation. Donor States should establish effective monitoring mechanisms to assess the human rights impact of ODA policies and projects and embedded complaint mechanisms for violations of socio-economic rights in development cooperation projects.[138] In respect of Indigenous peoples, if their socio-economic rights are affected by ODA, they 'should receive compensation for damages or losses' and more radically 'receive a share of the profits from' the projects.[139] This is also one of the few examples of CESCR considering remedies for failing to cooperate and is evidence of the potential for radical remedies. It also highlights how remedies for failing to cooperate could link back to Article 11 by providing individuals and groups with the resources needed for improving living conditions.

vii. Climate Change

CESCR has recently released two Statements on climate change which call on States to 'cooperate in good faith' in devising global responses to climate

[133] 'General Comment No. 25' (n 20) para 79.
[134] 'CO: UK' (n 54) para 14.
[135] 'CO: France' (n 83) para 17.
[136] CESCR, 'CO: Cameroon' (2020) E/C.12/CMR/CO/4 para 16.
[137] ibid para 17(b); 'CO: UK' (n 54) para 15.
[138] 'CO: UK' (n 54) para 15.
[139] 'CO: Cameroon' (n 136) para 17(b).

change.[140] In both of these documents CESCR focuses on the obligations of developed States. Financial incentives or investments to private actors operating extraterritorially, such as the fossil fuel industry, that contribute to climate change should be discontinued, and States should offer protection mechanism for migrant workers displaced by climate change.[141] CESCR holds that as part of the duty of international assistance and cooperation, 'high-income State should support adaption efforts, particularly in developing countries, by facilitating the transfer of green technologies, and by contributing to the Green Climate Fund'.[142] It links these mitigation and adaption efforts to Article 15, not to Article 11. The connections and perhaps transformative and radical re-thinking on what constitute an adequate standard of living and continuous improvement of living conditions in the context of climate change have not yet been unpacked.

There are only a handful of occurrences where CESCR encourages States to cooperate to address the human rights violations inherent in climate change in the Concluding Observations. In one instance, CESCR recognised that Mauritius is bearing the brunt of the impact of climate change 'despite the fact that the State has made a negligible contribution to climate change'.[143] This is a textbook example of where and why international cooperation is needed and could, in theory, be a powerful avenue for building greater legitimacy for this duty. In the handful of cases where CESCR engages with climate change and cooperation in the Concluding Observations, it repeats facets of cooperation analysed above. It encourages States to adopt international and regional commitments and frameworks on climate change.[144] CESCR is also exploring how ODA can be harnessed towards redressing climate change.[145]

IV. CONCLUSION: CONTINUOUSLY IMPROVING COOPERATION

So, what can be taken away on the role of international cooperation in the right to continuous improvement of living conditions? On the positive side, CESCR is consistently holding States to account for international cooperation, but on the negative side, it largely ignores cooperation in light of continuous improvement of living conditions. Understanding both the nuances of CESCR's approach to cooperation and its blind spots, this chapter can hopefully act as a springboard

[140] CESCR and others, 'Statement on Human Rights and Climate Change' (2019) HRI/2019/1 [17]; CESCR, 'Statement on Climate Change and ICESCR' (2018) E/C.12/2018/1.

[141] CESCR and others (n 140) para 15.

[142] 'Statement on Climate Change and ICESCR' (n 140) para 7.

[143] 'CO: Mauritius' (n 107) para 9.

[144] CESCR, 'CO: Argentina' (2018) E/C.12/ARG/CO/4 paras 13–14; 'CO: Australia' (n 50) para 11; CESCR, 'CO: Ecuador' (2019) E/C.12/ECU/CO/4 paras 11–12; CESCR, 'CO: Belgium' (2020) E/C.12/BEL/CO/5 para 10.

[145] 'CO: Denmark' (n 92) paras 14–15; 'CO: Belgium' (n 144) paras 14–15.

for further engagement on the role of cooperation in the right to continuous improvement of living conditions.

Understanding the right to continuous improvement in connection with an obligation of cooperation could yield greater clarity on three unanswered questions on international cooperation. First, while CESCR is actively working to build up the legitimacy of a legal duty to cooperate, it has failed to draw on cooperation in the right to continuous improvement. This is a stark example of a missed opportunity to emphasise the centrality of cooperation in ICESCR. Second, CESCR is investigating the conditions upon which a State must cooperate and places obligations on States to seek and provide cooperation. Taking cooperation seriously under a right to continuous improvement raises challenges on identifying when a State is required to seek cooperation for continuous improvement. As the right is a continual obligation, pinning down theoretically coherent triggering criteria is a conceptual challenge. On the providing side of the equation, CESCR is recognising that there is a 'special responsibility' upon economically developed States. It is only at the beginning of refining what this special responsibility entails. Intriguingly, at this embryonic stage it is focusing on non-financial aspects. States with power or influence have a special responsibility to use this power to influence labour law in host-States or high-level international policy. There is space to understand how States' power and influence can be directed towards fulfilling the right to continuously improve.

Third, the core of CESCR's work on cooperation has been on unpacking the myriad of cooperative measures a State must undertake. There is a strong running thread to cooperate via international organisation and by ratifying international instruments. Interestingly, there are patterns to this cooperation as CESCR homes in on certain international organisations and only minimally engages with others. There is also very limited engagement with cooperation via regional human rights instruments. This could be the beginning of understanding the role of the legal and policy frameworks that are necessary to achieve the right to continuously improving living conditions. However, these inconsistencies are ripe for further research on CESCR's procedures and decision-making processes. CESCR's monitoring of certain aspects of cooperation is well developed – business and human rights – but only in its infancy in others – overseas development aid, migrant workers and climate change. As mentioned, there is little attention to cooperation being tied to rights to food (with the exception of protecting the land of small-scale farmers), clothing, housing or water or improving these aspects of an adequate standard of living. Although Article 11 explicitly calls on international cooperation to end hunger, to share scientific knowledge on food production and to create a system of equitable food distribution, there is virtually no reference to these aspects of cooperation in the work of CESCR in the last five years. In a similar vein, there are nods to an intersectional approach to cooperation, particularly with respect to Indigenous peoples, but much more is needed to ensure equality within international cooperation. And lastly, there is a creeping proceduralisation of cooperation through impact assessments and less regularly, through consultation. On one hand, this may be strategic to galvanise support for a legal duty to cooperate and could prompt meaningful engagement and change to improve rights protection, but on the other hand, this may dilute the transformative potential of cooperation.

Greater appreciation of the practice of CESCR is illuminating in continued theorising on cross-border obligations on socio-economic rights. The text of ICESCR recognises that no State acting alone can achieve the right to continuously improvement of living conditions. While cooperation is being taken seriously by CESCR, it is not devoting its energies to unpacking cooperation under Article 11. In the coming years, CESCR will continue to evolve cooperation and it is hoped more attention will be paid to how cooperation can facilitate a right to continuous improvement of living conditions.

4

The Right to Continuous Improvement of Living Conditions as a Response to Poverty

LUKE D GRAHAM

The world is at an existential crossroads involving a pandemic, a deep economic recession, devastating climate change, extreme inequality, and a movement challenging the prevalence of racism in many countries. A common thread running through all these challenges and exacerbating their consequences is the dramatic and longstanding neglect of extreme poverty and the systemic downplaying of the problem by many governments, economists, and human rights advocates.[1]

I. INTRODUCTION

PHILLIP ALSTON'S PARTHIAN shot – his final report as Special Rapporteur on extreme poverty and human rights – is rightly critical of current approaches to poverty eradication.[2] The parlous state of poverty eradication compounded by the effects of the Covid-19 pandemic – which 'will erase all poverty alleviation progress over the past three years, and will push 176 million people into poverty at the $3.20 poverty line'[3] – requires now more than ever that approaches to poverty eradication are reimagined.

One mechanism which can serve to address poverty is the neglected and underexplored right to continuous improvement of living conditions.

[1] P Alston, 'The Parlous State of Poverty Eradication: Report of the Special Rapporteur on Extreme Poverty and Human Rights (Advance Unedited Version)' (7 July 2020) UN Doc A/HRC/44/40 para 1 <https://www.ohchr.org/EN/HRBodies/HRC/RegularSessions/Session44/Documents/A_HRC_44_40_AUV.docx> accessed 23 July 2020. I am grateful to Sigrun Skogly for the thought provoking and fruitful discussions which we shared when this paper was initially drafted. I am grateful also for the incisive comments provided by the editors of this collection Beth Goldblatt and Jessie Hohmann which have clarified and focused this chapter. Any errors remain, solely, my own.

[2] ibid section II.

[3] ibid para 33.

Jessie Hohmann highlights that analysis of the Committee on Economic, Social, and Cultural Rights (CESCR's) approach to the right to continuous improvement of living conditions 'appears to reflect' a shift from a focus on 'overall development policy as a driver of improved living conditions as a right, to a right that is a response to poverty, and a greater focus on minimal standards, rather than on overall human development or flourishing'.[4] Despite this, there has been little substantive engagement with the implications of this for the right to continuous improvement of living conditions. Additionally, from the perspective of the right itself as opposed to poverty, it may be feared that such an approach is minimalistic, unambitious and limits the potential of this underexplored right.

In this chapter, I will explicitly engage the right to continuous improvement of living conditions from the perspective of poverty. This is to address several conceptual issues which stem from the right. These issues are the baseline from which improvement must be made, the limits on continuity of improvement, the rights-holders, and that which must be continuously improved. Some of these issues are highlighted for consideration by Skogly elsewhere in this volume[5] and I contend that poverty can serve as a useful framework through which to respond to these issues coherently and consistently.

In section II, poverty and extreme poverty are defined, before I argue that the baseline from which improvement must be made is the context-specific and relativist poverty threshold defined in section II. The implications of this baseline for the notion of continuity of the right will be explored in section III and I will argue that a poverty focus does not limit the notion of continuity within the right. Rather, the poverty lens allows for perpetual improvement. Beyond this, a poverty lens necessarily focuses on efforts towards improving material living conditions of the poor. However, as will be explored in section IV, such prioritisation does not deprive the non-poor of their status as rights holders and has positive implications for the more broadly understood living conditions of all. This broader understanding of living conditions – that is, that which must be continuously improved – is examined in section V, where I argue that the resources required to avoid poverty ought to represent the subject matter of this right. This is because approaching the right to continuous improvement of living conditions through the lens of a human rights-based approach to poverty results in a broad interpretation of the subject matter of this right, which in turn focuses upon the realisation of other human rights.

Based on this outlined analysis, in section VI I highlight how my conceptualisation of the right to continuous improvement of living conditions may apply in practice. That is, I demonstrate how in the context of Covid-19 a poverty-focused right to continuous improvement of living conditions can

[4] See Hohmann, chapter two in this volume.
[5] See Skogly, chapter eight in this volume.

serve to improve the living conditions of the rich and poor alike. In this sense, whilst the right is of an individual nature it may also be interpreted as a societal claim that the minimum conditions of living (the poverty threshold) within a society must be continuously improved.

As this chapter overview makes clear, the conceptual issues which I have highlighted are strongly interwoven and must be approached consistently. Therefore, in this chapter I view the right to the continuous improvement of living conditions through the lens of poverty and use this poverty lens as a framework through which to address the conceptual issues stemming from the right. Viewed in this way, the prevention and alleviation of poverty, whilst being of value in itself, can also be a stimulus for the implementation of fundamental social and economic rights including the right to the continuous improvement of living conditions. This is because the poverty lens can bring clarity to the right to continuous improvement of living conditions, whilst at the same time the right to continuous improvement of living conditions may bolster poverty eradication efforts.

II. POVERTY, EXTREME POVERTY AND LIVING CONDITIONS

Both poverty and extreme poverty carry specific meaning in the field of international human rights law and the living conditions faced by those experiencing poverty 'demonstrate violations of a large variety of human rights'.[6] The United Nations Committee on Economic, Social, and Cultural Rights (CESCR) endorses a 'multi-dimensional understanding of poverty', defining it:

> as a human condition characterized by sustained or chronic deprivation of the resources, capabilities, choices, security and power necessary for the enjoyment of an adequate standard of living and other civil, cultural, economic, political and social rights.[7]

As is clear from this statement, 'poverty is not solely an economic issue, but rather a multidimensional phenomenon that encompasses a lack of both income and the basic capabilities to live in dignity'.[8] This, in turn, has negative implications for the realisation of human rights and consequently living conditions.[9]

[6] S Skogly, 'Is There a Right Not to Be Poor?' (2002) 2 *Human Rights Law Review* 59, 74.

[7] CESCR, 'Substantive Issues Arising in The Implementation of The International Covenant on Economic, Social and Cultural Rights: Poverty and The International Covenant on Economic, Social and Cultural Rights' (13 May 2001) UN Doc E/C.12/2001/10, para 8.

[8] M Sepúlveda Carmona, 'Final Draft of the Guiding Principles on Extreme Poverty and Human Rights' (18 July 2012) UN Doc A/HRC/21/39, para 2.

[9] As will be addressed below, the focus on income-based approaches to poverty correlates to a view of the world in which opportunity and access to goods is always measured in terms of money. See nn 114–125.

Logically, poverty is less severe than extreme poverty. Sepúlveda Carmona observes that extreme poverty exists 'where a prolonged lack of basic security affects several aspects of people's lives simultaneously, severely compromising their chances of exercising or regaining their rights in the foreseeable future'.[10] On account of this, I suggest that one feature which distinguishes extreme poverty from poverty is inescapability. More clarity can be found by reference to the work of United Nations Independent Experts on the question of human rights and extreme poverty.

The first annual report of an independent expert on extreme poverty and human rights produced by A-M Lizin relies upon the definition of extreme poverty endorsed by Leandro Despouy in his role as UN Special Rapporteur on Prevention of Discrimination and Protection of Minorities.[11] Despouy endorses a definition of extreme poverty which foregrounds a lack of basic security:

> The lack of basic security connotes the absence of one or more factors enabling individuals and families to assume basic responsibilities and to enjoy fundamental rights. The situation may become widespread and result in more serious and permanent consequences. The lack of basic security leads to chronic poverty when it simultaneously affects several aspects of people's lives, when it is prolonged and when it severely compromises people's chances of regaining their rights and of reassuming their responsibilities in the foreseeable future.[12]

This definition highlights 'that the demarcation line between poverty and extreme poverty, although very real, may be fluid'.[13] Lizin later distinguished extreme poverty from mere poverty using the concept of social exclusion given that 'the extremely poor cannot express themselves or play a part in the communities in which they live'.[14] This is due to 'a total lack of resources and means of social integration'.[15]

It is the work of a later independent expert which offers a more comprehensive understanding of extreme poverty. Following the extension of the mandate of the Independent Expert on Extreme Poverty,[16] Arjun Sengupta was appointed as the new mandate holder. From 2005 to 2008, Sengupta produced four annual reports as independent expert on the question of human rights and extreme

[10] Sepúlveda Carmona (n 8) para 2.

[11] A-M. Lizin, 'Human Rights and Extreme Poverty' (29 Jan 1999) UN Doc E/CN.4/1999/48, paras 6–7.

[12] L Despouy 'Final report on human rights and extreme poverty' (28 June 1996) UN Doc E/CN.4/Sub.2/1996/13, Annex III.

[13] ibid.

[14] A-M Lizin, 'Report submitted by Ms. A.-M. Lizin, independent expert, pursuant to Commission resolution 1999/26' (25 February 2000) UN Doc E/CN.4/2000/52, para 8.

[15] ibid para 12.

[16] UNCHR Res 2004/23 (16 April 2004) UN Doc E/CN.4/RES/2004/23.

poverty.[17] In the fourth and final of these, Sengupta defined extreme poverty as 'the combination of income poverty, human development poverty and social exclusion'.[18]

Two approaches to determining who experiences severe poverty are highlighted by Sengupta. One approach classifies an individual to be suffering from extreme poverty if they suffer from all three categories of poverty (*income poverty*, *human development poverty* and *social exclusion*).[19] This is referred to as the overlap approach. This overlap approach classifies fewer individuals as suffering from extreme poverty and is narrower than the second approach. The second approach does not require any overlap between the three categories of poverty and regards sufferers of extreme poverty as individuals from 'each of these categories selected in terms of the severity of the conditions of deprivation'.[20] This later approach is referred to as the union approach. In his report, Sengupta does not prescribe one approach to the detriment of the other. This definition can be unpacked further by considering each of these three categories in turn.

A. Absolute Income Poverty

To determine *absolute income poverty* a minimum expenditure line 'could be based on a minimum daily amount of calorie intake from food necessary for survival in a reasonably healthy condition, supplemented by some minimum amount of non-food items regarded as essential *for a decent social existence*'.[21] In 2015 the World Bank set the international poverty line at US$1.90 per day with this figure being determined using the 'average of the national poverty lines in the poorest 15 countries'.[22] As such, under the absolute income poverty category of extreme poverty, an individual experiences extreme poverty if their income is less than US$1.90 per day. However, because the World Bank's international poverty line is determined using the average poverty lines of the poorest countries, the World Bank's extreme poverty standard 'is inadequate for capturing

[17] A Sengupta, 'Report of the independent expert on the question of human rights and extreme poverty' (11 February 2005) UN Doc E/CN.4/2005/49; A Sengupta, 'Report of the independent expert' (2 March 2006) UN Doc E/CN.4/2006/43; A Sengupta, 'Report of the independent expert' (31 May 2007) UN Doc A/HRC/5/3.

[18] A Sengupta, 'Promotion and Protection of All Human Rights, Civil, Political, Economic, Social and Cultural Rights, Including the Right to Development' (28 February 2008) UN Doc A/HRC/7/15, para 13.

[19] ibid 36.

[20] ibid 35.

[21] ibid 24. (My emphasis.)

[22] SP Marks, 'Poverty' in D Moeckli et al (ed), *International Human Rights Law* 3rd edn (OUP 2018) 599.

the realities of poverty on the ground'[23] and excludes, by definition, 'all poverty in developed countries'.[24] Below I criticise a focus on income alone in determining poverty as failing to adequately and fully encapsulate the experience of poverty and extreme poverty.[25] However, Sengupta's definition goes beyond income alone.

B. Human Development Poverty

The *human development poverty* category regards extreme poverty 'as extreme or severe deprivation'.[26] In this sense, extreme poverty can be regarded as extreme deprivation which limits an individual's ability to 'lead a life that she or he values with freedom of "being and doing"'.[27] The Human Development Indicators capture the deprivation of such freedoms.[28] These indicators have been labelled 'components of the concept of well-being'[29] and consider, inter alia, such issues as 'literacy rates or school enrolment ratios', which 'represent freedom from ignorance and the lack of education. Similarly, indices of life expectancy or infant mortality have been described as indicators of the freedom to lead a healthy life'.[30] It is clear that this aspect of Sengupta's definition parallels the conception of living conditions proposed by Beth Goldblatt in this collection, which focuses on enabling a decent life in the home and community.[31]

C. Social Exclusion

Sengupta's definition of extreme poverty is also relevant to the community aspect of Goldblatt's conception of living conditions. Similarly to Lizin's definition, Sengupta explicitly includes the concept of *social exclusion*.[32] The third category of extreme poverty is 'social exclusion, which is quite distinct from the other components, yet is an essential component of the concept of deprivation of well-being'.[33] It both affects and is affected by the level of different human

[23] P Alston, 'Report of the Special Rapporteur on Extreme Poverty and Human Rights' (11 August 2014) UN Doc A/69/297, para 7.
[24] ibid.
[25] See nn 114–125.
[26] Sengupta (n 18) para 27.
[27] ibid.
[28] ibid.
[29] ibid 26.
[30] ibid.
[31] See Goldblatt, chapter eleven in this volume.
[32] See nn 14–15.
[33] Sengupta (n 18) para 28.

development indicators and the level of income and is 'the opposite of social integration, where the poor, the unemployed, ethnic minorities and vulnerable groups have remained "outsiders" in the social hierarchy'.[34]

Ultimately, poverty is about a 'continuum of want',[35] which contributes to an 'inability to attain a minimal standard of living'.[36] This in turn has implications for living conditions. In international human rights law, the existing concept which engages minimum levels of rights realisation is the minimum core obligation. For Bilchitz, this constitutes a subsistence level.[37] Regarded as contested and complex,[38] the minimum core is an obligation of every state party to realise, 'as a matter of priority',[39] the 'minimum essential levels of each of the rights'[40] enshrined in the ICESCR. Further, it constitutes 'a right to basic socio-economic entitlements that can be claimed by everyone in desperate need',[41] a 'non-derogable foundation'[42] that must be guaranteed for all. Thus, it aims to provide a minimum level of social protection for all.[43] In theory, the minimum core obligation should be the minimum level of ICESCR rights realisation experienced by any individual.

Focusing on the right to an adequate standard of living understood holistically, all individuals should have dignified enjoyment of their basic needs.[44] Beyond basic rights and focusing on the right to an adequate standard of living, Hohmann argues that a minimum basic content exists concerning the right to an adequate standard of living and that this content 'ensures subsistence to all people in the form of food, clothing, housing and necessary conditions

[34] ibid.

[35] V George and I Howards, *Poverty amidst Affluence* (Edward Elgar Publishing 1991) 1.

[36] K Funken and P Cooper, *Old and New Poverty* (River Oram Press 1995) 43.

[37] D Bilchitz, 'Socio-Economic Rights, Economic Crisis, and Legal Doctrine' (2014) 14 *International Journal of Constitutional Law* 710, 719; see also D Bilchitz, 'Giving Socio-Economic Rights Teeth: The Minimum Core and Its Importance' (2002) 119 *The South African Law Journal* 484, 488.

[38] A Nolan, 'Budget Analysis and Economic and Social Rights' in E Riedel et al (ed), *Economic, Social, and Cultural Rights in International Law* (OUP 2014) 369–91, 374.

[39] CESCR, 'General Comment No. 3: The Nature of States Parties' Obligations' (14 December 1990) UN Doc E/1991/23, para 10.

[40] RE Robertson, 'Measuring State Compliance with the Obligation to Devote the "Maximum Available Resources" to Realizing Economic, Social, and Cultural Rights' (1994) 16 *Human Rights Quarterly* 692, 701 quoting CESCR UN Doc No E/C.12/1990/8 (16 November – 14 December 1990).

[41] O Fuo and A Du Plessis, 'In the Face of Judicial Deference: Taking the "Minimum Core" of Socio-Economic Rights to the Local Government Sphere' (2015) 19 *Law, Democracy & Development* 1, 5.

[42] M Odello and F Seatzu, *The UN Committee on Economic, Social and Cultural Rights: The Law Process and Practice* (Routledge 2013) 65.

[43] I Leijten, 'The German Right to an Existenzminimum, Human Dignity, and the Possibility of Minimum Core Socioeconomic Rights Protection' 16 *German Law Journal* 23, 36; see also EB Bluemel, 'The Implications of Formulating a Human Right to Water' (2004) 31 *Ecology Law Quarterly* 957, 976.

[44] A Eide, 'Adequate Standard of Living' in D Moeckli et al (ed), *International Human Rights Law* 3rd edn (OUP 2018) 187.

of care'.[45] Eide labels the enjoyment of these subsistence rights being minimally required for the enjoyment of an adequate standard of living.[46]

That which is minimally required to ensure subsistence engages the concept of basic or survival rights, which are also referred to as subsistence rights.[47] Bilchitz highlights that in its general comments the CESCR has 'adopted and modified Henry Shue's framework concerning the range of obligations that can be said to flow from fundamental socio-economic rights'.[48] However, Baxi recognises that the process of identifying what constitutes basic needs varies greatly.[49] Even so, 'the basic idea is to have available for consumption what is needed for a decent chance at a reasonably healthy and active life of more or less normal length, barring tragic interventions'.[50] Basic rights, according to Shue, are; 'the line beneath which no one is allowed to sink';[51] 'everyone's minimum reasonable demands upon the rest of humanity';[52] and more distinctively, rights of which the enjoyment, and realisation, is 'essential to the enjoyment of all other rights'.[53] Shue equates subsistence to 'minimal economic security' and defines this as; unpolluted air and water; adequate food, clothing, and shelter; and 'minimal preventive public health care'.[54] Thus, these are the resources which constitute Shue's basic rights and, beyond this, Sengupta highlights the ability to purchase necessities when lacking access to them.[55] This gives some indication of an absolute baseline from which to improve.

However, a key debate surrounding the minimum core obligation approach is whether the level of realisation required to satisfy this obligation is universal or relative. Some scholars question whether different standards exist between developing and developed nations.[56] Arguments in support of regarding the minimum core obligation as 'an absolute international minimum' suggest that allowing State specificity undermines the purpose of the minimum core obligation.[57]

[45] J Hohmann, *The Right to Housing: Law, Concepts, Possibilities* (Hart Publishing 2013) 7.

[46] A Eide, 'Economic, Social and Cultural Rights as Human Rights' in A Eide et al (ed), *Economic, Social and Cultural Rights: A Textbook* (Second Revised Edition, Kluwer International Law 2001) 17–18.

[47] G Giacca, *Economic, Social and Cultural Rights in Armed Conflict* (OUP 2014) 31.

[48] D Bilchitz, *Poverty and Fundamental Rights* (OUP 2007) 184.

[49] U Baxi, 'International Development, Global Impoverishment, and Human Rights' in S Sheeran and N Rodley (eds), *Routledge Handbook of International Human Rights Law* (Routledge 2013) 597–613, 600.

[50] H Shue, *Basic Rights* 2nd edn (Princeton University Press 1996) 23.

[51] ibid 18.

[52] ibid 19.

[53] ibid.

[54] ibid 23.

[55] A Sengupta, 'Poverty Eradication and Human Rights' in T Pogge (ed), *Freedom from Poverty as a Human Right* (OUP 2007) 335–36.

[56] M Ssenyonjo, *Economic, Social and Cultural Rights in International Law* (Hart Publishing 2006) 66; see also I Bantekas and L Oette, *International Human Rights: Law and Practice* 2nd edn (CUP 2016) 413.

[57] Ssenyonjo (n 56) 66.

Thus, a universal approach is required to give the concept meaning.[58] This can be supported by reference to the CESCR's General Comments No 3[59] and No 14,[60] which have been described as suggesting that the minimum core obligation is one of a universal nature[61] and the CESCR's purpose was to 'define a minimum floor'.[62]

However, in contrast, Young argues that 'additional principles over simple survival'[63] are required to make the minimum core obligation contextually appropriate. Young's view can be supported with reference to Sen's observation that the baseline of goods required for societal participation varies between societies and States.[64] This engages the absolute versus relative debate and, I argue further below, it is clear that the right to continuous improvement of living conditions tilts firmly towards relativist conceptions.[65] In this sense, the minimum core must be considered as going beyond mere survival and subsistence to consider additional factors.

In pursuance of this goal, absolutism can be reconciled with relativism. Such reconciliation ensures that the minimum core obligation can remain contextually appropriate. Bilchitz's 'relative minimum threshold approach'[66] allows for relativist standards of obligation to be set, with the sole exception being that these standards cannot be below the standard found in the minimum core obligation.[67] This approach can account for aspects of living conditions beyond mere subsistence.[68] This is because Bilchitz's approach would ensure a subsistence minimum whilst at the same time requiring a higher standard of realisation in contexts in which it is within the State's resources to ensure this. This would serve to prevent the stagnation of the minimum level.

Based on the exploration of poverty and extreme poverty in this section, it is perhaps unsurprising that understandings of all the rights in the ICESCR have shifted towards being seen as a response to poverty with 'a greater focus on minimal standards, rather than on overall human development or flourishing'.[69]

[58] K Lehmann, 'In Defense of the Constitutional Court: Litigating Socio-Economic Rights and the Myth of the Minimum Core' (2006) 22 *American University International Law Review* 163, 184.

[59] CESCR, 'General Comment No. 3' (n 39).

[60] CESCR, 'General Comment No. 14: The Right to the Highest Attainable Standard of Health (Article 12 of the International Covenant on Economic, Social and Cultural Rights)' (11 August 2000) UN Doc E/C.12/2000/4'.

[61] Lehmann (n 58) 183.

[62] P de Vos, 'The Right to Housing' in D Brand and C Heyns (eds), *Socio-Economic Rights in South Africa* (Pretoria University Law Press 2005) 85–106.

[63] KG Young, 'The Minimum Core of Economic and Social Rights: A Concept in Search of Content' (2008) 33 *Yale Journal of International Law* 113, 131.

[64] A Sen, *Inequality Reexamined* (Harvard University Press 1992) 115.

[65] See section III below.

[66] Bilchitz, 'Socio-Economic Rights, Economic Crisis, and Legal Doctrine' (n 37) 712.

[67] ibid 733.

[68] This analysis will be used in addressing the subject matter of the right in section V below.

[69] See Hohmann, chapter two in this volume.

In the remainder of this chapter, I explore the implications of this focus on poverty for the interpretation of the right to continuous improvement of living conditions.

III. POVERTY ERADICATION: A LIMIT ON CONTINUITY?

One area in which this poverty focus asks difficult questions of the right to continuous improvement of living conditions is as to the continuity of improvement. This is because if the right is merely a response to poverty it may be interpreted that the duties and obligations stemming from the right are dispensed with once poverty is eradicated. This would suggest that there exists no right to further improvement of living conditions for those not experiencing poverty. This touches upon the question of whether there exists a ceiling for the right to continuous improvement of living conditions. On this point, some parallels may be drawn to Skogly's exploration of the limits of continuity when considered alongside the rights of future generations.[70] I contend that the issue of whether such a ceiling exists can be resolved through employing the lens of poverty. The extent to which the right provides for (un)limited continuity of improvement must therefore be examined through this lens.

The phrasing of the right – combined with a lack of clarification by the CESCR – suggests that there is a right to the perpetual improvement of living conditions. So conceived, the right to continuous improvement of living conditions may conflict with a range of other human rights some of which are addressed elsewhere in this volume.[71] Additionally, the pursuit of further improvement may be limited by environmental considerations.[72] This undermines the conception of continuous improvement as relating to perpetual improvement and suggests that there are limits to what is meant by continuous with respect to this right. After all, infinite improvement of *material* conditions (like growth) cannot occur on a finite planet.[73] Based upon such sentiments, and with respect to the constant improvement provisions of the Declaration on the Right to Development, Löfquist observes that:

> a simple solution to this conceptual problem is to claim that the right to development cannot be an open-ended concept, and there is no right to continuous development. The right must include some kind of limit and theoretically, that limit can be high above current levels of well-being.[74]

[70] See Skogly, chapter eight in this volume. But see Lott, chapter seven in this volume.
[71] Skogly, chapter eight in this volume.
[72] L Löfquist, 'Climate Change, Justice and the Right to Development' (2011) 7 *Journal of Global Ethics* 251, 253.
[73] See Skogly, chapter eight in this volume. Below I will support the view that the subject matter of the right goes beyond material conditions alone to represent a broader understanding of living conditions. See section V.
[74] Löfquist (n 72) 258.

As opposed to a right to perpetual improvement, one proposed approach to determining such limits has been to limit continuity to the attainment of 'a certain minimum level of well-being'.[75] The poverty lens can be useful here. If the right to continuous improvement of living conditions is merely a response to poverty, as the CESCR's more recent engagement with the right appears to suggest,[76] the choice of poverty definition may limit the concept of continuity within the right. From the view that the right to continuous improvement of living conditions is a response to poverty, it may be interpreted that once poverty is eradicated the right becomes devoid of meaning. Although I do not support this view, I raise it to highlight that the way in which poverty is defined has the potential to limit the right.[77] Disagreement exists as to the correct approach to determining minimum standards of living. Such disagreement is also a feature of the poverty discourse. In defining poverty, a choice must be made 'between whether poverty ought to be about relative deprivation or subsistence needs'.[78] These definitions 'result in very different measures of the numbers of people who are poor in society'[79] as well as very different ideas of what poverty 'is' in essence.

Synonymous with objective poverty, absolute poverty is technically defined, as Langmore writes, as poverty measured against a fixed standard.[80] This fixed standard is, as Fouarge notes, 'clearly based on some notion of basic needs'.[81] Consequently, absolute poverty is 'sometimes referred to as subsistence poverty'[82] and, in the first instance, appears to represent material deprivation hindering survival. Based on the assumption that all individuals require the same basic necessities in order to survive,[83] an absolute poverty line does not alter as societal living standards increase.[84] Absolute conceptions of poverty, therefore, set an immovable and universal standard. Applying an absolutist-poverty lens to the right to continuous improvement of living conditions conceived as a response to poverty leads to the conclusion that once individuals reach a certain minimum level of well-being they possess no further right to improvement.[85] Such an approach explicitly limits the continuity of the right. Moreover, implicit in such

[75] ibid 259.
[76] See Hohmann, chapter two in this volume.
[77] See Fredman, chapter twelve in this volume.
[78] B Jordan, *A Theory of Poverty and Social Exclusion* (Policy Press 1996) 94.
[79] P Alcock, *Why We Need Welfare* (Policy Press 2016) 36; see also RJ Samuelson, 'Defining Poverty Up' (2010) 155 *Newsweek*.
[80] J Langmore, 'Reducing Poverty: The Implications of the 1995 Copenhagen Agreement for Research on Poverty' in D Gordon and P Townsend (eds), *Breadline Europe: The Measurement of Poverty* (Policy Press 2000) 36.
[81] D Fouarge, *Poverty and Subsidiarity in Europe* (Edward Elgar Publishing 2004) 115. For my overview of basic needs see above (nn 48–55).
[82] Alcock (n 79) 36.
[83] HPP Lotter, 'Defining Poverty as Distinctively Human' 63 *HTS* 1195, 1203–04.
[84] Fouarge (n 81) 115.
[85] Löfquist (n 72) 256.

an approach is the acceptance that a minimum level of living conditions can be set at a fixed universally applicable level. This can be interpreted to suggest that what individuals need to subsist – and thus avoid absolute poverty – will always be the same even in the future. Consequently, if the right to continuous improvement of living conditions is regarded as *merely* a response to poverty and, concurrently, poverty is defined using this absolutist approach, this would suggest that once the absolute poverty threshold is met an individual no longer has any claim to continued improvement of living conditions. This could be interpreted as a 'ceiling' for the right.[86]

In contrast to this, relative, or subjective, poverty is distinguishable from absolute poverty and allows for the determination of contextually appropriate deprivation thresholds.[87] Given that the contextually appropriate nature of relative approaches necessarily allows for understandings of poverty to go beyond mere subsistence, a tension exists between absolute and relative approaches to poverty. However, the advantages of the relative approach are clear. The relative approach 'links the extent and the experience of poverty to the position of people within the broader social order'[88] and accounts for evolving perceptions of basic needs.[89] This goes beyond 'the requirements of subsistence and essential consumption' and broadens the scope of income poverty by increasing the minimum expenditure line to such a level as to 'allow access to goods and services required to satisfy sociocultural norms'.[90]

As such, relative concepts of poverty are based on the notion that the poverty line cannot be fixed at one subsistence level but rather should rise over time in line with improvements in overall living standards.[91] As opposed to the fixed subsistence standard of the absolute approach to poverty, regarding the relative approach to poverty as the focus of the right to continuous improvement of living conditions does not extinguish claims to the right once minimum living conditions (the objective poverty line) are realised. This is indicative that if we are to regard the right to continuous improvement of living conditions as a response to poverty it *must* be as a response to relative and not objective poverty.

Furthermore, given the centrality of the right to an adequate standard of living to the CESCR's definition of poverty, it is clear that a relative approach most readily aligns with the human rights-based understandings of poverty.[92]

[86] See Skogly, chapter eight in this volume.

[87] Marks (n 22) 599.

[88] Alcock (n 79) 38.

[89] C Muller, 'Defining Poverty Lines as a Fraction of Central Tendency' (2006) 72 *Southern Economic Journal* 720, 720.

[90] Sengupta (n 18) para 25.

[91] Alcock (n 79) 36.

[92] See CESCR (n 7) The CESCR defines poverty 'as a human condition characterized by sustained or chronic deprivation of the resources, capabilities, choices, security and power *necessary for the enjoyment of an adequate standard of living* and other civil, cultural, economic, political and social rights'. (My emphasis.)

This can be supported further given Eide's contention that an adequate standard of living goes beyond the basic necessities referred to in the numerous international instruments, but exactly how far beyond is dependent upon the societal conditions under consideration and, as such, 'cannot be stated in general terms'.[93] For the right to continuous improvement of living conditions, the implication of the recognition that the right to an adequate standard of living goes beyond basic necessities is that the realisation of a minimum level of socio-economic rights should not be considered the limit of the right. This aligns with a plain and literal reading of the phrase continuous improvement of living conditions and the lack of engagement with this right has resulted in the absence of any definitive evidence which could justify anything but such a literal reading. Consequently, a relative approach to poverty suggests that the right to continuous improvement of living conditions as a response to poverty cannot be limited once a fixed universal level of minimal rights realisation (below full realisation) is achieved.[94] The eradication of poverty is not a 'ceiling' for the right.

Thus, in the future, if the rights forming the subject matter[95] of the right to continuous improvement of living conditions are 'fully' realised, three possible outcomes exist. The first of these outcomes is that the right to continuous improvement of living conditions becomes superfluous and that any claim to further improvement is eliminated. The second outcome is that the full realisation of the rights related to living standards we envision today in no way relate to the standards of living required of the future. This would require continuing improvement. The third outcome is that the right to continuous improvement of living conditions enters a state of hibernation only to awaken when societal and human rights advances (such as new standards of well-being, new resources and goods, and new rights to these advancements) occur. The second and third of these outcomes are preferred as they account for relativist understandings of living conditions, suggesting that there is no limit to the continuity of improvement within the right to continuous improvement of living conditions.

IV. PRIORITISING THE IMPOVERISHED

Building upon the analysis in the preceding section, a key conceptual issue concerning the right to continuous improvement of living conditions is the determination of who ought to be able to claim it. This has been raised as an

[93] Eide, 'Adequate Standard of Living' (n 44) 187.

[94] If living conditions are tied to the realisation of human rights, it is logical that if *all* human rights are fully realised for all then there is no scope for further improvement.

[95] The subject-matter of the right will be explored below. See section V.

issue by Craven[96] and addressed in greater detail by Löfquist.[97] If the right to continuous improvement of living conditions is a response to poverty it would appear to flow logically from this that the holders of the right are those experiencing poverty. Such a view lacks nuance, and this issue can be unpacked in considering Löfquist's contention that 'there are at least three distributive responses to the idea that we have a prima facie right to continuous improvement: (1) no one has this right; (2) only some people have this right and (3) everyone has this right'.[98]

As Löfquist observes, although initially seeming to be a radical claim:

> claiming that no one has a right to continuous improvement is compatible with the idea that everyone should have a right to subsist above a certain minimum level of well-being, an idea suggested by Henry Shue (1980) and his theory of basic rights. The claim is that when people reach this level, there is no right to further improvement.[99]

This aligns with the absolutist-poverty approach to the rights. However, an outright rejection of the right to continuous improvement living conditions which is premised upon the view that human rights merely convey the right to very basic entitlements does not account for the fact that – even if rights realisation meets this minimum level – rights-holders 'could still' Löfquist points out, 'be in a relatively bad situation'.[100] Thus, a need for continuity of improvement would still exist. This links to the analysis in the previous section, which held that poverty eradication alone is not the limit of the right to continuous improvement. Rather, we should aspire beyond this towards the full realisation of human rights.

More so, an outright rejection of the right based upon these grounds too readily ignores that the right to continuous improvement of living conditions was deliberately and explicitly codified into the ICESCR. The mere fact that realising this right would necessarily cause us to radically alter our existing socio-political order does not diminish the existence of this right.[101] As such, I reject the view that nobody holds the right to continuous improvement of living conditions and must, therefore, determine whether the right is held by either a limited category of persons or by all persons.

Turning to the proposition that only some individuals hold the right, it is arguably the most impoverished whose living conditions are most in need

[96] MCR Craven, *The International Covenant on Economic, Social, and Cultural Rights: A Perspective on Its Development* (Clarendon Press 1995) 295.

[97] Löfquist (n 72) 253.

[98] ibid 255.

[99] ibid 256.

[100] ibid.

[101] For a brief outline of the incompatibility of the current socio-political order and the realisation of ESCRs see J Wills, 'The World Turned Upside Down? Neo-Liberalism, Socioeconomic Rights, and Hegemony' (2014) 27 *Leiden Journal of International Law* 11, 11–13.

of improvement. Sepúlveda Carmona observes that with respect to policy and resource allocation 'States should accord due priority to the human rights of the most disadvantaged groups, especially persons living in extreme poverty'.[102] However, prioritising the poor may be perceived as improving the conditions of the poor at the expense of the rich. For example, Salomon and Arnott contend that 'human rights offers a theory of justice that focuses on the poor and therefore requires that we should distinguish between possible "losers" to improve the position of the poor, even at the expense of the rich'.[103] If such sentiments are accepted it is logical to accept that the category of persons who hold the right to continuous improvement of living conditions must be limited. However, such limitations may undermine the right's individual nature[104] and the universality of the rights.[105]

This analysis highlights that there are difficulties with all three approaches to determining who holds the right. Examining approaches to improvement in the field of development can serve to bring clarity to this issue. This is because the Declaration on the Right to Development is – alongside Article 11 of the ICESCR – one of two key instruments which make reference to continuous improvement. The Declaration aims 'at the "constant improvement of the well-being of the entire population and of all individuals."'[106] This would appear to support the view that all individuals have the right to continuous improvement of living conditions. However, it has been argued that if the right to continuous improvement of living conditions is universally held 'a rich person has a right, a moral demand, on other people to increase his or her wealth'.[107] If it is accepted that in order to realise the right some must 'lose', a universally held right to continuous improvement of living conditions could be argued to place into conflict the claims to continuous improvement of living conditions of the rich and the poor. As such, the view that everybody holds the right may be used to challenge redistributive policies which seek to improve the living conditions of the poor at the 'expense' of the rich.

This view rests upon two assumptions. Firstly, the assumption that if the right is universally held, it is incompatible with prioritisation. I do not believe this to be the case for two reasons. First, by drawing a distinction between the right to continuous improvement of living conditions and the obligations stemming from this right it can be argued that, although every individual has the right, no further obligations stem from the right beyond a certain category of persons (the impoverished). Second, prioritisation has been a feature of the

[102] Sepúlveda Carmona (n 8) para 51.
[103] ME Salomon and C Arnott, 'Better Development Decision-Making: Applying International Human Rights Law to Neoclassical Economics' (2014) 32 *Nordic Journal of Human Rights* 44, 62.
[104] Craven (n 96) 295.
[105] Löfquist (n 72) 257.
[106] Salomon and Arnott (n 103) 58.
[107] Löfquist (n 72) 253.

CESCR's approach to core obligations concerning other rights[108] and this has not deprived those who already enjoy adequate realisation of their rights of their status as rights-holders. As such, the right to continuous improvement of living conditions can be universally held whilst at the same time prioritising those most in need of their living conditions being improved. In addition, this view assumes that the subject matter of the right is narrowly defined and from this assumption living conditions are equated to wealth. As will be addressed in the following section, there are strong arguments to refute this narrow understanding of the subject matter of the right.

V. POVERTY AND THE SUBJECT MATTER OF THE RIGHT

My view that the right to continuous improvement of living conditions is held universally by all persons can be further supported by my analysis of the subject matter of the right. I highlight two existing approaches in this regard. Either the subject matter of the right refers to material conditions, or instead the right directly refers to well-being.[109] This debate rests on the fact Article 11 of the ICESCR and the Declaration to the Right to Development have been interpreted as taking different approaches.

The Declaration on the Right to Development specifies improvement in terms of well-being[110] whereas Article 11 of the ICESCR 'specifically refers to material objects as food, clothing and housing and does not refer to the concept of well-being'.[111] However, the concepts of material conditions and well-being need not be divorced from each other. Salomon contends that 'intermittent treaty references to the "continuous improvement" of living conditions' … 'should not be read in isolation but rather as part of a much larger post-1945 international effort to situate the *eradication of material deprivation* within a process of *human-centred development*'.[112] A process of human-centred development may be read widely to include both material conditions and well-being and the interrelationship between material conditions and well-being must not be undervalued.[113] This is because well-being is affected by material deprivation. More so, this lack of well-being may contribute to individuals facing material deprivation. Thus, both the subject matter of the right to continuous improvement of living conditions and poverty must go beyond income alone.

[108] CESCR, 'General Comment No. 3' (n 39) para 10.

[109] Löfquist (n 72) 253.

[110] United Nations General Assembly (UNGA), 'Declaration on the Right to Development' (4 December 1986) UN Doc A/RES/41/128, Art 2(3).

[111] Löfquist (n 72) 253.

[112] ME Salomon, 'Why Should It Matter That Others Have More? Poverty, Inequality, and the Potential of International Human Rights Law' (2011) 37 *Review of International Studies* 2137, 2152. (My emphasis.)

[113] See Goldblatt, chapter eleven in this volume.

The analysis in the previous section explored the implications of prioritisation in determining the holders of the right to continuous improvement of living conditions. Linking to this, the dichotomy between a universally held right to continuous improvement of living conditions and prioritisation can be further rejected. This dichotomy falsely (and narrowly) equates the subject matter of the right with wealth. If this dichotomy is accepted, it follows that prioritising the living conditions of some at the 'expense' of others deprives those who are not prioritised of their status as rights holders. Accepting that the subject matter of the right can be interpreted broadly and in turn rejecting the view that the subject matter of the right is wealth (or income alone) supports rejecting this dichotomy. It follows that prioritisation can occur without depriving those who are not prioritised of their status as holders of the right. In turn, the rejection of this dichotomy supports the view that all individuals are holders of the right. This reasoning accepts that a reduction in the total wealth of a millionaire or billionaire can in no way be regarded as undermining their right to continuous improvement of living conditions. This is because a reduction in total wealth would not be regarded as equating to a reduction of living conditions unless the reduction in wealth were so severe as to undermine the realisation of other economic, social and cultural rights.

Whilst I challenge the view that the subject matter of the right to continuous improvement of living conditions is wealth, this poses an issue for the conception of the right as a response to poverty. This is because poverty is often determined by reference to income-based measures with poverty being regarded as the income level separating 'the poor from the not poor'.[114] Consequently, poverty continues to be perceived exclusively, by many legal systems, as the income poverty of individuals.[115] This is evidenced by the fact that poverty rates have come to be 'defined in terms of household income'.[116] Thus, poverty and deprivation have been reduced to a shortage of money.[117] This is understandable in that lack of money and income can contribute to an individual being unable to access the basic necessities required to not experience poverty.[118] Further, income is easy to measure and is, therefore, a convenient method of poverty identification.[119]

Yet, this disregards and is despite the fact that income-based measurements of poverty assess only one aspect of deprivation.[120] Poverty is 'broader than

[114] R Doyle, 'Defining Poverty' (2003) 288 *Scientific America* 21, 31.

[115] S Goonesekere, 'Civil and Political Rights and Poverty Eradication' in G Van Bueren (ed), *Freedom from Poverty as a Human Right* (UNESCO Publishing 2010) 51–78, 52.

[116] D Gallie, 'The Quality of Working Life in Welfare Strategy' in G Esping-Andersen et al (ed), *Why We Need a New Welfare State* (OUP 2002) 96–129, 104.

[117] P Ashley, *The Money Problems of the Poor* (Heinemann Educational Books 1983) 2.

[118] K McFate et al, *Poverty, Inequality and the Future of Social Policy* (Russell Sage Foundation 1995) 137.

[119] Marks (n 22) 600.

[120] George and Howards (n 35) 57.

income data' alone[121] and this is irrefutably apparent from the existing human rights-based understandings of both poverty and extreme poverty addressed above.[122] Consequently, such a method of determining poverty has been criticised 'for using arbitrary thresholds as proxies for poverty'.[123] Additionally, income-only-based measurements of poverty have been criticised by Skogly, as incapable of capturing the significance and complexity of 'the rights of the poor and the violations thereof'.[124] Sen also posits that 'the reduction of income poverty alone cannot possibly be the ultimate motivation of antipoverty policy'.[125]

It follows that if the right to continuous improvement of living conditions is indeed regarded as a response to poverty, the subject matter of the right must go beyond income and consequently wealth alone to also consider 'the resources, capabilities, choices, security and power necessary for the enjoyment of an adequate standard of living and other civil, cultural, economic, political and social rights' which are highlighted by the CESCR as being representative of the experience of poverty.[126] In some contexts these resources, capabilities, choices, security and power are utterly detached from income and individuals can enjoy both an adequate standard of living and other civil, cultural, economic, political and social rights without reliance on income.[127] Eide posits that the essential point of an adequate standard of living:

> is that everyone shall be able, without shame and without unreasonable obstacles, to be a full participant in ordinary, everyday interaction with other people. This means, *inter alia*, that they shall be able to enjoy their basic needs under conditions of dignity. No one shall have to live under conditions whereby the only way to satisfy their needs is by degrading or depriving themselves of their basic freedoms, such as through begging, prostitution or bonded labour.[128]

As such, 'in purely material terms'[129] this implies living above the context-specific poverty line.[130] Understanding living above the context-specific poverty line as the essential point of an adequate standard of living, makes clear the

[121] Marks (n 22) 600.
[122] See (n 6–36)
[123] A Donald and E Mottershaw, 'Poverty, Inequality and Human Rights: Do Human Rights Make a Difference?' (Joseph Rowntree Foundation 2009) 12.
[124] Skogly (n 6) 63.
[125] A Sen, *Development as Freedom* (OUP 1999) 92.
[126] CESCR, UN Doc E/C.12/2001/10 (n 7) para 8.
[127] Thus, any focus on income – which stems from a vision of a world in which opportunity as well as access to goods and services is always measured in terms of money – excludes alternative ways of living where individuals are able to enjoy an adequate standard of living without reliance on market forces.
[128] A Eide, 'The Right to an Adequate Standard of Living Including the Right to Food' in A Eide et al (ed), *Economic, Social and Cultural Rights: A Textbook* 2nd rev edn (Kluwer International Law 2001) 133.
[129] ibid 133–34.
[130] ibid.

interrelationship between adequate standards of living and poverty thresholds. However, poverty lines necessarily go beyond merely the right to an adequate standard of living to include all social rights. Social rights are rights that 'improve the lives of individuals and communities'[131] and make 'it possible for all members of society to enjoy satisfactory conditions of life'.[132] Thus, approaching the right to continuous improvement of living conditions through the lens of a human rights-based approach to poverty results in a broad interpretation of the subject matter of the right, which in turn focuses upon the realisation of other human rights.

VI. POVERTY ERADICATION MEASURES AS IMPROVING THE LIVING CONDITIONS OF ALL IN SOCIETY

The dichotomy between wealth (income) and living standards can be rejected further in considering a broader conception of living conditions. For the already rich, the right to continuous improvement of living conditions may not meaningfully alter their individual material conditions of living but rather improved living conditions could mean living in a society which is increasingly happier and equal, with less poverty, less crime and less ill-health. Improving the material living conditions of the poor may, therefore, improve the broader living conditions of all in society – rich and poor alike.

This observation can be supported drawing upon the example of Covid-19. The Covid-19 crisis has powerfully highlighted the impact socio-economic inequality has across all of society. The poor have been disproportionately affected by this crisis across the world whether through, *inter alia*, exclusion from healthcare, cramped living conditions, greater physical vulnerability to the virus caused by a multitude of deprivations, and their occupations.

However, because Covid-19 is a *public* health crisis the increased vulnerability of the poor has had adverse implications for the rich. This is because the vulnerability of the poor has resulted in the poor and rich alike living in a society that is more susceptible to the transmission of – and the adverse health implications of – the virus. Society's increased susceptibility to the virus has worsened the consequences of the virus. This in turn has required the public health measures imposed across many States to be more restrictive and to last longer. As such, society's increased susceptibility to the virus has impacted upon the living conditions of the poor and rich alike. This is because public health measures must apply to all persons regardless of socio-economic status. It follows that improving the living conditions of the poor to resolve these vulnerabilities would better

[131] P Hunt, 'Social Rights Are Human Rights' (Centre for Welfare Reform 2017) 7 <https://www.centreforwelfarereform.org/uploads/attachment/584/social-rights-are-human-rights.pdf> accessed 20 September 2019.

[132] Eide, 'Economic, Social and Cultural Rights as Human Rights' (n 46) 13.

protect society at large and ensure the normality of day-to-day lives, in turn, resulting in an improvement of living conditions broadly understood.

This is but one example of how improving the living conditions of the poor improves the overall living conditions of society as a whole. Thus, the realisation of the right to continuous improvement of living conditions of the rich may manifest itself from the benefits of the realisation of this right for the poor. On the face of it, this constitutes a utilitarian argument in support of the right. However, as the analysis throughout this chapter makes clear, the right to continuous improvement of living conditions offers the potential to address poverty and consequently, given that poverty and inequality are inextricably linked,[133] make societies more equal. In understanding poverty as the non-realisation of a range of human rights, it follows that reduced poverty – and the greater equality which would stem from this – are conducive to improved realisation of human rights within society. Given this strong case for asserting that a more equal society is inherently a better one in human rights terms, the potential of the right in regard to fostering greater equality constitutes a more principled and normative argument – beyond this utilitarian one alone – in support of the right to continuous improvement of living conditions.

VII. CONCLUSION

One approach to the right to continuous improvement of living conditions is to regard it as a response to poverty. It may be feared that such an approach is minimalistic, unambitious and limits the potential of this underexplored right. In this chapter, I have addressed several conceptual issues underpinning the right to continuous improvement of living conditions through the lens of poverty to assuage these fears.

Thus, whilst the poverty-based approach to this right provides a consistent framework from which to clarify conceptual issues, in this chapter I argue that the poverty-lens does not limit the potential of the right to continuous improvement of living conditions. The example of Covid-19, drawn upon above, demonstrates that a response to poverty has something to offer, by way of improvement to the rights and living conditions of everybody. Viewed through the lens of poverty, the baseline from which to improve, the limits on the continuity of improvement, the holders of the right, and that which must be continuously improved, become clear.

Given that poverty has been tied to adequate standards of living, a strong argument can be made that the baseline from which improvement must be made is the context-specific poverty threshold. Taking an absolute, as opposed to a relative,

[133] V Lang and H Lingnau, 'Defining and Measuring Poverty and Inequality Post-2015' (2015) 27 *Journal of International Development* 399, 404.

approach to poverty could be interpreted as suggesting a limit to the continuity of improvement. However, taking a relative approach to poverty suggests that in any society (or global order) in which there exists socioeconomic inequality there will always be scope for improvement. As such, the eradication of absolute poverty would not act as a limit for the right. Necessarily, this poverty lens prioritises the improvement of material conditions of the poor. This prioritisation does not deprive the non-poor of their status as rights-holders but rather may contribute to the improvement of their living conditions more broadly understood. In regarding living conditions as going beyond material living conditions, continuously improving the minimally acceptable living conditions in any society has a whole range of benefits for everybody in that society although the improvement in material conditions would be most strongly felt by the poor. Viewed through the poverty lens, this broad conception of living conditions can be used to consider living conditions – that is, the subject matter of the right – as everything included in the definition of poverty used by the CESCR. This therefore requires the improvement of 'the resources, capabilities, choices, security and power necessary for the enjoyment of an adequate standard of living and other civil, cultural, economic, political and social rights'.[134] Thus, whilst the lens of poverty adds value to understandings of the right to continuous improvement of living conditions, this right offers the potential to be used as a new tool in the fight against poverty.

In conclusion, conceptualising the right to continuous improvement of living conditions as a response to poverty – as the CECSR has done – and unpacking the implications of this understanding suggests that the right to continuous improvement of living conditions is a societal claim that the minimum conditions of living (the poverty threshold) within a society must be continuously improved. Twinned with a relative approach to poverty, this understanding of the right serves to ensure that the subject matter of the right to continuous improvement of living conditions can evolve in response to new standards and conditions of living. Thus, the right to continuous improvement of living conditions is crucial to preventing stagnation of rights realisation and ensuring the *perpetual* relevance of the ICESCR.

[134] CESCR (n 7) para 8.

5

Is Financial Inclusion a Proxy for Continuously Improving Living Conditions?

JUAN PABLO BOHOSLAVSKY AND FRANCISCO CANTAMUTTO

I. INTRODUCTION

ONE OF THE outstanding characteristics of the current stage of world capitalism is the ubiquitous presence of finance regulating forms of accumulation. This chapter focuses on the debt of households. The ability to borrow within the limits of one's own financial capacity may improve people's living standards, allowing access to services that would otherwise be out of reach; and it may play a role in activating and supporting the economy. Household or individual debt may, at times, also facilitate social mobility or integration, and it can be a determinant factor in ensuring social inclusion. This is so-called financial inclusion working well. There is no lack of case studies that can present examples of success.[1]

The narrative of financialisation contains the explicit assumption that financial inclusion leads to the realisation of borrowers' human rights and that, in turn, an increasing volume of financial resources available to individuals and households is paralleled by the continuous improvement of their living conditions. Some go further, proposing financial inclusion as a human right itself, as it strengthens individual autonomy and provides resources (ie money) to acquire the services that fulfil a proper standard of living.[2] This chapter discusses this assumption.

There are two aspects that lead us to question that assumption. First, the fact that private debt can not only be the cause of human rights violations but also their consequence: poverty, inequality and States not ensuring the realisation of

[1] For a wide sample of successful cases, see the Centre for Financial Inclusion <https://www.centerforfinancialinclusion.org>. See also the Global Partnership for Financial Inclusion <https://www.gpfi.org>.

[2] J Queralt, 'A Human Right to Financial Inclusion' in H Gaisbauer, G Schweiger and C Sedmak (eds), *Ethical Issues in Poverty Alleviation* (Springer International Publishing 2016).

economic and social rights in a context of increasing financialisation of public goods push people into private debt. Second, the scale of over-indebtedness, abusive contractual terms and collection practices which become a burden and a threat for individuals or households, potentially quickly turn into a trap for many, putting the realisation of human rights in jeopardy.

If financial inclusion means to make available credit to households, we can have a first glimpse of its scale by looking at some measurements at an aggregated level. The figure presents two series, covering the period 1980 to 2018: the participation of the top 1% of the adult population in current income and total stock of loans and debt securities issued by households as a share of GDP. What is shown there is that household debt rose constantly until 2009, reaching an amazing peak of three quarters of GDP, and has stayed nearly constant since then with very little decrease. At the same time, the share of the top richest people has increased over time until 2007, and has shown a really mild decline since then. Thus, the success in financial inclusion, ie the rise in household debt, has gone hand in hand with increasing economic inequality in the entire world. That seems to be the opposite of closing the gap. Because of the data provided, we cannot infer causality between both trends.[3]

Figure Household debt (as share of GDP) and top 1% share in current income, 1980–2018

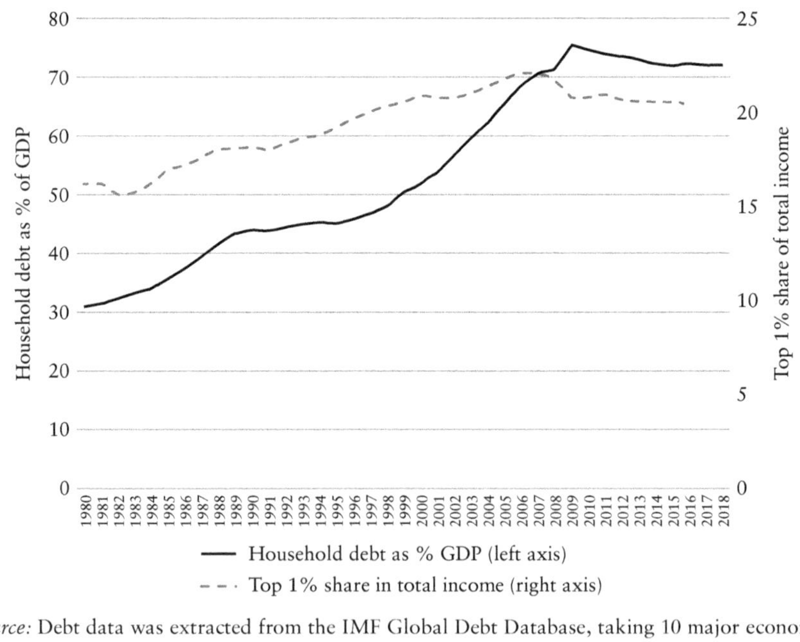

Source: Debt data was extracted from the IMF Global Debt Database, taking 10 major economies with continuous data in the period considered. Distribution data was taken from World Inequality Database as the world index. The IMF Global Debt Database is available at <https://www.imf.org/external/datamapper/HH_LS@GDD/SWE>. The World Inequality Database is available at <https://wid.world/es/series>.

This information tells us that, in any case, inequality and household indebtedness have grown at the same rate, no more and no less than this. However, here we understand that this points out the limitations of the financial inclusion strategy to guarantee or promote a fairer world. To the extent that greater indebtedness increases the income of the richest, we suspect that it is likely to be in their interest to promote financialisation. On the other hand, it does not seem logical to assume that the remaining 99%, who take over a smaller part of the income and see their debt grow, could thus be improving their living conditions. The task undertaken in the rest of the chapter is to explain this link, showing how debt actually hinders the guarantee of the right to live better. Financialisation highlights the power of financial markets and the notion of self-management in improving one's own living conditions, obfuscating States' obligations to take appropriate steps to progressively realise economic, social and cultural rights. Overall, this course of the economy does not appear to have benefited the large majority, since, on the contrary, in addition to intensifying inequality, instability and uncertainty have increased. It does not seem that the growing financialisation has supported an improvement in the living conditions of the people.

In this chapter we will look at household indebtedness within this framework of analysis. We will seek to provide evidence from various disciplinary sources to show how it is linked with negative human rights implications of microcredit; health, education and housing-related debts; abusive collection practices, including the criminalisation of debtors; consumers and migration-related debts; and debt bondage.

'Financial inclusion', seen by many as proxy for the improvement of living conditions, seems in fact to be often both a cause and a consequence of human rights violations. If this is true, this chapter will study the legal implications of the right to the continuous improvement of living conditions in the contractual relations and regulatory frameworks regarding private indebtedness. State commitment to the right to the continuous improvement of living conditions should emphasise direct responsibility in terms of ensuring that basic needs are met, instead of just promoting compensatory short-term mechanisms such as credit.

This chapter is organised as follows. Section II explains the main features of the current stage of world capitalism. Section III focuses on household debt as a hazard to human rights and their violation as the cause of indebtedness. Section IV proposes a typology of household debts to contribute to understanding the particular links between financial inclusion and human rights. Finally, Section V links the previous findings to explore their impacts on the right to the continuous improvement of living conditions.

[3] See A Mian, L Straub and A Sufi, 'The Saving Glut of the Rich and the Rise in Household Debt' (2020) National Bureau of Economic Research Working Paper 26941 <https://www.nber.org/papers/w26941>.

II. FINANCIAL CAPITALISM

One of the outstanding characteristics of the current stage of world capitalism is the ubiquitous presence of finance regulating forms of accumulation. Although it is a clear trend seen since the break-up of the Bretton Woods agreements, this phenomenon – described as financialisation – has expanded intensely since the last global financial crisis, which erupted in 2008. Thanks to strong deregulation, the financial business has – with its logic being the organisation of public accounts – shaped the provision of public services, the corporate administration of companies and even the finances of households. This scenario emerges from a specific history which is outlined below.

The role of finance in historical capitalism has changed over time. Already at the beginning of the twentieth century, those who studied imperialism recorded the merger between industrial and banking capital, imposing a financial logic for the operation of companies. In fact, this link marked the outbreak of the Great Depression in the 1930s, the corollary of which was the imposition of various limitations on the functioning of the financial sector around the world. It was on this basis that the Bretton Woods agreements of 1944 forged the central guidelines of the international financial architecture.[4] Subject to these rules, global capitalism expanded rapidly for almost three decades.

In the early 1970s, this framework began to crack.[5] The inconvertibility of the dollar in 1971 and its devaluation in 1973 marked a turning point, opening the way to a decade of stagnation and inflation. This milestone is relevant because it was a turning point in economic policies worldwide. Hand in hand with the most orthodox interpretations, a series of reforms aimed at deregulating and liberalising the economy were promoted, redefining the role of the State in favour of more concentrated capital. These changes gave capital a great advantage in imposing its desires over the people's will. Under the threat of going elsewhere, corporations began to get tax breaks, greater labour and legal flexibility, less social controls, etc. States increasingly put themselves at the service of attracting and tempting capital, instead of granting their people's rights.[6] This was not a retraction of the State, but a change of its functions.[7]

[4] B Steil, *The Battle of Bretton Woods: John Maynard Keynes, Harry Dexter White and the Making of a New World Order* (Princeton University Press 2013).

[5] For an analysis of structural and historical determinations that ended those agreements, see F Block, *The Origins of International Economic Disorder: A Study of United States International Monetary Policy from World War II to the Present* (University of California Press 1977); E Hobsbawm, *The Age of Extremes: A History of the World, 1914-1991* (Random House 1996).

[6] P Hirst and G Thompson, 'Globalization and the Future of the Nation State' (1995) 24(3) *Economy and Society* 408–42.

[7] It is commonly said that the State shrank during neoliberalism. This is not true. States grew in size in most countries and made extensive interventions in the market, with active public policies. In fact, the very deregulation of economies was a strong intervention in the way markets worked. The main change was that States intervened in a more biased way, ie in favour of large, financialised firms.

Debt played a key role in this change. The need to invest the so-called 'Eurodollars' and 'petrodollars' pushed several Third World States to take loans, even unneeded ones. This was particularly the case of Latin America. Sovereign debt grew, becoming unsustainable, which led to a deep crisis throughout the 1980s. This event conditioned the reform of the world financial system. Through the Baker and Brady plans, the restructuring of Latin American debt functioned as a gateway to a new stage in financial deregulation, by providing incentives for bond markets and allowing new players to participate in this type of investment.[8]

This implied that debt could be bought and sold infinitely, without knowing who the creditor was. As a guarantee for these operations, countries committed themselves before multilateral credit agencies to observe their recommendations, and in particular, to advance with structural reforms. Specifically, the International Monetary Fund (IMF) played the role of auditing the accounts of the countries and suggesting what economic policies would be most appropriate. Its axis, in line with monetarist recommendations, was the stabilisation of prices, instead of growth or fulfilment of economic needs.

As a complement to the above, a genuine international system of rights to protect investments grew. The investment protection system consists of a complex set of bilateral and multilateral treaties, which grant multiple rights to companies in order to attract investments – even if the results do not seem to support this.[9] There are currently more than 3,000 treaties in force around the world that allow companies to sue States whenever they feel their interests have been affected; States, on the other hand, often do not have the same rights. In addition, a large number of free trade or trade partnership agreements were signed, which facilitated the movement of goods in the world. Even though treaties focus on investment or trade, investment funds have taken advantage of their terms to initiate lawsuits against debtor countries.[10]

This change in priorities is not exclusively due to prevailing ideas, but to a structural crisis of capitalism. In fact, the stage that opened up in the

[8] The plans mentioned above guided the restructuring of Third World debts in the late 1980s and 1990s. The latter is an especially important milestone in the consolidation of contemporary international financial architecture. It promoted the use of bonds to address sovereign debt, expanded secondary markets, and merged financial and productive capitals. See J Ross, *Why Not Default? The Political Economy of Sovereign Debt* (Princeton University Press 2019); O Ugarteche and A Acosta, 'Post Bretton Woods: Los problemas de la economía global, y el tribunal internacional de arbitraje de deuda soberana' in A Acosta and F Falconí (eds), *Asedios a lo imposible: Propuestas económicas en construcción* (FLACSO 2005).

[9] M Saguier and L Ghiotto, 'Las empresas transnacionales: un punto de encuentro para la Economía Política Internacional de América Latina' (2018) 30(2) *Desafíos* 159–90.

[10] For an explanation of why international arbitration is not an economically or legally adequate forum in which to settle sovereign debt disputes, see JP Bohoslavsky and E Guntrip, 'Unanticipated Consequences: The Human Rights Implications of Bringing Sovereign Debt Disputes Within Investment Treaty Arbitration' in L Sachs, L Johnson and J Coleman (eds), *Yearbook on Investment Law and Policy* (Oxford University Press 2018) 492–535.

1980s represents a new historical phase, which we can call neoliberal globalisation. Thanks to the structural reforms, the financial link between different forms of capital became overwhelming. In addition to increasing trade flows in the world, there was a strong pressure to commodify resources, services and rights. That is, to transform as many social links as possible into commodities subject to market transactions. This opened up enormous possibilities for new businesses, tempting capital that could not find alternative placements. This could include privatisation of public enterprises or unsustainable exploitation of mining and agriculture on a large scale, among others.[11]

The tension marked by financial logic was not exclusive to macroeconomic regulation. Various studies have shown that business management has become increasingly financial. This phenomenon, also known as financialisation, has many characteristics.[12]

We do not seek here to exhaust the discussion of corporate financialisation, but to point out how in the space of production the same type of logic was imposed on the States by means of sovereign debt. Since the crisis that broke out in 2008, these two types of debt – sovereign and private (corporate and household) – have grown to levels previously unheard of on a global scale, thanks to the cheap credit available through the monetary policies (quantitative easing) applied by the major powers.

According to the International Institute of Finance Report,[13] global debt reached an astonishing total of $258 trillion in Q1 2020. This is over 331% of global GDP. This is almost 50 percentage points ($90 trillion) higher than at the onset of the 2008 financial crisis. Non-financial sectors account for most of this increase in total debt, where sovereign debt and non-financial corporate sectors explain most of it. The crisis, far from being resolved, was displaced in time by the same mechanisms that produced it: the dissociation between production and consumption leveraged by finance – splitting reward and risk.

In short, the crisis of the 1970s gave rise to a set of structural transformations relevant to understanding the problem of household debt and its relationship to the fulfilment of human rights. First, it is clear that there was a change in the functions of the State, which abandoned the role of 'protector' of social rights to become a business facilitator. Second, as we highlight in this chapter, the use of

[11] D Harvey, 'Neoliberalism as Creative Destruction' (2007) 610(1) *The Annals of the American Academy of Political and Social Science*. Other scholars who have also raised attention to the fact that created scarcity is key to explaining the expansion of capitalism suggest that de-commodification is a valid goal to economic policies, even if it diminishes GDP growth. See eg J Hickle, 'Degrowth: A Call for Radical Abundance' (2018) <www.jasonhickel.org/blog/2018/10/27/degrowth-a-call-for-radical-abundance>.

[12] M Abeles, P Caldentey and S Valdecantos (eds), *Estudios sobre financierización en América Latina* (CEPAL, 2018); P Mader, D Mertens and N Van Der Zwan (eds), *The Routledge International Handbook of Financialization* (Routledge 2020).

[13] See E Tiftik and K Mahmood, 'Institute of International Finance, "Sharp spike in debt ratios"' (*Institute of International Finance*, 16 July 2020) <www.iif.com/Portals/0/Files/content/Research/Global%20Debt%20Monitor_July2020.pdf>.

debt as a pressure mechanism in favour of creditors, which limits the apparently affordable set of economic policies. Third, the financialisation of households went hand in hand with structural reforms, which fostered inequality and the loss of social rights (especially, but not only, labour rights). Fourth, in particular, it fostered the commodification of previously State-provided services. In other words, they are part of the same structural-historical process. Finally, it shows that household indebtedness is just one expression of a broader phenomenon.

III. HOUSEHOLDS' DEBT

Despite their stated objectives, the most significant result of the structural reforms has been a lower overall growth rate along with an increase in inequality. This is not surprising, since the opening up of economies offers capital a powerful mechanism for putting pressure on societies and States. Although the subject is hotly debated, evidence indicates that the economic expansion of some countries (BRICS centrally) reduced the global income gap, as observations within countries consistently show greater inequality.[14] All over the world, inequality rose in the last decade. Credit Suisse's 2019 global wealth report[15] shows that while the richest 10% own as much as 82% of global wealth, the bottom half collectively accounted for less than 1%. The top 1% alone owns 45% of global wealth. The report shows that the ultra-rich elite had lost some share in total wealth until the 2008 crisis, and rose from there. It can be assumed that some of the measured wealth was in fact debt-sustained, and therefore collapsed after the crisis. Oxfam has drawn attention to the fact that 'the world's 2,153 billionaires have more wealth than the 4.6 billion people who make up 60 percent of the planet's population'.[16]

The growing ability of the richest strata of the world's population to accumulate wealth has raised global concern.[17] Criticism of the richest '1%' has taken centre stage in multiple social movements over the past decade. It is remarkable that in 2014 the best-selling book was Thomas Picketty's *Capital in the Twenty-First Century*, which explores the issue from a progressive perspective.[18]

[14] B Alper and A Oktayer, 'Globalization And Poverty: A Panel Evidencia from Worldwide Countries' in U Çağlar, H Şimşek and I Şiriner (eds), *Current Debates in Economic Growth & Public Finance & Game Theory* (IJOPEC 2019) 11–22; Z Darvas, 'Global Interpersonal Income Inequality Decline: The Role of China and India' (2019) 121 *World Development* 16–32; B Milanovic, *Global Inequality: A New Approach for the Age of Globalization* (Harvard University Press 2016).

[15] Credit Suisse, 'Global Wealth Report 2019' (October 2019) <www.credit-suisse.com/media/assets/corporate/docs/about-us/research/publications/global-wealth-report-2019-en.pdf>.

[16] Oxfam, 'World's billionaires have more wealth than 4.6 billion people' (20 January 2020) <www.oxfam.org/en/press-releases/worlds-billionaires-have-more-wealth-46-billion-people>.

[17] The wealth of the richest percentile is systematically underestimated in surveys. See eg V Hlasny, 'Unit Nonresponse Bias in Inequality Measurement: Worldwide Analysis Using Luxembourg Income Study Database' (2020) 101(2) *Social Science Quarterly* 712.

[18] T Picketty, *Capital in the Twenty-First Century* (Harvard University Press 2014).

To serve this truly global elite, a whole range of financial services has been consolidated, capable of managing resources across borders. Tax havens provide a special service for hiding this wealth, not only among the elite, but also for the very operation of transnational corporations.[19]

As stated by the United Nations Human Rights Council,[20] the issue of foreign debt, both public and private, is closely linked with increasing inequality worldwide and with the obstacles to sustainable human development resulting from the debt burden, including in achieving the 2030 Agenda for Sustainable Development through adequate financing. Global household debt reached $48.1 trillion in 2020, from $35 trillion in 2007.[21] This is estimated to be about 62% of global GDP. In this vein, the General Assembly has already warned[22] of rising private and public indebtedness in many developing countries, and stressed the need for continuing efforts to address systemic fragilities and imbalances and to reform and strengthen the international financial system.

Under the umbrella of' individual and household debt', many forms of private debts can be considered, as can various types of creditors and debtors. Some of these might even refer to small family businesses borrowing through formal and informal channels. The most direct and egregious violations of human rights suffered by private borrowers are committed in the context of individual and household debts,[23] particularly in the case of persons and households living in poverty or marginalised, or those who are forced into a 'debt trap'.

A number of studies has pointed to a close relationship between the accumulation of private debt, macroeconomic instability and sovereign debt crises: private debt booms in some countries have been associated with economic downturns and often serve as an accurate indicator of financial instability.[24] Similarly, increasing inequality may lead to private over-borrowing and over-lending, which can in turn have an impact on financial stability, potentially resulting in a debt crisis over time.[25]

Individual and household debt accounts for a significant portion of private debt in most countries, and may be the result of a series of economic measures, such as privatisation of public services or austerity measures, or labour market flexibilisation, which drives down the wages of unskilled workers and fuel inequality.[26]

[19] Global Justice Network particularly stresses this issue. See eg <www.globaljusticenetwork.com/>.

[20] OHCHR Res/40/8 (27 December 2018).

[21] See Tiftik and Mahmood (n 13).

[22] UN General Assembly (21 December 2016) UN Doc A/RES/71/215.

[23] UNGA (3 January 2020) UN Doc A/HRC/43/45.

[24] JP Bohoslavsky, 'Economic Inequality, Debt Crises and Human Rights' (2016) 41 *Yale Journal of International Law* (2016) 177 (2016) 158–59.

[25] ibid.

[26] JM Servet and H Saiag, 'Household Over-indebtedness in Northern and Southern Countries: A Macro-Perspective' in S Morvant-Roux, M Villarreal and I Guérin (eds), *Microfinance, Debt and Over-Indebtedness* (Routledge 2014) 26.

As the gap between nominal income and cash needs has widened, households have increasingly turned to debt to fulfil their consumption needs. In 2018, the OECD average household debt was 126% of household net disposable income.[27] This is an expression of the weakness of household incomes, unable to reach consumption standards, and also of risky exposure to financial arrangements. For example, a sudden rise in interest rates would have a huge impact on a household's ability to manage its burden. Nevertheless, the problem of household indebtedness, specifically mortgage loans, came to the fore with the 2008 crisis. In general, the public policies implemented were not geared towards sustained wage increases or large housing solution programmes. Instead, bank bailouts were implemented, nationalising the debt. While this relieved the debt of households in the richest countries, this was not what happened in emerging economies.[28]

In these countries the expansion of consumer credit has significantly contributed to GDP growth while many consumers have fallen into a cycle of overindebtedness and poverty due to those loans.[29] Even the IMF has acknowledged that growing household debt may hold back economic recovery, which is already weak, prolonging the current phase of low growth,[30] a consequence of the financialisation of the economy. In a recent study, the IMF has gone further, recognising that increase in financialisation might in fact be sharpening inequality.[31]

High household debt can also have a negative impact on the economy. At a certain point, indebtedness puts a strain on productivity, consumption and growth, leading to an unsustainable disequilibrium.[32] If private debt is too high, consumers and businesses have to divert a greater portion of their income to cover interests and principal on that debt, spending and investing less as a result. In a number of financial crises, the rising level of consumer debt has triggered investment asset bubbles, leading to a financial meltdown. In many cases, part of private debt is nationalised through bailout programmes, which deepen public sector imbalances and may lead to sovereign debt crises.[33] The unprecedented

[27] OECD, 'How's Life? 2020' (2020) <www.oecd.org/statistics/how-s-life-23089679.htm>.

[28] E Tiftik and K Mahmood, 'High and Rising Debt Levels: Should We Worry? Global Debt Monitor Slide Deck' (2019) *Institute of International Finance Quarterly Global Debt Monitor*.

[29] Household debt has risen in emerging economies, especially in China and India. See eg M Badia and P Dudine, 'New Data on World Debt: A Dive into Country Numbers' (IMFBlog, 17 December 2019) <https://blogs.imf.org/2019/12/17/new-data-on-world-debt-a-dive-into-country-numbers/>.

[30] International Monetary Fund (IMF), 'Global Financial Stability Report' (2019) <www.imf.org/en/Publications/GFSR> 53.

[31] M Čihák and R Sahay, 'Financial Services and Inequality' (2020) IMF Staff Discusión Notes SDN/20/XX <www.imf.org/en/Publications/Staff-Discussion-Notes/Issues/2020/01/16/Finance-and-Inequality-45129>.

[32] IMF (n 30) 78; Servet and Saiag (n 26) 28.

[33] UN Conference on Trade and Development (UNCFTD), 'Trade and Development Report' (2017) 100, 106.

explosion of private debt indeed constitutes the single largest contingent liability on public debt in the event of a debt crisis.[34]

A correlation between private debt and inequality has been widely recognised. It has been shown that household debt and top income share are positively correlated; income inequality therefore widens as private debt grows.[35] According to the credit-demand line of reasoning, private debt increases as households try to maintain certain absolute or relative levels of consumption while facing growing inequality; in other words, people borrow more extensively to maintain their standard of living. Moreover, household borrowing has become a key mechanism in social reproduction. Indeed, because of the commodification and privatisation process, credit has become increasingly important to have access to basic public services, such as education and health care. Unequal access to credit can therefore exacerbate existing social and economic inequalities.[36] Finally, private debt exacerbates inequality by increasing incomes for financial sector workers, particularly managers and executives, in relation to non-financial sector workers, as well as by driving returns for those who hold the concentrated ownership of financial assets.[37]

A common policy response in a financial crisis has been to protect financial institutions and large corporations, which, by default, shields the wealthier households owning their assets, rather than middle- and low-income households.[38] Austerity measures usually affect those in vulnerable situations, such as the poorest, not creditors. For women, access (or lack thereof) to social protection and private debt are closely connected. As they start off poorer and with vulnerability in access to the labour market, women tend to be specially benefited by social policies, so their access to credit can be jeopardised by cuts to welfare benefits.[39]

Rising levels of inequality may, in turn, directly or indirectly contribute to an increase in public debt and financial crises. Regressive taxation and sluggish economic growth may diminish public revenue and lead to more reliance on external borrowing, which may eventually degenerate into a sovereign debt crisis. Empirical studies demonstrate that there is indeed a positive correlation between income inequality, fiscal deficit and mounting sovereign debt.[40]

[34] ibid 76.

[35] ibid 103–04.

[36] L Rethel, 'Financialisation and the Malaysian Political Economy' (2010) 7(4) *Globalizations* 489–506.

[37] J Wood, 'Can Household Debt Influence Income Inequality? Evidence from Britain: 1966–2016' (2019) 22(4) *British Journal of Politics and International Relations* 22–46.

[38] UNCTAD (n 33) 108.

[39] J Callegari, P Liedgren and C Kullberg, 'Gendered Debt: A Scoping Study Review of Research on Debt Acquisition and Management in Single and Couple Households' (2019) 23 *European Journal of Social Work* 9.

[40] UN Independent Expert on Debt and Human Rights, 'Inequality, Financial Crises and Human Rights' (2016) UN Doc A/HRC/31/60.

It is important to note that not only has inequality increased within countries, but there has also been an intense growth in poverty at the global level. So much so that the problem has moved to the centre of the public policy agenda. In 2000, the United Nations agreed on the Millennium Development Goals, the first of which was to eradicate poverty. Although there was some progress, a decade and a half later these goals had not been met, and new goals, called Sustainable Development Goals, were renegotiated. Beyond the expression of a goal, this prominence in the agenda expresses the persistence of the problem.[41]

Both the World Bank and the IMF insist in their agendas on the progressive nature of financial inclusion, despite this contradicting some of the evidence they refer to. Understood as greater access to credit for all, it is increasingly presented as a solution to many human rights problems – whether to start a business to earn a living, to obtain appropriate health care or to have access to employment opportunities. In the 1990s, Muhammad Yunus, who pioneered the concept of microcredit, even argued that access to credit was a 'basic human right for all', although serious efforts to construct such a claim from law were never made.

Financialisation highlights the power of financial markets and the notion of self-management in improving one's own living conditions, obfuscating States' obligations to take appropriate steps to progressively realise economic, social and cultural rights. Instead of providing public services or ensure decent wage levels, the State has played an active role in promoting financialisation of households. The State is responsible for the economic policy that generates impoverishment, in addition to failing to protect basic social rights. In this way, it pushes households – especially the poorest – into debt to cover their needs. But beyond that, the State also appears as a direct lender, through multiple channels. The most perverse recent developments are those that link the use of social programmes as collateral for receiving credit: the State provides minimal social assistance, which is used as insurance for loans provided by the State itself.[42] This is a perverse way of 'educating' those who suffer the greatest deprivation. Finally, by endorsing the deregulation of finance, it helps to admit predatory or abusive practices by financial companies.

Financialisation of households is premised on the assumption that providing access to credit might solve some of the market's imperfections, letting people invest in the best opportunities left because of the lack of information or assets. Further, as financial education is always encouraged within the growth of credit, it assumes this education will correct people's behaviour to better

[41] For further discussion, see Graham, chapter four in this volume and Fredman, chapter twelve in this volume.

[42] L Lavinas, *The Takeover of Social Policy by Financialization: The Brazilian Paradox* (Palgrave Macmillan 2017).

meet intertemporal consumption needs.[43] Which is more or less to say that poor people are responsible for their bad choices. Even the gender gap seems to be addressed by lending more to women.[44] Yet, if a company pays a woman less than it pays a man – but gives her a loan on top, to reach the same nominal level as her male colleague, this does not ensure equal treatment. As long as she does not own this difference, she remains unequal and additionally becomes indebted.

It must be stressed that no connection is presented in these proposals to provide credit to the poor between pro-market structural reforms and the increase on inequality and poverty. This argument seems to assume that people make their economic choices in a vacuum, not in historically grounded societies; as if debtors decide to take credit without considering their social or economic context. If wages are to be reduced and social security is cut to increase capital engagement, it is unlikely that people who live on selling their labour can live better.[45] Credit does not seem to aim at reducing income inequality or poverty. Instead, credit seems to solve a need of capitalism as a system – that is, it feeds the purchasing power of consumers, preventing a lack of aggregate demand from resulting in an immediate crisis. As their living standards move away from what contemporary technology enables – and how rich people live – credit appears as a defensive mechanism to meet social consumption standards.[46] Moreover, indebted people seem to be more ready to accept bad jobs to pay their liabilities. Debt functions as a disciplinary resource for capitalists, with a particular bonus; it seems to come as a demand from the disciplined instead of an imposition of the mighty who take advantage of it.

Still, credit can work in some cases. There are many good projects that would not be implemented just because they have no collateral to apply for credit. As financialisation deepens, it is more likely that these projects will became real, as they gain access to credit. However, this approach ignores the determinations that cause people to lack collateral in the first place. They lack resources because the same reforms that support financialisation as a panacea have impoverished them. Encouraging new business is unlikely to be a way out for the majority, as

[43] Banco Mundial, 'New World Bank Group Report Charts Road Map for Financial Inclusion' (11 November 2013) <www.bancomundial.org/es/news/feature/2013/11/11/New-World-Bank-Group-Report-Charts-Road-Map-for-Financial-Inclusion>.

[44] M Čihák and R Sahay, 'Women in Finance: A Case for Closing Gaps' (2020) IMF Staff Discusión Notes SDN/20/XX <www.imf.org/en/Publications/Staff-Discussion-Notes/Issues/2018/09/17/women-in-finance-a-case-for-closing-gaps-45136>.

[45] See further Lamarche, chapter six in this volume.

[46] J Perraton, 'Macroeconomic Implications of Inequality and Household Debt: European Evidence' in LP Rochon and V Monvoisin (eds), *Finance, Growth and Inequality: Post-Keynesian Perspectives* (Edward Elgar Publishing 2019) 93–110; B Berberoglu (ed), *The Global Capitalist Crisis and Its Aftermath: The Causes and Consequences of the Great Recession of 2008-2009* (Ashgate Publishing 2014); M Roberts, *The Long Depression: Marxism and the Global Crisis of Capitalism* (Haymarket Books 2016).

each project must deal with an economy increasingly exposed to global competition, with greater technological and educational distances and lobbying capacity to protect investments. In other words, some projects are likely to be successful, but it is even more likely that those projects will be a minority.

Overall, the main point made in this section is that household debt has been directly associated with the rise in inequality, the change in public policies contrary to people's welfare, and the commodification of a number of public services and goods. This is an economist's way of saying that household debt rose because human rights were not guaranteed, with the right to the continuous improvement of living conditions being directly threatened.

IV. A TYPOLOGY OF DEBTS

Accurate and comprehensive global, regional or sometimes domestic data about household private debt and default rates are not entirely available. Many cases of informal or even illegal lending and borrowing at the individual and household levels are not registered, accounted for, or adequately estimated. In certain countries the informal economy is huge, and a large part of private household debt is likely to be kept out of financial, banking and non-banking systems. Another part of household debt can be intertwined within larger estimates of illicit financial flows, such as all debt owed to migrant smugglers and transit debts owed to corrupt authorities at the border. Therefore, a purely quantitative approach to private debt and human rights would be highly unsatisfactory in contexts such as these.[47]

There is a huge number of reasons to require credit. We seek to put some order into the types of situations that require credit but the list cannot be exhaustive. As people's living standards have been delayed in relationship to aggregate growth and technological capabilities, many of the reasons for becoming indebted are linked to meet decent living conditions. Welfare States were designed on the assumption that goods and services were bought using the money earned in the form of wages, or alternatively, were provided by the State. In underdeveloped economies it is not unusual that informal communitarian arrangements allow people to subsist outside of the provision through the market or the State.[48] But neoliberal globalisation has destroyed almost all of these access channels to fulfil these needs. Real wages have not remained sufficient to buy the goods and services, and increasingly privatisation and commodification of services have

[47] See generally UN Independent Expert on Debt and Human Rights (3 January 2020), 'Private Debt and Human Rights' OHCHR UN Doc A/HRC/43/45.

[48] It is not unusual in poor areas that neighbours help each other to fulfil basic needs such as eating or taking care of elders, the sick or children. Their mutual recognition in the face of adversity and the need to consolidate protection networks over time forge bonds of solidarity.

diminished State and community provision. Therefore, people need an extra supply of money just to retain a decent level of consumption.[49]

In this sense, the *provision of food* appears to be an unsettling reason for requesting credit. Lack of food, inadequate access to nutritious food, malnutrition and hunger seriously affect the physical health of people, especially children, pregnant women, the chronically ill and older persons. Even more, for people who are late in their payments or in default, bills and hunger are too often connected, sometimes forcing them to resort to 'payday loans' and food aid.

In a similar fashion, people use credit for paying for *health* services. Health-related debt – a growing cause of financial insecurity and impoverishment in many households around the world, be it due to maternity services, unexpected hospitalisation, a chronic disease or the need for costly or rare medication or frequent use of services and facilities – often arises from high out-of-pocket medical expenses that people cannot afford. The primary factor underlying high out-of-pocket expenses is lack of access to adequate essential health care, services or facilities: more than 50% of the global population has no access to adequate essential health care and, in most countries, the accessibility and affordability of essential health care are limited or not guaranteed. In many countries, health packages may cover too few interventions, may not cover medicines, or provide insufficient financial protection; health insurance does not necessarily protect the insured from medical debt. This debt typology is even more relevant in the context of the Covid-19 pandemic.

Millions of households around the world make hard choices for the *education* of children and adolescents, often based on economic considerations and their total dependence on access to credit. In certain cases, households have to decide which member of the family is more 'deserving' of education, which can at times mean only the eldest child, or the boy rather than the girl. The call to prevent the risk of overindebtedness reflects a mounting situation around the world, and may often refer to debt for secondary education too. Student loans have also been on the rise, as the public education systems in many countries have faced austerity, private schools have expanded and the cost of education has grown rapidly in real terms.[50] As the UN Special Rapporteur on the right to education has highlighted,[51] for-profit schools may seek to maximise profits through high fees or to cut costs by, for example, reducing the most expensive parts of the curriculum, expelling learners that need the most support, or not properly maintaining school premises.

[49] For further discussion on the role of the State in the provision of certain services and goods see Goldblatt, chapter eleven in this volume.

[50] M Lim, Michael, M Hui and J Sundaram, 'Transforming Society, Financialization Destroys Social Solidarity' (*Inter Press Service*, 4 June 2019) <www.ipsnews.net/2019/06/transforming-society-financialization-destroys-social-solidarity/>.

[51] UN Special Rapporteur on the Right to Education, 'Right to education and SDG 4 in the context to the growth of private actors in education' (2019) UN Doc A/HRC/41/37.

Student loans for tertiary education are usually perceived as a positive investment and 'good debt', as they could go a long way towards better educational qualifications and employment opportunities, and may provide financial stability for the individual and the entire household. Evidence suggests, however, that college loans no longer guarantee social mobility and financial stability. The increasingly concentrated labour market, growing precariousness, and stagnant wage growth mean that graduates often have difficulties finding employment that enables them to pay off debt.[52]

In a similar way as described for health or education, many other public services are no longer provided by the State, nor guaranteed as rights. Arguing State inefficiency, basic services such as water, electricity or gas have surrendered to corporate interests and are now sold as market commodities. Continuously privatised around the world, in response to neoliberal recommendations, these services are managed as private business, therefore setting profitability as the main goal, and failing to meet the needs of impoverished people.[53] In order to pay bills to access water or electricity, some households turn to credit. This means that the realisation of access to basic services is restricted to being able to pay and not guaranteed as a right.

Housing financialisation, predatory lending and unpayable household mortgage debt, at the root of the 2008 financial crisis, illustrate the links between household debt and the deregulation of financial markets, to the detriment of people, with devastating consequences in terms of thousands of foreclosures, and widespread cases of eviction, displacement and homelessness, across countries in the North and increasingly also in the global South. Unregulated land markets and corporate financialisation make real estate speculation an attractive investment, frequently with government support, regardless of its social effects. In underdeveloped countries, commodity booms usually go hand in hand with land prices rising, displacing people from their houses. When foreign investment also aims at securing the supply of certain primary goods, the former effect is increased. The gap between job earnings and housing prices has grown, making housing unaffordable for the vast majority.

As previously explained, available consumption goods have expanded in the last decades due to technological progress. Nevertheless, for people to keep on buying *durable and non durable goods* credit needs to be at hand. Credit cards and banks are a widespread option, but a limited one. Both work on the basis of the existence of some collateral of the debtor; assets or some constant source of income (ie wages) that provide the promise to repay. That is why other non-bank financial institutions have risen to meet the demand, giving credit to people

[52] M Corkery and S Cowley, 'Household Debt Makes a Comeback in the U.S.' (*New York Times*, 17 May 2017).

[53] Global case tracking is available at Privatization Watch, a publication by the Public Services International <www.world-psi.org/en/privatization-watch-newsletter-all-issues>.

with lower or no collateral. Advertised as 'solely signature' needed, they offer extremely expensive credit to people who cannot access bank loans. These firms usually have a greater geographical dispersion, so as to achieve proximity to potential customers.

Another reason for access to debt are *small entrepreneur investments*. Not only family-owned SMEs, but also microbusiness, even informal ones, need credit for supplies and eventually machines or improvement of facilities. This kind of credit is also needed for stockpiles that many people need who, rejected from the labour market due to age, skills, gender or other reasons, intend to survive by risking their money in their own small enterprises. The huge informal sector of economies, especially in underdeveloped countries, functions this way. Microcredit proposals of financial inclusion aim to take advantage of this risky business. Of course, most of these projects have a high probability of failure, because of the difficulties involved in competing for small shares of the market with little capital and the technological gap. Creditors facilitate this failure by imposing high interest rates.

Migration also carries debt issues. Migration-related debt may be taken on to pay for the costs of migrating to another country, with or without documents. It can include payment of documentation, travel by various means, assistance in crossing borders, or even bribing authorities during transit or paying for smugglers when migrating without documentation. Such debt is frequently an issue for the entire (extended) family, and creates generational links and obligations across elders and younger members.

The more debt a family member incurs for economic migration, the more likely it is that this victim of human trafficking ends up in a never-ending debt-driven cycle, fed by the hope of avoiding the loss of collateral. Psychological and physical pressure, sexual harassment, death threats and other means of intimidation against relatives who stay behind are frequently features of the abuse exercised by collectors and smugglers. Individuals and families therefore go beyond their network to borrow, turning to high-interest loans from unregulated or loosely regulated institutional actors, such as *prestamistas* (moneylenders), notaries, cooperatives or banks, using land, homes, vehicles, or goods as collateral.[54] In such a context, some might consider remigration the only option for debt repayment.

Even in the case of formal migration, some countries do not allow recent migrants to work for a certain period, which aggravates the families' economic situation while having to repay migration-related debts. Furthermore, refugees and asylum seekers can incur new debts when arriving to a country as they face a range of financial challenges to meet their basic needs.

[54] L Heidbrink, 'the Coercive Power of Debt: Migration and Deportation of Guatemala Indigenous Youth' (2019) 24(1) *Journal of Latin America and Caribbean Anthropology* 263–81.

The repayment of credit is another reason to become more indebted. This includes debts repaid by instalments and regular (revolving) credit. The impossible equation of diminishing earnings and debt provides no way out. Debt repayment expresses the feedback logic of the problem: debts are contracted to pay living expenses, which in turn generate an expense at the time of payment, which reduces the meagre income available, forcing the taking of more debt. With the little they earn they have to pay back these loans, and reapply for new loans because they really cannot afford to live. This encourages defaults, which in turn cuts off other possible avenues of access to funds. Unless there is a sudden change in income, debt-taking generally seems to be associated with a continuous mechanism over time, rather than a one-off operation.

V. HOUSEHOLD DEBT AND THE RIGHT TO THE CONTINUOUS IMPROVEMENT OF LIVING CONDITIONS

Article 11(1) of the International Covenant on Economic, Social and Cultural Rights recognises the right of everyone to an adequate standard of living for himself and his family, including food and housing, and to the *continuous improvement of living conditions*.[55] This article should be read in conjunction with Article 2(2) of the Covenant, providing for the exercise of any right under the Covenant without discrimination of any kind. What are the implications of the right to the continuous improvement of living conditions in the context of private debt? In order to answer this question we need to integrate both macro and micro views of the causal links involved.

On the one hand, the explosion of private household debt in many countries is the direct result of two parallel and intertwined phenomena: first, the social services are being increasingly 'financialised' or reduced to commodities; and, second, the State, in promoting that transformation, is failing to abide by its human rights obligations, in particular in the field of economic, social and cultural rights. The human rights framework is fundamentally based on the notion that States (and to some extent private actors) have obligations to respect, protect and fulfil human rights, ensuring equality and combating discrimination.[56] Financialisation can in practice work as the antithesis of such a framework, as it rests on the idea of the individual's responsibility to take appropriate steps to ensure an adequate standard of living and access to essential goods and services for themselves. In other words, financial inclusion can actually hide the fact that living conditions are worsening due to structural (economic and social) conditions.

[55] International Covenant on Economic, Social and Cultural Rights, 16 December 1996, 993 UNTS 3.

[56] See OHCHR (3 January 2020) UN Doc A/HRC/43/45. See ICESCR (Art 2.2) and ICCPR (Art 26).

On the other hand, debt is not *per se* a human rights problem, even less a violation. What raises concerns is when indebtedness is either caused by or causes human rights violations, affecting in particular those in a situation of marginalisation or vulnerability. Again, even when financial inclusion is regularly presented as a proxy for improving living conditions, when we look at debtors' personal experiences we find that worsening conditions can lead to borrowing and, in turn, borrowing can indeed be followed by worsening conditions.

The principles of equality and non-discrimination lie at the heart of international human rights law. Understanding the implications of household indebtedness on the enjoyment of rights, such as to health, education, housing or access to water and electricity, and the right to continuous improvement of living conditions, inevitably leads to a detailed assessment of what the enjoyment of various human rights require from a financial perspective. Individuals or households trapped in the spiral of debt and economic vulnerability have to confront formidable economic forces or actors, high degrees of inequality, low levels of accountability, increasingly financialised services and limited access to mechanisms of justice or redress.

Frequently, individuals or groups of individuals face discrimination owing to their economic and social situation or status, which can be direct or indirect, or compounded by other forms of discrimination. This arbitrary treatment is given on account of their belonging to a certain economic or social group or strata within society in relation to their debt situation[57] and they may be stigmatised, marginalised or criminalised because of their incapacity to pay debt or because of the debt in their household.[58] To some extent, the very low levels of social protection and public expenditure in this area,[59] and the progressive weakening of remuneration systems for workers in formal employment are to a great extent the reason why millions of people seek recourse to credit in order to secure essential services, and are caught in a never-ending debt circle. The Committee on Economic, Social and Cultural Rights (CESCR) has referred to the 'redistributive character' of social security, which plays an important role in poverty reduction and promoting social inclusion.[60] Closely linked, the right to work encompasses the right to a remuneration that provides all workers with a decent living for themselves and their families. As explained by the CESCR in 2016,[61] remuneration must be sufficient to enable workers and their families to enjoy other rights in the Covenant.

[57] Unlike collateral, the amount paid for the risk-premium (mostly determined by the availability and quality of collateral) is not returned once the debt has been paid. This practice leads to different pricing for the same product and therefore discrimination based on property. O Pahnecke and JP Bohoslavsky, 'Interest Rates and Human Rights – Reinterpreting Risk Premiums to Adjust the Financial Economy' (2021) 46 *Yale Journal of International Law* 1.

[58] UN Committee on Economic, Social and Cultural Rights (CESCR), 'General Comment No. 22' (2016), E/C.12/GC/22.

[59] International Labour Organisation, 'World Social Protection Report 2017-2019' (2017).

[60] CESCR, 'General Comment No. 19' (2008), E/C.12/GC/19.

[61] CESCR, 'General Comment No. 23' (2016), E/C.12/GC/23.

Affordability, accessibility and quality are essential elements for the definition of the rights to housing, health and education.[62] Conversely, lack of access to health services, facilities and goods is most often defined by economic limitations on the one hand (low wages, poverty, high living costs, inflation) and high costs of medicines, hospitals or medical attention on the other. Despite being presented as a means to access to otherwise unreachable services or goods, what happens in fact is that the gap between income and prices stays high, and people are left with a credit burden because of this. This is a reinforcement of the disciplinary bias of debt: as there is no other way to accede to basic services, the payment of debt becomes essential to preserve that access. So high prices are paid for goods and services, and also high interest on the debts.

In addition to other serious human rights concerns with a potential impact on a range of rights, including the right to life,[63] liberty and security, several of the issues relating to debt collection pose crucial questions with regard to access to justice, and to procedures and mechanisms by which both public and private actors might claim debts. Article 26 of the International Covenant on Civil and Political Rights is clear in providing for equality before the law, without any discrimination, and to the equal protection of the law.

The Guiding Principles on Business and Human Rights[64] are relevant to the impact of business activities on human rights, including banking and financial private lenders and other private lending actors. According to the Guiding Principles, States have a duty to protect against human rights abuses within their territory and/or jurisdiction by third parties, including business enterprises. In turn, corporations must not violate human rights, while States have a duty to take steps to prevent and to investigate, punish and redress abuses through legislation, regulations, policies and adjudication. Furthermore, States have an obligation to ensure access to effective remedial mechanisms for persons whose rights have been violated by business activities within their territory.

VI. CONCLUDING REMARKS

The scale, frequency and seriousness of the economic, social and cultural rights violations that normally lead to or are a consequence of individual or household indebtedness should prevent us from identifying financial inclusion as a proxy of improving living conditions. Then, it is not surprising that the

[62] CESCR, 'General Comment No. 14' (2000), E/C.12/2000/4.

[63] For further discussion on the links between women's suicide rates and debt levels, see eg Tamilnadu Federation of Women Farmers' Rights, 'Rural distress on women farmer: an impact study' (7–17 January 2017) <www.tnlabour.in/wp-content/uploads/2017/02/180117-women-farmes-studyf-1.pdf>.

[64] UN Special Representative on Human Rights and Business, 'Guiding principles on business and human rights' (2011) UN Doc A/HRC/17/31, Annex.

brutal increase of private debt at an aggregate level in the last two decades has not been paralleled by a proportional decreased inequality between and within countries.

The expansion of finance over the last decades has been explicitly pushed by multilateral financial institutions, among which the idea of financial inclusion has even been promoted as an economic policy tool to address the world's poverty problems. There are two main drivers of the increase in private indebtedness. First, the flourishing supply side of finance, with deregulation and increasing financialisation being its facilitating instruments; second, the reconfiguration of many human needs for social reproduction that become unmet needs paralleled by a colossal failure of the State to ensure economic, social and cultural rights for all. This can lead to a perverse vicious circle. If so, then the 'financial inclusion', propagated as a proxy for improvement of living conditions, seems in fact to be both a cause and a consequence of human rights violations. Overall, the increasing financialisation of the economy does not appear to have benefited the large majority, since, on the contrary, in addition to intensifying inequality, instability and uncertainty have increased.

The revival of the right to continuous improvement of living conditions can advance human rights at two complementary levels in the field studied in this chapter: (a) preventing, minimising and compensating specific, concrete human rights violations in the context of private debt and (b) helping frame and legalise discussions on how structural inequalities and violations of fundamental economic and social rights are intrinsically linked to an increasing commodification and financialisation of human rights. Indeed, household debts seem to hide (or even legitimatise) poverty and radical inequalities. If the right to continuous improvement of living conditions is to play a more prominent role in the coming years in the international and national legal discourse in order to advance social changes, we need to be able to differentiate improving living conditions from access to credit (and being indebted). All of the above should not be taken as an outright rejection of all forms of household debt. There are several initiatives that promote social inclusion and economic opportunities through credit – and many of them actually work. In general, it can be said that this is the case of those projects that are directly linked to socially or economically productive investments and/or that deepen the social ties of communities. This type of credit is not necessarily characterised by its profitability in terms of high interest. However, this is not the kind of credit that has mostly spread in recent decades in the world, which explains the growth of household indebtedness. As long as the systematic violation of human rights is sustained through exclusion, discrimination and inequality, credit by itself cannot but reproduce the conditions that promote it.

This allows us to highlight once again that credit has flourished in a context in which the persistent violation of economic and social rights has been the norm. Scarce and precarious access to sufficient income to cover basic needs has been a driving force behind household credit. Therefore, debt is transformed into short-term relief, which quickly becomes a burden that prevents a sustainable improvement in living conditions. This is exactly the opposite of what the right to continuous improvement of living conditions is meant to achieve. The State has been a promoter of this phenomenon, not only by increasingly deregulating finances, but ultimately by its systematic failure to protect and promote social and economic rights for all.

6

The Right to the Continuous Improvement of Living Conditions and Progressive Realisation

The Case of the Right to Social Security in Canada

LUCIE LAMARCHE

I. INTRODUCTION

THE RIGHT TO the continuous improvement of living conditions in Article 11(1) of the International Covenant on Economic, Social and Cultural Rights (ICESCR)[1] concerns issues of distributive justice. It requires an international social, political and economic order that facilitates the material and democratic realisation of such right. It calls for inclusive, non-discriminatory and sustainable social spending at the national and supra-national levels. In this chapter I argue that it is a meta right which requires the assessment of each of the social rights guaranteed by the ICESCR in the light of Article 2 of the Covenant, which forbids regressive measures that impede the progressive realisation of social rights. One of these rights is the right to social security, which is more than a worker's right. As a social right, it relies on many different technical means that serve the overarching purpose of guaranteeing the human right to continuous improvement of living conditions. Section II of this chapter explores the historical trajectory of the right to social security and concludes that it has been in search of a purpose for too long. A contemporary challenge is to reconcile a technical right, such as the right to social security provided for by Article 9 of ICESCR, with both Articles 11 and 2 of the Covenant. How can the right to social security be benchmarked in order to assess both the

[1] International Covenant on Economic, Social and Cultural Rights, 16 December 1996, 993 UNTS 3.

right to the continuous improvement of living conditions and the obligation of a State Party not to claw back the level of realisation of the rights guaranteed by the Covenant?

States Parties to the Covenant too often use the argument of an urgent need for austerity measures as an excuse to legitimise claw back processes in regard to the realisation of the right to social security. During the same time that the Committee on Economic, Social and Cultural Rights (CESCR), responsible for the monitoring of the Covenant, has debated the notions of regressive and progressive realisation of all rights guaranteed by the Covenant, successive governments have put in place new means of delivering social security and social protection. These reforms do not necessarily depend on the political acknowledgment of a need for austerity measures. Consequently, such changes raise an important question: are social protection regimes being retrenched or recalibrated? In order to address this issue, in section III of this chapter I will look to the Canadian experience. The Canadian political discourse departed from the justification of austerity a decade ago. Nevertheless, the Canadian social protection regime has been deeply transformed. If one accepts the fact that the right to social security serves the meta right to the continuous improvement of living conditions, how should we assess the notions of retrenchment and of recalibration of the specific right to social security and to social protection in Canada?

Section IV of this chapter focuses on ICESCR and on its interpretation in the context of economic reforms and of the ideology of austerity. The CESCR went through different stages in interpreting the States Parties' main obligation stated in Article 2 of the treaty. Article 2 provides for the obligation to take steps, individually and through international assistance and co-operation, to the maximum of its available resources, with a view to achieving progressively the full realisation of the rights recognised in the Covenant. How did the Committee assess the new justifications offered by States Parties in order to explain regression or recalibration of the new mechanisms for the realisation of social rights, including the right to social security? Again, the chapter will use the dialogue between Canada and the CESCR as a case study.

After a decade of confusion, it seems that the CESCR has gone back to basics. Measures that reduce protections in the context of the transformation of the social state must be assessed for what they are: retrogression. Even more so, it seems that the Committee is promoting, as a matter of State obligations, the duty to allocate not only adequate resources, but also more resources to the realisation of social rights. Taxation, international cooperation and an appropriate percentage of GDP allocated to social spending have recently been at the forefront of the assessment by the CESCR of State compliance in regard to the ICESCR. In conclusion, the means by which a State Party implements the right to social security makes sense only if more resources are mobilised in order to also guarantee the meta right to the continuous improvement of living conditions.

II. SOCIAL RIGHTS, HUMAN NEEDS AND THE RIGHT TO SOCIAL SECURITY: UNDERSTANDING THE RIGHT TO THE CONTINUOUS IMPROVEMENT OF LIVING CONDITIONS AS A META RIGHT

A. Social Rights as Technical Means in Search of a Purpose

Social rights guaranteed by the Universal Declaration of Human Rights (UDHR)[2] and subsequently by the ICESCR concern human needs (food, clothing, housing, education, health care and necessary social services, decent work and income availability) served by technical means. Such means refer to the broad range of public policies, including legislative measures, which translate human needs into legal claims. Social security schemes clearly fall into such categorisation.

However, are social rights only about human needs? Is the only end game of social rights the satisfaction of human needs? These questions also apply to the right to social security. A contextual analysis of both the UDHR and of the ICESCR, as well as of the foundational work accomplished by the International Labour Organisation (ILO) suggests a more transformative, if not radical, reading. The Declaration of Philadelphia of 1944[3] states that all human beings have the right to pursue both *their material well-being* and their *spiritual development* in conditions of freedom and dignity, of economic security and equal opportunity. The Preamble of the ICESCR affirms that all rights guaranteed by the Covenant derive from the *inherent dignity* of the human person. Article 22 of the UDHR echoes this ambition by stating that the right to social security is indispensable for the dignity and the free development of the personality of everyone, as a member of the society.

Clearly, the satisfaction of human needs as human rights cannot be restricted to immediate material needs. It encompasses all dimensions of human dignity for all as a matter of living conditions. Article 11 of the ICESCR guarantees not only basic living conditions but also the right to the continuous improvement of such conditions. Article 11 of the Covenant carries an intriguing history in regard to the drafting process.[4] It provides for two distinct rights: the right to an adequate standard of living and another to the continuous improvement of living conditions. The *travaux préparatoires* tell us that the India representative insisted on providing necessary precision to the right to an adequate standard of living: adequate food, clothing and housing. This list of some components of the right is incomplete when compared to Article 25 of the UDHR (right to

[2] *Universal Declaration of Human Rights* UNGA Res 217 A(III) (UDHR).

[3] International Labour Organization (ILO), *Declaration concerning the aims and purposes of the International Labour Organisation* (10 May 1944).

[4] Lucie Lamarche, *Perspectives occidentales du droit international des droits économiques de la personne* (Bruylant 1995).

a standard of living), which addresses a long list of social rights. The right to the continuous improvement of living conditions is a new concept introduced by Article 11. Could this right be seen as a consequence right (deemed to be respected if the right to an adequate standard of living is respected)? Such interpretation would limit the understanding of all social rights to the satisfaction of human needs. Is it more appropriate to consider the right to the continuous improvement of living conditions as an ordinary right on par with other rights guaranteed by the ICESCR? Such an interpretation is also merely an issue of consequence as it assumes that non-regressive measures in the realisation of all rights guaranteed by the ICESCR is the principal benchmark for assessing the continuity of the improvement of living conditions. In order to avoid a circular understanding of this right, I believe it has to be seen as a meta right. The specific content of such right is the requirement for the continuous improvement of all social and economic rights. This interpretation echoes favourably with Article 28 of the UDHR, which affirms the need for a social and international order in which the rights and freedoms set forth in this Declaration can be fully realised. In addition, it offers a purpose to the main obligation of States Parties towards the Covenant, which is expressed in Article 2. In other words, the Parties have to realise progressively all rights guaranteed by the Covenant to the maximum of their available resources – as well as the resources of the international community – because every person has a right to the full realisation of all social and economic rights.[5] This goal requires continuous efforts as well as the monitoring of regressive initiatives. Consequently, the autonomous right to such improvement is a meta right conditional to the realisation of all other social rights as long as the content of those other social rights acknowledge the specific requirement of such meta right.

Article 2 of the ICESCR reveals its complexity in all contexts, in the North and in the South. The requirement for States to mobilise all resources to the maximum available extent in order to achieve progressively the full realisation of all the rights recognised in the Covenant is not a matter of domestic opinion or ideology, be it economic or political. Public policies must be governed by both the level of realisation of a right and by their duty to respect the meta right

[5] At the time of the drafting of the Covenants (both on civil and political and on economic, social and cultural rights), the discussion about the possibility of a precise meaning and content for each social right coincided with the march of the Global South demanding a New International Economic Order (NIEO). Social rights, understood as not only justiciable rights, but even more so, as rights that create specific obligations for the international community of states were at the heart of the NIEO Agenda. M Mazurek and P Betts, 'When Rights Were Social' (2012) *Humanity* 291; MA Glendon, 'The Rule of Law in the Universal Declaration of Human Rights' (2004) *Northwestern Journal of International Human Rights* 1; R Burke, 'Some Rights are more Equal than Others: the Third World and the Transformations of Economic and Social Rights' (2012) *Humanity* 427, note 44. For a different analysis, see A Anghie, 'Inequality, Human Rights and the New International Economic Order' (2019) *Humanity* 429. And for discussion of the obligation of international cooperation in Article 11(1) see Campbell, chapter three in this volume.

to the continuous improvement of living conditions, understood as a tangible and intangible right. This explains why Article 4 of the ICESCR, the limitation clause, states that such limitations must be compatible with the nature of these rights and solely for the purpose of promoting the general welfare in a democratic society. The dynamic suggested by the ICESCR clearly echoes Article 28 of the UDHR. Such reading of the international law of human rights as requiring a particular international and national economic order demands a clear – although contextualised – understanding of the content of each right, including the right to continuous improvement of living conditions. As Bilchitz stated, evaluating setbacks and progress in matters of social rights requires clear reference points and benchmarks.[6] It is not a matter of opinion.

B. The Human Right to Social Security in Need of the Meta Right to the Continuous Improvement of Living Conditions

The right to social security has been seen historically as a technical right, a clear expression of social rights as a mean to reach an end. The drafting Committee of the ICESCR totally relied on the ILO social security experts in their formulation of the right. The right to social security, guaranteed by Article 9 of the ICESCR, invites some criticism.

In 1952, the ILO had adopted the Social Security (Minimum Standards) Convention (No 102).[7] The Convention is a synthesis of all social security conventions adopted by the institution before World War II. It provides for a variety of ways to deliver social security (from the lowest level of income replacement in the case of universal coverage, to the highest one in the case of insurance plans designed for specific categories of skilled workers) and it enumerates the social risks[8] in need of social security coverage. Convention No 102 does not submit the right to social security to any progressivity requirement. On the contrary, a threshold is provided for each enumerated risk. Such threshold defines the level of vertical (the percentage of wages' replacement) and horizontal (percentage of designated persons covered by the social security scheme) equity required.[9]

ILO Convention No 102 offers the possibility of minimal universal coverage on a risk-by-risk basis and it privileges the protection of categories of

[6] D Bilchitz, 'Socio-Economic Rights, Economic Crisis, and Legal Doctrine' (2014) *International Journal of Constitutional Law* 710.

[7] International Labour Organization (ILO), *Social Security (Minimum Standards) Convention, C102*, 28 June 1952.

[8] Article 2(a)(ii) of Convention No 102 n 9, provides for the branches of social security that a State member shall comply with at minimum in order to ratify the Convention.

[9] L Lamarche, 'Human Rights, Social Security and Migrant Workers' in R Blanpain, PA Ortiz, M Olivier and G Vonk (eds), *Social Security and Migrant Workers* (Wolters Kluwer 2014).

workers as a way to reach the appropriate level of national coverage, again, on a risk-by-risk basis.[10] This approach clearly departs from the ambition of Article 9 of the ICESCR, which guarantees the right to social security to every person. The ILO itself recognised over time that Convention No 102 excludes more than it includes.[11] In addition, the Convention is highly gendered. The worker is implicitly the male worker and a social security scheme must be designed in order to protect him and his family.[12] As a result, the continental European model exported to the then colonies or recent ex-colonies created a complex web of political favouritism in the South. Army and police members as well as workers belonging to sectors supporting a political regime were clearly advantaged by, for example, pension plans.[13]

The ILO social security experts acknowledged over time that Convention No 102 failed effectively to provide universal access to social security for all workers[14] thereby reinforcing the figure of the wageworker as the unique person that can claim the right to social security. In addition, Convention No 102 does not capture both the complex relation between the formal and informal sectors of the economy and the one between paid and unpaid work, such as care or social reproduction. Consequently, the right to social security, designed as a human right in the twentieth century, encouraged a dynamic of exclusion-inclusion that did not pay a lot of attention to the human rights framework: promoting human dignity and the continuous improvement of living conditions for all. This is understandable if one accepts the idea that such right was conceptualised as a labour right.

Needless to say that the world had changed by the time of the entry in force of the ICESCR in 1976. Social rights had been under attack. In the Global South, successive generations of structural adjustments programmes decimated the uneven progress accomplished in regard to the development of social security mechanisms.[15] The New International Economic Order Agenda gave way to the fight against extreme poverty, which focused on the satisfaction of basic needs.[16]

[10] An analogy can also be drawn here with Arts 12 and 13 of the original *European Social Charter* CETS no 35.

[11] In 2005, ILO estimated that only one in five people in the world had adequate social security coverage of any sort.

[12] L Lamarche, 'Le PIDESC, les femmes et le droit à la sécurité sociale: considérations et propositions pour un droit universel à la sécurité sociale' (2002) *CJWL* 53.

[13] As example, see IACHR, *'Five Pensioners' v Perú*. Merits, Reparations and Costs, Series C No 98, 28 February 2003.

[14] W van Ginneken, 'Extending Social Security: Policies for Developing Countries' (2003) *International Labour Review* 276.

[15] *Promotion and Protection of All Human Rights, Civil, Political, Social and Cultural Rights, including the right to Development*, Report of the independent expert on the question of human rights and extreme poverty, UN Doc A/HRC/11/9, paras 10–65.

[16] L Lamarche, *Beyond the Rhetoric of Social Rights for the Poor: the Need to Promote a Methodology aimed at Reinforcing International and National Institutions*, 2004, available at SSRN <https://papers.ssrn.com/sol3/papers.cfm?abstract_id=3605601>.

In the North, austerity policies[17] and the neoliberal ideology conferred the character of 'suspect rights' on social, economic and labour rights.

The contemporary challenge is to reconcile a technical right – the right to social security provided for by Article 9 of ICESCR – with both Articles 11 and 2 of the Covenant. How can the right be benchmarked in order to comply with: (1) the right to the continuous improvement of living conditions, which implies the need for a fair international economic order as well as the recognition of a multidimensional citizenship and the satisfaction of human needs; and (2) the obligation of a State Party not to claw back the level of realisation of the rights guaranteed by the Covenant, including the right to social security?

This chapter uses the Canadian example as a case study in order to illustrate the complexity of this issue. According to the OECD Social Spending Survey, Canada ranks 24 out of 37 member countries in regard to the percentage of GDP allocated to such spending (17.3 per cent).[18] This is a lower percentage than the United Kingdom or Australia. Canada is a rich country and its Constitution is silent about social rights. Considering the shortcomings of the right to social security as a human right, the next section will end with a troubling question: is Canada involved in retrenchment of the right to social security or is it recalibrating it?[19] How can the ICESCR and more specifically the meta right to the continuous improvement of living conditions help in answering this question?

III. THE RECENT CREATION AND RAPID TRANSFORMATION OF A CANADIAN SOCIAL PROTECTION REGIME: TRANSFORMATIVE OR REGRESSIVE?[20]

A. Exiting World War II

Foreseeing the end of a booming war economy, in 1942, Prime Minister Mackenzie King commissioned the Marsh Report on social security.[21] The Marsh commission took its inspiration from the Beveridge Report implemented in the United Kingdom.[22] The Marsh Report proposed building a social security

[17] L Elliott, 'Austerity policies do more harm than good, IMF study concludes' *The Guardian* (London 27 May 2016).

[18] OECD Data, Social Spending <https://data.oecd.org/socialexp/social-spending.htm>.

[19] I borrow this expression from C Saraceno, 'Retrenching, recalibrating, pre-distributing. The welfare state facing old and new inequalities' (2019) Structural Change and Economic Dynamics 35.

[20] L Lamarche, 'From a social protection Regime to an Income Security Agenda: Canada at the Crossroads' in M Westerveld and M Olivier (eds), *Social Security outside the Realm of the Labour Contract, Informal work and employee-like workers* (Edward Elgar 2019).

[21] Canada, *Report on Social Security for Canada*, University of Toronto Press 1975 ('the Marsh Report').

[22] William Beveridge, *Social Insurance and Allied Services* (McMillan 1942).

regime (at that point non-existent) on two guiding principles: (1) a decent level of wages replacement; and (2) a supplement to insufficient family income. Marsh designed the different means to address those two goals: (a) demo grants (described as universal payments based on a single condition, such as the presence of children in family or a condition of age, which are not means tested) and (b) social insurance (whereas employers and employees, and even in cases, such as unemployment benefits, the State, would contribute to a mutualised fund). The proposal did not include means-tested assistance measures, which were an exclusive provincial matter. Eventually, such assistance measures would become the fourth pillar of the Canadian social protection regime.

The missing piece in this national picture was health care. The universality of the health coverage programme in Canada is a strong national value. The programme is accessible to all residents. This one system for all, clearly inspired by the British model, expanded to the point of including out-of-hospital services in all provinces, a coverage completed in 1967.[23] The House of Commons adopted the Canada Health Act in 1984.[24] The Act accomplished two major changes: (1) the cost sharing of health expenses between the federal government and provinces and territories and (2) the introduction of a general prohibition of care for fees.[25]

The real novelty of the 1970s in Canada was the introduction of a universal means-tested social assistance programme, led by provinces, but cost-shared with the federal government. Under CAP (Canada Assistance Plan),[26] a province can cost share its social assistance budget only if the programme is based solely on a means tested condition. Although with slightly different rates of benefits, all provinces adopted a social assistance scheme.

This quick overview of the Canadian social protection architecture reveals a system based on four different approaches to social protection: contributory, tax-based, universal and means-tested. Although Canada did not ratify ILO Convention No 102, it can be said that the Canadian model – or at least the initial or founding model – was in conformity with the possibilities offered by the treaty. Consequently, when the time to consider the ratification of the ICESCR came, Canada concluded, without any careful analysis, that the support provided for by its social security system largely exceeded the expectations required by the Covenant. In fact, the aim was to maintain or guarantee a basic level of economic living conditions rather than to improve it.[27]

[23] Medical Care Act SC 1966–1967 c 64.

[24] Canada Health Act SC 1984 c 6.

[25] Recently confirmed in *Cambie Surgeries Corporation v British Columbia (Attorney General)* 2020 BCSC 1310.

[26] Canada Assistance Plan SC 1966–67, c 45.

[27] An exception should be noted in the case of contributory schemes, designed for some categories of industrial wageworkers, which delivered – and still deliver – better protection than any other schemes profiled as more universal, although not totally universal.

B. From Social Security to the War against Poverty: The Neoliberal Agenda in the Making

As in the case of many other developed countries, the economic crisis of 1972, often described as the Great Inflation crisis, hit Canada and the pockets of working families. The 1970 Croll Report on Poverty raised an alarm bell: Canadian households were poorer than expected – was it not the time to move towards a strategy of income security?[28] It was in this context that the notion of a guaranteed basic income gained popularity in Canada.[29] The input of social sciences clearly nourished this discussion by promoting the idea of an official poverty line as the ultimate benchmark in order to assess poverty. It took different names: the MBM (market basket measure) or LICO (low income cut offs measure), as examples.

At the time, economists were predicting not only a slowdown of the Canadian economy, but also a transformation and a *precarisation*[30] of the attachment to the labour market. Workers and non-workers would have to adapt to a more open economy. Canada was engaging in a trade agreement with the USA, which would lead in 1987 to the adoption of the first Free Trade Agreement,[31] followed by the North American Free Trade Agreement (NAFTA) in 1994.[32] The MacDonald Report of 1985[33] (Royal Commission on the Economic Union and Development Prospects for Canada) clearly was setting the stage for the posturing of a more competitive Canada in the context of global trade.

Starting in 1977, universal demo grants ended. Provincial governments started to rely on refundable tax credits[34] aimed at supporting the available income of low-income families. Families and children were at the core of such strategy. At the same time, a significant process of claw back in existing benefits was implemented. The claw back method concerned contributory as well as universal programmes.[35] The figure of families in need – often single parent families – replaced the one of the wageworker, leaving behind those who were

[28] Canada, Report of the Special Senate Committee on Poverty, *Poverty in Canada* (Ottawa 1970).

[29] D Hum and W Simpson, 'Economic Response to a Guaranteed Annual Income: Experience from Canada and United States' (1993) *Journal of Labor Economics* S263.

[30] Using the expression from G Standing, *The Precariat, The New Dangerous Class* (Bloomsbury Academic 2014).

[31] Canada United States Free Trade Agreement SC 1988, c. 65, Annex Part A <www.international.gc.ca/trade-commerce/assets/pdfs/agreements-accords/cusfta-e.pdf>.

[32] North American Free Trade Agreement 32 ILM 289, 605 (1993).

[33] Canada, Privy Council, *Report – Royal Commission on the Economic Union and Development Prospects for Canada*, Vol 1, 1985 <www.publications.gc.ca/collections/collection_2014/bcp-pco/Z1-1983-1-1-1-eng.pdf>.

[34] A refundable credit is a tax credit one gets by way of tax return, no matter what the tax liability is.

[35] For a detailed analysis, see Canadian Centre for Policy Alternatives, *Canada's Declining Social Safety Net, the Case of EI Reform* 2009 <www.policyalternatives.ca/publications/reports/canadas-declining-social-safety-net>.

not parents as well as the new and growing population of non-resident, although documented, migrant workers.

In sum, available income of all types progressively became the key operating concept for accessing social benefits, which were made available in the form of refundable tax credits. Traditional programmes were not abolished but they offered diminished returns to contributors and non-contributors.

From then on, the poverty line[36] would largely govern the distributive impact of social protection. Such transformation raises a fundamental question in regard to the ICESCR as it addresses only the immediate obligation of a State Party to the ICESCR to provide the essential and minimal content of all social and economic rights, including social security, rather than the broader one of progressively realising all rights to the maximum of available resources.

This paradigmatic change coincided with the implementation of austerity measures in Canada. In 1995, Prime Minister Martin launched a first austerity budget that contained all the usual decisions attached to such agenda: public services cuts; privatisations; cutbacks in social benefits; huge emphasis of public debt repayment; etc.[37] All provinces followed on this sad and detrimental path.

C. Social Security and Tax Credits: A Brave New World

Between 1995 and 2015, the austerity agenda gave way to a new one: the budget-balanced approach. Such approach sounded more reasonable to many voters but what had been lost would not come back. Canada is nowadays relying more and more on tax credits[38] to address poverty as a social risk. This strategy downplays the relevancy of the normative approach historically promoted by the ILO. Tax credits transit through the exercise of the annual income tax report. They are susceptible to annual changes depending on Budget bills. Tax decisions are automated and, to say the least, often undecipherable. Therefore, it is increasingly accepted that any person that works at any type of work or that receives a revenue from any kind of productive – and declared – activity can be poor. Governments would put it differently and say that the purpose of

[36] In 2019, the federal government adopted the Poverty Reduction Act SC 2019, c 29, s 315. The main purpose of this law is to adopt and define a Canadian poverty line. Statistics Canada adopted the Market Basket Measure (MBM) as the national measure of low income based on the cost of a specified basket of goods and services representing a modest, basic standard of living. See <www12.statcan.gc.ca/nhs-enm/2011/ref/dict/pop165-eng.cfm>.

[37] The Canadian Encyclopedia, *Martin's 1995 budget* at <www.thecanadianencyclopedia.ca/en/Article/martins-1995-budget>.

[38] Canada is also aligning itself with its neighbour, the United States. The USA has a long experience with the Earned Income Tax Credit (EITC) programme. For an evaluation: K Ryan, 'EITC as Income (In)Stability' (2014) *Florida Tax Review* 583; SD Holt, 'Keeping it in Context: Earned Income Tax Credit Compliance and Treatment of the Working Poor' (2006) *Connecticut Public Interest Law Journal* 183 and L Book, 'The IRS's EITC Compliance Regime: Taxpayers Caught in the Net' (2002) *Oregon Law Review* 351.

social protection measures is to keep the working poor above the established poverty line. Implicitly, this paradigm confirms the legitimacy of all forms of work: short-term contracts; independent; platform or gig economy. The system will react to declared income shown in a personal income tax declaration more than it cares about the decency of the work from which one is receiving wages. It is not that labour standards are vanishing. Violations of workers' basic rights are still justiciable, in theory. It is not either that contributory regimes, such as unemployment or contributory pensions, do not exist anymore. They are simply reserved for the elite of the working class, unionised or not.

Interestingly, this income-tax-driven social security scheme provides better horizontal equity (percentage of households that may benefit) than previous approaches. It is nevertheless totally structured around the official poverty line as a benchmark. There is more horizontal equity but a very weak impact on distributive justice. To put it differently, it is a more efficient answer to basic needs – which is not to say it is perfect – but there is much less consideration for the human right to the continuous improvement of living conditions. In addition, this transformation comes with a new understanding of the State duty to implement progressively all rights guaranteed by the ICESCR. It limits the notion of progressivity to one goal: pulling up all households above the official poverty line through tax credits.

A tax credit has no race, no gender, no geography and no history of social exclusion or discrimination. It solely relies on a social insurance number and a tax report. This totally confuses the Left (asking for more social justice) and the Right (highly critical of the cost of traditional social programmes). The public answer to the Covid-19 crisis illustrates this brave new world. Between March and September 2020 Canada spent approximately eighty billion dollars in a crisis programme named CERB (Canadian Emergency Response Benefit). This reached about four million Canadians. CERB suspended the application of the Unemployment Act.[39] Many see CERB as a test for the introduction in Canada of a guaranteed income programme, which would not look a lot different to the sum of the tax credits already available.

In July 2020, and in the context of the pandemic, the federal Office of the Parliamentary Budget released a document that costs an eventual Canadian guaranteed income programme, which would also put an end to provincial social assistance programmes.[40] Those programmes, it has to be acknowledged, are associated with the most degrading conditions. They operate with the help of heavy social control mechanisms to the detriment of the most vulnerable of the Canadian society. In fact, fewer and fewer women and families rely on social assistance due to the significance of tax credits and especially tax credits dedicated to children.

[39] Information up to date as of 1 September 2020.

[40] Canada, Office of the Parliamentary Budget Officer, *Costing a Guaranteed Basic Income during the COVID Pandemic*, 7 July 2020.

It is no exaggeration to say that in regard to its social security system, Canada is at a crossroads. A slow but steady transformation occurred over the last four decades. It moved from a four pillars architecture (demo-grants, contributory schemes, universal health access and residuary social assistance) to a two-tier system: contributory benefits for less than 40 per cent of the population (mainly in regard of pensions) and an income supplementation that relies on tax credits for the rest. Health care has to be analysed as a stand-alone system as it is universal. Nevertheless, health care expenses put an immense fiscal pressure on provinces that are constantly struggling with the federal government in order to get more financial support. In some provinces, such as Quebec, 40 per cent of the entire basket of services has been privatised, directly or indirectly. These changes affect the goal of a right to social security – providing for adequate protection for all social risks and the means to achieve this. Tax credits are anything but reliable, predictable and sustainable. A budget bill can wipe them out at any time. Tax credits are intrusive and require a high level of tax literacy. Finally, tax credits designed for poor households are barely justiciable and tax jurisdictions are not sympathetic to human rights arguments.

In other words, tax credits as a social security tool echo the political philosophy of subsidiarity that serves as a pillar of the Canadian social security system. Translated in the words of the ICESCR, tax credits serve the goal of the immediate realisation of the minimum core content of the right to social security while at the same time disregarding the obligation to progressively realise, to the maximum of the available resources, all rights guaranteed by the Covenant, and in particular, the right to the continuous improvement of living conditions of right holders. Tax credits disregard the requirement of decent work while at the same time reinforcing the entitlement to better living conditions to the benefit of an elite earning class that can still contribute to contributory social security schemes and benefit from them. When contemplating the principle of the interdependence of all human rights, tax credits are more regressive than progressive. Accordingly, this technical means of delivering social security and protection denies the role of the right to the continuous improvement of living conditions as a meta right applying to other social rights in the ICESCR.

That being said, and with the exception of the Covid context, the discourse of austerity or of economic crisis is not at the heart of this more contemporary transformation in Canada. It is the continuation of a longer-standing trajectory. In addition, the analogy between the wave of cash transfer programmes promoted as an answer to the dramatic consequences of structural adjustments programmes in the South since the 1980s[41] and the specific form of cash transfers represented by tax credits in the North is obvious.

As we consider tax credits as a contemporary expression of social security in Canada, it is worth verifying if and how the ICESCR Experts' Committee

[41] Report of the independent expert on the question of human rights and extreme poverty, UN Doc A/64/279.

(CESCR) evaluates such a shift in social security delivery. Also, and keeping in mind this new context, how does the CESCR, if at all, promote an interdependent reading of Articles 9 and 11 of the ICESCR and of the right to the continuous improvement of living conditions? The next section addresses those issues.

IV. LOOKING FOR A CONTEMPORARY READING OF OBLIGATIONS UNDER THE ICESCR: FROM THE ADEQUATE ALLOCATION OF RESOURCES TO MORE RESOURCES

A. ICESCR, Duty of Non-Retrogression and New Justifications

The Committee on Economic, Social and Cultural Rights (CESCR), established under the United Nations Economic and Social Council (ECOSOC),[42] carries out the monitoring functions assigned to ECOSOC in Part IV of the Covenant. The creation of the CESCR coincided with the implementation all around the world of structural adjustments policies associated with the neoliberal model and with the ideology of austerity. On top of the usual arguments concerning States Parties' autonomy and sovereignty, this context largely explains the reasons why States quarrelled with the CESCR about the scope and the interpretation of Article 2(1) of the Covenant. States Parties considered that reasons why they were not progressively implementing or were halting such implementation of all rights guaranteed by the ICESCR should not be scrutinised by the CESCR as they were outside the scope of Article 2.

The CESCR saw it differently. As Alston, then Chair of the CESCR, and Quinn put it in an Article published in 1987,[43] the requirement of progressive realisation of all rights guaranteed by the Covenant if, in itself, a limitation, is no justification for failing when resources are available.[44] They said that 'vagaries of economic circumstances is not an escape hatch' for States to lessen their obligations.[45] Accordingly, 'a state party's subjective determination as to what constitutes an adequate resource allocation is not entitled to complete deference'.[46] Referring to the *travaux préparatoires*, the authors concluded that the framers of the ICESCR did not intend to 'let states arbitrarily and artificially determine for themselves the level of commitment required by the Covenant'.[47]

[42] ECOSOC Resolution 1985/17 of 28 May 1985.
[43] P Alston and G Quinn, 'The Nature and Scope of States Parties' Obligations under the International Covenant on Economic, Social and Cultural Rights' (1987) *Human Rights Quarterly* 156.
[44] ibid 174.
[45] ibid 175.
[46] ibid 178.
[47] ibid 179.

The CESCR transformed this doctrinal proposition in interpretive jurisprudence when it adopted General Comment No 3 in 1990.[48] Paragraph 9 of General Comment No 3 states that retrogressive measures need to be fully justified by reference to the totality of rights guaranteed in the ICESCR. Paragraph 12 of the same Comment refers to situations of severe constraints and emphasises the need for a State Party to adopt targeted programmes aimed at providing specific protections.

When considering the case of rich countries, it is useful to distinguish undetermined concepts, such as an economic crisis leading to urgency measures, from austerity measures.[49] Austerity measures leave permanent scars to social and economic rights and serve as an excuse or a rationale for limiting the realisation of such rights to the threshold of the minimum core obligations attached to the rights guaranteed by the Covenant. This is even truer when a State Party abandons the discourse of the need for austerity measures and when a government shows budget surpluses instead of deficit, because of budget-balanced strategies. In such context, it seems that the real tension is between the need to realise the totality of rights, when paying attention to each of them, and the risk of limiting the scope of economic and social rights to their minimal core content, as a post-austerity answer to the fight against poverty. Such tension brings us back to the autonomy of the right to the continuous improvement of living conditions as a meta right. It illustrates the complexity of the task for the CESCR when its members are expected to assess not only the adequate allocation of necessary resources in order for social and economic rights to be progressively realised but also the duty of States Parties to generate such resources. It seems that the CESCR understands such complexity and recently started to address the issue, as will be demonstrated in the case of Canada.

B. Implementing the Right to Continuous Improvement of Living Conditions does not Stop with the Poverty Line

Can we resolve the tension between progressive and regressive social security schemes by relying on Article 9 of the Covenant that guarantees a right to social security, including social insurance? The CESCR has interpreted the right to social security in General Comment No 19 adopted in 2008.[50]

[48] General Comment No 3: 'The nature of States parties' obligations (Art 2, para 1, of the Covenant)', UN Doc HRI/GEN/1/Rev.9 (Vol I) 7.

[49] For an interesting discussion about the interpretation of States Parties' obligations under the ICESCR in times of economic crisis see BTC Warwick, 'Socio-Economic Rights during Economic Crisis: A Changed Approach to Non-Retrogression' (2016) *International & Comparative Law Quarterly* 249 and J Wills and BTC Warwick, 'Contesting Austerity: the Potential and Pitfalls of Socioeconomic Rights Discourse' (2016) *Indiana Journal of Global Legal Studies* 629.

[50] General Comment No. 19, 'The Right to Social Security (Article 9)', UN Doc HRI/GEN/1/Rev.9 (Vol I) 152.

As with other rights interpreted by General Comments, adequacy constitutes an important element of the right to social security. Paragraph 22 of General Comment No 19 reads as follow:

> Benefits, whether in cash or in kind, must be adequate in amount and duration in order that everyone may realize his or her rights to family protection and assistance, an adequate standard of living and adequate access to health care, as contained in Articles 10, 11 and 12 of the Covenant. States parties must also pay full respect to the principle of human dignity contained in the preamble of the Covenant, and the principle of non-discrimination, so as to avoid any adverse effect on the levels of benefits and the form in which they are provided. Methods applied should ensure the adequacy of benefits. The adequacy criteria should be monitored regularly to ensure that beneficiaries are able to afford the goods and services they require to realize their Covenant rights.

Such usage of adequacy as a benchmark of the right to social security sends us back to ILO Convention No 102 where, but for health care (because benefits are often provided in kind for residents or citizens and members of their family),[51] social security benefits are designed to guarantee an equal access to market goods. In fact, austerity measures transformed many social goods into market goods. Consequently, a critical view is that such interpretation limits the scope of progressivity in the realisation of the right to social security to the cost of living indexation of benefits. Paragraph 42 of General Comment No 19, when trying to resolve the tension between the twin benchmarks of progressive and regressive measures, states at para 42(e) that it would be prohibited to deploy a social security scheme that would deprive a group or an individual of access to the minimum essential level of social security. Can States Parties that have the means to deploy an efficient tax regime provide the right to social security only to the threshold of an official poverty line? As the CESCR once said, poverty is a cause and a consequence of violations of human rights.[52] Poverty is an unacceptable material fact and not a normative standard. The eradication of extreme and relative poverty is certainly an immediate obligation of States Parties to the ICESCR, but it is not the expression or the limit of their obligation to guarantee progressively the betterment of living conditions for all.

In 2015, the CESCR adopted a Statement about social protection floors where it stated that the negative effect of austerity measures must be compensated by an identification of the core content of a social protection floor.[53] In examining the scenario of retrogressive measures, when unavoidable, the CESCR insists on

[51] Excluding undocumented migrants and temporary visitors.

[52] 'Substantive Issues Arising in the Implementation of the International Covenant on Economic, Social and Cultural Rights: Poverty and the International Covenant on Economic, Social and Cultural Rights', UN Doc E/C.12/2001/10.

[53] 'Social Protection Floors: An Essential Element of the Right to Social Security and of the Sustainable Development Goals', Statement by the Committee on Economic, Social and Cultural rights, UN Doc E/C.12/2-15/1.

the need for such measures to be necessary and proportionate. The CESCR, it seems, did not find it appropriate to distinguish between retrogressive measures in an urgent context and those adopted in a context that is not one of crisis or urgency but one of sovereign choices promoting economic reforms inspired by the neoliberal agenda. Such omission supports the view that the scope of States' obligation to realise progressively all rights guaranteed by the ICESCR is limited to the core content of each right instead of its full and interdependent realisation.

This is why an interdependent reading of Articles 9 and 11 of the ICESCR matters, and even more so, the acknowledgment of the autonomy of the right to the continuous improvement of living conditions. The right to social security is a means to promote other human rights guaranteed by the Covenant. Restricting it to its minimum threshold overly narrows the extent of its reach. Accordingly, an assessment, 'right by right', of the allocation of the maximum of resources a State should allow to the realisation of all rights guaranteed by the Covenant, without the acknowledgment of the meta value of the right to the continuous improvement of living conditions, misses the centrality of human dignity to the human rights project. Right holders are more than a collection of formal and precarious workers looking for their place in a new economy. Public policies cannot limit social spending to whatever income supplement is required in order to access market goods that answer their basic needs. This policy approach is nevertheless the reality in Canada.

C. Is Canada Regressing or Adapting?

The fourth and fifth Periodic reports under the ICESCR were submitted by Canada in 2004 and 2005[54] after a decade of no reporting, which coincided with the first decade of austerity measures that Canadians suffered from.[55] The CESCR considered those Reports in May 2006.[56] Canada provided the CESCR with a picture of the Canadian economy totally focused on the need to eliminate the deficits recorded and to bring the fiscal situation under control. The report suggests that such strategy would subsequently allow a reinvestment in social programming. It alludes to austerity measures by stating that such measures increased the fiscal pressure on provinces, mainly responsible for the implementation of social and economic rights.[57] This argument was made in a context where the federal budgetary surplus was 9.1 billion dollars in 2003–2004, marking the seventh consecutive year of national balanced budgets.

[54] UN Doc E/C.12/4/Add.15, 28 October 2004.

[55] The third periodic report concerning rights covered by Arts 1 to 15 (UN Doc (E/1994/104/Add.17) was considered by the Committee on Economic, Social and Cultural Rights at its nineteenth session (UN Doc E/C.12/1998/SR.46–48; UN Doc E/C.12/1/Add.31) in 1998.

[56] UN Doc E/C.12/CAN/CO/4 and UN Doc E/C.12/CAN/CO/5.

[57] UN Doc E/C.12/CAN/CO/5, para 12.

In its Concluding Observations adopted in 2006, the CESCR strictly respected the interpretation of States Parties' obligations under Article 2 of the Covenant provided for by General Comment No 3.[58] The CESCR, without providing more guidance, invited Canada to examine all retrogressive measures adopted since 1995.[59]

The sixth Periodic Report presented by Canada in 2013[60] offers an analysis of the Canadian economy contradicted by facts.[61] In 2013, although Canada suffered like many other countries from the 2007–2008 recession, the numbers clearly showed that it had recovered. One of the means of recovery was to off-load responsibilities (by limiting recourse to spending power) to provincial and municipal governments. At the same time, the Federal government put money back into the pockets of middle class households by lowering taxes and accelerated the creation of new tax credits to the benefit of poorer households. How would the CESCR appreciate such new realities? Paragraph 10 of the Concluding Observations adopted by the CESCR in April 2016[62] represents a mix of messages that are hard to interpret:

> The Committee recommends that the State party increase national spending to guarantee Covenant rights to achieve the progressive realization of economic, social and cultural rights. The Committee urges the State party to adopt and implement a tax policy that is adequate and socially equitable and improves tax collection, to ensure the mobilization of resources sufficient for implementing economic, social and cultural rights, with special attention paid to disadvantaged and marginalized individuals and groups. In that regard, the Committee encourages the State party to collect disaggregated data based on the prohibited grounds of discrimination. The Committee recommends that the State party monitor closely the introduction of austerity measures by provinces and ensure that they do not undermine the minimum core content of all the Covenant rights, and that such austerity measures are not discriminatory and are temporary, necessary and proportionate. The Committee refers the State party to the letter sent by the Committee's Chairperson on austerity measures to all States parties on 16 May 2012.[63]

The CESCR struggled with two opposite realities: recession and economic reforms. It also confused the notions of recession and of urgency.[64] The 2016 situation in Canada could not be compared by any standard to a context that may legitimise halting the progressive realisation of any social and economic

[58] ibid para 44.
[59] UN Doc E/C.12/CAN/CO/4 and 5, 22 May 2006, paras 44 and 52.
[60] UN Doc E/C.12/CAN/6.
[61] ibid paras 13 and ff.
[62] UN Doc E/C.12/CAN/CO/6, para 10.
[63] UN Committee on Economic, Social and Cultural Rights, Letter dated 16 May 2012 addressed by the Chairperson of the Committee on Economic, Social and Cultural Rights to States parties to the International Covenant on Economic, Social and Cultural Rights, Protection of the Covenant rights in the context of the economic and financial crisis.
[64] For an explicit usage of the 'Austerity as Emergency' test provided for by this letter, see UN Doc GBR/CO/6, 2016, para 19.

right. Canada obviously privileged neoliberal economic reforms and was not facing recession. On the contrary, it was spending increasing amounts of money in creating tax credits (considered as tax expenditures) when at the same time collecting fewer and fewer taxes. Therefore, making a reference to the minimum core content of all the Covenant rights to be respected within a context of austerity supports a *de minimis* reading of every person's right not only to social security, but also, to a decent living and to the improvement of living conditions. Is it because economic reforms pushed people outside of social security programmes that they would only now be in need of the delivery of the core content of all their social rights?

Had the CESCR considered tax credits (non-refundable) within human rights framework new questions would have arisen. However, the CESCR contented itself in revisiting the less and less relevant question of social assistance:

> [T]he Committee recommends that the State party ensure that social assistance rates are increased in all provinces to levels that allow a decent living for beneficiaries and their families so as to ensure an effective income safety net.[65]

In Canada, social assistance never reached the necessary level of benefits in order to guarantee a decent living. Social assistance was designed, in fact, not to do so. At best, the contemporary debate is about providing – for a diminishing number of persons – a benefit that matches the national poverty line. Poor people are working people. They juggle consecutive precarious jobs and tax credits in order to survive. This reality did not have a lot to do with economic recession, until the Covid-19 pandemic.

D. Looking for a Contemporary Reading of the ICESCR

There are reasons to believe that the CESCR is starting to address up front what is really at stake in both the notion of progressive realisation of all rights guaranteed by the ICESCR and of the right to continuous improvement of living conditions, more specifically. Such realisation requires not only a fair allocation of resources but more resources. In fact, States Parties to the Covenant are nowadays trying to do more with a reduced – and more inequitable – tax base. In its Concluding Observations addressed to New Zealand in 2018, the CESCR departed from the ideology of austerity and tackled up front the challenges of neoliberal economic reforms:

> The Committee recommends that the State party take measures to ensure the maximization of the resources allocated for the realization of Covenant rights, including by making the necessary adjustments to the Public Finance Act (1989) by introducing human rights impact assessments. It also recommends that appropriate

[65] UN Doc E/C.12/CAN/CO/6, para 30.

> consideration of the Covenant obligations of the State party is established when fiscal and resource generation and allocation decisions are made ...[66]

This approach echoes the Guiding Principles on human rights impact assessments of economic reforms presented to the Human Rights Council in December 2018.[67] Principle 9 is about the progressive realisation of rights and the obligation to give effect to this goal using the maximum available resources. Commentary 9.3 reads as follows:

> States' obligation to mobilize resources includes: tackling tax evasion and avoidance; ensuring a progressive tax system, including by widening the tax base with regard to multinational corporations and the richest; avoiding international tax competition; improving the efficiency of tax collection; and reprioritizing expenditures to ensure, among other things, adequate funding of public services.

Guiding Principle 9.3 echoes Article 28 of the UDHR, which promises a 'social and international order in which the rights and freedoms ... can be fully realised', in a globalised and neoliberal context. There cannot be fair development at the global level without promoting an economic model that guarantees the availability of the necessary resources to the benefit of all. In matters relating to social security and to social protection, this aspiration translates not only into more horizontal equity, but also into more vertical equity. Such translation means less discrimination and exclusion.

The examination of Canada's 7th Periodic Report by the CESCR is scheduled for 2021 or 2022. The CESCR addressed a List of Issues to Canada in March 2020.[68] Some questions clearly express more concerns for the right to social security and to a decent standard of living outside the context of exceptional or urgent circumstances. The CESCR is curious about how Canada intends to mitigate the adverse impact of past austerity programmes concerning some specific components of the right to social security: health, pensions, disabilities and unemployment.[69] In other words, the CESCR is reminding the State Party of its obligation to expand not only the horizontal aspect of the right to social security (increasing the percentage of persons covered) but also, the vertical one (better benefits). Hereby, the CESCR is promoting the meta right to the continuous improvement of living conditions. Nowhere does the CESCR allude to respect only of the minimal content of the rights guaranteed by the ICESCR. Addressing discrimination due to exclusion seems to lead the CESCR's search for compliance by Canada. It seems that the CESCR is ready to reinforce and to reaffirm the purposive and comprehensive approach promoted by the ICESCR.

[66] UN Doc E/C.12/NZL/CO/4, paras 15 and 35.

[67] 'Guiding Principles on Human Rights Impact Assessments of Economic Reforms', UN Doc A/HRC/40/557.

[68] UN Doc E/C.12/CAN/QPR/7.

[69] ibid paras 18, 20 and 23. Regarding pensions, the Committee notes that the Canadian Pension Plan is currently below the Organization for Economic Cooperation and Development average.

As in the case of the Concluding Observations addressed to New Zealand in 2018,[70] the CESCR provides, in the case of Canada, a contemporary reading of the obligation for States Parties to allocate the maximum of resources that have to be and can be made available in order to realise the rights guaranteed by the Covenant. The CESCR then requires the following information:

(a) The proportion of the population below the poverty line as defined at the national level and the levels of inequality, defined as the ratio of the total income accruing to the richest decile of the population and the total income of the poorest 40 per cent of the population;
(b) The proportion of public revenue that is financed through taxes;
(c) Tax rates levied on corporate profits and on personal incomes, and value added tax (exclusive of value added tax on luxury items, tobacco, alcohol, sugary drinks and snacks, and petrol and diesel), the tax rates on energy use, and the percentage of total revenue from personal income taxes that is collected from the richest decile of the population;
(d) Public expenses as a percentage of gross domestic product and, within total public expenses, the proportion of the public budget that is dedicated to social priorities (employment, education, food, health, water and sanitation, social security, housing and culture);
(e) Inflation-adjusted absolute levels of social spending.[71]

It is safe to assume that Canada will consider such questions quite radical and will make a point of explaining how the strategy of tax credits represents a new way to implement many rights guaranteed by the ICESCR. In fact, tax credits do not answer any of the questions asked by the CESCR in the List of Issues addressed to Canada in March 2020. As a matter of social security and of social protection, Canada is thereby confusing the means and the end.

The end game is the continuous improvement of living conditions to the benefit of all rights holders. A more sustainable level of taxes levied by a State Party is essential to that end. However, it does not on its own provide the appropriate analytical framework for the CESCR to assess the choices made in regard to social protection methods by a State Party. As an example, Canada is in the process of recalibrating its social security regime with the explicit goal of guaranteeing to workers of the new economy an annual income above the poverty line. Although the fight against official poverty is a goal to be celebrated, this finality falls short of guaranteeing the enjoyment of the right to the continuous improvement of living conditions. Put in the context of social security as a subsidiary tool to market wages giving access to market goods, the recalibration of the Canadian social security regime shows an abandonment by Canada of its obligation to progressively implement all rights provided for by the Covenant: housing; decent work; health; education. Therefore, the function of the meta

[70] n 66.
[71] n 68, para 10.

right to the continuous improvement of living conditions, in combination with a State Party's duty to progressively realise all economic and social rights, is hereby denied.

V. CONCLUSION

This chapter was written during the early months of the international Covid-19 pandemic in 2020. We can expect that in the coming months and years, governments will be quick to invoke the health emergency context in order to mitigate their responsibilities towards social rights. This pandemic has revealed the terrible consequences of many past economic reforms. As an example, vulnerable workers, and mostly racialised women, were on the frontline of the health care struggle. In Canada, a significant percentage of unemployed were simply not eligible for social security benefits when restrictions and lockdowns took their jobs or their livelihood away. We discovered that poor housing, no access to health services and lack of social services and public services, work hand in hand in creating more discrimination and exclusion.

By relying on a fast-tracked budget bill, Canada answered the pandemic by creating a huge cash transfer programme (Canadian Emergency Response Benefit – CERB) that is easily accessible. It channelled this programme through the Income Tax system. In effect, CERB is an expedited version of past generations of tax credits. This chapter is not questioning the relevance of such a strategy in the context of a real emergency. Nevertheless, it overshadows the fact that many of the reasons and causes behind why some are suffering more than others during the pandemic pre-dated the pandemic.

Unfortunately, the Covid context may provide an environment favourable to the limitation of social rights to their minimal content for rich States. This is why it is necessary, in order not to neglect the States' duty to continuously progress in the realisation of all social rights, to explore the function and the content of the autonomous and meta right to the continuous improvement of living conditions. The questions addressed to Canada by the CESCR in its 2020 List of Issues contribute to such exploration. It is hoped that the new firmness coming from the Committee is robust enough to survive the myriad of reasons that the Covid crisis provides to States Parties in their attempts to halt the progressive realisation of all rights guaranteed by the Covenant.

7

Understanding Forgotten Rights

NAOMI LOTT

I. INTRODUCTION

THE RIGHT TO the continuous improvement of living conditions sits alongside the right to an adequate standard of living in Article 11(1) of the International Covenant on Economic, Social and Cultural Rights (ICESCR).[1] Despite over 40 years of enforcement of ICESCR, there has been a dearth of engagement with the right by the Committee on Economic, Social and Cultural Rights (CESCR) and by scholars. In this chapter I will examine the key factors that have resulted in the right to the continuous improvement of living conditions being 'forgotten'. Throughout the chapter analogies are drawn with the right to play, widely regarded as a 'forgotten' right, in order to evidence and support the claims made.[2] I will argue that a focus on a minimum core 'set' of rights has resulted in the right to continuous improvement of living conditions being overlooked and risks a perception of the right as a luxury right. This chapter will demonstrate why this must not be the case, drawing upon the principle of human dignity and its centrality to the human rights project to justify greater attention being offered to the right. I will argue that advocacy and awareness raising by scholars, non-governmental organisations and the Committee on Economic, Social and Cultural Rights are important to overcome the possible perception of the right as a luxury.

I will then discuss the ambiguity of human rights. I acknowledge that there are some benefits and potentials in ambiguity in the drafting of human rights treaties, including achieving wide ratification of treaties and the temporal flexibility of human rights, prior to examining challenges posed by ambiguity and a lack of conceptual clarity. Ambiguity can, however, undermine the implementation

[1] International Covenant on Economic, Social and Cultural Rights, 16 December 1996, 993 UNTS 3 (ICESCR).

[2] The right to play is provided for in Article 31(1) of the UN Convention on the Rights of the Child, which reads: 'States Parties recognize the right of the child to rest and leisure, to engage in play and recreational activities appropriate to the age of the child and to participate freely in cultural life and the arts.' (Convention on the Rights of the Child, 20 November 1989, 1577 UNTS 3 (CRC)).

and realisation of rights in the ways intended by drafters of human rights treaties, and it threatens the enforceability and justiciability of human rights. There is a considerable threat that ambiguous rights may be forgotten, and this chapter highlights the ways in which the inherent lack of conceptual clarity of the right to the continuous improvement of living conditions has led to the right being overlooked by the CESCR, States Parties to the ICESCR and scholars. In light of this discussion, I will reflect on the importance of conceptual clarity and the particular need to develop such clarity for rights that have previously been 'forgotten', such as the right to the continuous improvement of living conditions. In order to redress the 'forgotten' nature of the right, meaningful engagement with the right must follow, by the CESCR and scholars alike, to provide greater conceptual clarity.

II. THE RIGHT TO THE CONTINUOUS IMPROVEMENT OF LIVING CONDITIONS AS A FORGOTTEN RIGHT

Hohmann has strongly evidenced the status of the right to the continuous improvement of living conditions as a forgotten right. She has extensively demonstrated the way in which the right has been overlooked by the Committee on Economic, Social and Cultural Rights (CESCR).[3] In order to identify the scope, content and obligations pertaining to the right to the continuous improvement of living conditions, it is necessary to recognise why and how it has come to be a 'forgotten' right. To understand this, analogies can be drawn from the situation of a widely accepted 'forgotten' right in children's rights: the right to play.[4] These rights differ in a great many ways in terms of their scope and content, yet their treatment and development have some similarities. Exploring this helps to understand why and how the right to the continuous improvement of living conditions has become a 'forgotten' right, and potential steps to redress this. This section examines two primary factors that have led to the right to the continuous improvement of living conditions being considered as forgotten: that the right may be viewed as a luxury, and that it is conceptually unclear.

[3] Hohmann, chapter two in this volume.

[4] The right to play is often referred to as a forgotten right, see P David, *A Commentary on the United Nations Convention on the Rights of the Child, Article 31: The Right to Leisure, Play and Culture* (Nijhoff 2006) para 42; R Hodgkin and P Newell, *Implementation Handbook for the Convention on the Rights of the Child* 3rd edn (UNICEF 2007) 469; A Voce, *Policy for Play* (Policy Press 2015) 8, 13.

The Committee on the Rights of the Child also refers to the right to play as 'neglected', alongside other Art 31 rights, in development programmes (Committee on the Rights of the Child, 'General Comment No. 17 on the right of the child to rest, leisure, play, recreational activities, cultural life and the arts (art. 31)' (2013) CRC/C/GC/17 (GC17) para 43), and as 'endangered' (Committee of the Rights of the Child, 'Day of General Discussion: Implementing Child Rights in Early Childhood' (17 September 2004) para 9).

A. Luxury

One commonality between the right to the continuous improvement of living conditions and the right to play is that they may, erroneously, be viewed to be luxury in nature. The historic lack of engagement with the rights supports this claim due to the fact that engagement with these rights has not been deemed necessary or urgent in comparison to other rights. Much of this stems from the wide acceptance of a minimum core 'set' of rights.[5]

This minimum core 'set' of rights primarily focuses on the implementation of civil and political rights, and in the context of economic, social and cultural rights is recognised as including 'essential foodstuffs', 'essential primary health care', 'basic shelter and housing' and 'the most basic forms of education'.[6] King argues that 'a *minimally* decent life' would need to address three core human interests: well-being, autonomy, and social participation, requiring 'provision of a bundle of resources satisfying', amongst others, 'a *healthy subsistence threshold*' that includes 'basic physical needs for shelter'.[7] In this chapter I contend that '*basic* physical needs for shelter', or '*basic* shelter and housing' as expressed by the CESCR,[8] should not qualify as sufficient for human dignity.[9] Instead, the realisation of the right to the continuous improvement of living conditions is necessary to meet the goals of human dignity.

Lists such as those provided by King and the CESCR serve to bolster a perception that some rights are more important than others. Brems, for example, argues that human rights literature and practice has resulted in a 'borderline' of rights that is continually pushed 'downwards'.[10] With a focus on minimal human rights guarantees, rights that may be perceived as beyond this minimum

[5] This differs from an understanding of the minimum core 'content' of rights. For more perspectives on a minimum core set of rights or set of fundamental rights see, for example, FS Müller, 'The Hierarchy of Human Rights and the Transcendental System of Right' (2018) *Human Rights Review* 47; T Koji, 'Emerging Hierarchy in International Human Rights and Beyond: From the Perspective of Non-derogable Rights' (2001) *European Journal of International Law* 917; T Farer, 'The Hierarchy of Human Rights' (1992) *American University International Law Review* 115; T Meron, 'On a Hierarchy of International Human Rights' (1986) *American Journal of International Law* 1. Harris shows how these two concepts (minimum core content and minimum core set) of rights have developed (M Harris, 'Downsizing Rights: Why the "Minimum Core" Concept in International Human Rights Law Should be Abandoned' (2013) *Public Interest Law Journal of New Zealand* 169).

[6] Committee on Economic, Social and Cultural Rights (2009) 'General Comment No. 3: The Nature of States Parties' Obligations' E/1991/23 (CESCR GC3) para 10. See Harris (n 5) for a critique of the Committee's classification and terminology here.

[7] J King, *Judging Social Rights,* (CUP 2012) 29 (emphasis in original) 4.

[8] CESCR GC3 para 10 (emphasis added).

[9] Schroeder outlines five separate notions of dignity, grouped under inviolable dignity and aspirational dignity, and covering religious, Kantian, aristocratic, comportment and meritorious dignity. (D Schroeder, 'Human Rights and Human Dignity: An Appeal to Separate the Conjoined Twins' (2012) 15 *Ethical Theory and Moral Practice* 323, especially 332.).

[10] E Brems, 'Human Rights: Minimum and Maximum Perspectives' (2009) 9 *Human Rights Law Review* 349, 350–51.

core 'set' of rights risk becoming ignored or overlooked, as is evidenced by the historic lack of engagement with the right to play, and the right to the continuous improvement of living conditions becoming largely forgotten.[11] As Brems argues, 'the borderline function of human rights in practice often becomes a bottom line'.[12] Since '[a]ll attention is focused on the borderline and on determining whether or not it is crossed, whatever happens on either side of the line becomes irrelevant'.[13]

In practice, the weight of attention on rights realisation remains heavily at the ground level. This is primarily due to State failure to realise rights obligations; it is claimed that for some States 'even minimum core standards are hard … to achieve'.[14] A 2019 Food and Agricultural Organisation (FAO) report suggests that '[m]ore than 820 million people in the world are still hungry today', with 'about 2 billion people' worldwide experiencing 'moderate or severe food insecurity'.[15] However, whilst addressing food insecurity is of course critical, difficulty in realising the minimum core 'set' of rights does not justify scant attention (or neglect) of human rights beyond this group of rights. This critique is supported by the Committee on the Rights of the Child who warn against, for example, the '[n]eglect of article 31 [including the right to play] in development programmes'.[16] The Committee states:

> Early childhood care and development work in many countries focuses exclusively on issues of child *survival* with no attention paid to the conditions that enable children to *thrive*. Programmes often only deal with nutrition, immunization and preschool education with little or no emphasis on play, recreation, culture and the arts.[17]

Such practice serves to render rights such as the right to play and the right to the continuous improvement of living conditions as luxury rights; a view that other rights are more important and that these can be addressed at a later date, once the minimum core 'set' of rights are realised. This must not be the case. These rights must not be viewed as 'next' to fulfil – this supports a hierarchy of rights that fails to reflect the raison d'être of human rights and the human

[11] Indeed, even a chapter calling for movement beyond the minimum threshold of rights, and a fuller understanding of the right to adequate living standards expanding beyond the minimum core, neglects to refer to the right to the continuous improvement of living conditions (G MacNaughton, 'Beyond a Minimum Threshold: The Right to Social Equality' in Lanse Minkler, *The State of Economic and Social Human Rights: A Global Overview* (Cambridge University Press 2013) 283 defines adequate housing as 'more than just minimal shelter from the weather; it must also provide security and privacy, as well as serve social functions').

[12] Brems (n 10) 353.

[13] ibid 354.

[14] E Wiles, 'Aspirational Principles or Enforceable Rights? The Future for Socio-Economic Rights in National Law' (2006) *American University International Law Review* 35, 60.

[15] FAO, IFAD, UNICEF, WFP and WHO, *The State of Food Security and Nutrition in the World 2019. Safeguarding against economic slowdowns and downturns* (FAO, 2019) vii.

[16] Committee on the Rights of the Child, GC17 (n 4) para 43.

[17] ibid (emphasis added).

rights project.[18] The human rights project is based upon notions of freedom, equality, well-being and human dignity.[19] Habermas states that the Universal Declaration of Human Rights 'speaks of human dignity and human rights in the same breath'.[20] Human dignity has been described as 'the foundational concept of human rights'.[21] Reference to human dignity in the preambles of most of the core United Nations human rights treaties reflects this.[22] Human dignity centres on the belief that 'human beings, due to qualities they possess, have a special value or distinctive worth, that in each case and without exception should be respected and nourished'.[23]

Recognition of rights such as the right to the continuous improvement of living conditions and the right to play is necessary to achieve the aims of the human rights project, and realisation of these rights is necessary to 'secure … that human persons enjoy a dignified life'.[24] Therefore, when considering these rights through a comprehensive lens of the human rights project, these rights become vital and cannot be viewed as luxury rights. These rights reflect the goals of the human rights project viewed holistically.[25] What is it to have minimal

[18] MacNaughton (n 11) 281 suggests that a hierarchy of rights 'is inconsistent with the UN's position that all rights are equal'.

[19] These principles are core to the Universal Declaration of Human Rights (adopted 10 December 1948) UNGA Res 217 A(III) (UDHR).

[20] J Habermas, 'The Concept of Human Dignity and the Realistic Utopia of Human Rights' in C Corradetti (ed), *Philosophical Dimensions of Human Rights: Some Contemporary Views* (Springer 2012) 63.

[21] J Donnelly, *Universal Human Rights in Theory and Practice*, (Cornell University Press 2013) 28.

[22] Dignity is referred to in the preambles of the Universal Declaration of Human Rights, 10 December 1948, UNGA Res 217 A(III) (UDHR), ICESCR (n 1), International Covenant on Civil and Political Rights, 16 December 1966, 999 UNTS 171 (ICCPR), CRC (n 2), Convention on the Elimination of All Forms of Discrimination Against Women, 18 December 1979, 1249 UNTS 13 (CEDAW), Convention on the Rights of Persons with Disabilities, 24 January 2007, A/RES/61/106 (CRPD), International Convention on the Elimination of All Forms of Racial Discrimination, 21 December 1965, 660 UNTS 195 (ICERD), Convention Against Torture and Other Cruel, Inhuman or Degrading Treatment or Punishment, 10 December 1984, 1465 UNTS 85 (CAT). It does not appear in the preambles of the International Convention on the Protection of the Rights of All Migrant Workers and International Convention for the Protection of All Persons from Enforced Disappearance; however, these treaties refer to human dignity elsewhere. (The International Convention on the Protection of the Rights of All Migrant Workers refers to 'inherent human dignity of the human person' in Article 17(1) and 'principles of … human dignity' in Article 70. The International Convention for the Protection of All Persons from Enforced Disappearance refers to human dignity in Arts 19(2) and 24(5)).

[23] G Hughes, 'The Concept of Dignity in the Universal Declaration of Human Rights' (2011) 39 *Journal of Religious Ethics* 1, 3.

[24] P Gilabert, 'Human Rights, Human Dignity and Power' in R Cruft, M Liao and M Renzo (eds), *Philosophical Foundations of Human Rights* (OUP 2015) 200 (refers to this as 'condition-dignity'. He also refers to 'status-dignity' which can be described as '[t]he claim of human dignity is that simply being human makes one worthy or deserving of respect; that there is an inherent worth that demands respect in all of us'); Donnelly (n 21) 29.

[25] Play is proven as necessary for child development (cognitive, social, emotional, and physical). The Committee has confirmed the fundamental importance of play for the child, recognised also in the travaux préparatoires of the Convention on the Rights of the Child. (N Lott, 'The Right to Play', PhD Thesis, University of Nottingham (2020) ch 4; Committee on the Rights of the Child, GC17 (n 4)).

food, shelter and water but no hope of the improvement of living conditions? What is it for a child to have basic survival needs met with no ability to play? What is it to say that a minimum is sufficient? It perpetuates inequality, and limits dignity, freedom and well-being. This is due to the fact that human dignity requires more than simply survival, as evident in the Committee on the Rights of the Child's statement above. Donnelly and Whelan articulate this argument clearly, stating:

> We have human rights not to what as animals we need naturally for survival. We have human rights to what we need for a life of dignity. The human nature that is the source of human rights is a moral account of human *possibility*. It reflects what human beings *might become*, not what they "are" in some scientifically determinable sense or what they have been historically.[26]

Thus, by ignoring some rights and privileging others (those that we need as animals for survival), we fail to acknowledge and provide for the broader needs of a human being for a life of dignity. Donnelly and Whelan's statement further relates to the right to the continuous improvement of living conditions as this right focuses on future possibility – it is not about the immediate, nor can it be a 'quick fix'. The promise offered by the right to the continuous improvement of living conditions is that of hope and progress; it fulfils the aim of human dignity at a deeper and richer level. This progressive or future-focused foundation of the right reflects the aims of human rights as set out in the UDHR.[27] This future-focus of the right may further contribute to its status as forgotten or luxury, as it moves beyond 'basic' survival needs. Nevertheless, human rights were not intended to focus simply on basic survival (biological) needs, but rather are to include 'a (broader) *human* need'.[28] This is reflected also in the Committee on the Rights of the Child's statement above regarding the right to play, where it refers to a need to address 'conditions that enable children to thrive'.[29]

Donnelly states that '[h]uman rights reflect a particular specification of certain minimum preconditions for a life of dignity in the contemporary world'.[30] Donnelly and Whelan argue that '[u]nless (nearly) *all* internationally recognized human rights are respected, a life full of dignity is unlikely to be a realistic possibility … The gross and systematic denial of *any* of these rights is an unacceptable denial of human dignity'.[31] The neglect of the right to the continuous improvement of living conditions is thus a 'gross and systematic denial' of the right and thus an unacceptable denial of human dignity.

[26] J Donnelly and DJ Whelan, *International Human Rights* (Routledge 2020) (emphasis added).

[27] UDHR (n 22) Preamble ('determined to promote social progress and better standards of life in larger freedom').

[28] L Morales, 'The Discontent of Social and Economic Rights' (2018) 24 *Res Publica* 257, 261 (emphasis added).

[29] Committee on the Rights of the Child, GC17 (n 4) para 43.

[30] Donnelly (n 21) 133.

[31] Donnelly and Whelan (n 26).

MacNaughton states that 'the International Bill of Rights guarantees the rights deemed by the members of the UN to be *necessary for human dignity, not for survival*'.[32] On this basis, it is 'difficult to sustain a threshold of core rights that are by definition less than what the Bill proclaims is necessary for human dignity'.[33] Thus, the current focus on a minimum core 'set' of rights is 'inconsistent with both human dignity and the holistic framework of the International Bill of Human Rights'.[34] Movement away from this focus on a minimum core 'set' of rights and towards full acknowledgement of rights such as the right to the continuous improvement of living conditions is also necessary to overcome injustice and to see 'equality in dignity'.[35] The Vienna Declaration on Human Rights states that all human rights must be treated as 'universal, indivisible and interdependent and interrelated. The international community must treat human rights globally in a fair and equal manner, on the same footing, and with the same emphasis'.[36] The current practice towards human rights, of favouring some rights over others, thus contravenes this principle of indivisibility and fails to treat all human rights equally.

In this section I have argued that the historic lack of engagement with the right to the continuous improvement of living conditions, and the right to play, stems from an understanding of the rights as 'luxury'. They have not been traditionally included in lists that describe minimal human rights requirements, or the minimum core 'set' of rights, due to a focus on survival needs. Providing, through practice and engagement, a hierarchy or rights results in a situation that focuses on meeting 'basic' needs and rights first, with an implied view of addressing second-level or 'luxury' rights next. The reality of this as evidenced by human rights practice is that as States struggle to meet or ignore the requirements of the established minimum core 'set' of rights, other rights remain overlooked. In this section I have argued that the practice of focusing on a minimum core 'set' of rights serves to lower the borderline of human rights, and risks that rights excluded from this set of rights are forgotten. The discussion above evidences

[32] MacNaughton (n 11) 281 (emphasis added) (she cites, for example: ICESCR Article 13 – full development of personality and dignity; 12(1) – highest attainable standard of health; 11(1) – the right to the continuous improvement of living conditions; 2(1) – maximum resources/full realisation).

[33] MacNaughton (n 11) 281–82.

[34] ibid.

[35] As called for in Article 1 UDHR, and E Pribytkova, 'A Decent Social Minimum as a Matter of Justice' in HP Gaisbauer, G Schweiger and C Sedmak (eds), *Ethical Issues in Poverty Alleviation* (Springer 2016) 45 (She states 'I consider equality of status to be capable of serving as the desired intercultural core of human dignity'); MacNaughton similarly argues that the minimum core threshold fails to account for 'the importance of equality to people or the adverse impacts of inequality on individuals and societies', and states, in arguing for a right to social equality, that the 'minimal threshold approaches do not reflect the central idea in the holistic framework of the international Bill of Human Rights that everyone is born *equal* in dignity and rights (UDHR, Article 1)' (emphasis added) MacNaughton (n 11) 291.

[36] UN General Assembly, Vienna Declaration and Programme of Action, 12 July 1993, A/CONF. 157/23 para.5.

that a notion of human rights that reflects the goals of the human rights project requires engagement with rights such as the right to the continuous improvement of living conditions and the right to play, as respect and realisation of these rights are necessary for human dignity. Having addressed this key factor that has led to the right to the continuous improvement of living conditions being considered as forgotten, I now turn to examine another key factor – the inherent ambiguity and lack of conceptual clarity of the right.

B. Inherently Conceptually Unclear

Socio-economic rights have widely been criticised as characteristically conceptually unclear. They have been described as 'abstract',[37] 'vague',[38] 'ambiguous' and 'indeterminate'.[39] At this stage it is worth noting that socio-economic rights are not exclusively ambiguous – in practice civil and political rights have also shown themselves to suffer from a lack of clarity.[40] Alston argues that that 'many civil and political rights formulation are equally vague'.[41] This lack of conceptual clarity is partly due to the aim of having universal, or near-universal, ratification of human rights treaties. Ambiguity in the human rights treaty provisions allows for State- or context-specific interpretation of rights, within the remit of the general object and purpose of the treaty. It is evident that allowing for some ambiguity in treaty provisions has had a positive impact on the ratification of human rights treaties.[42] Ambiguity also allows for temporal flexibility. The world was a vastly different place at the time of drafting the International Bill of Rights with, for example, the internet yet to be invented and issues such as climate change still to become global concerns to the extent they are today. The ambiguity of human rights provisions thus allows for their scope and implementation to adapt to new challenges and opportunities over time. The ambiguity of human rights is therefore, to some extent, deliberate and offers some considerable advantages. However, it also poses significant challenges.

Prior to discussing the challenges of ambiguity, it is necessary to draw out aspects of the right to the continuous improvement of living conditions that are particularly unclear. This will frame the subsequent discussion and demonstrate

[37] See eg Habermas (n 20) 65.

[38] See eg E Riedel, G Giacca and C Golay, 'The Development of Economic, Social and Cultural Rights in International Law', in E Riedel, G Giacca and C Golay (eds), *Economic, Social and Cultural Rights in International Law: Contemporary Issues and Challenges* (OUP 2014) 22.

[39] Morales (n 28) 258.

[40] Regional human rights courts such as the European Court of Human Rights have, for example, devoted significant effort to defining rights such as freedom from torture, the right to life and freedom of expression.

[41] P Alston 'The Committee on Economic, Social and Cultural Rights' in F Mégret and P Alston (eds), *The United Nations and Human Rights: A Critical Appraisal* (OUP 2020) 460–61). He also describes ICESCR rights as lacking in conceptual clarity (440).

[42] For example, the ICCPR has 173 State Parties, ICESCR 171, and the CRC 196.

why this discussion applies to the right. First, as noted the right to the continuous improvement of living conditions is found 'alongside' the right to adequate standard of living conditions. However, the provision itself is ambiguous as to the relationship between these two rights. Is the right to the continuous improvement of living conditions in fact a stand-alone right, sitting 'alongside' others, or is it rather an aspect or element of the right to an adequate standard of living? This is a particular problem facing provisions that list a number of rights therein, such as the provision that includes the right to play. Article 31(1) of the Convention on the Rights of the Child reads as follows:

> States parties recognize the right of the child to rest and leisure, to engage in play and recreational activities appropriate to the age of the child and to participate freely in cultural life and the arts.

Article 31(1) lists five unique rights; however the text itself is unclear on how these rights relate to each other, or how they differ from each other. This ambiguity surrounding Article 31(1) has begun to be overcome through scholarly debate, and discussion and guidance by the Committee on the Rights of the Child. This is yet to occur to a considerable degree regarding the right to the continuous improvement of living conditions, serving to prolong its lack of conceptual clarity. One area where the right has received attention by the Committee on Economic, Social and Cultural Rights (CESCR) is within the reporting guidelines for State Party reports. Here the Committee on Economic, Social and Cultural Rights hints at aspects of the content of the right. The CESCR focuses on national measures to combat poverty, suggesting that the right to the continuous improvement of living conditions is linked to exiting poverty.[43] This contrasts with the reporting guidelines for State Party reports relating to the UNCRC, where the Committee on the Rights of the Child does not provide any insight into the content of the right to play within the reporting guidelines.[44]

A second area of ambiguity regarding the right to the continuous improvement of living conditions is closely related to the first. The phrasing of the right as referring to the 'continuous improvement' of living conditions leads to a lack of clarity over whether or not 'continuous improvement' of living conditions is a specific application of, or a furthering of, the obligation of progressive realisation. It raises questions such as: is the right to the continuous improvement of living conditions indeed a right in its own right? Is it an extension of other more widely recognised rights? Or is it simply a reiteration or specific application of

[43] CESCR, 'Guidelines on Treaty-Specific Documents to Be Submitted by States Parties under Articles 16 and 17 of the International Covenant on Economic, Social and Cultural Rights', 24 March 2009, UN Doc E/C.12/2008/2, at 10. And see Hohmann, chapter two in this volume.

[44] Although, it could be suggested that the Committee's decision to place the right to play with the right to education has narrowed the content of the right to that of play for the purposes of, or exclusive to the context of, education, as discussed further below.

the concept of progressive realisation? This chapter is written from the perspective that the continuous improvement of living conditions is a right. This reflects the articulation of the right to the continuous improvement of living conditions within the reporting guidelines for ICESCR.

A lack of conceptual clarity risks undermining the implementation and realisation of rights in the ways intended by the drafters. Alston writes:

> The various rights recognized in the Covenant are spelled out with varying degrees of specificity, partly as a result of differing approaches advocated by the relevant UN Specialized Agencies during the drafting process.[45] But even those formulations that go into some detail leave much to be determined through practice and interpretation.[46]

As rights are interpreted by treaty bodies or States Parties, and applied to unique contexts, over time there is considerable risk that the meaning and purpose of the right gets lost in translation. The child's right to play provides a good example of this. The drafters intended the right to play to be protected for both the holistic development of the child and as an activity related to the drafters' conception of childhood.[47] The drafters placed importance on both the intrinsic and the instrumental, or educational, value of play.[48] Furthermore, after much discussion during the drafting processes of the 1959 Declaration on the Rights of the Child and the subsequent Convention, it was decided that the right to play should be separated from the provision on the right to education.[49] Nevertheless, a lack of conceptual clarity through engagement with the right has led to the right to play being grouped with the right to education in the State Party reporting process.[50] This has in turn led to the right to play being discussed by the Committee on the Rights of the Child and States Parties primarily in the context of education, or being overlooked completely.[51] Considering this in light of Alston's statement would suggest that the right to play has been 'determined' to be limited largely to education purposes and settings. This is in stark contrast to the intentions of the drafters, evidencing that the meaning and purpose of conceptually unclear rights may become blurred over time. Ambiguity over the scope and content of the right to the continuous improvement of living conditions means this right risks facing the same fate.

Ambiguity of rights threatens enforceability and justiciability. 'Without legal enforceability, it is widely believed that socio-economic rights will remain

[45] This echoes the arguments made in the previous paragraph of the benefits of ambiguity for consensus.

[46] Alston (n 41) 460.

[47] Lott (n 25) ch 4.

[48] ibid.

[49] ibid.

[50] Committee on the Rights of the Child, 'General Guidelines Regarding the Form and Content of Initial Reports to be Submitted by States Parties under Article 44, Paragraph 1(a), of the Convention', 30 October 1991, CRC/C/5, para 21.

[51] Lott (n 25) ch 4.

ineffectual as legal entities.'[52] Whilst general arguments suggesting that socio-economic rights are unenforceable have been refuted,[53] this issue highlights the need for, or at least the benefit of, conceptual clarity. Without clarity over the scope and content of a specific right it is harder for courts to adjudicate on rights violations. Thus, a lack of clarity over the scope and content of the right to the continuous improvement of living conditions risks undermining the enforceability and justiciability of the right. In order to adjudicate on rights violations the content of rights must be 'spelled out in concrete terms in each particular case'.[54] The search for a concrete and precise content of a right can lead to '[l]owering the borderline' of rights content 'out of a desire to take into account different contextual possibilities'.[55] As stated by Morales, '[t]he minimum core conception of social rights serves as a response to the pervasive objection that the content of socio-economic claims remains indeterminate'.[56] Whilst 'the appeal of border control type human rights monitoring is in its clarity',[57] this threatens to rob rights of their intended purpose by narrowing their scope. As described above, this outcome is evident in the treatment of the right to play, with the right to play erroneously being directed primarily to the context of education (and principally for that of young children), failing to acknowledge its broader scope and content. As the content of the right to the continuous improvement of living conditions is unclear, there is a real risk that without a thorough examination of its intended content the right may be applied narrowly and the intended purpose of the right may be lost.

A further, related, challenge facing ambiguous rights rests upon measurability – or immeasurability. Being able to measure human rights is valuable as it enables the monitoring of implementation and violations of rights.[58] Whilst scholars have shown that both negative and positive rights can be measured,[59] a lack of clarity over the scope and content of a right inevitably presents problems for measurement. If we are unsure of the scope and content of a right, how are we to understand if, when or how it has been implemented or violated? How are we to agree indicators for conceptually unclear rights? Taking the right to play as an example, the concept of 'play' itself is riddled with ambiguity, with many scholars attempting and failing to agree on an operational definition.[60]

[52] Wiles (n 14) 36; MA Baderin and R McCorquodale, 'The International Covenant on Economic, Social and Cultural Rights: Forty Years of Development' in MA Baderin and R McCorquodale (eds), *Economic, Social and Cultural Rights in Action* (OUP 2007) 10.

[53] A Nolan, *Children's Socio-Economic Rights, Democracy and the Courts* (Hart 2011) 24, 30–32.

[54] Habermas (n 20).

[55] Brems (n 10) 352.

[56] Morales (n 28) 258.

[57] ibid 350.

[58] T Landman, 'Measuring Human Rights: Principle, Practice and Policy' (2004) 26 *Human Rights Quarterly* 906.

[59] ibid 923.

[60] Lott (n 25) ch 1. See also eg B Sutton-Smith B, *The Ambiguity of Play* (HUP 1997), S Brown, *Play: How it Shapes the Brain, Opens the Imagination, and Invigorates the Soul* (Avery 2000) 16.

This poses a significant challenge when attempting to understand the scope and content of the right, as 'play' remains an ambiguous concept. The lack of clarity over the scope and content of the right to play has led to a narrowed focus on play for the purposes of education or in educational settings. A further in-depth examination of the scope and content of the right to play demonstrates that its application should be much broader, taking into consideration children's play in all areas of life, impacting upon transport, planning and other policy areas as well. A fuller understanding of the right therefore reveals other areas of measurement necessary for monitoring the implementation of the right. Likewise, there are obvious questions to be posed regarding measurement for violations of the right. It is commonly accepted that children will play in all manner of scenarios and environments.[61] If it is the case that children will engage in play even in very difficult contexts, how can violations of the right be measured? Similar questions can be posed of the right to the continuous improvement of living conditions, beginning with those surrounding the scope and content of the right. What is to be understood as 'living conditions', and what is to be understood by 'continuous improvement'? What measures are required to implement the right? Without further examination of the right, and a clear articulation of the scope and content of the right, it is not possible to measure the implementation or violations of the right for the purposes of monitoring.

Taking these points into consideration it is unsurprising that a lack of conceptual clarity for some rights increases the likelihood that they will be forgotten. This is due to the fact that rights with clear, or more easily defined, normative content will be prioritised for implementation, monitoring and scholarly critique. It is understandable, therefore, that rights such as the right to play and the right to the continuous improvement of living conditions have been overlooked in favour of more 'clear-cut' rights, such as the rights to social security, education and health. Whilst a great deal of scholarly attention has gone into developing the normative content of these rights, the starting point for these rights is also somewhat clearer, partly due to much clearer language in the text of the provisions. The lack of engagement, implementation and monitoring of the right to the continuous improvement of living conditions, by the Committee on Economic, Social and Cultural Rights and scholars alike,[62] evidences that this right has succumbed to the same fate of being overlooked and forgotten as that previously faced by the right to play, in part due to the fact that it is inherently conceptually unclear – the parameters of the right are difficult to draw, and measurement of its implementation is uncertain.

[61] Committee on the Rights of the Child, GC17 (n 4) para 32.
[62] Hohmann and Goldblatt, introduction to this volume; Hohmann, chapter two in this volume.

III. OVERCOMING THE CHALLENGES FACING THE RIGHT TO THE CONTINUOUS IMPROVEMENT OF LIVING CONDITIONS

This section turns to address the steps that can be taken to overcome the challenges facing the right to the continuous improvement of living conditions as a forgotten right. In this chapter I have shown that the right to the continuous improvement of living conditions may have succumbed to this fate due to a perception of the right as luxury – as it sits outside of the generally accepted minimum core 'set' of rights – and due to the fact that it is inherently conceptually unclear. The right must not be viewed as a luxury due to its relationship with the concept of human dignity, upon which the project of human rights rests. Conceptual clarity for the right to the continuous improvement of living conditions is thus important.

Baderin and McCorquodale note that '[s]ince 1989, the ESCR Committee has provided considerable conceptual clarity and elaboration to the nature and scope of many ESC rights contained in the ICESCR'.[63] This has not been the case for the right to the continuous improvement of living conditions.[64] This lack of engagement by the Committee on Economic, Social and Cultural Rights has served to entrench the forgotten nature of the right and perpetuate the lack of engagement with the right by scholars and States. This lack of engagement also perpetuates a perception of luxury surrounding the right, as it can be assumed that the right has not been deemed worthy of attention or not deemed vital enough to warrant attention. Thus, the key way to overcome the challenges facing the right to the continuous improvement of living conditions is for the Committee on Economic, Social and Cultural Rights to engage with the right in a meaningful manner.

The value of treaty body engagement with a forgotten right has been seen in regard to the right to play. Prior to the publication of 'General Comment No. 17 on the right of the child to rest, leisure, play, recreational activities, cultural life and the arts', the Committee on the Rights of the Child had offered scant attention to the right to play in its General Comments and Concluding Observations.[65] Through engaging at a meaningful level with the right to play, the Committee was able to highlight the right's vital nature and broad scope. Since the publication of General Comment No 17, the Committee on the Rights of the Child has engaged more consistently (although there is still much room for improvement) with the right to play,[66] continuing to provide conceptual clarity and elaboration

[63] Baderin and McCorquodale (n 52) 11.

[64] Hohmann, chapter two in this volume.

[65] Committee on the Rights of the Child, GC17 (n 4); Lott (n 25) ch 4 provides an in-depth study of all General Comments and Concluding Observations prior to April 2020 for analysis of the Committee's engagement with the right to play.

[66] ibid.

of the nature and scope of the right. In doing so, the Committee on the Rights of the Child has begun to overturn the right to play's status as luxury or forgotten. One notable example of this shift in rhetoric is evident in the Committee on the Rights of the Child's neglect of the right to play in 'General Comment No. 4 on adolescent health and development in the context of the Convention on the Rights of the Child'[67] published prior to General Comment No 17, and its subsequent engagement with the right in 'General Comment No. 20 on the implementation of the rights of the child during adolescence', where the Committee emphasised the importance of play for adolescence.[68] Furthermore, through meaningful discussion of the right to play within General Comment No 17, the Committee on the Rights of the Child was able to address, in part, previous practice that had served to undermine the drafters' intentions for the right such as through highlighting the holistic value and broad scope of obligations pertaining to the right to play, as opposed to limiting its scope to education contexts. Meaningful engagement with the right to the continuous improvement of living conditions by the Committee on Economic, Social and Cultural Rights, similar to that provided by the Committee on the Rights of the Child in relation to the right to play, thus has considerable potential for overturning its status as forgotten and addressing the lack of conceptual clarity surrounding the right.

The right to the continuous improvement of living conditions must also be employed in the rhetoric of development organisations, advocacy groups and non-governmental organisations (NGOs) promoting the implementation of human rights, and particularly socio-economic rights. Groups such as the International Play Association were critical in lobbying the Committee on the Rights of the Child to address the right to play. Similarly, NGOs have played a crucial role in encouraging States to implement their obligations pertaining to the right to play. For example, NGOs were critical to the incorporation of the right to play in the legislative framework of Tanzania and have been key in encouraging local and national action to implement the right to play in the United Kingdom.[69] The greater the attention offered to the right through advocacy and awareness campaigns, the more likely the right will be engaged with by the CESCR, and by States in their reporting practices. With an increased awareness of the right and engagement with the right by the CESCR it is more likely States parties will consider and implement the right in practice.

[67] Committee on the Rights of the Child, 'General Comment No. 4: Adolescent Health and Development in the Context of the Convention on the Rights of the Child' (2003) CRC/GC/2003/4.

[68] Committee on the Rights of the Child, 'General Comment No. 20 on the Implementation of the Rights of the Child during Adolescence' (2016) CRC/C/GC/20, para 75.

[69] Lott (n 25) ch 6 (a multiple case study examines the incorporation and implementation of the right to play in Tanzania and the United Kingdom).

IV. CONCLUSION

In this chapter I have argued that the right to the continuous improvement of living conditions has been forgotten partly due to the heavy focus on a minimum core 'set' of rights, and partly due to the inherent ambiguity in the phrasing of the right. The notion of a minimum core 'set' of rights was intended to obviate ambiguity, but has resulted in lowering the borderline of rights and an abandonment of more progressive or ambitious rights critical for human dignity, including the right to the continuous improvement of living conditions. The fact that discussion of 'forgotten' rights is necessary proves the urgency of a movement away from the focus on a minimum core 'set' of rights. Drawing on the experience of the right to play, I suggest that the primary way to overcome the forgotten nature of the right is through meaningful engagement with the right by the CESCR. Additionally, the right to the continuous improvement of living conditions must be discussed by scholars and promoted by NGOs. Academic discussion of the right should provide appropriate critique of its scope and content, the steps required to implement the right, the intentions of the drafters, and the criteria by which its implementation or violation can be measured. It should also serve to elaborate upon and clarify the application of the human rights framework to the right, such as how concepts such as progressive realisation and non-retrogression apply and relate to the right to the continuous improvement of living conditions. An elaboration of the meaning of the right to the continuous improvement of living conditions could lead to fruitful new directions for the interpretation of the Covenant.

8

The Right to Continuous Improvement of Living Conditions and Human Rights of Future Generations – A Circle Impossible to Square?

SIGRUN I SKOGLY

I. INTRODUCTION

THE RIGHT TO continuous improvement of living conditions is provided for in Article 11 of the International Covenant on Economic, Social and Cultural Rights (ICESCR),[1] and is one of the rights mentioned as part of the concept of a right to an adequate standard of living. As detailed by Jessie Hohmann and Beth Goldblatt the right – as a distinct part of Article 11 – has not received much attention from States, the UN Committee on Economic, Social and Cultural Rights ('the Committee' or CESCR), or from the academic community.[2] Consequently, what the right entails from a normative perspective, and the corresponding obligations, have not been developed in any detail, compared to the other rights in the ICESCR.[3]

[1] International Covenant on Economic, Social and Cultural Rights (adopted 16 December 1966, entered into force 3 January 1976) 93 UNTS 3.

[2] Hohmann and Goldblatt, introduction to this volume.

[3] Most of the rights provided for in ICESCR have been subject to General Comments (GCs) adopted by the CESCR. These include the right to adequate food as a human right (CESCR, 'General Comment No. 12: The Right to Adequate Food (Art.11)' (12 May 1999) UN Doc E/C.12/1999/5); the right to adequate housing (CESCR, 'General Comment No. 4: The Right to Adequate Housing (Art. 11(1)) of the Covenant' (13 December 1991) UN Doc E/1992/23); the right to health (CESCR, 'CESCR General Comment No. 14: The Right to the Highest Attainable Standard of Health (Art. 12)' (11 August 2000) UN Doc E/C.12/2000/4); and the right to water (CESCR, 'General Comment No.15: The Right to Water (Arts. 11 and 12 of the Covenant)' (20 January 2013) UN Doc E/C.12/2002/11). However, it should be noted that the right to an adequate standard of living has not been subject to such scrutiny by the Committee, hence uncertainty about the link between the adequate standard of living on the one hand and right to continuous improvement of living conditions on the other remain. All General Comments are available through the Committee's website Office of the United Nations High Commissioner for Human Rights (OHCHR) 'Committee on Economic, Social, and Cultural Rights' <https://www.ohchr.org/en/hrbodies/cescr/pages/cescrindex.aspx>.

Another concept emerging within human rights circles is the human rights of future generations,[4] referring to the rights of current youth and children when they grow into adulthood, as well as other people who will live in the future.[5] Unlike the right to continuous improvement of living conditions, this concept is not codified in any human rights treaties. However, growing attention is being paid to this concept, both in the context of human rights related to environmental degradation (such as a right to a clean environment, and human rights effects of climate change, for instance), and in a broader sense of intergenerational justice. While lacking international codification as a right, as of 2019, 120 countries' constitutions make some reference to environmental posterity protection provisions,[6] with a few making explicit mention of the rights of future generations regarding the environment.[7] In a world facing exhaustion of finite resources, radical changes to our climate that will significantly impact upon the ability to grow food, and to preserve fishing resources, the effects on human rights for future generations may be severe. Other predicted future impacts on human rights include increased flows of refugees and internally displaced people due to rising sea levels and other climate-related causes, and technological advances may affect our way of life in fundamental manners. With such predicted changes, it is pertinent to ask whether we are paying sufficient attention to how future generations may be able to enjoy their human rights.

In this chapter, I will address one of the junctures between these two concepts, namely whether or how the right to continuous improvement of living conditions can be complied with, while at the same time addressing the rights of future generations. I will explore these tensions with a focus on the requirement in the ICESCR Article 2(1) that States Parties undertake to use the 'maximum of available resources' to implement the rights in the Covenant. There may clearly be tensions related to resource use when we address these two human rights issues. An important factor is the amount of resources we use to comply with the human rights of the current generation, while at the same time secure resource availability in the future. What the right to continuous improvement of living conditions and maximum of available resources have in common is that the attention (to the extent it has been given) tends to be focused on

[4] In a statement in 2019, the UN High Commissioner held that, 'the principle of intergenerational equity recognized in the Paris Agreement places a duty on us to act as responsible stewards of our environment, and ensure that future generations can fulfil their human rights'. See also M Bachelet, 'ONE UN Side event: SDG 16 and realising the right to participate – empowering people as agents of more effective climate change' (25th Session of the Conference of the Parties, Madrid, 9 December 2019) <https://www.ohchr.org/en/NewsEvents/Pages/DisplayNews.aspx?NewsID=25413&LangID=E>.

[5] R Künnemann, 'Human Rights of Future Generations – Draft Research Paper' (on file with author, 2019) 1.

[6] J Tremmel, 'Whose Constitution? Constitutional Self-Determination and Generational Change' (2019) 32(1) *Ratio Juris* 49, 61.

[7] ibid.

the access to and spending of financial and natural resources, and increasing material consumption. Addressing the human rights of future generations, this attention to increased spending may need to be rethought. Analysing the right to continuous improvement of living conditions and the human rights of future generations together necessitates attention to questions such as sustainability, retrogression, planetary boundaries and a human rights floor and ceiling.

Before addressing the requirement of employing the 'maximum of available resources' it is necessary to dwell on the content of the right to continuous improvement of living conditions (section II), and how we understand the rights of future generations (section III). Section IV will then be devoted to the tension between the right to continuous improvement of living conditions and the rights of future generations on a general level, while focusing on how we can address the concept of 'maximum available resources', in light of the right to continuous improvement of living conditions as well as human rights of future generations, and how this concept may be applied to cater for both rights. As the two concepts (the right to continuous improvement and human rights of future generations) both lack specific interpretation and appear as new in the international human rights debates, in this chapter I do not aspire to give the ultimate answers, but rather to identify questions that need to be asked and researched to enable us to understand the relationship between the two rights. I will argue that we need to approach the 'maximum of available resources' differently, to enable a possible joint approach to the right to continuous improvement of living conditions and human rights of future generations.

II. THE UNDERSTANDING OF THE 'RIGHT TO CONTINUOUS IMPROVEMENT OF LIVING CONDITIONS' AS A HUMAN RIGHT

As has been thoroughly addressed by Jessie Hohmann in her chapter in this volume,[8] the right to continuous improvement in living conditions has not been subject to much attention or scrutiny by the international human rights community up to now. This is the case for the UN human rights system, as well as civil society and the academic community.[9] Consequently, it is at this stage very hard to determine specifically what is meant by the concept, and indeed its limitations. But some reflections can be made as to the understanding of 'continuous', 'improvements' and also 'living conditions'. We should also consider the extent to which the right is limited by its connection to the overarching concept in Article 11, namely the right to an adequate standard of living.

[8] Hohmann, chapter two in this volume.

[9] It is telling that in B Saul, D Kinley and J Mowbray's important work on the ICESCR, a 100-page chapter on ICESCR Art 11, the right to continuous improvement of living conditions is mentioned only once and there is no discussion on the right. See B Saul, D Kinley, and J Mowbray, *International Covenant on Economic Social and Cultural Rights: Commentary, Cases and Materials* (OUP 2016) 861.

A key question is how we understand 'improvement', as improvement related to human rights enjoyment does not necessarily imply more material goods. There are other aspects of quality of life that can be considered improvement, even if material goods are not increased. This point may seem highly 'academic' in a world where close to 700 million people live in extreme poverty[10] and where many others lack access to essential material goods such as food, water, housing, and education to reach an adequate standard of living. This question relates closely to recent debates over the human rights impact of increasingly unequal societies,[11] and this is clearly of relevance to the discussion on the right to continuous improvement of living conditions. Alston holds that it is necessary to 'clearly recognize that there are limits to the degree of inequality that can be reconciled with notions of equality, dignity and commitments to human rights for everyone'.[12]

Closely linked to our understanding and interpretation of 'improvement' is our understanding of 'living conditions'. Living conditions do not only relate to access to adequate food, clothing, housing, and water, but also to personal security, working conditions, rest, leisure time and other aspects of our lives covered by the provisions in international human rights law more broadly. However, the content of living conditions goes even further than that and covers aspects such as social interaction with family and friends, and the opportunity to enjoy nature, art and culture.

The third concept in the provision to be considered is 'continuous'.[13] This could be seen as an indefinite concept; that there is never a point at which the living conditions are of such a standard that the continuation may no longer be applicable. However, such an approach would be utopian and not take into account the necessary limitations imposed upon us by finite resources and the human rights of the generations coming after us.[14]

One way of addressing this tension would be to address the right to the continuous improvement of living conditions in light of the overarching right in

[10] According to the World Bank 698 million people lived below the international poverty line of US$ 1.90 a day in 2017. See 'Poverty' Poverty Overview (worldbank.org) <https://www.worldbank.org/en/topic/poverty/overview> last updated 20 October 2020.

[11] P Alston, 'Extreme Inequality as the Antithesis of Human Rights' (*Opendemocracy*, 27 October 2015) <https://www.opendemocracy.net/en/openglobalrights-openpage/extreme-inequality-as-antithesis-of-human-rights/>; S Moyn, 'Human Rights and the Age of Inequality,' (*Opendemocracy*, 27 October 2015) <https://www.opendemocracy.net/en/openglobalrights-openpage/human-rights-and-age-of-inequality/>; M Leach, K Raworth and J Rockström, 'Between Social and Planetary Boundaries: Navigating Pathways in Safe and Just Space for Humanity', *OECD – World Social Science Report 2013* (OECD, 15 November 2013) Chapter 6, 84–89; W Vandenhole, 'De-Growth and Sustainable Development: Rethinking Human Rights Law and Poverty Alleviation' (2018) 11 *Law and Development Review* 647.

[12] Alston (n 11).

[13] Hohmann, chapter two in this volume.

[14] For a further discussion on this issue, see L Löfquist, 'Climate Change, Justice and the Right to Development' (2011) 7 *Journal of Global Ethics* 251.

Article 11, namely the right to an 'adequate standard of living'. In other words, do we have an unlimited right to improvement in our living conditions, or is this right only relevant to the point where we have achieved what is considered an adequate standard of living? As has been pointed out by Hohmann, the *travaux préparatoires* only gives limited indication of the intentions of the drafters, apart from expressing the need for achieving continuous improvement in living conditions.[15]

As is the case with the right to continuous improvement of living conditions, the right to an adequate standard of living has not received the specific attention of a General Comment related to its normative content and corresponding obligations from the Committee. However, it may be reasonable to argue that through the fulfilment of the composite rights (food, clothing, housing and water), combined with the fulfilment of the rights to the highest attainable standard of health,[16] and the right to education,[17] much of what would commonly be considered to be part of an adequate standard of living would be addressed. On the other hand, with such an emphasis on the material aspects, we may not be reflecting the wider content of the concept of 'continuous improvement of living conditions', which includes non-material elements such as clean air, leisure time, access to art and culture, etc. These are values that are not as easily measured as material goods, but still essential for our living conditions, and a life lived in dignity.[18]

Yet, in situations where we are looking at the right to continuous improvement of living conditions from an access to material goods perspective, there are still a number of questions to be raised. Do people whose living standards comply with the material understanding of adequacy still have a right to continuous improvement of their living conditions? Will there be priority for positive action from the government for the right to continuous improvement of living conditions for people whose living standards are not adequate according to the above definition, or does this right have an independent status so that people whose living standard has reached adequacy can still claim their right to the continuous improvement of living conditions?[19] Will a State fail in its obligations if its population enjoys the adequate standard of living as defined above, but it is unable to ensure that the population can continue to improve its living conditions?

The Committee has consistently emphasised that the various economic, social and cultural rights have a minimum core content with corresponding

[15] Hohmann, chapter two in this volume; M Craven, *The International Covenant on Economic, Social and Cultural Rights: A Perspective on its Development* (Clarendon Press 1995) 294–95.

[16] ICESCR (n 3) Art 12.

[17] ibid Art 13.

[18] UN General Assembly, Universal Declaration of Human Rights, 10 December 1948, 217 A (III), Art 1.

[19] Löfquist (n 14) 253–54.

core obligations.[20] This has been specified in a number of General Comments by the Committee.[21] However, the Committee has not been consistent in its terminology (sometimes using 'core content', sometimes 'minimum core content', and sometimes 'core obligations'). It would lead too far to go into this discussion in any detail, but it can reasonably be argued that this core content may represent a human rights 'floor' below which no-one should be living. In the context of the right to continuous improvement of living conditions, is there a similar human rights 'ceiling' above which the right would no longer apply? This may come across as a rhetorical question, and the answer may be 'of course'. After all, most people would accept that (multi)billionaires could legitimately see a significant decline in their living conditions before it becomes a human rights problem.[22] In practical terms though, if we have a right to 'continuous improvement of living conditions', at what point do we draw the line and argue that the right to continuous improvement no longer applies? This is a major question for our understanding of the right, and in particular if we see living conditions as representing material wealth. However, if the right is considered to go beyond material wealth and encompass non-material elements as mentioned above, the right to continuous improvement of living conditions would still have relevance for people whose material standard of living measures up to 'adequate' in the understanding of the ICESCR.

From the material wealth perspective, these questions really concern whether we address human rights implementation from a minimum or a maximum perspective;[23] or, indeed, whether there are spheres beyond what would be considered complete fulfilment of rights. It is evident that there are huge numbers of individuals in the world who do not live in conditions that can be considered to reflect the above definition of adequate standard of living and, for them, the right to continuous improvement of living conditions is certainly highly relevant and pertinent. But what about those that have living standards that are fully adequate – and beyond. Do we still have the right to the continuous improvement of living conditions? From a moral-philosophical perspective, this is a far more difficult question to respond to in the affirmative. Writing in the context of environment and the right to development, Löfquist holds that if 'some people have a vastly better situation than other people, there is something wrong with

[20] D Bilchitz, 'Giving Socio-Economic Rights Teeth: The Minimum Core and Its Importance' (2002) 119 *The South African Law Journal* 484; KG Young, 'The Minimum Core of Economic and Social Rights: A Concept in Search of Content' (2008) 33 *Yale Journal of International Law* 113; A Chapman and S Russell, *Core Obligations: Building a framework for economic, social and cultural rights* (Intersentia 2002).

[21] See generally CESCR, 'General Comment No. 3: The Nature of States Parties' Obligations (Art. 2, Para. 1, of the Covenant)' (14 December 1990) UN Doc E/1991/23 para 10; GC No 12 (n 3) paras 6, 8 and 33; GC No 14 (n 3) paras 19, 43 and 44; General Comment No 15 (n 3) paras 6 and 37.

[22] Löfquist (n 14) 255.

[23] Graham, chapter four in this volume.

the idea that both those who are very well off and those who have very little can have the same right to development'.[24] On the contrary, it may be pertinent to argue that given the finite resources in the world, and the excessive use of resources by a minority of the world's population,[25] the right to a continuous improvement of living conditions no longer applies to them. In essence, this part of the world's population has reached the level of adequacy and more, and therefore they may have reached a human rights ceiling beyond which the right to continuous improvement of living conditions no longer features.

The understanding of the right to continuous improvement of living conditions as reflected above, and in particular the concept of 'continuous improvement' and a possible human rights ceiling have not been directly addressed by the Committee, but relate to the understanding of retrogression or retrogressive measures taken by States, and how they impact upon the right.

The Committee have consistently held that retrogressive measures by States contravene their obligations, and should only be taken as a last resort and States have to explain why such measures were necessary.[26] However, for whom are retrogressive measures prohibited? Is this for everyone, or only for those whose adequate standard of living (and other economic, social and cultural rights) are not fulfilled? Are retrogressive measures that target those beyond the human rights ceiling permissible?

As early as 1990, the Committee referred to retrogression in its General Comment No 3 on the Nature of States Parties' Obligations. In this General Comment it was held that:

> … any deliberately retrogressive measures … would require the most careful consideration and would need to be fully justified by reference to the totality of the rights provided for in the Covenant and in the context of the full use of the maximum available resources.[27]

Even though this paragraph mentions that any retrogressive measures need to be taken with the 'most careful consideration', justified by the reference to the totality of the rights provided in the Covenant, and 'in the context of the full use of the maximum available resources', this sentence has been interpreted 'as establishing a doctrine which forbids the erosion of progress made by States

[24] Löfquist (n 14) 251.

[25] 'An average consumption rate per person means the amount of oils and other resources that the average person consumes a year. In rich countries those rates are up to 30 times as high as they are in poor countries': J Diamond, 'High consumption by some nations puts all of us at risk' (*National Geographic Magazine*, December 2018) <https://www.nationalgeographic.com/magazine/2018/12/inequality-rich-poor-essay-jared-diamond/>.

[26] CESCR has referred to the non-permission of retrogressive measures, *inter alia* in General Comment No 3 (n 21). For an in-depth analysis of the Committee's approach see BTC Warwick, 'Unwinding Retrogression: Examining the Practice of the Committee on Economic, Social and Cultural Rights' (2019) 19 *Human Rights Law Review* 467.

[27] General Comment No 3 (n 21) para 9.

(a "prohibition on backwards steps")'.[28] A statement from the Committee in 2016 contains a somewhat more nuanced approach:

> If the adoption of retrogressive measures is unavoidable, such measures should be necessary and proportionate, in the sense that the adoption of any other policy or failure to act would be more detrimental to economic, social and cultural rights. They should remain in place only insofar as they are necessary; they should not result in discrimination; they should mitigate inequalities that can grow in times of crisis and ensure that the rights of disadvantaged and marginalized individuals and groups are not disproportionately affected; and they should not affect the minimum core content of the rights protected under the Covenant.[29]

As is clear from these quotes, the concerns of the Committee have (rightly) been to focus on retrogression or backward steps that affect vulnerable groups in society. The second quote from 2016 includes a reference to non-discrimination, and that States should 'mitigate inequalities' and the need to ensure that the rights of 'disadvantaged and marginalized individuals and groups are not disproportionately affected'. Consequently, the attention is on the negative effects on the most deprived in society. In the passages quoted and indeed the many other instances where the Committee refers to non-retrogression, they do not – understandably – consider the position of the wealthiest parts of the population.

As will be seen in the next section, the question of a 'human rights ceiling', and the related concerns of retrogression do not only affect our understanding of continuous improvement of living conditions, they are also highly relevant for the discussion on human rights of future generations, and the 'planetary boundaries' that we are facing.

III. HUMAN RIGHTS OF FUTURE GENERATIONS

As specified in the introduction, when we use the term 'human rights of future generations' we are considering the rights of current youth and children, and other people who will live in the future.[30] A child is a human being currently protected by general human rights law, in addition to the specific rights of the child. However, children will grow up and become adults in a world that may face significant challenges related to individuals' human rights enjoyment due to the conduct of people acting today, over whose actions the children of today have no say.[31]

[28] Warwick (n 26) 468.

[29] CESCR, 'Statement: Public debt, austerity measures and the International Covenant on Economic, Social and Cultural Rights' (22 July 2016) UN Doc E/C.12/2016/1, para 4.

[30] Künnemann (n 5).

[31] T Skillington, 'Changing Perspectives on Natural Resource Heritage, Human Rights, and Intergenerational Justice' (2019) 24(3) *International Journal of Human Rights* 615, 615; M Düwell and G Bos, 'Human Rights and Future People – Possibilities of Argumentation' (2016) 15(2) *Journal of Human Rights* 231, 239.

There are a number of challenges to future generations' human rights enjoyment that stem from the conduct of the present generation. For instance, ongoing environmental degradation through pollution and climate change will have significant impact upon future generations' abilities to enjoy their human rights.[32] Environmental change is likely to cause degradation of agricultural land and the ability to grow sufficient and nutritionally sound food will be significantly reduced;[33] the availability of land on which to live and work will be reduced due to sea level rises;[34] a large number of people will be internally displaced, which may result in conflict and struggles over limited resources;[35] the development and use of technology may have significant impact upon future generations' rights to privacy,[36] to receive and impart information, and to take part in the government of their own countries. These are but a few of the potential human rights challenges. In essence, many of the consequences of current action or inaction will have direct impacts upon future generations' human rights – including the right to an adequate standard of living, and its composite rights.

In the emerging debate on human rights of future generations, a number of issues are being discussed, such as whether individuals who do not yet exist may have *rights*,[37] whether they may have legal standing,[38] and how their rights can be claimed.[39] While important for our understanding of legal rights of future generations, this chapter will not enter into this debate, but rather focus on some specific concepts that have relevance for our understanding of the link to the right to continuous improvement of living conditions.

Just as the question of who is covered by the right to continuous improvement of living conditions relates to the universality of human rights, so does the question of human rights of future generations. The understanding of universality is not limited to geographic reach, or a reach to all people irrespective of race, sex, language, religion, etc, but it also has a temporal element in that the human rights protection and enjoyment as envisaged in the UN Charter and the Universal Declaration of Human Rights apply to current as well as future

[32] B Lewis, 'Human Rights Duties towards Future Generations and the Potential for Achieving Climate Justice' (2016) 34(3) *Netherlands Quarterly of Human Rights* 206, 209–13.

[33] European Environmental Agency, 'Soil, Land and Climate Change' (2019) <https://www.eea.europa.eu/signals/signals-2019-content-list/articles/soil-land-and-climate-change>.

[34] International Panel on Climate Change, *Climate Change 2014: Synthesis Report* (2014) <https://www.ipcc.ch/site/assets/uploads/2018/05/SYR_AR5_FINAL_full_wcover.pdf> 4.

[35] B Thompson, 'Climate change and displacement' (*United Nations High Commissioner for Refugees (UNHCR)*, 15 October 2019) <https://www.unhcr.org/uk/news/stories/2019/10/5da5e18c4/climate-change-and-displacement.html>.

[36] L Rainnie and J Anderson, 'The Future of Privacy' (*Pew Research Centre Internet & Technology*, 18 December 2014 <https://www.pewresearch.org/internet/2014/12/18/future-of-privacy/>.

[37] Skillington (n 31) 616–20. See also Lewis (n 32) 206–26.

[38] B Mank, 'Standing and Future Generations: Does Massachusetts v. EPA Open Standing for Generations to Come?' (2009) University of Cincinnati College of Law, Faculty Articles and Other Publications Paper 272 <http://scholarship.law.uc.edu/fac_pubs/272>.

[39] Düwell and Bos (n 31).

people. This is a logical continuation of life – we as a current generation enjoy our human rights, which were proclaimed and codified before our birth. The conduct of past generations has enabled us to enjoy human rights as a future generation. The Preamble of the Universal Declaration on Human Rights provides the 'recognition of the inherent dignity and of the equal and inalienable rights of all members of the human family is the foundation of freedom, justice and peace in the world …'.[40] Weiss holds that 'the reference to all members of the human family has a temporal dimension which brings all generations within its scope. The reference to equal and inalienable rights affirms the basic equality of such generations in the human family.'[41]

This temporal universality of human rights is linked to the understanding of intergenerational justice. Shelton uses this term and holds that the humans who live today have special obligations as 'custodians or trustees' of the planet and that these obligations pertain to the survival of humans as a species.[42] This would mean that as rights holders, future generations should be able to 'inherit the Earth in as good a condition as did their ancestors and with at least comparable access to its resources'.[43] The other side of this coin, would mean that the current generation would be under an obligation to ensure that the Earth's conditions and resources are such that future generations are able to live their lives with full enjoyment of their human rights.

In light of this temporal universality and intergenerational justice approach, the debate on the human rights of future generations addresses how the decisions and behaviour of current people (individuals, corporations, as well as governments) may impact upon the ability of future generations to enjoy human rights in an equal manner to current populations. There is, of course, a clear tension regarding these questions, in that many people within current populations do not have their human rights fulfilled, including their right to an adequate standard of living. There is a real concern that addressing human rights of future generations may take the attention away from the plight of current generations, or may indeed be used as arguments for limiting the rights' enjoyment of current generations.[44] Consequently, when addressing the right to continuous improvement of living conditions for current generations in light of the rights of future generations, it is imperative to ensure that the fulfilment of the human rights for those currently suffering from violations and non-fulfilment of these rights

[40] Universal Declaration of Human Rights (adopted 10 December 1948 UNGA Res 217 A(III) (UDHR) Preamble.

[41] EB Weiss, 'In Fairness to Future Generations and Sustainable Development' (1992) 8(1) *American University International Law Review* 19, 21.

[42] D Shelton, 'Describing the Elephant: International Justice and Environmental Law' in J Ebbesson and P Okowa (eds), *Environmental Law and Justice in Context* (Cambridge University Press 2009) 62. See also Weiss (n 41) 20.

[43] Weiss (n 41) 21.

[44] Skillington (n 31) above provides a detailed analysis of the debates between those who favour rights fulfilment of current generations, and those who argue that this would be contrary to intergenerational justice and rights of future generations.

is not set aside on the pretext of securing the human rights for future generations. The challenge is consequently to find a way to secure the rights of current generations, while at the same time ensure that we do not prevent future generations from enjoying theirs.

IV. TENSIONS BETWEEN THE RIGHT TO CONTINUOUS IMPROVEMENT OF LIVING CONDITIONS AND HUMAN RIGHTS OF FUTURE GENERATIONS

From the discussion in the two previous sections, it becomes clear that there are tensions between the two concepts of the right to continuous improvement of living conditions and the rights of future generations. One of the key tensions concerns the use of resources, and how we interpret the requirement of Article 2(1) of the ICESCR to use the 'maximum of available resources' to implement economic, social and cultural rights, and to improve current living conditions. Even if we only focus on people whose living standards are not adequate according to a human rights approach as discussed above, the use of further resources, both financial and material will be required. However, the use of further resources, and in particular natural resources, will be highly detrimental to the ability of future generations to realise their human rights. Research clearly shows that current resource use (even assuming no further increases) is beyond what the Earth can sustain. In an article from 2018, Watt refers to research that shows that 'we have consumed a year's worth of carbon, food, water, fibre, land and timber in a record 212 days'.[45]

Consequently, one of the significant challenges when we seek convergence between the right to continuous improvement of living conditions and the human rights of future generations will be to find a way in which living conditions can be improved within existing resource limits, many of which have already been exceeded.[46] This shows a serious challenge related to sustainability of standards of living. However, this tension also shows, as was alluded to above, that we may need to consider the improvement in living conditions only for those segments of the world population who have not yet achieved an adequate standard of living. This may also challenge our approach to economic growth. Vandenhole holds that 'economic growth does not necessarily lead to economic development, let alone human development, and has typically come at a huge environmental cost'.[47] Such environmental cost is likely to have significant impact upon future generations' ability to enjoy their human rights.

[45] J Watts, 'Earth's resources consumed in ever greater destructive volumes' (*The Guardian*, 23 July 2018) <https://www.theguardian.com/environment/2018/jul/23/earths-resources-consumed-in-ever-greater-destructive-volumes>.

[46] See generally K Raworth, *Doughnut Economics* (Random House Business Books 2017).

[47] Vandenhole (n 11) 650. See also JP Bohoslavsky and F Cantamutto, chapter five in this volume.

There are therefore two specific areas of concern that need to be addressed if the tension between the rights to continuous improvement of living conditions and those of future generations may be eased: the question of how we use resources, and what this will mean in terms of sustainable development.

A. The Application of 'Maximum of Available Resources'

As already mentioned, the approach to 'the maximum of available resources' when implementing economic, social and cultural rights often focuses on the availability of financial resources. Hence, richer countries will have more resources to devote to such implementation than poorer countries. This approach has often been taken by the Committee, and is understandable: focusing on financial resources can be done relatively easily using available 'objective' data, and applying such data may be considered less interference in domestic policies than commenting on the use of other resources. It should be noted, however, that in recent years the Committee has shown a more nuanced approach to resources and the impact their use may have on economic, social and cultural rights. For instance, in their recent Concluding Observations on Norway's report, the Committee held that it 'is concerned about the licences the State party has issued in recent years for the exploration and exploitation of petroleum and natural gas reserves in the Arctic Ocean and the Barents Sea and the impact of those activities on global warming (art. 2 (1))'.[48] In earlier Concluding Observations related to Australia, the Committee:

> recommends that the State party revise its climate change and energy policies, as indicated during the dialogue. It recommends that the State party take immediate measures aimed at reversing the current trend of increasing absolute emissions of greenhouse gases, and pursue alternative and renewable energy production. The Committee also encourages the State party to review its position in support of coal mines and coal exports.[49]

This approach reflects the approach taken by some commentators. In an article from as early as 1994, Robertson carefully interpreted the concept of resources as going beyond a State's financial means,[50] including natural, human and technological resources.[51] Building on Robertson's arguments, I have previously held that resources and their use for implementation of economic, social, and cultural

[48] OHCHR 'Concluding Observations on the sixth periodic report of Norway' (2 April 2020) UN Doc E/C.12/NOR/CO/6, para 10.

[49] OHCHR, 'Concluding Observations on the fifth periodic report of Australia' (11 July 2017) UN Doc E/C.12/AUS/CO/5, para 12.

[50] RE Robertson, 'Measuring State Compliance with the Obligation to Devote the 'Maximum of Available Resources' to Realizing Economic, Social and Cultural Rights' (1994) 16 *Human Rights Quarterly* 693.

[51] ibid 695–96.

rights need to be considered on the basis of their quality as well as quantity.[52] In essence, it is not only the amount of resources dedicated to human rights implementation that is of importance, but also *how* such resources are being used and deployed. It is essential that resources are targeted to those that are in most need of support, that the deployment of resources are carried out in a transparent, participatory, non-discriminatory and accountable manner. There are too many examples where financial resources are committed, but not enough concern is devoted to ensuring that the outcome is one where the human rights situation is actually improved. In other words, it is essential to ensure that resources are used in a manner that complies with the obligation of result as well as the obligation of conduct.[53] However, in my earlier work I did not consider the application of resources from a sustainability or intergenerational justice perspective. In the decade that has passed, the need to reconsider what is understood by *available* resources, and indeed what can be considered *maximum* has become far more obvious.

In this context, the *availability* of resources needs to be considered based on what can reasonably be used currently, without jeopardising what will be available in the future. For instance, we may have significant resources of fish 'available' in our oceans, but we can only consider the maritime resources available to us to be the amount that can be used while at the same time securing the reproduction of these resources, ie avoiding over-fishing. Thus, what is available is not only a matter of what we can access, but equally what we can use without depleting resources. This is a huge challenge, and even more difficult with resources that are finite and are not renewable or do not renew themselves. There is an added complexity in that such resources are often found in poorer parts of the world, but claimed by richer States in conjunction with multinational corporations. Consequently, there is an additional challenge to consider availability from a redistributive perspective: it is not only a matter of what may be available, but equally important, who gets to benefit from it.[54]

Similarly, the way we understand *maximum* is not only a matter of the total amount of resources, but what amount can be used without prejudice to the next generation. However, the human rights benefits from the use of the maximum available resources may be enhanced by investing financial resources in human rights conducive policies (such as health, food, education), rather than in spending which is less human rights productive. Furthermore, the investment in the use of natural resources should be done to ensure that the benefits from

[52] S Skogly, 'The Requirement of Using the "Maximum of Available Resources" for Human Rights Realisation: a Question of Quality as well as Quantity?' (2012) 12(3) *Human Rights Law Review* 393.

[53] CESCR General Comment No 3 (n 21) para 1.

[54] For instance, Laura Spinney discusses how deforestation in the global south has time-limited benefits for the local population, while carries significant long-term detrimental effects for them. L Spinney, 'The Colonialist Thinking that Skews our View of Deforestation' (*The Guardian*, 22 December 2020).

the exploration and exploitation of these resources are used to improve the human rights situation of the population, and at the same time that such exploration and exploitation is limited to sustainable levels to secure the availability of resources for future generations. It should also be mentioned that the amount of resources available for human rights implementation, including the implementation of the right to continuous improvement of living conditions, can be increased through redistributive policy decisions by governments, such as taxation policy, investment in renewable energy,[55] and the fight against corruption.

B. Sustainability

Furthermore, the question of the right to continuous improvement of living conditions and the concern for human rights for future generations overlap with the issue of sustainable development. The Report of the World Commission on Environment and Development, *Our Common Future* (the Brundtland Report), from 1988, defines sustainable development as 'development that meets the needs of the present without compromising the ability of future generations to meet their own needs'.[56] The report did not use this concept in a human rights framework, but rather that of human needs. Nevertheless, sustainability is considered in light of the needs of current and future generations. Hence, it can be argued that the understanding of the World Commission more than 30 years ago saw sustainability as a concept that would limit the freedom of manoeuvre for current development policies by the needs of future generations.

This can be translated into human rights language. By applying the word 'rights' rather than 'needs', the Brundtland quote would read: sustainable development is development that meets the *rights* of the present without compromising the ability of future generations to *enjoy their own rights*. To make the enjoyment of economic, social and cultural rights sustainable for future generations, there is clearly a limitation added to the concept of the application of resources. This has been recognised, *inter alia*, in the UN General Assembly Agenda 2030 Resolution, which contains the Sustainable Development Goals, where it is stated that:

> We are determined to protect the planet from degradation, including *through sustainable consumption* and production, *sustainably managing its natural resources* and taking urgent action on climate change, so that it can support the needs of the present and future generations.[57]

[55] See Alston (n 11).

[56] UN, 'Report of the World Commission on Environment and Development: Our Common Future' (1987) UN Doc A/42/427 (Annex) ch 2, para 1 <http://www.un-documents.net/ocf-02.htm>.

[57] UN General Assembly, 'Transforming our world: the 2030 Agenda for Sustainable Development', 21 October 2015, A/RES/70/1, Preamble (emphasis added).

If we see resources as going beyond financial resources and including natural resources such as minerals that are mined, land that is used for agriculture, oceans used for fisheries, and the air that is used for travel, it is clear that the use of these resources to the 'maximum' is difficult to align with the above understanding of sustainability and the possibility of future generations to enjoy their economic and social rights, including the right to an adequate standard of living. Rather, the depletion of mineral resources through excessive consumption; destruction of land as a result of overly intensive agricultural production; overfishing in our oceans; and significant air pollution represents direct destruction or overuse of our resources. Such destruction or overuse means that future generations will be unable to secure their rights to food, water and health. In short, they will be unable to secure their right to an adequate standard of living.

If we accept that we need to restrict the use of resources to levels that are sustainable for future generations, this will necessarily impact upon what is available to ensure continuous improvement of living conditions for all currently, at least if the right to continuous improvement of living conditions is considered to mainly address material consumption. However, if we understand the right to continuous improvement of living conditions as being limited by the fulfilment of an adequate standard of living as addressed above, the opportunity to use resources in a more sustainable manner is more feasible. Some authors address these issues from the perspective of de-growth,[58] and argue that sustainable development needs a balance of 'economic growth with environmental and social considerations'.[59] Vandenhole challenges the way in which international human rights law has tried to work within the parameters of the current high growth approach and argues that:

> only if human rights law undergoes a paradigmatic shift in the understanding of socio-economic human rights and its role in development, beyond growth assumptions and with a stronger focus on redistribution, it may keep [the] transformative potential in post-growth or growth agnostic economies.[60]

Hence, Vandenhole here sees the need for redistribution to enable sustainable development.

Consequently, the understanding of what we mean by 'maximum available resources' in the context of a right to the continuous improvement of living conditions and sustainability for the rights of future generations need to be redefined. We will not only need to consider the actual amount that is available, but also more carefully consider how much of the amount available can sustainably

[58] In tackling questions related to human deprivation and ecological degradation, Raworth does not argue 'de-growth' per se, but advocates an economy 'that promotes human prosperity whether GDP is going up, down, or holding steady'. Raworth (n 46) 245.
[59] Vandenhole (n 11) 648.
[60] ibid 651.

be used at the present time in order to ensure that future generations are not negatively affected by excessive use of resources by this generation.

V. CONCLUDING REMARKS

To conclude, the question then becomes how such a limitation of what can be considered 'maximum of available resources' will affect our approach to the right to continuous improvement of living conditions. Redistribution is increasingly called for by human rights scholars,[61] and this may be necessary to enable sustainable use of resources to give future generations the opportunity to secure their human rights. However, a call for redistribution may be difficult if we approach the right to continuous improvement of living conditions from an unlimited perspective. Accepting that redistribution is part of the implementation of human rights for all (current and future generations) may involve a more nuanced approach to the content of the right to continuous improvement of living conditions and also to implementation measures such as the use of resources and the 'prohibition' of retrogressive measures. However, caution is necessary to ensure that the redistribution and retrogressive measures are targeted towards those who have reached the human rights ceiling.

While improvement in material well-being and access to better and more food, easier access to clean water, and housing that is compatible with personal health and security, is still a big challenge for many people around the world, it may also be necessary for many of us to reconsider what 'improvement' of living conditions is about. If we always equate improvement in living conditions with economic growth (in society and for individuals), we are in danger of falling into (or rather remaining in) a trap highlighted by Robert F Kennedy in 1968. In his famous speech at the University of Kansas, he illustrated how the way in which we count our Gross National Product (which is often used as a measure of standard of living) contains many elements that are destructive to society and individuals, such as the sale of tobacco and the generation of pollution that pose a threat to health and the sale of handguns that can kill, while other values that impact on our standard of living are excluded:

> … the gross national product does not allow for the health of our children, the quality of their education or the joy of their play. It does not include the beauty of our poetry or the strength of our marriages, the intelligence of our public debate or the integrity of our public officials. It measures neither our wit nor our courage, neither our wisdom nor our learning, neither our compassion nor our devotion to our country, it measures everything in short, except that which makes life worthwhile.[62]

[61] P Alston, 'Report of the Special Rapporteur on extreme poverty and human rights' (27 May 2015) UN Doc A/HRC/29/31 para 56(c); M Leach, K Raworth and J Rockström (n 11) 89.

[62] RF Kennedy, 'Remarks at the University of Kansas, March 18, 1968' (University of Kansas, 18 March 1968) <https://www.jfklibrary.org/learn/about-jfk/the-kennedy-family/robert-f-kennedy/robert-f-kennedy-speeches/remarks-at-the-university-of-kansas-march-18-1968>.

In this quote, Kennedy captures much of what are important, but often 'invisible', aspects of our living conditions. In the calls for redistribution and sustainability, it will be necessary to approach the complexities of our societies in a different manner, and use the resources available to enhance the social well-being of everyone. This can for instance take the form of investment in renewable energy to reduce pollution and secure supply for the future; the preservation of natural resources for the enjoyment of broader society; and other forms of improvements that will benefit society in a sustainable manner, such as redistribution of sources of wealth.[63]

In the title of this chapter, I asked if the tension between the right to continuous improvement of living conditions and the human rights of future generations represents a circle that cannot be squared. As I have argued, if we seek to ensure that future generations will be able to enjoy their human rights, while at the same time provide for the right to continuous improvement of living conditions for people that currently live below the 'human rights ceiling', it will be necessary to reduce the resource use for those above this ceiling. Furthermore, the resources that are used for current generations should be treated with more care. Depleting finite resources currently available to ensure human rights fulfilment of current generations will not be in accordance with intergenerational justice. Even more serious is the fact that much of the currently 'available' resources are not depleted to ensure current human rights compliance, but rather to enable overconsumption amongst those who have already reached the human rights ceiling.[64] Consequently, we need to rethink our use of resources, including for the implementation of economic, social and cultural rights. This will mean that what can be considered as 'maximum' and 'available' will have to be viewed in light of sustainability for future generations.

[63] Raworth (n 46) 177.
[64] For a discussion of such a scenario, see Düwell and Bos (n 31) 235.

9

New Synergies and Possibilities in the Inter-American Court of Human Rights

From Dignified Life to the Right to Continuous Improvement of Living Conditions

ISAAC DE PAZ GONZÁLEZ

I. INTRODUCTION

ONE OF THE most innovative categories introduced by the Inter-American Court of Human Rights (IACtHR) through its case law is the concept of the '*vida digna*' or 'dignified life'. In cases expounding the *vida digna*, the Court unveiled the causal relationship between States' positive obligations regarding the right to life and children's meaningful life within society. In various judgments from the years 2001 to 2010, the IACtHR recognised situations where States did not provide a minimum threshold of material well-being and, consequently, victims lost their lives. Nevertheless, in subsequent cases which had similar facts, the Court has made only isolated reference to the *vida digna* and the concept has not undergone further jurisprudential development or extensive consideration. In a different way, but in pursuit of well-being for victims, from 2013 to date the IACtHR has been directly interpreting the content of economic and social rights enshrined in Articles 21, 26 and 29 of the American Convention on Human Rights (ACHR),[1] linked to

[1] Article 21 of the ACHR states: 'Everyone has the right to the use and enjoyment of his property. The law may subordinate such use and enjoyment to the interest of society.' This is tied, in cases involving Indigenous peoples, to Arts 6, 7, 12–15 of the ILO's Indigenous and Tribal Peoples Convention 169. Article 26 ACHR establishes 'The States Parties undertake to adopt measures, both

interpretations of human rights in the international covenants. Such an interpretation has been consistent in invoking international human rights standards, and has been a stable trend in recent IACtHR social rights judgments. For the purposes of this chapter, I consider it as a new synergy that could set the floor for an Inter-American approach to the right to continuous improvement of living conditions.

A preliminary assumption is that, due to the systematic and evolving interpretation of education, health, social security and indigenous rights, forthcoming judgments could shift the IACtHR's jurisprudence in the direction of the right to continuous improvement of living conditions. My argument points out the emerging categories provided by the IACtHR derived from the standards on accessibility, progressivity and availability developed by the Committee on Economic, Social and Cultural Rights (CESCR), which have fixed the contours of social rights in international law. Under this framework, I establish that there are new synergies and conceptual elements that could create a robust Inter-American foundation for the right to continuous improvement of living conditions within its contentious jurisdiction.

The overall justification for focusing on the improvement of living conditions in Latin America arises from the existing levels of poverty and growing inequalities across the region.[2] In fact, most ACHR Member States share common denominators on the following issues: high numbers of the population live with low rates of access to higher education, with no basic services, no social protection, and a lack of health services. Furthermore, ongoing gender violence and the 2020 Covid-19 pandemic have worsened such conditions.[3] From Mexico to Argentina, the Inter-American Commission on Human Rights (IACHR) has been monitoring critical human rights issues provoked by economic deprivation, including in Central America.[4] Additionally, during the last few years,

internally and through international cooperation, especially those of an economic and technical nature, with a view to achieving progressively, by legislation or other appropriate means, the full realization of the rights implicit in the economic, social, educational, scientific, and cultural standards set forth in the Charter of the Organization of American States as amended by the Protocol of Buenos Aires'; and Art 29(d) ACHR states that 'No provision of this Convention shall be interpreted as: … excluding or limiting the effect that the American Declaration of the Rights and Duties of Man and other international acts of the same nature may have.'

[2] In spite of positive factors such as its biodiversity, the high production of gold, silver, and copper, its strong labour force and its young population, the region experiences economic problems derived from a model of unequal distribution of income between the richest and the poorest populations. *Informe de avance cuatrienal sobre el progreso y los desafíos regionales de la Agenda 2030 para el Desarrollo Sostenible en América Latina y el Caribe* (Comisión Económica para America Latina y el Caribe 2019) 118–20.

[3] See *Resolution 1/2020, Pandemic and Human Rights in the Americas*, IACtHR (Adopted on 10 April 2020), noting the severe and already existing risks in Member States.

[4] In the last 20 years, Mexico has had high levels of violence, forced disappearances, extrajudicial executions and gross human rights violations. See *Concluding observations on the sixth periodic report of Mexico* (Human Rights Committee, CCPR/C/MEX/CO/6, 4 December 2019). In Guatemala, El Salvador, Honduras and Nicaragua, increasing patterns of discrimination, evictions, harassment and killings of Indigenous peoples and human rights defenders can be seen.

there have been additional pressures such as environmental damage in Latin America; the post-conflict situation in Colombia; political upheaval in Bolivia; and judicialisation of politics in Peru.[5] Chile is not an exception: in the last two years, within the context of social protests, the vast majority of the population has been asking for new socio-economic policies to be included in the forthcoming Chilean constitution.[6]

Given the situation in the American continent, the IACtHR becomes a key forum to study the possibility of making the right to continuous improvement of living conditions visible both at the judicial and the legislative levels. It offers the possibility of opening up a discussion that pays attention to existing regional and constitutional approaches on social rights, which are already recognised by Member States, bringing them into a new narrative on the right to life having international law and the IACtHR's jurisprudence as guidance.

Prior to exploring the main features of the IACtHR's approach to *vida digna* and social rights, it is necessary to comment that, so far, we cannot identify jurisprudential, normative developments or theoretical discussions on the right to the continuous improvement of living conditions within the Inter-American arena. The only possible normative concepts that could enrich the proposals for an Inter-American foundation of the right to continuous improvement of living conditions are the unique constitutional dimensions from the Ecuadorian and Bolivian 'good living' principles, which entail a wide range of Indigenous cosmogonies linked to the harmonious individual and communitarian life of peoples, making themselves part of the motherland-environment.[7]

Inter-American Commission on Human Rights (IACHR), *Internal displacement in the Northern Triangle of Central America: Public Policy Guidelines* (OAS/Ser.L/V/II, 2018) para 54. The current situation pushes thousands of peoples to walk across Honduras and Guatemala (in '*caravanas*') to reach the Mexico-United States border seeking asylum.

[5] In Brazil, for instance, environmental defenders and Indigenous communities are struggling against deforestation provoked by Brazilian executive power and third parties. See 'IACHR Concludes Visit to Brazil', www.oas.org/en/iachr/media_center/PReleases/2018/238.asp, accessed 20 June 2020. In Colombia, the scope of integral reparations for victims are highly dependent on judicial proceedings. See M Cárdenas Poveda, 'Criterios para reparar a las víctimas del conflicto armado desde la perspectiva de la administración pública y del juez administrativo colombiano' (2019) 68 *Vniversitas* 1. In the aftermath of the coup against Evo Morales in late 2019, Bolivia faced political polarisation, ethnic discrimination, and excessive use of force provoked by the rupture of the rule of law. See IACHR, 'The IACHR presents its preliminary observations following its visit to Bolivia and requests an urgent international investigation take place into the serious human rights violations that have occurred in the country since the October 2019 elections (10 December 2019) <https://www.oas.org/en/iachr/media_center/PReleases/2019/321.asp> accessed 27 February 2021. In relation to Peru, in October 2019, President Vizcarra dissolved Parliament and called for a general election. In January 2019, the Peruvian Constitutional Court declared the closure lawful. See *Case 0006-2019 CC/TC, Sentencia del Tribunal Constitucional de Perú* [9 January 2020]. In November of 2020, the Peruvian congress ousted President Vizcarra.

[6] See eg the Global Initiative for Economic, Social and Cultural Rights, 'Chile said it loud and clear: a new constitution for a new social pact' <www.gi-escr.org/latest-news/chile-towards-guaranteeing-dignity>.

[7] See D Bonilla-Maldonado, 'El constitucionalismo radical ambiental y la diversidad cultural en América Latina. Los derechos de la naturaleza y el buen vivir en Ecuador y Bolivia' (2019) 42 *Revista*

Taking the empirical evidence of the Inter-American judgments, in this chapter I will study the meaning and elements of the *vida digna* along with the possibility of connecting such original elements with the new IACtHR doctrine on economic and social rights, in order to set guidelines that might point towards an approach to the right to continuous improvement of living conditions. Under this framework, I argue that the IACtHR could set substantive and procedural conditions which would extensively protect life, and this could be done through the international interpretations of both economic and social rights, and the right to continuous improvement of living conditions. I posit that an Inter-American approach to the right to continuous improvement of living conditions entails a virtuous circle of well-being based on a complete understanding of the right to life that includes education, health services, a safe environment, social security, non-discrimination and economic welfare.

Following this introduction, the chapter is structured in three sections. In section II, I study the substantive and procedural advances of the IACtHR's *vida digna* concept, pointing out its components: States' positive actions; its applicability in situations of vulnerability; and States' duties of progressive development. In the next section (section III), I refer to various judgments related to economic and social rights in which economic discrimination, intersectionality, and the adequate standard of life emerged as relevant concepts to define concrete State obligations. In the final section (section IV), I outline key features and synergies of the initial elements of *vida digna*, in combination with specific social rights duties, which could start off an academic, legal and judicial Inter-American discussion on the right to continuous improvement of living conditions.

II. DIGNIFIED LIFE AS A DEPARTURE POINT FOR THE RIGHT TO CONTINUOUS IMPROVEMENT OF LIVING CONDITIONS

Initially, we must take into consideration that, unlike the debates on the adequate standard of living derived from Article 11 of the International Covenant on Economic, Social and Cultural Rights[8] (ICESCR), minimum core obligations, and the right to social equality,[9] which are all relatively well developed at the international level, the concepts of living conditions and *vida digna* in the

Derecho del Estado 3. See Articles 8–10 of the Bolivian Constitution and Articles 3(5) and 14 of Ecuador's Constitution.

[8] International Covenant on Economic, Social and Cultural Rights, 16 December 1996, 993 UNTS 3. For a fuller debate on the origins and the overlooked normative aspects of an adequate standard of living, see Hohmann, chapter two in this volume.

[9] G MacNaughton, 'Beyond a Minimum Threshold. The Right to Social Equality' in L Minkler, *The State of Social and Economic and Social Human Rights* (CUP 2013) 295.

Inter-American context have had only a few indirect mentions and allusions both at practical and theoretical levels.[10]

An IACHR thematic report highlights the necessity of increasing a human rights-based approach to education, economic inclusion, health, and housing to address poverty and create a standard of living based on the availability of and access to basic services.[11] The objective of this multidimensional approach promoted by the IACHR is to put a minimum 'public policy' floor[12] on healthful, productive and dignified life, focusing on the particular needs of persons, groups and communities who are discriminated against.[13] At the same time, Inter-American scholars agree on how progressive the interpretation of Article 4 ACHR has been in cases linked to the quality of life under the scope of social rights,[14] and they agree on the elements underpinning the violations of the right to a dignified life: a group (or individuals) with lack of basic services, whose situation is known by the State, and the causal relationship between such omissions and the aggravating conditions impacting on the victims' lives.[15]

I now turn to consider in more detail the jurisprudence of the dignified life at the IACtHR.

A. The Forgotten Jurisprudence on Dignified Life

At the historic moment of the first landmark decision *Street Children v Guatemala*,[16] the concept of 'vida digna' emerged in the jurisprudence of the IACtHR giving an expansive interpretation of Article 4 ACHR. Article 4 ACHR is simply phrased '1. Every person has the right to have his life respected … No one shall be arbitrarily deprived of his life'.

Street Children is an example of the Inter-American search for an active status for the right to life and dignity, and is based on normative and philosophical

[10] On the qualities of *vida digna* pursuing material wellbeing based on the same legal foundations of social rights, see M Beloff and L Clérico, 'Derecho a condiciones de existencia digna y situación de vulnerabilidad en la jurisprudencia de la Corte Interamericana' (2016) 1 *Estudios Constitucionales* 139. Recent Inter-American discussion on social rights avoids the *vida digna* approach, eg E Ferrer Mac-Gregor et al, *Inclusión, ius commune y justiciabilidad de los DESCA en la jurisprudencia interamericana. El caso Lagos del Campo y los nuevos desafíos* (Instituto de Estudios Constitucionales del Estado de Querétaro 2018).

[11] IACHR, *Poverty and Human Rights* (2017) paras 57, 74–78, 91.

[12] For instance, the extensive guidance on the rights to social security, health, education, work and trade unions, adequate food, a healthy environment and the benefits of culture according to the IACHR, *Progress Indicators for Measuring Rights Under the Protocol of San Salvador* 2nd edn (2015).

[13] ibid paras 97, 108.

[14] Beloff and Clérico (n 10) 141.

[15] JM Pasqualucci, 'The Right to a Dignified Life (Vida Digna): The Integration of Economic and Social Rights with Civil and Political Rights in the Inter-American Human Rights System' (2008) 31 *Hastings International and Comparative Law Review* 26.

[16] *Street Children v Guatemala* [19 November 1999] IACtHR, Merits.

dimensions rejecting the unequal distribution of social goods.[17] The central question – one that remains unanswered by the IACtHR – was to identify which positive obligations should be carried out by States in protecting children's capabilities in a society.[18] Although set out as the indirect economic and social rights justiciability model,[19] the first substantive considerations in *Street Children* paved the road for a bold interpretation of Articles 4 and 19 ACHR, connected to the Convention on the Rights of the Child (CRC).[20] Within this framework, the IACtHR established that States have positive duties to prevent children from living in misery on the streets. Thus, the Court stated that it wished:

> to record the particular gravity of the fact that a State Party to this Convention can be charged with having applied or tolerated a systematic practice of violence against at risk children in its territory. When States violate the rights of at risk children, … it makes them victims of a double aggression. First, such States do not prevent them from living in misery, thus depriving them of the minimum conditions for a dignified life and preventing them from the 'full and harmonious development of their personality', even though every child has the right to harbor a project of life that should be tended and encouraged by the public authorities so that it may develop this project for its personal benefit and that of the society to which it belongs. Second, they violate their physical, mental and moral integrity and even their lives.[21]

However, in *Street Children*, the IACtHR did not declare legally binding obligations derived from Articles 26 and 29(d) ACHR that could create a complete interpretative ground floor of an adequate standard of living.[22] Hence, *Street Children* showed some interpretative deficiencies of the Court's early approach to dignified life: its lack of an argumentative connection to the concept of adequate standard of living, envisaged in Article 11 ICESCR, and a lack of analysis of the provision for the child's development recognized in Article 27(2) CRC. In the same narrow way, in *Reeducation Institute v Paraguay*[23] the IACtHR reasoned on the dimensions of dignified life which are even more relevant for

[17] See Beloff and Clérico (n 10) 139, 150. In my view, the IACtHR relies on what Valentini calls 'status dignity' (possessed by human beings comprising stringent normative demands) and highlights that States are primarily responsible for human rights. L Valentini, 'Dignity and Human Rights: A Reconceptualisation' (2017) 37 *Oxford Journal of Legal Studies* 862, cf 862, 865, 868.

[18] Although critical debates point out the need to move beyond the rhetorical level to create anti-poverty measures based on children's rights, see A Nolan, 'Poverty and Children's Rights' in J Todres and S M King, *The Oxford Handbook of Children's Rights Law* (OUP 2020).

[19] I De Paz González, *The Social Rights Jurisprudence of the Inter-American Court of Human Rights. Shadow and Light in International Human Rights Law* (Edward Elgar 2018) 146.

[20] *Street Children* (n 16), para 195. Taking advantage of the brief and general provisions of Art 19 ACHR that states 'Every minor child has the right to the measures of protection required by his condition as a minor on the part of his family, society, and the state', the IACtHR has linked it to the whole content of the Convention on the Rights of the Child.

[21] ibid para 191, footnotes omitted.

[22] The IACtHR overlooked the petition from victims' representatives asking for Guatemala to take legislative and administrative measures and public policies to provide integral protection for street children. *Street Children v Guatemala* [26 May 2001] IACtHR, Reparations, para 95(a).

[23] [2 September 2004] IACtHR, Merits, paras 159–60.

children deprived of liberty because of the impact on their project of life,[24] and the further difficulties when re-entering society.[25]

Later on, in a series of cases on Indigenous rights (*Yakye Axa v Paraguay*,[26] *Sawhoyamaxa v Paraguay*[27] and *Xákmok Kásek v Paraguay*[28]), the IACtHR settled further normative aspects and an overall feature of dignified life. That is, a situation of vulnerability previously known by the State, that might suppress conditions for individual and even communal development.[29] Furthermore, *Sawhoyamaxa* addressed a context in which the community's living situation caused severe deprivation for children, women and the elderly. These conditions included unemployment, illiteracy, morbidity rates caused by preventable illnesses, malnutrition, precarious conditions in their dwelling places and environment, alongside economic, geographic and cultural marginalisation.[30] However, *Sawhoyamaxa* left aside the reasoning on the violation of Articles 21 and 26 ACHR, and the right to a cultural identity was not mentioned as an integral part of the subsistence of the community.[31] In contrast, *Xákmok Kásek v Paraguay* went further and analysed the adequate standard of living of the community subsisting in a whole context of vulnerability: without land, water, food, or healthcare services, and without access to educative facilities and services, all of which, the Court argued, must be approached using a multicultural approach.[32] Finally, *Xákmok Kásek* pointed out that poverty is a barrier to the enjoyment of other rights, as well as the ability to participate on the basis of equality, in every aspect of society's cultural life.[33]

In spite of the normative arguments developed in these cases, the IACtHR did not establish a uniform basis for the concept of *vida digna*, since the consequences for declaring a violation of Articles 4 and 1(1) ACHR were different in *Street Children*, *Yakye Axa*, *Sawhoyamaxa* and *Xákmok Kásek*. Moreover, the IACtHR did not focus on what kind of specific measures (anchored within the ACHR or other treaties) must be adopted by Member States to repair economic marginalisation, while ameliorating vulnerability situations suffered by children, women and Indigenous peoples.

During the period of 2009–2016, the IACtHR entered into deep discussions on ESR justiciability, but seem to have abandoned the dignified life approach

[24] ibid para 171.
[25] ibid paras 173–74.
[26] *Yakye Axa v Paraguay* [17 June 2005] IACtHR, Merits.
[27] *Sawhoyamaxa v Paraguay* [29 March 2006] IACtHR, Merits.
[28] *Xákmok Kasék v Paraguay* [24 August 2010] IACtHR, Merits.
[29] In this regard, dignified life has always been linked to groups in situations of vulnerability. See Beloff and Clérico (n 10) 141.
[30] *Sawhoyamaxa* (n 27) paras 73–69 and 73–72.
[31] Related to their cosmogony, their pre-existing condition in the State, and their communitarian subsistence. See the advances on their right to proper consultation, cultural identity and property highlighted by the Indigenous case law discussed in De Paz González (n 19) 45–50.
[32] *Xákmok Kásek v Paraguay* (n 28) paras 194–217.
[33] ibid para 216.

when dealing with cases of groups and persons in extreme vulnerability.[34] Some cases from this period were factually similar to those the Court had previously identified as raising the *vida digna*, such as discrimination and violence suffered by those already vulnerable to discrimination such as women, living in a context of poverty, lacking access to public services.[35] These factors could have been analysed through the *vida digna* normative elements, but the IACtHR overlooked this.

In 2015, the direct interpretation and justiciability of the right to education came onto the scene in the case of *Talia Gonzales Lluy et al v Ecuador*.[36] This case contained the perfect factual and normative scenario to unveil a new route that would highlight how the adequate standard of life could be protected when medical malpractice unchains multidimensional damages in a child's life. The key point in the case (besides Talia's health condition) was how the State's omissions worsened her quality of life, increasing her level of poverty, excluding her from educative services and creating barriers for her family to find housing.[37] The IACtHR observed that, due to the violation of her right to health, the intensity of the discrimination she was subjected to aggravated her condition of being a child, female and poor. These intersectional factors worsened Talia's integral development as a person in the social milieu.[38]

Another case in which the IACtHR invoked international sources on adequate standard of living was *Yarce v Colombia*.[39] This case presented the difficulty of how to protect a right to housing, which is not set out in the ACHR or in the Protocol of San Salvador.[40] In his concurring opinion, Justice Ferrer Mac-Gregor drew a dynamic and evolutionary interpretation of Articles 4 and 21 ACHR read in line with the legally binding provisions related to health, housing, social measures, education, culture, decent living conditions, work and social security enshrined within Articles XI, XII, XIII, XIV and XXIII of

[34] Antkowiak points out that the Court avoided much discussion on dignified life and acknowledges a declining emphasis in *Chinchilla Sandoval* and *Cuscul Pivaral*. See TM Antkowiak, 'A "Dignified Life" and the Resurgence of Social Rights' (2020) 18 *Northwestern Journal of Human Rights* 24.

[35] The most prominent was *Gonzalez and others (Cotton Field) v Mexico* [2009] Merits, paras 114, 122, 130, 146. *Cotton Field* and *Street Children* have in common the same patterns of violence, the State's omissions, and failures within the criminal system/investigations, as well as the lack of effective duties to prevent violations of children's social rights.

[36] *Gonzales Lluy et al v Ecuador* [1 September 2015] IACtHR, Merits.

[37] ibid paras 155, 175, 291–92.

[38] Intersectionality as a method and oriented-practice has been used within the CEDAW framework on women in its General Recommendation 28, 33, 34 and 35. See I Truscan and J Bourke-Martignoni, 'International Human Rights Law and Intersectional Discrimination' (2016) *ERR Sixteen* 104, 124.

[39] *Yarce and others v Colombia* [22 November 2016] IACtHR, Merits.

[40] ibid paras 76–90. Under the integral and evolutionary interpretation of economic and social rights, the Protocol of San Salvador is a limited normative resource that must be read in light of the rest of the Inter-American *corpus iuris*. Otherwise – according to Art 19(6) of the Protocol – justiciability would be narrowly confined to education and labour rights.

the American Declaration of the Rights and Duties of Man (ADRDM), linked to Articles 1, 2, 26 and 29 of the ACHR, which demonstrate the persistent legal-political will of Member States to respect and protect all categories of human rights. The reasoned vote established that housing rights were violated. The facts revealed that the victim's houses were gradually looted and destroyed. The Court held that property rights must be viewed as indivisible from economic and social rights, and are violated when housing is affected as it was in this case.[41] The damage affected legal security of tenure, and the physical habitability of their houses. The Court held that the normative basis for an Inter-American right to housing can be found within the content of Articles 26 ACHR, Article XI of the ADRDM and Article 34-k OAS Charter.[42]

Justice Ferrer-Mac-Gregor's concurring opinion in *Yarce*, however, noted that the IACtHR overlooks its own precedents on economic damages – and the vulnerability context highlighted in cases where the intrusive activity of perpetrators destroyed victims' property.[43] Hence, in order to be effective, the interpretation of Articles 21 and 22 ACHR, and the above-mentioned AMRDM social rights, must take into consideration facts of vulnerability: economic deprivation, lack of basic services, gender violence, insecurity, extrajudicial executions and other conditions provoked by actions, omissions and orders of the State.

In my view, the earliest cases on dignified life decided by the IACtHR, discussed above, contained an original interpretation of Article 4 ACHR, but – at the same time – failed to invoke or engage with concepts on decent living and adequate standards coming out of Article 11 ICESCR.[44] However, *vida digna* emerged as a part of the indirect interpretation of social rights, and unveiled the legal possibility to discuss its relationship with the concept of living conditions in the Inter-American understanding of the right to life, on a level playing field, for children.

[41] *Yarce and others v Colombia*, Concurring Opinion of Justice Eduardo Ferrer Mac-Gregor, para 41.

[42] ibid paras 99–101, 145, 148. From *Suarez Peralta* to *Lhaka Honhat*, through his concurring opinions, Justice Ferrer Mac-Gregor posits a systematic and evolutionary interpretation, derived from the regional and international treaties signed by Member States demonstrating a consistent legal and political will that grants an autonomous existence of each right and therefore its justiciability before national and regional courts.

[43] Noting the cases of *El Mozote Massacres v El Salvador* [25 October 2012] IACtHR, Merits; *Massacres of the Cacarica River Basin v Colombia* [20 November 2013] IACtHR, Merits; *Yakye Axa* (n 26) and *Sawhoyamaxa* (n 27); the cases of *Barrios Family v Venezuela* and *Uzcategui et al v Venezuela* [3 September 2012]. IACtHR, *Yarce and others v Colombia*, Merits, paras 43–46.

[44] There are no current approaches to the right to an adequate standard of living in Mexico, Chile or Brazil. The exception is the Colombian Constitutional Court, where we find judgments on dignified life and 'decent housing' for persons with disabilities in the cases T-416/01(Judgment 26 April 2001), T-664/10 (Judgment 20 August 2010), T-239/2016 (Judgment 16 May 2016).

B. Economic Position and the Right to Continuous Improvement of Living Conditions

Until 2016, there were significant Inter-American allusions to, and arguments based on, international interpretations of the adequate standard of living. These shaped the contours of Indigenous rights, the right to life, to social security and education at the IACtHR. However, there remained a substantial a gap between such considerations, and a common denominator presented in many cases: victims suffered economic exclusion and poverty, which facilitated the human rights violations they suffered.

In 2016, the IACtHR issued its judgment in *Hacienda Brazil Verde v Brazil*,[45] in which the concept of economic discrimination blossomed as a normative category enshrined within Article 1(1) ACHR. Article 1(1) states:

> 1. The States Parties to this Convention undertake to respect the rights and freedoms recognized herein and to ensure to all persons subject to their jurisdiction the free and full exercise of those rights and freedoms, without any discrimination for reasons of race, color, sex, language, religion, political or other opinion, national or social origin, economic status, birth, or any other social condition.

In the merits of *Brazil Verde*, the IACtHR recognised patterns of historic discrimination on grounds of economic status (poverty) suffered by the enslaved people. It relied on Articles 1(1), 3, 5, 6(1) and 7 ACHR. Justices Ferrer Mac-Gregor and Odio Benito highlighted the individual conditions of the victims and the context in which the human rights violations occurred: illiteracy, poverty, no access to justice and economic deprivation.[46]

Considering the prohibition of discrimination due to economic status enshrined in Article 1 ACHR, the reasoned vote also distinguishes four aspects of structural discrimination already noted by the IACtHR in other cases. First, a group of persons who have been historically excluded. Second, inability to access basic conditions of human development stemming from this exclusion. Third, the fact that intergenerational exclusion suffered by the victims may be located in a specific geographical zone. Finally, that the group of persons are affected by direct or indirect actions and State omissions.[47] In a substantive way, the reasoning set the scheme of discrimination on grounds of economic position linked to the lack of basic necessities: housing, education, health, public services, culture

[45] *Hacienda Brazil Verde Brazil v Brazil* [20 October 2016] IACtHR.

[46] A background of victims living in poverty can be observed in the merits of *Reeducation Institute v Paraguay* [19 November 2009] IACtHR; *Servellon García v Honduras* [21 September 2006] IACtHR; *Moiwana v Suriname* [15 June 2005] IACtHR; *Ximenes Lopes v Brazil* [4 July 2006] IACtHR; *Rosendo Cantú et al v México* [31 August 2010] IACtHR; *Furlan and others v Argentina* [31 August 2012] IACtHR; *Yean and Bosico v Dominican Republic* [8 September 2005] IACtHR; *Gonzales Lluy* (n 36), *Brazil Verde* (n 45) cf *Separate Opinion of Justices E Ferrer Mac-Gregor and E Odio Benito*, paras 27–42.

[47] *Brazil Verde* (n 45) para 80.

and social security, 'goods that configure the individual economic condition'.[48] This approach would provide a consolidated framework in fostering a social rights scheme when structural conditions of marginalisation – on the whole life of individuals or groups neglected by States for a long period – are exposed before courts. The reasoning highlighted how the economic position (poverty) of the victims opened up the potential for them to be subjected to slavery, as the ultimate violation of their human rights.[49]

Brazil Verde thus offers two essential normative features of economic discrimination as a matter subject to legal scrutiny. The first, and substantive one, is that the prohibition of economic discrimination has an autonomous normative ground in the ACHR. The second emerges from the multiple omissions, lack of due diligence, and lack of legislation that prevents rights holders from obtaining a life under better conditions of work, housing, education and so on. However, the majority of the court held that economic position was not justiciable, and that only the right to non-discrimination was violated.[50] Nonetheless, *Brazil Verde* was a useful development in the IACtHR's reasoning. It established a causal relationship between the victim's dignity, and the economic context of the victim in which the human rights violations occurred.

III. DIRECT JUSTICIABILITY OF ECONOMIC AND SOCIAL RIGHTS AND THE RIGHT TO CONTINUOUS IMPROVEMENT OF LIVING CONDITIONS: SYNERGIES

In late 2017, the IACtHR issued two landmark decisions on the justiciability of economic and social rights: *Lagos del Campo v Peru*[51] and *Petroperu v Peru*,[52] in which the Court declared for the first time the violation of social rights envisaged in Articles 1, 2(1) 26, and 29(d) ACHR, in connection with the San Salvador Protocol.[53] Following its expansive trend in interpreting social rights, the IACtHR delivered the advisory opinion OC-23/17. The Opinion sets out a framework which includes duties to protect, prevent damages and grant environmental rights, which were linked to health (including both physical and spiritual dimensions of well-being) in order to ensure a dignified life.[54]

OC-23/17 focused on how States have specific duties to protect the right to life and personal integrity when they carry on activities that produce industrial

[48] ibid para 54.
[49] ibid paras 91, 100.
[50] ibid para 508.
[51] [31 August 2017] IACtHR, Merits.
[52] [23 November 2017] IACtHR, Merits.
[53] See the method of direct interpretation of *Lagos del Campo* discussed in De Paz González (n 19) 158–60.
[54] The dignified life approach resurfaced in OC-23/17 linked to due diligence duties of international humanitarian and environmental law, and centred on the life, health, and personal integrity of the human being. OC-23/17 [2017] IACtHR, paras 109–10, 123–30.

waste in ways that affect the quality of access to water, food sources and consequently may endanger subsistence of individuals and communities.[55] The IACtHR referred to operative conditions on the due diligence principle regarding environmental rights, arising under international law. These included the prevention and precautionary principles, duties to cooperate with other States, and procedural duties to protect environmental and the other human rights, recognising their interdependence.[56] The IACtHR argued that procedural guarantees of the right to life are essential when activities and projects could damage the environment, and thus the integrity of life for individuals and groups. In this vein, the court linked the right to a safe environment to the right to information and political participation (when dealing with infrastructure projects from the early stages of the activities), and the Court highlighted the importance of making remedies effective when environmental rights violations occur.[57]

In my view, OC-23/17 opened a new approach that connects the current scope of the right to life in procedural terms to implement, develop and interpret environmental duties in domestic jurisdictions.[58] These new guidelines refresh the interdependence of civil, political and social rights. For instance, the right to political participation is linked to the right to health and to the right to a safe environment, on the legal basis of Articles 1(1) 4, 13, 8, 25, 26, and 29 ACHR, linked to international law.

A. Jurisprudential Basis to Set a Normative Floor for the Right to Continuous Improvement of Living Conditions

Between 2018 and early 2020, the IACtHR issued a number of important decisions expanding its economic and social rights doctrine: *Poblete Vilches v Chile*, *Cuscul Pivaral v Guatemala*,[59] *Muelle Flores v Peru*[60] and *Lhaka Honhat communities v Argentina*.[61] These judgments set out economic and social rights parameters which could define contours of a right to continuous improvement of living conditions. The starting point is to acknowledge that, so far, the new IACtHR doctrine on social rights only has implicit elements that could set a floor for the right to continuous improvement of living conditions.

[55] ibid para 117.
[56] ibid para 125.
[57] ibid para 211.
[58] So far, only the Mexican Supreme Court has invoked the legal basis of OC-23/17 and dimensions of individual/communal protection of the environment to halt an eco-park which would have destroyed a mangrove (and its environmental services) in Tamaulipas. See *Amparo en Revisión 307/2016* (2018) *Suprema Corte de Justicia de la Nación, 1ª Sala*, paras 70–80.
[59] *Cuscul Pivaral v Guatemala* [23 August 2018] IACtHR, Merits.
[60] *Muelle Flores v Peru* [6 March 2019] IACtHR, Merits.
[61] *Lhaka Honhat v Argentina* [6 February 2020] IACtHR, Merits.

Therefore, two positive indicators setting the cornerstone for the right to continuous improvement of living conditions can be seen. The first one is the integration of Article 26 ACHR with the right to education, Indigenous rights, environmental rights, health rights, social security and the right to food, envisaged within international human rights law. The second is the argumentative basis for the adequate standards (such as availability, accessibility and progressivity) provided in the CESCR's General Comments, which are regularly invoked by the Court and linked to Articles 26 and 29(d) ACHR. This trend is very likely to continue in future judgments, to create a complete basis of duties to merge substantive and procedural guidelines on social rights and the right to continuous improvement of living conditions, in situations which may include the ingredient of economic discrimination.

The above-mentioned indicators are being developed in recent social rights cases. For instance, in *Poblete Vilches v Chile* the IACtHR took the 'adequate standards' approach provided by the CESCR to study violations of Article 26 ACHR. The IACtHR hooked up guidelines of availability, accessibility, quality and acceptability to the substantial and procedural elements of the right to health[62] and settled three conditions of 'essential health services' that States must provide to their population. That is, they must be provided on an integral quality basis, they must be efficient, and there must be continuous improvement in the provision of them. These normative considerations apply for both public and private services.[63] Another important argument of the IACtHR in *Poblete Vilches* is the essential value of health services for elderly people in emergency situations, and the integral quality of health services they must have.[64] The value given to health services can be seen in two critical situations: quality of health services improves every aspect of an elderly person's life and it is also useful to ameliorate vulnerability situations which exist due to their physical, economic and potential ill health limitations.[65] In the background, *Poblete Vilches* demonstrates a key point on Chilean health services when dealing with elderly people: such services must be provided – by public or private agencies – in terms of immediate obligations under non-discriminatory basis.[66]

Following this trend, *Cuscul Pivaral v Guatemala* directly interrogated the State's obligations of progressive realisation. The outcome was twofold: It provided an autonomous interpretation of the right to health and recognised the consequences of the lack of healthcare services on the life of persons

[62] The substantial arguments were drawn from CESCR's General Comments 3, 5, 6, 15, 16, 18, 19 and 20. *Poblete Vilches v Chile* [2018] IACtHR, Merits, paras 115, 121. Footnotes omitted.
[63] ibid para 118.
[64] ibid paras 126–27, 174.
[65] ibid paras 131, 140.
[66] ibid 175.

living with HIV.[67] For the very first time in the IACtHR, *Cuscul Pivaral* invoked the international legal basis of progressivity when States deal with healthcare services for persons suffering a mortal disease, and held that Guatemala must apply them not only by legal but by technical and operative means.[68] In order to strengthen its arguments, the IACtHR reasoned that international normative sources make the right to health 'operative' under the 'adequate standards' of availability, accessibility and quality of health services established in CESCR's General comment No 14.[69] It connected these standards to Articles 2, 26 and 29(d) ACHR. Through this approach, the IACtHR considered the requirements of Article 2(1) ICESCR and CESCR's General Comment No 14.[70]

Another example of how the IACtHR has taken argumentative insights from international human rights law and the CESCR's approach to adequate standards, is *Muelle Flores v Peru*. In this case, the IACtHR unveiled the existing content of social security derived from Articles 45(b) OAS Charter and Article xvi of the ADRDM, which it connected to the concrete adequate standards of social security in CESCR General Comment No 19.[71] This method allowed the IACtHR to set out normative scope for the right to social security (which is not mentioned in the ACHR). Secondly, following CESCR General Comment No 3, the IACtHR shaped two types of obligations: those of immediate character (eg to provide social security on the basis of equality) and those of a progressive nature, requiring improvement and the taking of steps toward the realisation of the right.[72] The IACtHR identified elements of an adequate standard of social security. These are: (i) access to a pension system supervised by the State (whether public or private) which provides adequate economic and health benefits for living; (ii) the system must meet criteria of accessibility and availability; (iii) the scheme must provide benefits for elderly people; finally (iv) effective remedies must be provided.[73] Following this reasoning, the IACtHR declared a violation of the rights to personal integrity, access to justice, and to social security.[74] In sum, *Muelle Flores* showed that a deprivation of pension to an older person, and that person's exclusion from health services diminishes the person's standard of living, due to age and weak economic position.

[67] The judgment strongly emphasises the autonomy of social rights envisaged in Art 26 ACHR, and the right to health recognised in several instruments of international human rights law. Separate Opinion of RF Caldas and Concurring Opinion of E Ferrer MacGregor. *Cuscul Pivaral* (n 59) paras 74, 98, 127. However, in the merits, the Court concluded that the claims to dignified life were already analysed within the framework of the right to health. ibid, Merits, para 160.

[68] *Cuscul Pivaral* (n 59) paras 100, 141–48.

[69] ibid para 106.

[70] ibid paras 80, 106.

[71] The substantive content reads: 'b) Work is a right and a social duty, it gives dignity to the one who performs it, and it should be performed under conditions, including a system of fair wages, that ensure life, health, and a decent standard of living for the worker and his family …'.

[72] *Muelle Flores* (n 60) paras 187–90.

[73] ibid para 192.

[74] ibid para 208.

The merits of *Muelle Flores* offer at least three new elements that can create a new set of specific duties attaching to the adequate standards of each social right. The first element is the autonomous analysis of each right envisaged within Article 26, linked to other international treaties according to Article 29(d) ACHR. The second is to read in 'adequate standards' according to CESCR's guidelines on availability and accessibility of services. The third is the procedural method the Court uses to study the interdependent relation between the scope of progressivity of each social right (at both communitarian and individual levels) and the effectiveness of the measures taken by States to prevent persons/groups suffering exclusion of basic services and economic deprivation.

As observed in *Muelle Flores* and *Cuscul Pivaral*, the IACtHR is attempting to develop systematic ways to give an autonomous interpretation to economic and social rights, considering the binding effects of international law on those rights. The new social rights judgments show how the IACtHR is taking specific guidelines, principles and criteria from the CESCR's adequate standards methodology, which are reinforcing the justiciability and interpretation of social rights at the Inter-American forum. On the one hand, international sources fill the gaps in Article 26 and provide specific content on the aims and normative content of education, Indigenous rights, housing, healthcare and social security in terms of accessibility, quality, progressivity and adaptability. On the other, the IACtHR provides a set of duties for States to persuade them to enact legislation and public policies and create remedies or provide reparations for economic and social rights violations, according to the general obligations of Articles 1, 2 and 63 ACHR.

Turning to a final judgment, on Indigenous rights, we can see noteworthy points on the economic and social rights violations of a group of 132 communities of the Argentinian *Chaco*, whose land and territories were invaded by meat producers and state infrastructure. In *Lhaka Honhat v Argentina*, the IACtHR deployed three new important arguments. The first is a complete approach to Indigenous territorial (property) rights linked to sufficient and nutritious food, and including a right to a consultation process, which the Court argued must be understood as an integral part of their cultural rights. The second refers to the importance of environment and cultural rights, as a part of an adequate right to life, including the integral elements of adequate food and water. The third is the set of specific reparations ordered by the IACtHR to reintegrate and improve enjoyment of each right breached.[75]

The core reasoning in *Lhaka Honhat* was the normative recognition of the right to cultural identity, linked to the community's property and means

[75] The judgment established specific remedies, reparations and plans to be implemented by Argentina on the legal tenure of lands, cultural damage, consultation process, water, and the environment. *Lhaka Honhat* (n 61) paras 307, 321–49.

of subsistence, under three 'adequate standards' international guidelines:[76] adequate access to food, quality of water and a safe environment within the territories of the community. Regarding environmental rights, water and health rights, the IACtHR recalled the duties of prevention, supervision and accountability in OC-23/17, considering the critical situation and damage caused within the territory of the 132 communities, and ordered Argentina to repair such damage, creating action plans to prevent further violations and preserve natural resources.[77]

On the adequate standard of food, the IACtHR defined general obligations recognised in the content of Articles 34(j) OAS Charter, Article 11 ICESCR, and the concrete provisions on security, availability and protection of adequate access to food, envisaged in CESCR General Comment No 12. On the right to water (considered as a public good) and its schemes of availability, quality and accessibility, the Court's reasoning was guided by CESCR General Comment No 15, emphasising duties to ameliorate critical conditions in the communities which were facing interference with and pollution of their water resources caused by third parties.[78]

To sum up, current IACtHR approaches to economic and social rights are connected to the content and rules of interpretation of Articles 26 and 29 ACHR, and linked to positive obligations for the rights that are set out at the international level and that define concrete ways of complying with an adequate standard of education, healthcare services, social security and labour rights. The above-mentioned cases are being approached by the IACtHR through the lens of economic and social rights with a genuine method of direct and internationalist interpretation, and here we can find emerging synergies to study intersectional factors that lead to lack of health services, lack of education, unsafe environment, discrimination and poverty of the victims.

B. Legal Provisions and Possibilities for the Right to Continuous Improvement of Living Conditions

Bearing in mind the IACtHR's recent economic and social rights jurisprudence and the adoption of CESCR guidelines under the general obligations of Articles 1 and 2, and the specific social rights obligations in Articles 26 and 29 ACHR, the question is whether the argumentative and legal foundations are enough to set a floor for the right to continuous improvement of living conditions in the Inter-American Court?

To answer the question, we must consider two factors. The first is the increasing integration of economic and social rights derived from Articles 26

[76] ibid, paras 207–9.
[77] ibid.
[78] ibid paras 220–30.

and 29 ACHR and the international provisions, through attention to the CESCR's General Comments regarding adequate standards on accessibility, adaptability, affordability and progressivity as general principles. These categories have been the regular basis of the IACtHR's reasoning in *Poblete Vilches v Chile*, *Muelle Flores v Peru*, *Cuscul Pivaral v Guatemala*, and *Lhaka Honhat v Argentina*.The second is the economic element of non-discrimination regarding 'economic status' enshrined in Article 1 ACHR. This one has been invoked in cases where discrimination, exclusion and economic deprivation of victims made them vulnerable, while decreasing their capacity to access an adequate standard of life, such as in *Brazil Verde*.[79]

To determine if the right to continuous improvement of living conditions can be integrated with the economic and social rights doctrine of the IACtHR, one must consider what concrete substantive and procedural guidelines can be articulated on the same basis. My general assumption is that the old doctrine of *vida digna* or dignified life can be reshuffled in cases where a State has responsibility to ameliorate conditions of vulnerability of those who claim violations, who are living in situations lacking healthcare services, education, social security, housing, drinking water, and so on. As a result of the cases previously analysed, I propose the following framework of concrete directives towards the right to continuous improvement of living conditions.[80]

My framework has four key aspects. The first is a procedural analysis of a vulnerability context that must be carried out under the intersectionality method to unveil those convergent factors which operate together to increase human rights violations and decrease the quality of victims' living conditions. The outcome of an intersectionality method would have legal consequences with twofold objectives. The first is to determine specific reparations for each violation experienced by the victims/survivors. The second would allow the IACtHR to make certain orders seeking legislative and public remedies to improve the living conditions involved in the cases.

Second, the normative integration of the content set out in Articles 1, 2, 26 and 29(d) ACHR, connected to the interpretation of Articles 2(1) and 11(1) ICESCR and 27(2) CRC, may be entrenched in a set of positive obligations on States, to avoid economic status as a form of discrimination. In addition, such normative aspects must be complemented through the application of the CESCR's general comments to specify duties for health, education, housing, Indigenous and children's rights. This should be done under a specific framework

[79] See discussion at section II.B above.

[80] In advance, we must consider the ambiguity and conceptual unclearness of the right, which has undermined its implementation at international and national levels. For this reason, academic discussion and proposals are needed to provide clarity. On the lack of conceptual clarity see Lott, chapter seven in this volume, who explains how the lack of clarity on the right's scope and content has negatively impacted the right's implementation, despite the ICESCR's 40-year history.

of the 'adequate standards' of availability, accessibility, progressivity and quality for each right.

Third, the economic approach that shapes the right to continuous improvement of living conditions under an Inter-American legal perspective, must be understood as part of the 'full exercise' obligations established in Article 1 ACHR. According to the prohibition of economic discrimination recognised in Article 1 ACHR, and following the Separate Opinion of Justices Ferrer Mac-Gregor and Odio Benito in *Brazil Verde*, poverty presents three aspects: it is often associated with persons in contexts of vulnerability; it implies multiple discriminatory conditions; and poverty itself should be seen as a human rights violation.[81]

Fourth, bearing in mind that all ACHR current Member States to have accepted ACHR contentious jurisdiction have also ratified ICESCR,[82] under the interpretative directives of Article 29(d) ACHR,[83] the IACtHR is able to consider the concept of 'adequate standard of living' envisaged in Article 11 ICESCR. In this way, the IACtHR can provide effective guidance on adequate housing, health, education and food, in order to shape its own jurisprudential basis of the right to continuous improvement of living conditions, as it has already done with direct economic and social rights interpretation. In fact, such legal reasoning has been articulated by the IACtHR in a more visible way in *Lhaka Honhat v Argentina*, through the interdependent approach and reparations for cultural-environmental rights: the right to food, the right to drinking water and the territorial rights of the communities, which must be satisfied and respected by Argentina and third parties.

C. Towards an Inter-American Right to Continuous Improvement of Living Conditions

On the substantive content of the right to continuous improvement of living conditions, Goldblatt points to the main features of 'living conditions' as 'those goods/supports to enable a decent life'.[84] The IACtHR recognises that provision of education, health services, social security and cultural life (especially for Indigenous peoples) are part of States' general and specific obligations and, therefore, justiciable. This set of social rights could be integrated as the minimum floor for every person or group to ensure the 'conditions' required

[81] *Brazil Verde, Reasoned vote of Justices Ferrer Mac-Gregor and Odio Benito* (n 46) para 44.

[82] See the list at <https://indicators.ohchr.org> accessed 19 June 2020.

[83] Which states: 'No provision of this Convention shall be interpreted as: … excluding or limiting the effect that the American Declaration of the Rights and Duties of Man and other international acts of the same nature may have'.

[84] See Goldblatt, chapter eleven in this volume.

to achieve a decent life. At the same time, the integration of social rights with the right to continuous improvement of living conditions might unchain more effective ways of making reparations once intersectional violations of human rights are identified.

The economic element of the Inter-American approach that could provide a basis for the right to continuous improvement of living conditions and its normative attempt to tackle poverty, is the prohibition of economic discrimination. Graham discuss how the right to continuous improvement of living conditions provides a human rights-based approach to poverty and 'results in a broad interpretation of the subject matter of the right, which in turn focuses upon the realisation of other human rights'.[85] Showing a genuine concern for how poverty affects the most vulnerable, the Inter-American jurisprudence shows that poverty itself is a form of discrimination (based on economic status), which unchains other human rights violations. This conception therefore requires a systematic reading of Articles 1, 4, 26 and 29 ACHR, to give complete meaning to the 'right to life' as requiring economic inclusion in order to fulfil other human rights at the level of adequacy.[86]

The second element rests on the connection between Articles 26 and 29(d) ACHR and the clauses of 'adequate standard of living', enshrined in Article 11 ICESCR. Through a series of cases, the IACtHR has built strong arguments on economic and social rights, using the CESCR's comments in order to define specific obligations or qualities that States must consider on education, health services, social security, Indigenous rights and the right to a healthy environment.[87] Through this approach, the IACtHR has informed and enriched its own jurisprudence using international law in a very consistent way, although within national courts of the region there are no major references to the CESCR's opinions to measure the influx of international jurisprudence. However, I consider that under a universalist and indivisible conception of human rights, a two-way traffic of arguments from both the IACtHR and national courts to treaty bodies must be carried out to expand on the content of and obligations for social rights.[88]

[85] See Graham, chapter four in this volume.

[86] For instance, employment, social security, access to justice, education, a safe environment, political rights and so on.

[87] With respect to Indigenous rights, as of its early Indigenous case-law (including the right to a proper consultation), the IACtHR frequently takes ILO standards as a reference to justify its interpretation in a given context of the case and reinforce its credibility. See B Duhaime and É Décoste, 'De Genève à San José: les normes de l'OIT et le système interaméricain de protection des droits humains' (2020) 159 *Revue internationale du Travail* 540.

[88] In fact, within its opinions, the CESCR has not taken the IACtHR's legal reasoning on social rights as a matter of reference. Possibly because the IACtHR's contentious jurisdictions and the CESCR have different sets of rules (for instance, a State's acceptance of the Additional Protocol) and standards when creating jurisprudence. Within national courts of Latin America, general comments are barely mentioned.

The third element is the improvement of living conditions. The term 'aligns with the idea of progressive realisation',[89] and this is not an unfamiliar Inter-American concept. In *Cuscul Pivaral*, the IACtHR recognised that the progressivity principle legally binds Member States to take concrete and effective steps to improve economic and social rights conditions. Through a systematic reading of Articles 26 ACHR and 11 ICESCR, the IACtHR can adopt the concept and qualities related to 'improvement of living conditions' within its legal reasoning to pin down how Member States are protecting – or not – social rights and the right to life itself.

Objections to the right to continuous improvement of living conditions may surface from two possible critiques: its lack of an accurate legal entitlement within the ACHR, and its lack of adequacy to solve a big issue such as poverty. Moreover, we must consider its current underdevelopment in international human rights theory and practice.[90] However, the lack of legal entitlement can be solved through the evolutive and systematic, teleological and universalist interpretation of the ACHR. Regarding the problem of poverty, it is true that law alone cannot solve it, but it is a useful tool to identify blind areas of public policy, and legal arguments can be used to clarify State obligations on the subject.

The IACtHR has showed itself willing to invoke CESCR's General Comments to give a concrete shape and meaning to adequate standards on health, education, social security and Indigenous rights, implicitly referred to in Articles 21, 26 and 29 ACHR. Thus, due to the IACtHR's direct interpretation of social rights and its growing allusions to the CESCR's work to specify State duties on the issue, the right to continuous improvement of living conditions has tangible chances to be integrated into the Inter-American system, both at conceptual and normative levels.

IV. CONCLUSION

Looking at the current landscape of poverty and deprivation within ACHR Member States, the right to continuous improvement of living conditions fits well into discussions to continue the direct effect of economic and social rights at the Inter-American level. This direct effect is anchored in the general and specific obligations derived from Articles 1, 2, 4, 26 and 29 ACHR, and inextricably linked to the progressive obligations provided by Articles 2 and 11 ICESCR. Such a conception will refresh the Inter-American understanding of the 'dignified life' approach in a useful and significant way in current cases before the court.

[89] Goldblatt, chapter eleven in this volume.

[90] But, as Hohmann points out, the CESCR is issuing guidelines, general comments and concluding observations containing implicit assumptions on poverty, progressive obligations and adequate standards to improve state's practice and *opinio juris*. See Hohmann, chapter two in this volume.

As has been explained in this chapter we can draw out an emerging interpretation of social rights with various substantive guidelines: the prohibition on economic discrimination, the adequate standards of each social right, and the progressivity principle. Such guidelines come from the content of Articles 26 and 29 ACHR linked to Article 11 of ICESCR. From this normative integration, an Inter-American right to continuous improvement of living conditions may blossom. Throughout the proposed framework, IACtHR might shape new dimensions of the right to life, understood in terms of a meaningful existence of both individuals and communities from Latin America. Drawing on the Inter-American experience, and progressive approaches to economic and social rights, the right to continuous improvement of living conditions is the missing link at this very critical moment in which millions of people from ACHR Member States plead for decent socioeconomic conditions of life.

10

(Dis)Continuous Improvement

Canada, Indigenous Peoples, Lobster and Child Welfare

JEFFERY HEWITT[1]

I. OVERVIEW

IN THIS CHAPTER I survey ways by which Canada limits Indigenous peoples' access to a right to continuous improvement of living conditions in Article 11(1) of the International Covenant on Economic Social and Cultural Rights (ICESCR).[2] As a frame for this examination, I consider a 1999 Supreme Court of Canada decision on eighteenth century peace and friendship treaties, and a 2016 Canadian human rights tribunal watershed decision citing Canada's discrimination against First Nation children in the child welfare system. Together these two case studies show how access to a right to continuous improvement of living conditions in Canada is limited with respect to Indigenous peoples by the State. They arguably offer insight into the ways in which Canada interprets a right to continuous improvement of living conditions without regard for Indigenous peoples, laws and perspectives. Taken together these case studies also demonstrate some of the ways in which rights in Article 11(1) are regressing.

[1] A different version of select portions of this chapter first appeared in my LLM thesis 'The Failure of the Canadian Human Rights Regime to Provide Remedies for Indigenous Peoples: Enough Time Has Passed' (2015). I have updated those portions here. I am also grateful for the research work of Emily King. I am grateful for both Luke Graham and Meghan Campbell's comments, thoughtful interventions, and supportive discussions, as well as comments and patience from Jessie Hohmann and Beth Goldblatt. Any errors are solely mine.

[2] International Covenant on Economic, Social and Cultural Rights, 16 December 1996, 993 UNTS 3 which provides: 'The States Parties to the present Covenant recognize the right of everyone to an adequate standard of living for himself and his family, including adequate food, clothing and housing, and to the continuous improvement of living conditions …'.

For the purposes of this chapter, the right to continuous improvement of living conditions is considered a human right held both collectively and individually by everyone, including Indigenous peoples. A right to continuous improvement of living conditions is characterised as inclusive of other economic, social and cultural rights,[3] which are to be ensured by the State, not restricted.[4] Economic, social and cultural rights are also guaranteed in a range of other international human rights instruments, including the United Nations Declaration on the Rights of Indigenous Peoples (UNDRIP).[5] However, Canada has yet to implement the UNDRIP domestically.[6]

I juxtapose Canada's action or inaction with respect to Indigenous peoples and ICESCR's right to continuous improvement of living conditions with Indigenous laws present both at the time of the treaties considered by the Supreme Court of Canada in *Marshall*[7] and as evidenced in the *Caring Society* decision[8] of the Canadian Human Rights Tribunal (CHRT). Finally, I conclude with an offering of a few potential remedies as a means of opening up more access for Indigenous peoples to a right to continuous improvement of living conditions, including the adoption of the UNDRIP to ensure that the State honours treaties with Indigenous peoples in a way that balances the current asymmetrical relations as defined exclusively by the State.

Like other legal orders, Indigenous legal orders are structured within larger economic, social and cultural frameworks. This is echoed in the wording of the Preamble of the ICESCR, which states:

> Recognizing that, in accordance with the Universal Declaration of Human Rights, the ideal of free human beings enjoying freedom from fear and want can only be achieved if conditions are created whereby everyone may enjoy his economic, social and cultural rights, as well as his civil and political rights ...[9]

[3] In relation to characterising the right as a freedom, the Preamble of the Covenant recognises economic, social and cultural rights derive from the 'inherent dignity of the human person' and that 'the ideal of free human beings enjoying freedom of fear and want can only be achieved if conditions are created whereby everyone may enjoy his economic, social and cultural rights, as well as civil and political rights'. Furthermore, the overarching principles of the Covenant are: (1) equality and non-discrimination in regard to the enjoyment of all the rights set forth in the treaty; and (2) States Parties have an obligation to respect, protect and fulfil economic, social and cultural rights.

[4] For more see Committee on Economic, Social and Cultural Rights, General Comment No 21, 'Right of everyone to take part in a cultural life (Art 15, para 1a, of the Convention on Economic, Social and Cultural Rights)', 21 December 2009, E/C.12/GC/21. Article 15(1) provides further context for Art 11(1) in relation to Indigenous peoples.

[5] United Nations Declaration on the Rights of Indigenous Peoples, 13 December 2007 (A/RES/61/295), including Arts 1, 2, 4, and 17.

[6] At the time of writing, the UNDRIP is currently being tabled in Canada as Bill C-15, <https://parl.ca/DocumentViewer/en/43-2/bill/C-15/first-reading>. I leave a critical examination of Bill C-15 and Canada's approaches to implementing UNDRIP through s 35(1), of the Constitution Act, 1982 for a future paper.

[7] *R v Marshall* [1999] 3 SCR 456.

[8] *First Nations Child and Family Caring Society of Canada v Canada (AG)*, 2016 CHRT 2.

[9] ICESCR (n 2), Preamble, para 4.

Legal orders are not the same as legal systems, the latter of which are the institutions and apparatuses necessary to implement, enforce, and uphold a broader legal order.[10] International documents such as the ICESCR, the United Nations' Universal Declaration of Human Rights (UDHR),[11] and the UNDRIP are generated through States, which historically exclude Indigenous Nations. With the exception of UNDRIP, Indigenous peoples were not directly involved in drafting and voted on none of these. Indigenous peoples were also not centrally involved in the construction of the western-based legal structures such as courts and tribunals, established solely for the purposes of interpreting such agreements.

In what is now known as Canada there are multi-juridical systems, namely common law, civil law and Indigenous legal orders.[12] However, common and civil legal systems, constructed without the participation of Indigenous peoples, are not sufficiently equipped to engage with Indigenous legal orders. Indigenous legal orders not only structurally differ given the different worldviews upon which they are premised,[13] but also interpret and respond to international documents differently than Canadian legal systems. In short, Indigenous legal structures would not be occupied with performing legal gymnastics that uphold the mythology of the doctrine of discovery[14] giving rise to the assertion of Crown sovereignty over Indigenous peoples in Canada. How might this exclusion of Indigenous participation in international and domestic legal systems impact Article 11(1) of the ICESCR in relation to Indigenous peoples? In part, the answer lies in Canada's master narrative of Crown sovereignty over Indigenous lands, resources and peoples. Rather than recognise and engage with Indigenous laws as law and Indigenous nations as nations, the general Canadian approach – by and large – has been to place the Canadian legal system and Indigenous legal orders in a 'reconciliation' conversation, as though they are on par with one another. They are not. Indeed, the Supreme Court of Canada has positioned section 35 of the Constitution Act, 1982 as a means to reconcile Indigenous peoples and laws to the sovereignty of the Crown. Yet, the Court does not offer a clear legal analysis for its ongoing acceptance of Crown sovereignty[15] or for assuming the validity of the doctrine of discovery.

Such a constitutional 'dialogue' persists in that it offers promises of progress but may merely be a diversion of the imperial power.[16] As we shall see with

[10] V Napoleon, 'Thinking about Indigenous Legal Orders', *Dialogues on Human Rights and Legal Pluralism* (Dordrecht 2013) 229–45.

[11] UN General Assembly, *Universal Declaration of Human Rights*, 10 December 1948, 217 A (III).

[12] J Borrows, *Canada's Indigenous Constitution* (University of Toronto Press 2010).

[13] L Little Bear, 'Jagged Worldviews Colliding' (2000) *Reclaiming Indigenous Voice and Vision* 77.

[14] For more on the doctrine of discovery see: RJ Miller, 'The Doctrine of Discovery in American Indian Law' (2005) 42 *Idaho Law Review* 1.

[15] J Borrows, 'Frozen Rights in Canada: Constitutional Interpretation and the Trickster' (1997) 22(1) *American Indian Law Review* 37–64.

[16] For a good primer on Indigenous peoples and Canadian law see C Vowel, *Indigenous Writes: A Guide to First Nations, Métis, and Inuit Issues in Canada* (Portage & Main Press 2016).

respect to treaties, for example, this allows western legal orders and systems to offer only a western-based pathway for Indigenous peoples' claims while simultaneously asserting universality of western laws and systems. Among the outcomes is an ongoing suppression of Indigenous legal orders and a failing of Canada to comply with its own rule of law. This coordinated approach to diminishing Indigenous claims and asserting Canadian law over Indigenous peoples minimises access to a right to continuous improvement of living conditions. In this chapter I will discuss how in *Marshall* we see Canada interfering with economic freedoms, and in the *Caring Society* decision there is a denial of social and cultural freedoms along with economic injustice. Canada might cite a handful of economically successful First Nations as a national 'success' in relation to a continuous improvement of living conditions for Indigenous peoples. This would ignore the economic reality that many Indigenous communities continue to be dependent on the State for core funding and services. It also belies the use of Canadian law to suppress Indigenous peoples' access to the ICESCR's Article 11, as illustrated through the following two case studies.

In this chapter, I argue that rather than cast Indigenous peoples as a perpetual problem to be solved, Indigenous laws and ways of being could more effectively contribute to the meaning of a right to continuous improvement of living conditions.

II. CASE STUDY NO 1 – *R V MARSHALL*

Treaties between Indigenous peoples and the Crown were negotiated over the course of almost two centuries, starting with the so-called peace and friendship treaties of the mid-eighteenth century in what is now Canada's east coast. Treaties and treaty interpretation continue to generate considerable legal attention in Canada's legal system.[17] However, there are relatively few scholarly contributions that explore treaties between States (such as Canada) and Indigenous nations, as treaties at international law.[18] Yet, treaties allowed for the subsequent settlement of Canada[19] with what the Royal Proclamation 1763

[17] For a good discussion on treaties between the Crown and Indigenous peoples in Canada see J Borrows and M Coyle (eds), *The Right Relationship: Reimagining the Implementation of Historical Treaties* (University of Toronto Press 2017).

[18] See J Nichols, 'Sui Generis Sovereignties: The Relationship between Treaty Interpretation and Canadian Sovereignty' (Centre for International Governance Innovation 2018); SH Venne, 'Treaties made in good faith' (2007) 34(1) *Canadian Review of Comparative Literature/Revue Canadienne de Littérature Comparée*; J Borrows and LI Rotman, 'The sui generis Nature of Aboriginal Rights: Does it Make a Difference' (1997) 36 *Alberta Law Review* 9; J Sákéj and H Youngblood, 'Sui generis and Treaty Citizenship' (2002) 6(4) *Citizenship Studies* 415–40.

[19] For a more in-depth discussion on treaties, land rights and the settlement of Canada see: J Borrows, 'Domesticating doctrines: Aboriginal peoples after the Royal Commission' (2000) 46 *McGill Law Journal* 615; M Asch, *On Being Here to Stay: Treaties and Aboriginal Rights in Canada* (University of Toronto Press 2014).

states as 'Nations or Tribes of Indians'.[20] This language of nations situates Crown recognition of Indigenous nations as nations possessed of requisite authority to engage in treaty making.

The Supreme Court of Canada (SCC) has ruled Canada's obligations under treaties are ongoing and not relegated to historical record.[21] The same Court has also declared treaties *sui generis* – different.[22] This has ultimately allowed Canada and its courts to be the sole arbitrator of treaty interpretation for treaties to which Canada (as successor from the English Crown), is only one party. It has also allowed Canadian courts to unilaterally determine the Indigenous perspective, which ultimately distorts treaties and sets aside Indigenous laws that originally allowed for the making of such treaties.[23]

Consider, for example, *Marshall*.[24] In 1999 the SCC interpreted Peace and Friendship treaties of 1760 and 1761 (the 'treaties'), as between the British Crown and the Mi'kmaq, Maliseet and Passamaquoddy Nations. It was asserted that the treaties preserved a Mi'kmaq right to fish.[25] It is worth noting, these treaties were negotiated in the years immediately prior to the Royal Proclamation, 1763, as the English Crown was at war with French forces in North America and the treaties assisted in providing a local food supply to British truck houses (a trade and supply centre for goods). In this context, the Crown understood the international element of treaty-making with the Mi'kmaq Nation and the necessity of peaceful relationships – allowing the Crown to focus on its then battles with the French. These particular treaties were negotiated to secure peace and friendship with the Mi'kmaq Nation. Such treaty relationships, as interpreted by Indigenous scholars Sharon Venne and John Borrows, incorporated a mutual exchange and reciprocity within the treaties' meaning.[26]

In this particular case, Donald Marshall, Jr was charged under the Fisheries Act[27] in 1993 with both fishing for and selling eels without a licence, as well as fishing with prohibited nets outside of the regulated fishing season. Marshall admitted to these acts and, as a member of the Mi'kmaq Nation, claimed both a treaty right and an Aboriginal right in accordance with section 35(1), Constitution Act, 1982.[28] The trial judge ruled against Marshall, finding no such

[20] Royal Proclamation, 1763, para 1. <https://www.sfu.ca/~palys/The%20Royal%20Proclamation.pdf>.

[21] *Mikisew Cree First Nation v Canada (Minister of Canadian Heritage)* [2005] 3 SCR 388.

[22] *Guerin v The Queen* [1984] 2 SCR 335 was the first ruling by the Supreme Court of Canada that described treaties between the Crown and Indigenous nations as being *sui generis*, within two years of the enactment of Canada's Constitution Act, 1982.

[23] Venne (n 18).

[24] *Marshall* (n 7).

[25] Also for the Maliseet and Passamaquoddy Nations as signatories.

[26] Venne (n 18); and J Borrows, 'Ground-rules: Indigenous Treaties in Canada and New Zealand'. Available at SSRN: <https://ssrn.com/abstract=2744928>.

[27] Fisheries Act, RSC 1985, c F-14.

[28] Section 35(1), Constitution Act, 1982, states: 'The existing aboriginal and treaty rights of the aboriginal peoples of Canada are hereby recognized and affirmed.'

treaty or Aboriginal right. The provincial appellate court upheld the trial decision. In 1999, the SCC ultimately considered the legal issue as to whether the 1760–61 treaties relied upon by Marshall granted a treaty right that included a right to catch and sell fish. The SCC overturned the prior decisions and found a limited treaty right to trade in support of a livelihood. Specifically, the SCC found the treaties included a Mi'kmaq right to a 'moderate' livelihood which includes:

> … such basics as 'food, clothing and housing, supplemented by a few amenities', but not the accumulation of wealth … It addresses day-to-day needs. This was the common intention in 1760. It is fair that it be given this interpretation today.[29]

The SCC did not opine on the meaning of 'moderate' but rather left that for Canada to take up with the Mi'kmaq Nation. To be clear, even if a 'moderate' livelihood in the context of *Marshall* meets with a standard of adequacy within Article 11(1), this does not permit the State to disregard all of the elements of the Article with respect to a right to a continuous improvement of living conditions.

The SCC established a 'large and liberal'[30] approach to treaty interpretation, which includes a determination on treaty meaning that best reconciles the interests of all parties – the Crown and Indigenous parties – at the time the treaty was negotiated and executed. This liberal interpretive approach in *Marshall* reaffirmed the SCC's reasoning in the 1996 decision of *R v Badger* wherein the Court stated treaties must 'be liberally construed and any uncertainties, ambiguities or doubtful expressions should be resolve in favour' of Indigenous parties.[31] However, rather than advance this large and liberal approach in relation to the issues in *Marshall*, and resolve the matter in favour of Indigenous parties, the SCC resolved the case in favour of the Crown. For example, the SCC could have set out the legal rationale and tests for determining how such livelihood rights might be valued in a modern world (ie value of fish to the Mi'kmaq economy during the eighteenth century in twentieth century amounts, etc). The SCC could have considered Mi'kmaq laws and rationale for entering into the treaties. Perhaps this would have included non-economic values as well such as sustainability and management of fish stocks in accordance with Mi'kmaq science and environmental management practices or the role fishing played within Mi'kmaq community structures. The SCC could have provided the State with a timeframe in which to negotiate or regulate fishing rights in accordance with both federal and Mi'kmaq laws, but instead left it open ended exclusively in favour of the State's agenda. In sum, the overall effect of the ruling was to narrowly interpret the treaties in favour of Canada, which embarked

[29] *Marshall* (n 7) para 59.
[30] ibid para 78.
[31] *R v Badger* [1996] 1 SCR 771, para 52.

on a period of massive economic and State expansion between the eighteenth and twentieth centuries, while requiring the Mi'kmaq to remain bounded to a moderate livelihood. As such, the impact of the decision is to limit access to a right to continuous improvement of living conditions for Indigenous peoples versus all other Canadians.

Such restrictions on Indigenous peoples' access to a right to continuous improvement of living conditions are further revealed following the decision in *Marshall*, in the Crown's failure to act in 1999 and change anything about the fishing rights of the Mi'kmaq nation. By the autumn of 2020, the Mi'kmaq had issued approximately five lobster fishing permits to its own members, which comprised about 300 lobster traps in total. The response from commercial lobster fisheries owning over 350,000 traps collectively, was asymmetrical, with threats and acts of violence against the small Mi'kmaq fishing boats.[32] For weeks, predominately white mobs gathered to terrorise Mi'kmaq people with relative impunity. The federal government, at the point of growing public concern over the handling of this escalating situation, appointed a 'Federal Special Representative, a neutral third-party who will communicate with and rebuild trust between commercial and Indigenous fishers … so parties can move forward toward a positive resolution'.[33]

In other words, the Crown failed to comply with even the most basic of its treaty obligations which led to the 1999 *Marshall* decision; spent the 21 years following the Supreme Court of Canada's judgment without implementation of fishing rights through negotiations with the Mi'kmaq Nation; passively allowed the situation to escalate into further violence aimed at Indigenous peoples; and then declared neutrality rather than accepting its own treaty obligations and responsibilities. The Crown's failure to act in accordance with *Marshall* resulted in the wholesale denial of even fundamentals of 'such basics as "food, clothing and housing, supplemented by a few amenities"',[34] let alone 'the accumulation of wealth'.[35] In other words, while Canada was free to evolve, the Mi'kmaq were to be frozen in time at the moment of signing the peace and friendship treaties and thereby effectively denied a right to continuous improvement of living conditions.

Even in a unilateral reimagining of treaties, the Court provided the Crown with a regulatory path of managing Mi'kmaq treaty rights by stating:

> Catch limits that could reasonably be expected to produce a moderate livelihood for individual Mi'kmaq families at present-day standards can be established by

[32] S Kilpatrick, Canadian Press, 'Mi'kmaq fisheries under attack: The story in Nova Scotia so far, and the treaty rights behind it', published 19 October 2020, updated 28 October 2020 <https://www.theglobeandmail.com/canada/article-mikmaq-fisheries-nova-scotia-treaty-rights-explainer/>.

[33] News release, 23 October 2020 <https://www.newswire.ca/news-releases/government-of-canada-appoints-federal-special-representative-to-facilitate-discussions-between-commercial-lobster-industry-and-first-nations-in-atlantic-canada-801133191.html>.

[34] *Marshall* (n 7).

[35] ibid.

> regulation and enforced without violating the treaty right. In that case, regulations would accommodate the treaty right. Such regulations would *not* constitute an infringement that would have to be justified …[36]

Still, the Crown failed to act in the wake of *Marshall*. Negotiating over the meaning of the Court's decision with the Mi'kmaq could have resulted in access to a right to continuous improvement of living conditions in 'present-day standards', which the Court did not define.

In keeping with the Court's 'large and liberal' interpretive approach, 'present day standards' must also be considered from the Mi'kmaq perspective. Similarly, consistent with *Badger*, treaty disputes must be resolved in favour of Indigenous parties. In relation to these peace and friendship treaties, it is vital to remember that Mi'kmaq laws were complex and allowed for multi-juridical systems to coexist, which were values deeply integrated into Mi'kmaq relations.[37] For the Mi'kmaq Nation, law '… is not a separate entity but operates within social and cultural organisation, and must be considered within political, economic, social and spiritual frameworks of power'.[38] This would have been the understanding of their law by the Mi'kmaq in negotiating and entering into the treaties with the Crown.

Allowing the Crown to both evolve post-war with the French since the eighteenth century into the twenty-first century while insisting Indigenous peoples – in this instance the Mi'kmaq Nation – remain 'moderate' upholds the doctrine of discovery and assumption of Crown sovereignty, which was not a term of these treaties. It supports a narrative of supremacy over Indigenous peoples and presumes Indigenous peoples do not have a right to continuous improvement of living conditions – should such improvement be anything beyond 'moderate'. It allows the Crown to do nothing.

It did not have to be this way. The Crown could have moved to protect the human rights and the dignity of the Mi'kmaq fishers and peoples from the racism at the outset or at least when it began to escalate. Instead, the Crown continued its pivot away from its own treaty obligations as affirmed by the Supreme Court of Canada and invented a narrative of a local dispute between Mi'kmaq fishers and commercial fisheries.

Though encouraging the Crown to negotiate with the Mi'kmaq Nation and beneficiaries of the treaties, the *Marshall* judgment is also a reminder of the originalist approach the Court often adopts when interpreting treaties.[39] This reasoning allows a moderate livelihood as a ceiling by which Indigenous signatories are bound, while the Crown acts with impunity. The Court in *Marshall*

[36] ibid para 60.

[37] LJ McMillan, 'Koqqwaja'ltimk: Mi'kmaq Legal Consciousness' PhD dissertation, University of British Columbia, 2002, at 413.

[38] ibid 11.

[39] J Borrows, 'Frozen Rights in Canada: Constitutional Interpretation and the Trickster' (1997) 22(1) *American Indian Law Review* 37–64.

does not consider applicable Mi'kmaq laws that would have established and regulated Mi'kmaq fishing and trade practices long before and after contact with the Crown. As noted earlier, without the benefit of considering Mi'kmaq laws and approaches to treaty-making, which would have given fuller meaning to a 'large and liberal' approach in practice, the Mi'kmaq side of the treaty equation was notably absent. The SCC did not consider Mi'kmaq laws on key matters in dispute such as management of fisheries, use of Mi'kmaq scientific or environmental knowledge, and sustainability practices (such as permitting 350 lobster traps versus 350,000). There is simply no analysis of Mi'kmaq laws in *Marshall* even though that law was relevant to the establishment of the treaties, though such trade with the Crown in the treaties is part of the facts the Court addresses in the case. Even though the SCC failed to engage with Mi'kmaq laws in *Marshall* when interpreting the contours of the peace and friendship treaties when the State failed to act, which escalated the conflict, this does not mean that Canada should fail to include Indigenous legal orders when implementing a right to continuous improvement of living conditions. Canada could, as the SCC opines (but does not itself follow) in *Marshall*, take a large and liberal approach consistent with Article 11(1), in favour of the Indigenous parties, in this instance the Mi'kmaq Nation.

It seems, however, that a *sui generis* approach on display in *Marshall* allows for one party to the treaties to interpret the agreements through Canadian law, setting aside Indigenous laws. Treaty disputes could be resolved differently. Formal legal institutions that are Indigenous in structure and substance could interpret the treaties through relevant, applicable Indigenous laws by Indigenous decision-makers,[40] without which such imbalanced treaty decisions that continue to favour the Crown will continue. As such, treaty obligations, interpretation, and meaning becomes another reason for Canada to want to place Indigenous legal orders inside the Canadian legal system rather than respect Indigenous laws as laws to be interpreted through Indigenous legal systems. It also allows the Crown to spend over 21 years without applying its own highest court rulings and to declare itself neutral when called to task. It allows Canada to unilaterally restrict Indigenous peoples' access to ICESCR's right to continuous improvement of living conditions without consideration of Indigenous peoples' interests and without the benefit of interpreting such rights through Indigenous laws.

III. CASE STUDY NO 2 – *CARING SOCIETY ET AL V ATTORNEY GENERAL OF CANADA*

But treaties and their subsequent interpretation are not the only legal space in which Canada fails to advance a right to continuous improvement of living

[40] Venne (n 18).

conditions for Indigenous peoples. Consider Canada's actions in relation to Indigenous peoples and Article 11(1), within the Canadian human rights framework.

In 2007, the First Nations Child and Family Caring Society of Canada and the Assembly of First Nations filed a complaint under the Canadian Human Rights Act (the Complaint).[41] The Complaint alleged that the federal government of Canada had discriminated against First Nation children in care through inequitable funding to over 163,000 First Nations children. Canada initially challenged the Complaint on procedural grounds in an effort to have the matter dismissed.[42] Ultimately, it proceeded on the merits. In early 2016, the Canadian Human Rights Tribunal (CHRT) found Canada discriminates against First Nation children in care. The CHRT ordered immediate, interim and long-term remedies.[43] While the then newly formed Trudeau government announced it would not seek a judicial review of the ruling, Canada has subsequently not complied with the decision. Instead, the CHRT has issued nine subsequent non-compliance orders against Canada.[44] As we saw with *Marshall*, Canada has a history of inaction in relation to contributing to the improvement of living conditions of Indigenous peoples. Similarly, within Canada's own human rights law, the country's discrimination against First Nation children in care continues without repercussion for the State. How did we get here?

A considerable body of critical scholarship and various laws illustrate that racism in Canada against Indigenous peoples is intricately linked with long-standing and ongoing colonial assertions of superiority over Indigenous peoples, and woven into the constitutional narrative.[45] This master story was on display in *Marshall* vis-à-vis the unilateral interpretation of treaties by Canadian courts and the Crown's failure to uphold its own treaty obligations. Indeed, almost two centuries after the treaties considered in Marshall and the Royal Proclamation, 1763 – both of which recognised Indigenous nations as nations – Canada committed to the protection of human rights through becoming a signatory to the UDHR.[46] During the post-Second World War peace efforts, new ideas entered the international and legal lexicons, such as 'human rights'[47]

[41] *Caring Society* (n 8).

[42] For more on the procedural history of the Complaint see <https://fncaringsociety.com/i-am-witness-tribunal-timeline-and-documents> accessed 17 May 2021.

[43] *Caring Society* (n 8).

[44] For a list and copy of the CHRT's compliance orders, see <https://fncaringsociety.com/chrt-orders> accessed 17 May 2021.

[45] For more see: C Backhouse, *Colour-Coded: A Legal History of Racism in Canada, 1900–1950* (University of Toronto Press 1999); GS Coulthard, 'Subjects of Empire: Indigenous Peoples and the "Politics of Recognition" in Canada' (2007) 6(4) *Contemporary Political Theory* 437–60; S Razack (ed), *Race, Space, and the Law: Unmapping a White Settler Society* (Between the Lines 2002).

[46] A Moravcsik, 'The Origins of Human Rights Regimes: Democratic Delegation in Postwar Europe' (2000) 54(2) *International Organization* 217–52.

[47] J Morsink, The Universal Declaration of Human Rights: Origins, Drafting, and Intent (University of Pennsylvania Press 1999).

through the newly formed United Nations and the UDHR. At the time of enactment, the UDHR was so foundational in the codification of human rights that it served 'directly and indirectly as a model for many domestic constitutions, laws, regulations, and policies that protect fundamental human rights'.[48]

Yet, Canada has not had a history of applying human rights universally, particularly in relation to Indigenous Peoples.[49] Initially passed into law in 1977, and amended from time to time, the Canadian Human Rights Act (CHRA),[50] applies to those working for or receiving benefit from the federal government. First Nation 'Bands' are, in accordance with the provisions of the Indian Act,[51] a federal agency, and were exempted from the CHRA. The effect was to exclude Indigenous peoples from accessing the same human rights protections afforded to all other Canadians. It was not until a 2008 legislative amendment repealing section 67 of the CHRA[52] that Indigenous peoples were able to bring human rights complaints against the federal government and its agencies in the same way as others. In sum, there could be no continuous improvement in the living conditions of Indigenous peoples who were not recognised as subjects of Canadian human rights law. Why exclude Indigenous peoples until 2008?

Canada's Constitution Act, 1876 lists Indigenous peoples as a federal responsibility.[53] In exercising this control over Indigenous peoples, Canada introduced the Indian Act[54] in 1876. This federal legislation is fraught with problems and prejudice, which remain today. If there was ever any doubt as to the Indian Act's purpose, Duncan Campbell Scott, Deputy Superintendent of the Department of Indian Affairs from 1913 to 1932, infamously stated:

> I want to get rid of the Indian problem. I do not think as a matter of fact, that the country ought to continuously protect a class of people who are able to stand alone … Our objective is to continue until there is not a single Indian in Canada that has not been absorbed into the body politic and there is no Indian question, and no Indian Department, that is the whole object of this Bill [the Indian Act].[55]

[48] H Hannum, 'The Status of the Universal Declaration of Human Rights in National and International Law' (1995–1996) 25 *Georgia Journal of International and Comparative Law* 287.

[49] SJ Anaya, *Indigenous Peoples in International Law* (Oxford University Press 2004).

[50] Canadian Human Rights Act, RSC 1985, c H-6.

[51] Indian Act, RSC, 1985, c I-5, s 2(1). Many First Nations are deemed to be 'Bands' under the Indian Act, which outlawed Indigenous governance systems.

[52] Section 67 of the CHRA read: 'Nothing in this Act affects any provision of the *Indian Act* or any provision made under or pursuant to that Act.'

[53] The Constitution Act, 1867, 30 & 31 Vic, c 3, s 91(24) concerns Indians and lands reserved for Indians.

[54] The Indian Act, 1876 was a consolidation of laws that were previously enacted pre-confederation and was passed under s 19(24), Constitution Act, 1867. The Act replaced Upper Canada's Gradual Civilization Act, 1857 and the Gradual Enfranchisement Act, 1869. The Act creates reserve lands and its initial purpose was to administer Indians in a manner that forces Indians to renounce their status under the Act and become members of Canada's civilized society – also known as enfranchisement. The Act has gone through numerous amendments over the years from 1877 up to and including 2013.

[55] J Leslie, *The Historical Development of the Indian Act* 2nd edn (Department of Indian Affairs and Northern Development, Treaties and Historical Research Branch, 1978) 114. The Bill referred

Through constitutional and legislative means, between the 1870s to the mid 1990s, approximately 150,000 Indigenous children attended residential schools.[56] The residential school system was introduced by Canada's first Prime Minister, Sir John A MacDonald who, as justification for the forced removal of Indigenous children from their families versus building schools in First Nation communities so children could live with their parents like other Canadian children, stated:

> When the school is on the **reserve**, the child lives with its parents, who are savages, and though he may learn to read and write, his habits and training and mode of thought are Indian. He is simply a savage who can read and write.[57]

In 2008, the year the federal human rights law was amended to include Indigenous peoples, Canada also formally apologised to First Nations people for the residential school legacy[58] and promised the taking of Indigenous children would never happen again. But the apology has not changed the ongoing impacts and multigenerational effects of centuries of violence;[59] the Indian Act continues to be valid legislation; and as set out in the Caring Society Complaint, First Nation children in care continue to be disproportionately represented (and underfunded). Even with the formation in 2008 of Canada's Truth and Reconciliation Commission and its subsequent reports,[60] including the 2015 Calls to Action,[61] progress is slow.[62]

Indigenous children continue to be more than eight times more likely than their counterparts to be placed in care,[63] which is greater than the incidence of Indigenous children in residential schools. Children in foster care are also more likely to suffer serious mental health issues and serious physical harm as well as being multiple times more likely to die preventable deaths than children in the

to in the quote was a Bill to amend the Indian Act in even more restrictive measures, including enfranchisement.

[56] N Trocmé, D Knoke and C Blackstock, 'Pathways to the Overrepresentation of Aboriginal Children in Canada's Child Welfare System' (2004) 78(4) *Social Service Review* 577–600; and see also C Walker, 'New Documents May Shed Light on Residential School Deaths', 7 January 2014, *CBC News* <http://www.cbc.ca/news/aboriginal/new-documents-may-shed-light-on-residential-school-deaths-1.2487015>.

[57] Prime Minister Sir John A. Macdonald, Official report of the debates of the House of Commons of the Dominion of Canada, 9 May 1883, 1107–08.

[58] Former Prime Minister Stephen Harper, Statement of Apology to Former Students of Indian Residential Schools, 11 June 2008.

[59] A Bombay, K Matheson and H Anisman, 'The Intergenerational Effects of Indian Residential Schools: Implications for the Concept of Historical Trauma' (2014) 51(3) *Transcultural Psychiatry* 320–38; B Jacobs, 'Response to Canada's apology to residential school survivors' (2008) 26(3) *Canadian Woman Studies*.

[60] <https://nctr.ca/records/reports/> accessed 17 May 2021.

[61] <http://trc.ca/assets/pdf/Calls_to_Action_English2.pdf> accessed 17 May 2021.

[62] <https://yellowheadinstitute.org/2019/12/17/calls-to-action-accountability-a-status-update-on-reconciliation/> accessed 17 May 2021.

[63] Trocmé, above n 56; Auditor General, 2003–2011 reporting on First Nation housing and related poverty issues; <http://www.oag-bvg.gc.ca/internet/English/parl_oag_200304_06_e_12912.html> and <http://www.oag-bvg.gc.ca/internet/English/parl_oag_201106_04_e_35372.html>.

general population.[64] The State underfunding of child welfare services aimed at Indigenous children and families directly results in the deplorable living conditions of Indigenous youth in State care.[65] Such factors collude to minimise the ability to create healthy Indigenous families.[66]

The last residential school closed in Canada in 1996, 20 years after the ICESCR came into effect in 1976, and 12 years before Indigenous peoples would be included in human rights law. In other words, even as the ICESCR was executed, Canada spent the years shoring up its long-standing position against a right to continuous improvement of living conditions for Indigenous peoples by continuing to deny Indigenous peoples their human rights; actively separating Indigenous families by removing children; and seeking to separate Indigenous children from their parents, community and culture. The Caring Society Complaint concerning Indigenous children under care challenged Canada's deeply embedded racism against Indigenous peoples and was the first significant complaint following the inclusion of Indigenous peoples in Canada's human rights legislation.

The CHRT decision required Canada to equalise funding for Indigenous child welfare programmes to be equal to their provincial counterparts. While on the surface the Complaint alleges discrimination in funding for child welfare services, it is a window into Canada's colonialist past from pre-Confederation to rendering Indigenous peoples a federal constitutional responsibility, along with copyright and the postal service.[67] The CHRT decision recognises the legacy of the Indian Residential School policy; the impacts of intergenerational trauma on Indigenous families and communities; the predictable outcomes of colonial policies that target and exclude Indigenous peoples;[68] and the ongoing disproportionately high numbers of First Nation children in the country's child welfare system.[69] The federal government's ongoing failure to comply with the CHRT ruling is demonstrative of Canada's long-standing history of failing Indigenous peoples and intentionally structuring a system that commodifies Indigenous

[64] Ted Hughes (2006) *BC Child and Youth Review Report* <https://cwrp.ca/sites/default/files/publications/en/BC-HuguesReviewReport.pdf>.

[65] Among other things, this includes the 'housing' of Indigenous minors in State care in hotels such as in Manitoba. Lyle Stafford, 'Recent hotel stays highlight Manitoba's child-welfare challenges'<https://www.theglobeandmail.com/news/national/recent-hotel-stays-highlight-manitobas-child-welfare-challenges/article29306928/>; see also British Columbia's former Child Advocate, Mary Ellen Turpel-Lafond, 'Current child welfare system doesn't work for Indigenous kids: former B.C. advocate' <https://www.theglobeandmail.com/news/national/recent-hotel-stays-highlight-manitobas-child-welfare-challenges/article29306928/>.

[66] C Blackstock, N Trocmé and M Bennett, 'Child Maltreatment Investigations Among Aboriginal and Non-Aboriginal Families in Canada' (2004) 10(4) *Violence Against Women* 901–16.

[67] Constitution Act, 1867 (n 53) s 91.

[68] A Bombay, K Matheson and H Anisman, 'Intergenerational Trauma' (2009) 5 *Journal de la santé autochtone* 6.

[69] A Bombay, K Matheson and H Anisman, 'The Impact of Stressors on Second Generation Indian Residential School Survivors' (2011) 48(4) *Transcultural Psychiatry* 367.

children as a State responsibility while simultaneously denying Indigenous peoples equal application of Canadian human rights laws within a Canadian legal system. This is extraordinary and ongoing.

In a 2017 exposé *Uprooted* (a year after the CHRT decision finding that Canada discriminates against Indigenous children), the publicly owned news outlet the Canadian Broadcasting Corporation reported that disproportionately large numbers of Innu children in Newfoundland and Labrador (one of Canada's provinces), were being removed from their families and placed in non-Innu foster homes.[70] The report revealed that payment to non-Innu foster families caring for Innu children in the child welfare system served as an economic pipeline for a predominately white town.[71] There are multiple investors in this system that mines Indigenous children to sustain an industry. For example, in *Uprooted*, a social worker believed the system is 'successful' when Innu siblings are placed together in a foster home hundreds of kilometres from their families.[72] Recall too that the Caring Society Complaint was about an underfunding of Indigenous children in care, and yet still there is an industry – even at a discount. The CHRT also ordered long-term systemic remedies that address intergenerational trauma from the residential school system still impacting many Indigenous families,[73] as well as the colonialist underpinnings that result in so many First Nation children entering the system in the first instance.

The narrative that the system works to 'save' Indigenous children from their own families[74] is one that ignores how the very same system continuously replicates the same outcomes year after year discriminating against Indigenous children and families. Rather than experiencing continuous improvement, Indigenous families are continuously controlled and impoverished, treated as unhealthy and dangerous. This ongoing colonial narrative blames Indigenous families while upholding a caring account of non-Indigenous foster homes. It ignores the country's history of intentionally keeping Indigenous peoples out of the economy while simultaneously building an economic industry using Indigenous bodies. It ignores social and cultural rights of Indigenous children and families by removing Indigenous social and cultural rights seen through Indigenous worldviews and replacing them with a colonial worldview. In the name of saving the Indigenous children, it fails to admit that the Canadian laws that generated the problems cannot also solve them. Canada seemingly does not want to understand that Indigenous peoples and Indigenous laws are

[70] T Roberts, 28 February 2017, CBC, *Uprooted* <https://www.cbc.ca/news2/interactives/uprooted/>.
[71] ibid.
[72] ibid.
[73] Report of Parliament's Standing Committee on Public Accounts, Chapter 4, First Nations Child and Family Services Program – Indian and Northern Affairs Canada of the May 2008 Report of the Auditor General, 40th Parliament, 2nd Session (Ottawa: Communication Canada 2009) 5.
[74] ibid.

the solution, not the problem as Duncan Campbell-Scott framed it. It wilfully refuses to confront the fact that Canada's residential schools have led to generational effects that now flows Indigenous children into the child welfare system, thereby maintaining cycles of poverty and family fragmentation. All of this conspires to illustrate some of the ways Canada precludes Indigenous peoples' access to a right to continuous improvement of living conditions.

The intergenerational complexities attributed to Indian residential schools continue to be seen today. The impacts of taking children has damaged Indigenous families, communities and nations, as well as the entire country. Taking a child is not solely about the child. In the Caring Society Complaint, Elder Robert Joseph[75] testified before the Tribunal and explained the importance of children among his people, the Kwakwaka'wakw. He offered insight into Kwakwaka'wakw law, which the CHRT included in their decision. He described the *Heiltsu gula* – the 'Enough Time Has Passed' ceremony.[76] Joseph explained to the Tribunal that when a child is born to the Kwakwaka'wakw, they are thought to be deciding whether to stay in the mortal world or return to the spirit world,[77] and must be surrounded with love as an enticement to stay.[78] After 10 months, the *Heiltsu gula* is performed, which involves an entire village and guests, who serve as witnesses as the family affirms they ensure the child will be loved, cared for, and kept safe.[79]

There is a role for everyone in the child's life. Women step forward declaring their commitment to mentor the child in the meaning of life among the people, and to show the child what love means.[80] Parents carry their child and lead the extended family into the *Gukwdzi*.[81] Okra is smudged on the faces of the child and all those inside the *Gukwdzi* are invited to become part of the child's life, marking the responsibilities on the many individuals who commit to caring and providing for the child throughout their life.[82] Men step forward and offer mentorship, committing to remain part of the child's life forever.[83] Songs are sung.[84] The child and the people are bound.[85] The *Heiltsu gula* is reflective of the Kwakwaka'wakw's beliefs that children are central to the universe.[86]

[75] Elder Robert Joseph testified on behalf of the Complainants in the Caring Society's complaint. He is an hereditary Chief of the Gwa wa enuk First Nation and attended residential school in Alert Bay, off the coast of Vancouver Island.
[76] Complaint, Elder Joseph, transcripts from the hearing of the Caring Society complaint, page 14–15, Vol 42.
[77] ibid.
[78] ibid 14.
[79] ibid 14–15.
[80] ibid 17.
[81] ibid.
[82] ibid 18.
[83] ibid 19.
[84] ibid.
[85] ibid.
[86] ibid 16.

The warmth and creation of an ethic of caring in Kwakwaka'wakw law through the *Heiltsu gula* stands in stark contrast to the Indian Act that authorised residential schools, where children underwent an immediate and violent transition from being at the centre of the universe, to non-entities. Children no longer carried a name but were assigned a number,[87] they were not valued for who they were but rather were brutally transformed towards a colonialist end.[88] That First Nation children were stolen was wrong and 'one of the greatest tragedies … was that the children never experienced love; [it] was simply absent in their lives for a long time'.[89] Stealing other people's children is not a civil action as purported by MacDonald in the creation of Indian residential schools. It is savage.

As with *Marshall* in relation to treaty interpretation, I have also attempted to illustrate through the Caring Society Complaint that Canada's human rights framework maintains a system that fails Indigenous peoples in relation to continuous improvement of living conditions. Among the outcomes is a denial of a right to continuous improvement of living conditions for Indigenous peoples that is otherwise available to Canadians. The Crown's ongoing failure to comply with the CHRT's decision, which found that Canada discriminates against First Nation children in care through underfunding, is part of the deeper systemic problems. These are structural problems that conspire to deny Indigenous peoples a right to continuous improvement of living conditions, and their other economic, social and cultural rights. As per the Caring Society decision by the CHRT, First Nation children in care are entitled to live in their own social structures and within their own cultures. They are also entitled to equal budgetary allocations for services, including child welfare. Canada thus denies these children's economic, social and cultural rights and violates its obligation to realise their right to continuous improvement of living conditions.

Many Indigenous peoples are still experiencing intergenerational trauma inflicted by the State in residential schools and the child welfare system, yet despite the best efforts of the colonisers Indigenous laws continue to survive, be transmitted and shared, such as by Elder Joseph. Through the example of the *Heiltsu gula*, as described to the CHRT by Elder Joseph, Indigenous laws on child welfare should be appreciated for their beauty and humanity. As one example of an Indigenous law, the *Heiltsu gula* generates a large kinship web of caring for a child so that if some in the child's family may fail, there are many others in the family and community who also carry responsibilities to love and care for the child. This is the opposite of Canada's ongoing forced removal of Indigenous children from their families, communities and culture, that instead places them in a non-Kwakwaka'wakw house. It is an act of denial of access to

[87] B Sellars, *They Called Me Number One* (Talonbooks 2012).
[88] ibid 35.
[89] ibid 16.

the freedom of Indigenous families and their children to live within their own cultures and laws. It is a denial of how Indigenous laws, not the Canadian legal system, hold solutions to exercise the right to the continuous improvement of living conditions for Indigenous peoples.

IV. CONCLUSION

This chapter has shown that whether in treaties or human rights, in relation to Indigenous peoples and a right to continuous improvement of living conditions, Canada consistently refuses to follow the Supreme Court's direction in *Marshall* and negotiate implementation of the treaties' terms in a modern context. In addition, the State has continued to fail to end discrimination against First Nation children in care, which it was ordered to do by Canada's own human rights tribunal. In sum, deny, delay and redirect are tactics Canada has deployed in response to both *Marshall* and the CHRT in relation to limiting access of Indigenous peoples to the continuous improvement of their living conditions as required by Article 11(1) of the ICESCR.

Canada can and should choose otherwise. Though not an exhaustive list, by way of more appropriate responses and remedies to increase access to a right to continuous improvement of living conditions for Indigenous peoples, Canada can, first, adopt the UNDRIP outside a constitutional framework. Among other things, the UNDRIP calls for the recognition of Indigenous laws and the formation of Indigenous legal institutions,[90] which could interpret treaties through Indigenous perspectives, using Indigenous laws; as well as an Indigenous right to culture and language,[91] which in the residential schools was intentionally removed. Second, honour the treaties, which are international agreements between nations, versus upholding the legal invention that the treaties are *sui generis*, which has resulted in the unequal treatment of Indigenous peoples. This includes giving equal weight to Indigenous understandings of treaties. Third, engage directly with Indigenous peoples and Indigenous laws alongside Canadian law by recognising Indigenous legal orders as orders and Canadian legal systems as a system that does not unilaterally determine and interpret treaties for both the State and the Indigenous signatories. Fourth, comply with Canada's human rights legislation and implement the decision of the CHRT in relation to child welfare and thereby close the socio-economic gap between Canada and Indigenous peoples. Fifth, fundamentally shift from State-centred approaches to Indigenous child welfare with recognition of Indigenous laws as holding Indigenous-centred responses to child welfare. This is more than

[90] UNDRIP (n 5) Arts, 4, 5 and 8.
[91] ibid Art 5.

Canada's 'recognition' of Indigenous laws in its Bill C-92,[92] which became law at the end of 2019, that ultimately favours State law over Indigenous laws.[93] Sixth, reconcile the relationship with Indigenous peoples as partners in confederation versus subjects of it. This can occur if it is accepted that Indigenous peoples contributed all of the lands now known as Canada and, like the treaties made in good faith,[94] those lands and resources are to be shared in the same spirit.

Such fundamental changes are not a comprehensive list but are a necessary beginning because it is not acceptable to deny Indigenous peoples a right to continuous improvement of living conditions, as called for by Article 11(1) of the International Covenant on Economic, Social and Cultural Rights.

[92] An Act respecting First Nations, Inuit and Métis children, Youth and Families, SC 2019, c 24.
[93] <https://yellowheadinstitute.org/wp-content/uploads/2019/07/the-promise-and-pitfalls-of-c-92-report.pdf> accessed 17 May 2021.
[94] Venne (n 18).

11

The Work of Living

Social Reproduction and the Right to the Continuous Improvement of Living Conditions

BETH GOLDBLATT

I. INTRODUCTION

THE LOCKDOWN OF millions of people in their homes due to the Covid-19 global pandemic has had a massive and immediate impact on the working lives of many. Vast numbers of people have lost their employment, businesses and means of subsistence within days of stay at home orders. The lucky ones to retain their jobs have seen many of their workplaces shift from the office into the home with a range of consequences following this blurring of the spaces of production and reproduction. For others in sectors deemed essential such as health care, food production and delivery, work has continued outside of the home, albeit with modifications and new stresses, supporting the maintenance of society. While remote work aided by technology is already a growing feature of the contemporary landscape the shift to work from home has been sudden, huge, and for many, challenging. This is particularly so for those with caring responsibilities who lost many of the supports previously relied on such as schooling, child care and other care assistance for the elderly, people with disabilities and the sick. In many societies those supports were already lacking or had been undermined by years of austerity cuts. For those doing work in the home, the influx of newly unemployed family members, children and others in need has added to their load, strained their resources and heightened relationship tensions.[1] Policymakers and employers have 'requisitioned' our homes according to Fiona Jenkins:

> Acting as if home is a costless resource that is free for appropriation in an emergency, ignoring how home functions as a site of relatively invisible gendered relations of

[1] C Miller, 'Nearly Half of Men Say They Do Most of the Home Schooling. 3 Percent of Women Agree' (*New York Times*, 6 May 2020) <https://www.nytimes.com/2020/05/06/upshot/

care and labour and imagining home as a largely frictionless site of interpersonal relations, come all too naturally, especially in a crisis.[2]

Whether this crisis has created a moment of rupture in the social and economic fabric of neoliberal capitalism, as some suggest,[3] remains to be seen. But at least momentarily it has dramatically reshaped public and private spaces, with potentially lasting impacts, both positive and negative.[4] It is an important time to consider the meaning of 'work' and 'home' in understanding how these concepts inform international human rights. This chapter attempts to interpret and critically engage with the under-explored right 'to the continuous improvement of living conditions' in Article 11 of the UN's International Covenant on Economic, Social and Cultural Rights (ICESCR).[5] Trying to shed light on this neglected right might assist us in achieving the foundational goals of international human rights which are based, among other things, on faith in the 'dignity and worth of the human person' and the promotion of 'social progress and better standards of life in larger freedom'.[6]

In this chapter I argue that the right to the continuous improvement of living conditions requires State support for and provision of the means to a better life. If living conditions are understood as comparable to but distinguishable from working conditions, then this suggests that life at home and/or in the community rather than in the workplace is the locus of this right. While food, clothing and housing, including services such as water and electricity, transport and infrastructure, together with an adequate standard of living, provided through

pandemic-chores-homeschooling-gender.html>. Thanks to Ruth Fletcher, Sandra Fredman, Jessie Hohmann, Sandra Liebenberg, Shirin Rai and Michael Thomson for their helpful comments on an earlier version of this paper.

[2] F Jenkins, 'Did our employers just requisition our homes?' (*Canberra Times*, 4 April 2020) <https://www.canberratimes.com.au/story/6701054/did-our-employers-just-requisition-our-homes/>. Also see F Jenkins and J Smith, 'Work-from-home during COVID-19: Accounting for the Care Economy to Build Back Better' (2021) 32(1) *The Economic and Labour Relations Review* 22.

[3] A Davis and N Klein, 'Movement Building in the Time of the Coronavirus: A Rising Majority Teach-In with Angela Davis & Naomi Klein' (*Raising Majority*, 2 April 2020) <https://therisingmajority.com/events/movement-building/>; G Monbiot, 'Covid-19 is nature's wake-up call to complacent civilisation' (*The Guardian*, 25 March 2020) <https://www.theguardian.com/commentisfree/2020/mar/25/covid-19-is-natures-wake-up-call-to-complacent-civilisation>; S Pahuja and J Baskin, 'Never Waste a Crisis: A Practical Guide?' (*Critical Legal Thinking*, 20 March 2020) <https://criticallegalthinking.com/2020/03/20/never-waste-a-crisis-a-practical-guide/>; A Roy, 'The pandemic is a portal' (*Financial Times*, 4 April 2020) <https://www.ft.com/content/10d8f5e8-74eb-11ea-95fe-fcd274e920ca>; M Davis, 'The Coronavirus Crisis Is a Monster Fueled by Capitalism' (*In These Times*, 20 March 2020) <https://inthesetimes.com/article/22394/coronavirus-crisis-capitalism-covid-19-monster-mike-davis>.

[4] M Wade, 'There's a Silver Lining for Fathers in the Covid Crisis' (*Sydney Morning Herald*, 26 April 2020) <https://www.smh.com.au/business/the-economy/there-s-a-silver-lining-for-fathers-in-the-covid-crisis-20200424-p54n1z.html>; Miller (n 1); Jenkins (n 2).

[5] International Covenant on Economic, Social and Cultural Rights (adopted 16 December 1966, entered force 3 January 1976) UNGA resolution 2200A (XXI) (ICESCR).

[6] Universal Declaration of Human Rights (adopted 10 December 1948) UNGA Res 217 A(III) (UDHR) Preamble.

work or social security, are essential to a good life, something more makes up the living conditions to which the right refers. The home and community, the space of this 'living', is also the realm of social reproduction where society remakes itself, usually through unpaid work that is gendered and intimate, but also drawing on the (poorly) paid labour of workers. I consider how mechanisms to acknowledge and support the often unseen work of care and to generate new relations of caring should be built into our understanding of the right to the continuous improvement of living conditions. The right should be informed by an awareness of the material, affective, embodied and communal dimensions of this work in the home, family and community in attempting to ensure that this necessary labour is neither commodified nor exploited but is shared, supported and transformed.

This argument is made based on an analysis of the language of the ICESCR informed by the concept of social reproduction. This chapter begins with a discussion of this concept as developed by feminist scholars, its centrality to the existence of our societies, and its erosion under current conditions of capitalism (section II). Understanding the reasons for the invisibility of social reproduction within existing economic relations helps to explain its limited acknowledgement within human rights. The aim of the chapter is to bring attention to social reproduction in the interpretation of the right to the continuous improvement of living conditions. It offers a method of rights interpretation that takes feminist utopian and performative imagining seriously and integrates it into practices of reading rights. Some of these feminist imaginings appear in three recent manifestoes: '*A Care Manifesto: (Part)-Time for All*' by Jennifer Nedelsky and Tom Malleson;[7] the '*Feminism for the 99%: A Manifesto*' by Nancy Fraser, Tithi Bhattacharya and Cinzia Arruzza;[8] and the Care Collective's *The Care Manifesto: The Politics of Interdependence*[9] (section III). In this chapter I consider how ideas common to these manifestoes can inform new readings of the right and promote its contribution to transforming social reproduction. I do this by critically mining the language of the ICESCR to offer an interpretation, informed by feminist theories, visions and calls to action, of what should be meant by 'living', 'conditions' and 'continuous improvement' and I consider who are the parties to the right (section IV). Finally, the chapter concludes with a brief reflection on how the concept of 'continuous improvement' relates to ideas of utopia and social revolution as processes which should inform struggles to transform social reproduction, including within and through human rights (section V).

[7] J Nedelsky and T Malleson, *A Care Manifesto: (Part)-Time for All* (forthcoming).

[8] N Fraser, T Bhattacharya and C Arruzza, *Feminism for the 99%: A Manifesto* (Verso 2019).

[9] The Care Collective (A Chatzidakis, J Hakim, J Littler, C Rottenberg and L Segal), *The Care Manifesto: The Politics of Interdependence* (Verso 2020). See also The Care Collective, 'COVID-19 pandemic: A Crisis of Care' (*Verso Books*, 26 March 2020) <https://www.versobooks.com/blogs/4617-covid-19-pandemic-a-crisis-of-care> which sets out ideas that are explored in the book.

II. SOCIAL REPRODUCTION

This section provides a brief exposition of the concept of social reproduction and its current, global manifestation. Feminist scholars have built on Marxism's focus on exploitation of the worker's labour in producing goods and services in the capitalist market by emphasising the (re)production of the worker within the family and society. This process of reproduction is essential to capitalism and structured to ensure its maintenance.[10] Feminists economists have argued that the labour that occurs in the reproductive sphere although unpaid and uncounted in the economy is in fact work.[11] Social reproduction involves different forms of work to create and maintain life without which society cannot survive. Hoskyns and Rai categorise these forms of work as: (1) biological reproduction; (2) unpaid production in the home which includes unpaid subsistence labour and work in family businesses; (3) voluntary work in the community to nurture and maintain society; (4) the reproduction of culture and ideology; and (5) the provision of sexual, emotional and affective services to maintain family and relationships.[12] This work includes socialisation of children, preparation of food, housework, care of the elderly, disabled, ill and young, collection of resources such as water and fuel, cultural and religious practices, and multiple other activities that contribute to human survival and development.

The sphere of reproduction is profoundly gendered and hence contributes not only to class exploitation but to gender and other forms of oppression in capitalist societies. The sexual division of labour between home and the market reinforced by liberalism's public/private divide treats social reproductive work as feminine, natural and marginal.[13] This same devaluing affects paid work involving care which is feminised, poorly paid, and often informal and insufficiently regulated. Federici explains that 'women have been designated as men's common, a natural source of wealth and services to be as freely appropriated by them as the capitalists have appropriated the wealth of nature'.[14] But this results in a contradiction, as Fraser argues, since capitalism's unending drive to accumulate 'threatens to destabilize the very reproductive processes and capacities'

[10] T Bhattacharya, 'Introduction: Mapping Social Reproduction Theory' in T Bhattacharya (ed), *Social Reproduction Theory: Remapping Class, Recentering Oppression* (Pluto Press 2017).

[11] M Waring, *If Women Counted: A New Feminist Economics* (Harper & Row 1988).

[12] C Hoskyns and SM Rai, 'Recasting the Global Political Economy: Counting Women's Unpaid Work' (2007) 12(3) *New Political Economy* 297, 300.

[13] C Pateman, 'Feminist Critiques of the Public/Private Dichotomy' in S Benn and G Gaus (eds), *Public and Private in Social Life* (Croom Helm 1983) 1; FE Olsen, 'The Family and the Market: A Study of Ideology and Legal Reform' (1983) 96(7) *Harvard Law Review* 1497.

[14] S Federici, 'Feminism and the Politics of the Commons in an Era of Primitive Accumulation' in Silvia Federici (ed), *Re-enchanting the World: Feminism and the Politics of the Commons* (PM Press 2018) 102, 122. Note that while this chapter fails to explore the relationship between humans, other forms of life, and the environment, this relationship is central to social reproduction and requires further consideration within a human rights framework.

that capital needs.[15] This creates a tendency towards crisis in social reproduction that runs alongside other crises of capitalism – economic, ecological and political.[16] The current crisis of care that manifests under contemporary financialised neoliberal capitalism is creating a deficit in care. This new, globalising regime fuelled by debt is 'promoting state and corporate disinvestment from social welfare while recruiting women into the paid workforce … externalizing care work onto families and communities while diminishing their capacity to perform it'.[17] The two-earner family is 'dualised' into those who can afford to pay for commodified care and those who are confronted with privatised care and must provide care services at low pay to those who can afford it, leading to national and global 'care chains'.[18] Sole parents, usually mothers, are particularly disadvantaged in this context, becoming a precarious underclass that is destined to fail because they cannot fit the neoliberal family model.[19]

The crisis in care has harsh impacts on those performing social reproductive work and those dependent on it, leading to what Rai, Hoskyns and Thomas term 'depletion through social reproduction'.[20] They define depletion as 'the level at which the resource outflows exceed resource inflows in carrying out social reproductive work over a threshold of sustainability, making it harmful for those engaged in this unvalued work'.[21] This leads to harmful impacts on individuals, households and communities: individuals suffer physical and mental harms; households face reduced human and other resources and less leisure; and communities lose neighbourliness, organisation and collective provisioning.[22] The extent of the depletion of those doing social reproductive work is directly linked to the erosion of State support and community capacity driven by the voracious demands of the market system. As Fraser explains the contradiction inherent in capital and care, the economic system is paradoxically destroying its own capacity to maintain itself.[23]

This critical understanding of social reproduction and its contemporary manifestation advanced by feminist theorists assists in understanding how it is gendered but also shaped by race, class and geography. It informs our understanding of the ICESCR, which is a product of its historical and political context, but also assists our efforts to interpret the Covenant within the current landscape and give new content to its provisions, in advancing a reading that might support transformative change.

[15] N Fraser, Contradictions of Capital and Care' (2016) 100 *New Left Review* 99, 103.

[16] ibid 99.

[17] ibid 112.

[18] ibid 112–14. See also B Ehrenreich and A Russell Hochschild, *Global Woman: Nannies, Maids and Sex Workers in the New Economy* (Granta Books 2003).

[19] W Brown, *Undoing the Demos: Neoliberalism's Stealth Revolution* (Zone Books 2015) 107.

[20] SM Rai, C Hoskyns and D Thomas, 'Depletion: The Cost of Social Reproduction' (2014) 16(1) *International Feminist Journal of Politics* 86.

[21] ibid 88–89.

[22] ibid 90–91.

[23] Fraser (n 15) 103.

III. IDEAS FROM RECENT MANIFESTOES TO INFORM THE DEVELOPMENT OF THE RIGHT

The crisis in care, increasingly evident all over the world, has been exacerbated and brought into stark focus due to the Covid-19 pandemic. Finding new ways of structuring the social reproduction of our societies has become urgent. Critical scholars and activists, seeking to challenge the ubiquity of current social organisation under neoliberal capitalism, have offered critiques, calls to action and new models of care in a recent turn to the creation of manifestoes.[24] Manifestoes, which are often shaped by utopian imaginings, offer alternative conceptions of social organisation. The idea of utopias, returned to in the conclusion, can inform feminist interpretations of human rights. The chapter now outlines three of these manifestoes to consider how they might contribute to the project of giving content to the right to the continuous improvement of living conditions through a focus on social reproduction.[25]

Canadian law and politics scholar Jennifer Nedelsky has worked with activist/academic Tom Malleson to write *A Care Manifesto: (Part)-Time for All*.[26] Their project is a response to unsustainable stress confronting families, inequality facing those performing care, alongside ignorance by policy makers around the work of care. They argue that to transform norms around work and care the following proposal should be adopted: 'all capable adults are expected to do paid work part-time (what we would now call part-time), no less than 12 and no more than 30 hours a week, and to do unpaid care work part time, a minimum of 22 hours a week'. Their proposal is based on the understanding that the structures of work and care are entirely linked. Yet the increase in female employment, longer work hours and more precarious conditions have not seen accompanying changes in the nature of care, leading to major stress on households with the harshest impacts on women. The denigration of care is also a product of policy makers who lack experience and thus understanding of the demands of care, but also its benefits in terms of the relationships it fosters and the satisfaction this provides. They suggest that the way to overcome this denigration is to ensure that everyone becomes a care provider. Where a person no longer has immediate care responsibilities such as to their children they will need to provide care to others in their community such as neighbours or members of shared interest groups. The authors suggest that this proposal will lead to more time for people to enjoy their lives, less production and consumption, and, as a result, environmental, mental health and other benefits. While the State will

[24] Feminist manifestoes are of course not new. For some examples see B Fahs, *Burn It Down! Feminist Manifestos for the Revolution* (Verso 2020).

[25] Due to constraints of space this chapter does not include a close engagement with these manifestos but rather takes from them, perhaps uncritically, a shared interest in utopian visions of new ways of understanding and structuring care.

[26] Nedelsky and Malleson (n 7).

need to play some role, Nedelsky and Malleson's idea is primarily about norm change and the promotion of a conversation about a different way of structuring work and care in society.[27] Without engaging closely with all elements of this proposal here, I am attracted by its emphasis on communal responsibility for care undertaken at the individual level while recognising that there may be other ways to socialise care.

Visions for different ways of structuring work and care are not new. Philosopher Nancy Fraser in her famous 1994 'thought experiment' imagined a post-industrial welfare state with radically different conditions of work and reproduction.[28] In the current context, she joined with Tithi Bhattacharya and Cinzia Arruzza in 2019 to develop a feminist manifesto aimed at mobilising feminist struggle for far-reaching social change. While Nedelesky and Malleson's manifesto is the basis for conversation and democratic deliberation towards norm change, *Feminism for the 99%* is a more radical call to action.[29] It aims to introduce a feminist lens and a contemporary reading into the challenge to replace the capitalist system. The goal is to:

> overcome the system's stubborn nexus of production and reproduction, its entwinement of profit-making with people-making, and its subordination of the second to the first. And this means abolishing the larger system that generates their symbiosis.[30]

It suggests that methods such as women's strikes, food riots, occupations and other forms of struggle, in alliance and solidarity with other oppressed groups, are needed to transform society. Its anti-reformist message is clear where it describes itself as:

> … a restless anticapitalist feminism – one that can never be satisfied with equivalences until we have equality, never satisfied with legal rights until we have justice, and never satisfied with democracy until individual freedom is calibrated on the basis of freedom for all.[31]

This manifesto points to the need for struggles to improve working conditions along with struggles 'for universal health care, for free education, for environmental justice and access to clean energy, and for housing and public

[27] They note however, that their proposal is not intended to privatise all care and that the State would still need to support or provide care in a range of ways and some paid care would still be necessary. Similarly, the State would need to ensure that workers were able to earn adequate wages under decent conditions alongside good public services such as transportation and access to social protection where needed.

[28] N Fraser, 'After the Family Wage: Gender Equity and the Welfare State' (1994) 22(4) *Political Theory* 591.

[29] Fraser, Bhattacharya, and Arruzza (n 8). For a critique of this Manifesto see Gülnur Acar Savran (*Catlakzemin*, 30 October 2020) 'On Feminism for the 99%: A Manifesto*' <https://en.catlakzemin.com/on-feminism-for-the-99-a-manifesto/> who argues that the Manifesto is insufficiently grounded in diverse feminist struggles and is limited in its analysis of patriarchy.

[30] ibid 81.

[31] ibid 85.

transportation'.[32] It has a greater focus on State provision of the goods and services necessary to support the gendered work of social reproduction and is suggestive of the need to link the demand for social and economic rights to fundamental reordering of society.

The third and very current manifesto is the *Care Manifesto* developed by a group that calls itself the Care Collective, which uses an expansive idea of care to frame its call for social transformation.[33] This manifesto suggests that the Covid-19 pandemic and the pre-existing crisis of 'carelessness' requires a new politics that 'puts care front and centre of life'. It defines care as not only the 'hands on' meeting of others' physical and emotional needs but 'an enduring social capacity and practice involving the nurturing of all that is necessary for the welfare and flourishing of human and non-human life'. This broad meaning aligns with the concept of social reproduction but with an added focus on other life on our planet. Placing care at the centre involves recognising that our survival is based on interdependence – we all need to give and receive care. The Care Collective proposes an 'ethics of promiscuous caring' where we think beyond the traditional nuclear family and expand our ideas of kinship. This requires institutional transformation and concrete improvements such as ending 'financial discrimination against single mothers, teaching boys emotional literacy and housework, and expanding care across communities'. This community-based care must be supported with public resources or *commons* in contrast to the trend towards privatisation in our societies. The Care Collective suggests that we need a caring State to provide resources and services as well as to facilitate more agency and democratic participation. This must be accompanied by caring economies where exchange relationships distribute resources to meet the needs of all and the collectivisation of care infrastructure. These should all be located within a caring world that recognises planetary dependence with 'sustainable economies and porous borders' that generates a 'transnational orientation of care towards the stranger'. The aim of the manifesto is to 'wrest back control from the power-grabbing 1% and their tyranny of social carelessness' to create a caring world.

This final manifesto reimagines the very idea of care by valorising interdependence and rethinking existing family forms by focusing on communal and collective life. This too is both challenging and inspiring in offering new ways to read human rights.

Without critically evaluating these manifestoes here, I have drawn on certain broad ideas from them to inform my interpretation of the right. These three manifestoes, while differing in a number of ways, share important commonalities in foregrounding efforts to restructure 'care' while also rethinking work and the economy. This supports my argument that references to 'work' and 'living'

[32] ibid 15.
[33] The Care Collective (n 9).

within the ICESCR should be read in a way that breaks down rather than maintains this unhelpful dichotomy. The manifestoes suggest that structuring care differently is not the task of the state alone, but is also the responsibility of individuals, communities and the market. The State has a role in regulating and enabling new forms of care as well as resourcing some of this care. Just as the right to work requires the State to create the conditions for fair and decent employment, so the right to the continuous improvement of living conditions requires the State to create the conditions for fair and decent living. The manifestoes suggest a radical break with the unsustainable and unjust approach to social reproduction that currently exists. A human rights framing that is similarly disruptive may encourage a re-examination of the assumptions behind the forms of social organisation represented in the ICESCR. This could result in new understandings of the rights within the Covenant, particularly the right to the continuous improvement of living conditions, and its transformative potential.

IV. INTERPRETING THE ICESCR

Drawing on the theories of social reproduction and the visions shaping the care manifestoes discussed above, in this section I will advance a critical analysis of the ICESCR and propose an interpretation of the right to the continuous improvement of living conditions that acknowledges the centrality of social reproduction to our existence.

The International Covenant on Economic, Social and Cultural Rights (ICESCR) is premised on the vision of the Universal Declaration of Human Rights (UDHR) based on 'the ideal of free human beings enjoying freedom from fear and want' under conditions where they can enjoy their human rights (economic, social, cultural, civil and political).[34] States have obligations to promote these rights and individuals, with duties to other individuals and their community, also have responsibilities 'to strive for the promotion and observance' of the rights in the ICESCR.[35] One of these rights is the 'right to the continuous improvement of living conditions'. Article 11(1) includes this right as follows:

> The States Parties to the present Covenant recognize the right of everyone to an adequate standard of living for himself and his family, including adequate food, clothing and housing, **and to the continuous improvement of living conditions.** The States Parties will take appropriate steps to ensure the realization of this right, recognizing to this effect the essential importance of international co-operation based on free consent. [my emphasis]

[34] ICESCR (n 5) Preamble.
[35] ibid.

This section presents a textual analysis of the meaning of 'the continuous improvement of living conditions' within the right, in the context of State and individual obligations and responsibilities within the ICESCR as a whole. Since this aspect of the right has been under-examined by scholars and given limited and patchy attention within the treaty system,[36] it requires thorough scrutiny. The task of interpretation requires answering: (1) what is meant by living conditions? (2) how do we understand the idea of improvement and what does it mean for this to be continuous? (3) to whom does this aspect of the right apply?

A. The Meaning of 'Living Conditions'

i. 'Living'

'Living conditions' could be understood as those features of life commonly valued by all humans. The right to the continuous improvement of living conditions would thus imply State provision of the means to a better life. But this definition of living conditions is overly broad and unhelpful. In addition, the idea of a good (or better) life – the subject of ongoing and unresolved debate within the field of philosophy – is culturally and geographically relative as well as historically contingent. We clearly need to drill down somewhat to elicit the meaning of this term in the Covenant. It seems appropriate, as well as consistent with approaches to the interpretation of legal texts, to examine how the words 'living' and 'conditions' have been used elsewhere in the ICESCR.

The idea of 'living' within the ICESCR appears to entrench the production/reproduction divide inscribed into the current economic system. The right to work in Article 6 of the ICESCR refers to the concept of 'living' as something that is generated by/from work. Article 6(1) talks of 'the right of everyone to the opportunity to gain his *living* by work which he freely chooses or accepts'.[37] 'Living' here seems to mean either 'income' or the life outside of work that is made possible through work. This raises questions about whether we live while we work and whether we work while we live. Marx, in his concept of alienation of labour under capitalism, argued that 'the worker … only feels himself outside his work, and in his work feels outside himself. He is at home when he is not working, and when he is working he is not at home'.[38] This separation of 'working' from 'living' in the ICESCR involves a splitting of the human experience into

[36] See Hohmann and Goldblatt, chapter one, and Hohmann, chapter two in this volume.

[37] My emphasis, and note the sexist language. However, the Committee on Economic, Social and Cultural Rights has used male and female pronouns in some parts of its interpretation of the right including him/her and his/her. See CESCR 'The Right to Work: General comment No. 18, on Article 6 of the International Covenant on Economic, Social and Cultural Rights' (24 November 2005) UN Doc E/C.12/GC/18, para 1.

[38] K Marx, *Economic and Philosophic Manuscripts of 1844* (Dover 2007) 72. This is discussed in Bhattacharya (n 10) 10.

work in service of production from all other aspects of life. It reinforces the distinction between production and reproduction by treating the activities that go on in the home and community surrounding paid labour as 'non-work'. It seems to view work that generates income as legitimate work deserving of rights protections while work in the home or unpaid work is excluded from this coverage. A recent correction to this view has been advanced by the Committee on Economic, Social and Cultural Rights (CESCR) in its General Comment No. 23 on Article 7 where it recognised that unpaid workers are 'workers' entitled to just and favourable conditions of work.[39]

The Covenant does recognise the reproductive sphere where it refers to the family as the 'natural and fundamental group unit of society' noting its responsibility for the 'care and education of dependent children' (Article 10(1)). But while Article 10(2) addresses protection of mothers with special mention of maternity leave for 'working mothers', it treats the idea of work as synonymous with paid work, ignoring the unpaid work of parenting. The ICESCR, while contributing to the division between production and reproduction, aims to improve conditions in both realms. A critical reading would suggest that the Covenant is simply mapping onto existing capitalist relations and supporting the home as a space of reproduction for the market. However, I suggest that a more transformative interpretation can be supported in contesting this meaning of the treaty.

This approach to the ICESCR could be enhanced by reading it together with the Convention on the Elimination of All Forms of Discrimination against Women (CEDAW) which goes significantly further in recognising the gendered space of social reproduction. Its Preamble, although focused mainly on childrearing, points to this as follows:

> Bearing in mind the great contribution of women to the welfare of the family and to the development of society, so far not fully recognized, the social significance of maternity and the role of both parents in the family and in the upbringing of children, and aware that the role of women in procreation should not be a basis for discrimination but that the upbringing of children requires a sharing of responsibility between men and women and society as a whole,
>
> Aware that a change in the traditional role of men as well as the role of women in society and in the family is needed to achieve full equality between men and women, …

[39] CESCR, 'General comment No. 23 (2016) on the right to just and favourable conditions of work (article 7 of the International Covenant on Economic, Social and Cultural Rights)' (27 April 2016) UN Doc E/C.12/GC/23, paras 4, 5, 47(j). The important decision of the Committee in *Marcia Cecilia Trujillo Calero v Ecuador*, CESCR, Communication 10/2015, UN Doc E/C.12/63/D/10/2015 (26 March 2018) also acknowledges that unpaid care is work for the purposes of social security. The devaluation of caring work has extended to paid domestic work with workers having to fight for the right to access the same working conditions as other workers, as illustrated in the recent South African Constitutional Court decision of *Mahlangu and Another v Minister of Labour and Others* 2021 (1) BCLR 1 (CC).

This acknowledgment in CEDAW leads to a right to State support for parents in Article 11(c):

> To encourage the provision of the necessary supporting social services to enable parents to combine family obligations with work responsibilities and participation in public life, in particular through promoting the establishment and development of a network of child-care facilities;

Like the ICESCR, CEDAW focuses on the role of the State to supplement the social reproductive work already being done in the home to enable participation within paid employment. The reference to 'participation in public life' does however suggest some acknowledgement of aspects of life that are important and that should be supported, other than paid work. While this is significant, support for those doing unpaid social reproductive work seems to be a gap, although Article 13(a) does refer to 'family benefits' as part of 'other areas of economic and social life' (Article 13). The needs of people doing unpaid work are acknowledged in CEDAW in relation to rural women: Article 14(1) talks about 'the significant roles which rural women play in the economic survival of their families, including their work in the non-monetized sectors of the economy'.[40] It is unfortunate that this is not similarly recognised in relation to urban women.[41] Article 14(2)(e) and (f) refer to some of the features of communal organisation that are often central to the social reproduction that occurs within households and the communities that surround them. Interestingly, Article 14(2)(h), still in relation to rural women, provides a right '[t]o enjoy adequate living conditions, particularly in relation to housing, sanitation, electricity and water supply, transport and communications'. CEDAW thus uses the language of 'living conditions' where ICESCR uses the phrase 'standard of living', with the elaboration in CEDAW suggesting this is primarily about State provision of basic services.[42]

[40] See further references to unpaid work and the care needs of rural women by the CEDAW Committee: Committee on the Elimination of Discrimination against Women, 'General recommendation No. 34 (2016) on the rights of rural women' (7 March 2016) UN Doc CEDAW/C/GC/34 paras 48, 52(h).

[41] Although the CEDAW Committee did recognise the unpaid work of rural and urban women in early General Recommendations. See eg CEDAW Committee 'General recommendation No. 16: Unpaid women workers in rural and urban family enterprises' (1991) 10th Session UN Doc A/46/38; CEDAW committee 'General recommendation No. 17: Measurement and quantification of the unremunerated domestic activities of women and their recognition in the GNP' (1991) 10th Session UN Doc A/46/38.

[42] However, the CEDAW Committee uses the phrase 'improvement of living conditions' in a fuller sense in a number of its country reports. In relation to refugees see CEDAW Committee 'Concluding observations of the Committee on the Elimination of Discrimination against Women' (20 July – 7 August 2009) UN Doc CEDAW/C/AZE/CO/4 para 37. In relation to Indigenous women and women of African descent see CEDAW Committee 'Concluding observations of the Committee on the Elimination of Discrimination against Women' (11–29 July 2011) UN Doc CEDAW/C/CRI/CO/5-6 para 39; CEDAW Committee, 'Concluding observations of the Committee on the Elimination of Discrimination against Women' (19 January–6 February) UN Doc CEDAW/C/GUA/CO/7; CEDAW Committee 'Concluding observations of the Committee on the Elimination of Discrimination against Women' (20 October–7 November 2008) UN Doc CEDAW/C/ECU/CO/7; CEDAW Committee

Despite this possibly conflicting or confusing use of different terminology across the two treaties, the broad and specific acknowledgment of social reproduction within CEDAW is helpful in informing an interpretation of the ICESCR that recognises this dimension of life.

Returning to the ICESCR, in elaborating on working conditions related to remuneration, Article 7 requires this remuneration to provide all workers 'as a minimum' with fair wages (Article 7(a)(i)) and 'a decent living for themselves and their families in accordance with the provisions of the present Covenant' (Article 7(a)(ii)). The sub-section dealing with fair wages, which concerns equal pay, particularly between men and women, uses the terms 'wages', 'remuneration' and 'pay' (Article 7(a)(i)). These terms all suggest a monetary measure that fairly compensates work performed. However the next sub-section suggests that the remuneration is directed at achieving something broader – the idea of a 'decent living' (Article 7(a)(ii)). This seems to support the argument that the ICESCR treats work as the means to, but somehow separate from, life. 'Living' is thus the thing that a worker is able to do once they have been remunerated for their services. Where such remuneration is just and favourable, it provides the worker and their family not only with a right to a 'living' but to a 'decent' one.

The idea of a 'decent living' in Article 7 needs to be reconciled with the idea of an 'adequate standard of living' in Article 11. Are decent and adequate synonymous? It seems arguable that 'decent' offers something more – it suggests ideas of a measure based on values rather than something more quantifiable which lies behind the idea of adequacy or 'enough'.[43] Does this idea of decency inform the interpretation of 'living' in the right to 'the continuous improvement of living conditions'? It is possible that the decent living for which fairly remunerated work must provide implies a hierarchy between those in society who can support themselves through (paid) work, and those who cannot. It is also possible that Article 11 envisages State obligations towards those unable to support themselves that guarantee an adequate standard of living rather than a decent one. This hierarchy is troubling in the inequality it appears to endorse – it seems to require more for paid workers than for other people in the society. But the addition of the clause 'the continuous improvement of living conditions' possibly saves Article 11 from this criticism by requiring something that goes beyond adequacy.

'Concluding observations of the Committee on the Elimination of Discrimination against Women' (2 February 2007) UN Doc CEDAW/C/NIC/CO/6.

[43] The questions of what the ICESCR requires for people's lives, whether based on dignity, decency or adequacy; and how to determine the required standards, remain open for debate and development. See ME Salomon, 'Why Should it Matter that Others Have More? Poverty, Inequality, and the Potential of International Human Rights Law' (2011) 37(5) *Review of International Studies* 2137.

The beneficiaries of Article 6 and 7 are, in global terms, a limited category of waged workers in the formal economy – informal/precarious and unpaid workers are not the envisaged subjects of this right.[44] The imagined worker to which this right applies is seen as a (male) breadwinner supporting a family. Article 11(1) seems to accompany the right to work, expecting employment to afford a decent living but requiring the State to step in to provide an adequate living where it does not (whether because incomes are too low, people cannot find work, or people are unable to work). Article 11 is thus closely linked to the right to social security in Article 9 and seems to fill the gaps left by both employment and social security. Curiously, while Article 7(a)(ii) is gender-neutral in its language ('themselves and their families') Article 11(1) uses the male pronoun ('himself and his family'). Article 11, with its focus on food and adequacy seems oriented to addressing poverty and hunger, particularly in developing countries where the formal economy is small and cannot comprehensively address disadvantage. Its language of 'continuous improvement' and the reference to international cooperation which harks back to Article 2 on progressive realisation reinforces this acknowledgment of rights not capable of immediate fulfilment.

The two references to 'living' within Article 11(1) should also be considered. The first part of the right talks of an 'adequate standard of living' which should be contrasted with 'living conditions' in the second part of the right. 'Standard' implies a level, a quantitative measure of adequacy which seems different from the more qualitative implications of the term 'living conditions'. Arguably this latter term suggests more than the material features of life (food, housing, clothing, etc) and includes all those aspects of human existence that make life worth 'living' – family, community, relationships, personal and communal actualisation and development. The conditions needed for this broader idea of living, that go beyond an 'adequate standard of living', should, it is suggested, support social reproduction – the activities that are essential to sustaining life in society.

ii. 'Conditions'

The right to 'just and favourable conditions of work' in Article 7 of the ICESCR provides insight into the meaning of 'conditions' within the Covenant. The word 'conditions' here implies that certain requirements must be met to make work fair and beneficial. Similarly, the Preamble to ICESCR says that ideals of freedom can only be achieved if 'the conditions are created whereby everyone may enjoy

[44] B Saul, D Kinley and J Mowbray, *The International Covenant on Economic, Social and Cultural Rights: Commentary, Cases and Materials* (OUP 2014) 394. For background on the right to work in international law see eg J Sarkin and M Koenig, 'Developing the Right to Work: Intersecting and Dialoguing Human Rights and Economic Policy' (2011) 33(1) *Human Rights Quarterly* 1.

his economic, social and cultural rights, as well as his civil and political rights'. This suggests that the later use of the word 'conditions' in Article 11(1) attaching to 'living' also implies the need for a set of requirements to be met to make 'living' – the realm of 'non-work' – a positive experience based on the fulfilment of certain rights. The conditions set out in Article 7 include: remuneration, health and safety, equal opportunity, and rest and leisure.

Arguably, similar conditions that are rights within the workplace should be rights within the home and community, particularly for those performing unpaid work. Thus, housework and care should be fairly allocated and supported in such a way that it can be performed without exhausting, debilitating[45] and depleting[46] those who perform it. Living conditions, if understood as similar or in parallel to working conditions are those requirements/supports that make living good/just. If we are to think about equivalent conditions in the home to those required at work – remuneration, health and safety, equal opportunity, and rest and leisure – then work in the home arguably should be compensated in some way, undertaken safely, and equally or fairly distributed, alongside time for rest and other leisure activities. These conditions, met by employers in the workplace, must be met by society in the home – hence they are the responsibility of the State, community and individuals.

iii. 'Living Conditions'

Article 6 and 7 dealing with 'work' and Article 11 are, it is suggested, not only closely related, but relate to two sides of the same human experience for which the rights in the ICESCR are designed to provide. They seem to separate work and life, seeing the former as the means to the latter. But the idea of social reproduction as work challenges this bifurcated approach. I suggest that 'living conditions' should be understood as those goods/supports needed to enable a decent life in the home and community being the location of both the activities of social reproduction (including caring, housework, voluntary and communal tasks) and of rest and leisure. Where activities of social reproduction are undertaken primarily by women, leading to unequal quality of life, then the conditions for (decent) living are not being met. Where the market increasingly places demands for long hours on workers and provides wages requiring two-worker families then the capacity for a decent life is limited. In addition, where the home stands in for the State as the site of social reproduction through withdrawal or failure to provide support such as child, elder, disability and health care, then those burdened with this (gendered and classed) work face further inequality of access to a decent life. 'Living conditions' within the right therefore requires fairer distribution of social reproductive work through changed

[45] JK Puar, *The Right to Maim: Debility, Capacity, Disability* (Duke University Press 2017).
[46] Rai et al (n 20).

conditions in the market and public provision and changed gender relations within the home.

B. The Meaning of 'Improvement' and 'Continuous'

The term 'improvement' suggests that the status quo is not as it should be. This is consistent with the use of the term in the right to health which requires the 'improvement of all aspects of environmental and industrial hygiene' (Article 12(2)(b)). This interpretation also aligns with the idea of progressive realisation in Article 2(1) which applies to all rights in the Covenant including Article 11. Clearly Article 11(1) is directed at addressing poverty and lack of development in relation to essential needs (adequate housing, nutrition and clothing) where these are inadequate; but it also envisages a more expansive project where society improves the way people live on an ongoing basis. This would likely include material goods such as transport and communication and services such as childcare (all mentioned in CEDAW) but could also include State programmes to enable greater civic participation or communal activity.

'Continuous improvement' suggests that the way we live is an ongoing process of social development involving evaluation and adjustment, response to new issues, development of new ideas, technologies and methods. It implies that we will learn from our mistakes, find ways to do things better, and try to do more than we did before. It does not see the endpoint of development or the vision of society informed by human rights as fixed but as an ongoing process of social evolution towards a better society.

The failure to support social reproduction and the gender oppression this produces are social problems in need of improvement. Transforming gender relations to create the basis for a fair and just society is a long-term project that is likely to require continuous efforts for improvement. I suggest that it is in fact key to improvement of living conditions and should be recognised as central to the interpretation of Article 11(1).

C. Parties to the Right

The right to the continuous improvement of living conditions impacts a number of parties. It creates obligations on States Parties as well as extra-State bodies where it refers to international co-operation (whether with other States, regional or international bodies).[47] The need for international responsibility to address global care chains and the impacts of transnational businesses on the social reproductive resources of workers, families and communities is

[47] See Campbell, chapter three in this volume.

pressingly urgent.[48] As has been pointed out as a critical concern with international human rights, employers and businesses are conspicuously absent as parties with responsibilities.[49] Yet low wages and harsh working conditions are key contributors to the current deficiencies of social reproduction, just as lack of State support is also complicit. The recognition of business as an agent in rights violations and in addressing these harms is key to an effective rights framework.

ICESCR Article 11 refers to 'everyone' as the beneficiary of the right but also talks about 'himself and his family'. The sexist phrasing (which contrasts to other terminology in the Covenant, as noted above) demonstrates that the drafters saw the primary recipient of the goods being provided by the State (housing, food, clothing and more) as a male household head. This is both problematic in its sexism and assumptions about the family but is also valuable in acknowledging that rights attach not just to individuals but to groups of socially connected people in relationships of mutual support. While the family may have been envisaged as male headed, nuclear, heterosexual, and so on, a more accurate representation of family and community could be read into the right.[50] This would allow it to be used more appropriately to support different types of households with different needs such as single parent households, older persons, people with disabilities, multi-generational extended families, etc. By imagining the household differently we can require greater responsibility from men for social reproductive work while also expecting the State to support the household.

A focus on family alone should also be resisted as many of the aspects of living that human rights should protect may be experienced collectively and communally. This relates, lastly, to the idea of individuals in the ICESCR having duties to other individuals and their community with responsibilities to promote the rights in the Covenant.[51] The State/subject divide between provider and receiver implied in Article 11(1) should not prevent an understanding of the right that sees the individual both depending on and contributing to their community to improve life. However, this idea of communal responsibility should not be used, as it frequently is, to burden people (often women and poor) with social

[48] See B Goldblatt and S Rai, 'Remedying Depletion through Social Reproduction: a Critical Engagement with the United Nations' Business and Human Rights Framework' (2020) 3(2) *European Journal of Politics and Gender* 185.

[49] U Baxi, 'Human Rights Responsibility of Multinational Corporations, Political Ecology of Injustice: Learning from Bhopal Thirty Plus?' (2015) 1(1) *Business and Human Rights Journal* 21. See CESCR, 'General comment No. 24 (2017) on State obligations under the International Covenant on Economic, Social and Cultural Rights in the context of business activities' (10 August 2017) UN Doc E/C.12/GC/24.

[50] However the CESCR has used gender neutral language in relation to the worker and their family. See CESCR, 'General comment No. 23 (2016) on the right to just and favourable conditions of work (article 7 of the International Covenant on Economic, Social and Cultural Rights)' (27 April 2016) UN Doc E/C.12/GC/23, para 18.

[51] ICESCR (n 5) Preamble.

reproductive duties that should either be provided or supported by the State, business and more privileged members of the society. The right should be used to ensure State support for community and for more communal forms of social organisation as envisaged by the three care manifestoes discussed above.

V. CONCLUSION: CONTINUOUS IMPROVEMENT AND UTOPIAN PROCESS

The language of the right to the continuous improvement of living conditions suggests that improving our lives is a project without end point. This idea of 'utopia as evolution – not a place, but a process of becoming'[52] is the message of Ursula Le Guin's celebrated novel, *The Dispossessed*. Shevek, the novel's protagonist, is an anarchist who advocates revolution as individual obligation: 'If it is seen as having any end, it will never truly begin'.[53] Refocusing the idea of 'living' within the right by thinking about the work of care/social reproduction creates the opportunity to imagine a different way of organising our lives. But our ideas should go beyond nostalgia towards historic forms of social reproduction and beyond our critique of the current form, to generate new approaches that fit the (constantly changing) context, as suggested in the care manifestoes discussed here. At the same time, Federici suggests that the seeds of future forms of organisation exist in the struggles to resist the present ones. She argues that 'embryonic' forms of communitarian social organisation anticipate 'a world beyond capitalism and placing at the center of social change the question of social reproduction'.[54] While middle class experiments with, for example, collective kitchens and communal housing design, have been attempted, Federici points to current examples where the world's poorest women have reorganised reproductive activities collectively and reappropriated material resources to achieve this. Similarly, Cooper, in *Everyday Utopias*, documents organised spaces that 'create the change they wish to encounter' through 'building alternatives to dominant practices', including through contesting feminist ideas of care.[55]

Such visions and practices may appear vague, idealistic and incremental in the context of the urgent crises of the climate, inequality and the pandemic. However, alternative visions of society are absolutely key at a time of disillusion and fear. Human rights, informed by such visions, can offer tangible frameworks

[52] J Rodgers, 'Fulfillment as a Function of Time, Or the Ambiguous Process of Utopia' in L Davis and PG Stillman (eds), *The New Utopian Politics of Ursula K. Le Guin's The Dispossessed* (Lexington Books 2005) 181.

[53] UK Le Guin, *The Dispossessed* (Orion Books 1972) 296. See also R Houghton and A O'Donoghue, '"Ourworld:" A feminist approach to global constitutionalism' (2020) 9(1) *Global Constitutionalism* 38 for a discussion of how Le Guin's science fiction informs global constitutionalism.

[54] S Federici, 'Introduction' in S Federici, *Re-enchanting the World: Feminism and the Politics of the Commons* (PM Press 2018) 1, 4.

[55] D Cooper, *Everyday Utopias: The Conceptual Life of Promising Spaces* (Duke University Press 2014) 2, Ch 5.

to guide change. Feminist engagement with rights emerges from a rich tradition that is both critical and utopian.[56] While rights are closely critiqued to demonstrate their patriarchal origins and applications, they are often contested and reimagined to bring about change. Engaging, as this chapter has done, with the right to the continuous improvement of living conditions, has involved both a critical reading of the ICESCR and a reimagining of what it might offer for new modes of social organisation. At a time of health crisis and enormous economic suffering, human rights should do more than promote human survival. They should offer a vision of a world ordered around the just reproduction of life.

[56] See N Lacey, 'Feminist Legal Theory and the Rights of Women' in K Knop (ed), *Gender and Human Rights* (OUP 2004) 13.

12

Measure for Measure

The Challenges of Measuring Continuous Improvement and Lessons from the Sustainable Development Goals

SANDRA FREDMAN

I. INTRODUCTION

THE OPTIMISM OF progress behind the right to the continuous improvement of living conditions in Article 11(1) of the International Covenant on Economic, Social and Cultural Rights (ICESCR)[1] resonates with the aspirations of the 2015 Sustainable Development Goals (SDG) Agenda, an ambitious 15-year programme to eradicate poverty in all its forms and dimensions. Spurred on by the disappointing record of its predecessor, the Millennium Development Goals (MDGs), the 2030 Agenda for Sustainable Development sets out a 'supremely ambitious and transformational vision'.[2] While the conception of continuous improvement of living conditions in Article 11(1) remains at a high level of abstraction, the SDG Agenda sets out a detailed set of goals aimed at achieving its vision by 2030, including gender equality, universal quality education, good health and well-being, the reduction of inequality and zero hunger. Moreover, for the first time, the SDG Agenda explicitly links development goals to a commitment to protect human rights and promote gender equality and the empowerment of women and girls.[3] This raises the question of whether the SDG

[1] International Covenant on Economic, Social and Cultural Rights (adopted 16 December 1966, entered into force 3 January 1976) UNGA Res 2200A(XXI).

[2] United Nations General Assembly 'Transforming our World: the 2030 Agenda for Sustainable Development' (25–27 September 2015) UN Doc A/RES/70/1 para 7 <https://sustainabledevelopment.un.org/post2015/transformingourworld>.

[3] ibid para 3.

Agenda has the potential to give content and a fixed timetable to the right to the continuous improvement of living conditions. At the same time, as we enter the final decade in the countdown to 2030, the challenges inherent in the idea of progress become ever clearer. Most importantly, the Covid-19 pandemic has forced us again to confront the question of whether the promise of progress is illusory.[4] Will the intense global health crisis caused by the Covid-19 pandemic and the consequent economic devastation extinguish the hopes of progress and the possibility of continuous improvement of living conditions as envisaged by Article 11(1)?[5] Or can we reshape a new world order which is fairer, more equal and more sustainable by keeping alive the commitment to a right to continuous improvement of living conditions which embodies these values?

In this chapter I use the experience of drafting and implementing the SDGs to examine the challenges facing an elaboration of the right to continuous improvement of living conditions at a time in which the possibility of progress is more tenuous than ever. In particular, the SDGs illuminate the extent to which the approach to measuring progress influences the content and impact of the ideal of progress, regardless of how visionary the latter might be. Although apparently technical, setting of targets and indicators to measure progress is complex and value-laden and is often used to steer the political agenda. In relation to the SDG monitoring framework, however, these values have not been made sufficiently explicit, or opened up to scrutiny and debate. Thus, while the detailed vision of the SDGs can inform the goals of the right to continuous improvement of living conditions, the SDG experience of measuring progress strongly suggests that, to avoid a similar obfuscation of values behind technical measures, the principles and values informing the elaboration of Article 11(1) need to be clarified. Most importantly, the aggregate approach to measuring the SDGs overlooks the importance of individual rights. Similarly, the SDGs' focus on the poorest and most disadvantaged pays too little attention to rising inequalities between the richest and poorest.

This is not to say that human rights values are themselves uncontested. Liberal values which regard human rights as primarily protecting individuals against State intervention may yield a highly restrictive interpretation of the right to continuous improvement of living conditions. I have argued elsewhere that human rights should hold out more than just the promise of freedom from State interference. They should also concern the extent to which people can enjoy this freedom. This in turn carries with it more than a formal idea of equality before the law, to include substantive equality. In addition, rather than the traditional

[4] M Mutua, 'What is TWAIL?' (2000) 94 Proceedings of the Annual Meeting *American Society of International Law* 31.

[5] Article 11(1) does not define 'living conditions'. For the purposes of the discussion in this chapter, I follow the broad framing of living conditions found in the SDGs, on the basis that there was a universal commitment to these goals in 2015.

individualism of human rights, I argue that we are social beings who can only achieve fulfilment through society. While the State needs to be restrained from abusing its power, only the State can supply what is needed for an individual to fully enjoy their human rights equally with others.[6] These three broad values of positive freedom, substantive equality and social solidarity[7] make sense of the right to continuous improvement of living conditions. The aim of continuous improvement should be to give everyone the possibility of enjoying their freedom, in line with the understanding of freedom put forward by Sen and Nussbaum.[8] At the same time, substantive equality requires attention to be paid to those who are excluded and marginalised. Continuous improvement should not be achieved for some and not others. Moreover, continuous improvement cannot occur by individual actions without State co-ordination, reflecting the value of social solidarity. The right to continuous improvement of living conditions therefore carries the promise of positive freedom for individuals, but only with a commitment to social solidarity and substantive equality through positive State action. When it comes to measuring progress under the right, the values of positive freedom, solidarity, and substantive equality in turn provide a searching tool to require State accountability for achieving the right.

I develop this argument by examining the experience of the SDGs in two main arenas: reproductive rights and caring work. Section II considers how the challenges of setting goals, measuring progress and determining obligations have been experienced in relation to the SDGs and how these learnings can affect the ways in which we give content and traction to the right to continuous improvement of living conditions. Section III argues that some of these difficulties can be addressed by infusing the right to continuous improvement of living conditions with notions of positive freedom, social solidarity and substantive equality. It argues in particular that the values of positive freedom, solidarity and substantive equality should be at the centre of the measurement framework. The SDGs have exposed the risks of measuring progress by means of indicators dependent on aggregate data, which obscure the real values at play. Instead, I argue that the right to continuous improvement of living conditions should be tethered to a set of substantive values, namely, in this context, positive freedom, social solidarity and substantive equality. In this way, monitoring the key concept of continuous improvement can remain firmly based on a qualitative, genuinely human rights-based approach. Most importantly, attention should be paid to State obligations to put in place appropriate structures and funding, rather than regarding data-gathering as a substitute for achievement.

[6] S Fredman, *Human Rights Transformed: Positive Rights and Positive Duties* (Oxford University Press 2008) ch 1.

[7] ibid.

[8] A Sen, *Development as Freedom* (Oxford University Press 1999); M Nussbaum, *Creating Capabilities* (Harvard University Press 2011).

II. DEFINING GOALS AND MEASURING PROGRESS: THE SDGS AND THE RIGHT TO CONTINUOUS IMPROVEMENT OF LIVING CONDITIONS

In giving content to the right to continuous improvement of living conditions, a central challenge is to find means of measuring progress. This in turn requires a sense of what would constitute improvement of living conditions and in what timescale, as well as who is responsible for taking steps to secure such improvement. These are challenges which are already familiar from the experience of other progressively realisable rights.[9] Attempts have been made to address these complexities, through the ideas of a minimum core and benchmarks and indicators, but these are contested and difficult to delineate.[10] Progressive realisation remains elusive, and in some contexts has fallen off the radar entirely.[11] The SDGs have locked down both a defined set of goals and the timetable to achieving them. However, this on its own does not resolve the difficulty in measuring and realising progress. Having set the goals of development after a detailed and wide-ranging consultation, a further process was set in place to measure progress.[12] This is done through targets and indicators, where the target is a subset of the overall goal, and the indicators refer to the data from which progress to the specific target will be assessed.

On its face, the task of selecting targets and indicators appears to be a technical one, and indeed has been assigned to technical committees in the SDG process. However, as Fukuda-Parr and McNeill have shown, the choice of measurement tool is value-laden and often politically driven.[13] While the open and transparent process of agreeing the SDGs led to potentially transformative and ambitious goals, there was a 'slippage of ambition' when targets and indicators were selected.[14] Fukuda-Parr and McNeill acknowledge that in some cases, this is due to genuine difficulty in defining a suitable indicator. However, in other

[9] ICESCR (n 1) Art 2(1).

[10] D Bilchitz, 'Towards a Reasonable Approach to the Minimum Core' (2003) 19 *South African Journal on Human Rights* 1; *Republic of South Africa v Grootboom* 2001 (1) SA 46 (South African Constitutional Court); Fredman (n 6) ch 3; UN Committee on Economic, Social and Cultural Rights, 'General Comment No. 3: The Nature of States Parties' Obligations (Art. 2, Para. 1, of the Covenant)' (14 December 1990) UN Doc E/1991/23; A Chapman, 'A Violations Approach for monitoring the International Covenant of Social, Economic and Cultural Rights' (1996) 18 *Human Rights Quarterly* 23; K Young, 'The Minimum Core of Economic and Social Rights: A Concept on Search of Content' (2008) 33 *Yale Journal of International Law* 113.

[11] *Mazibuko v City of Johannesburg* [2009] ZACC 28 (South African Constitutional Court); S Fredman, *Comparative Human Rights Law* (Oxford University Press 2018) 69–84; M Campbell, 'Monitoring women's socio-economic equality under ICESCR' (2018) 30 *Canadian Journal of Women and the Law* 82.

[12] UNGA 'Work of the Statistical Commission pertaining to the 2030 Agenda for Sustainable Development' (6 July 2017) UN Doc A/RES/71/313; UN Department of Economic and Social Affairs, 'Inter-agency and Expert Group on SDG Indicators' <https://unstats.un.org/sdgs/iaeg-sdgs/> accessed 17 May 2021.

[13] S Fukuda-Parr and D McNeill, 'Knowledge and Politics in Setting and Measuring the SDGs' (2019) 10 *Global Policy* 5.

[14] ibid 12.

cases, they argue, 'indicators are used to reorient or pervert the meaning of the goal.'[15] Although 'obscured behind the veil of an objective and technical choice', they demonstrate that the selection of indicators is frequently highly political.[16] Fukuda-Parr and McNeill specifically point to the targets and indicators for Goal 10, which aims to reduce inequality between and within countries. They argue that the strong norm on reducing inequality was undermined by targets and indicators which focus on the poor and excluded, rather than on extreme inequality. This in turn shuts issues of extreme inequality and concentrations of wealth and income out of the global debate.[17] To this is added a minimalist approach to the measurement of extreme poverty, as was trenchantly demonstrated by Philip Alston in his final report as UN Special Rapporteur for Extreme Poverty and Human Rights. The main reference point for extreme poverty in both the MDGs and the SDGs is the World Bank's measurement of poverty, known as the International Poverty Line (IPL). According to the report, the IPL, which is an average of national poverty lines adopted by some of the world's poorest countries, 'is explicitly designed to reflect a staggeringly low standard of living, well below any reasonable conception of a life with dignity'.[18] Because it is well below the national poverty lines in most countries, the IPL dramatically depresses the number of people regarded as living in extreme poverty. 'By single-mindedly focusing on the World Bank's flawed international poverty line', the report concludes, 'the international community mistakenly gauges progress in eliminating poverty by reference to a standard of miserable subsistence rather than an even minimally adequate standard of living'.[19]

These challenges are considered below in the context of two issues central to the continuous improvement of living conditions, which are also dealt with in the SDGs: reproductive justice and care work.

A. Reproductive Justice

Despite their centrality to both personal and social life, reproductive health rights are not expressly mentioned in ICESCR.[20] This absence has recently been compensated for to some extent by including sexual and reproductive health rights within the right to health in Article 12, elaborated in the Committee on Economic, Social and Cultural Rights' General Comment No 22 in 2016 (GC22).[21] GC22 also mentions other rights which are implicated in reproductive health,

[15] ibid 10
[16] ibid 61.
[17] ibid 61.
[18] Report of the Special Rapporteur on extreme poverty and human rights, 'The parlous state of poverty eradication' (Human Rights Council 44th session, 2 July 2020) para 12.
[19] ibid, para 1.
[20] ICESCR (n 1).
[21] Office of the High Commissioner for Human Rights, 'CCPR General Comment No. 22: Article 18 (Freedom of Thought, Conscience or Religion)' (30 July 1993) UN Doc CCPR/C/21/Rev.1/Add.4.

in ICESCR itself and in other international human rights documents. These include education, non-discrimination, right to work and just and favourable working conditions, as well as rights to life, liberty and security of the person, freedom from torture, and privacy and respect for family life.[22] GC22 stresses too that reproductive health implicates underlying social determinants, such as gender, poverty, ethnic origin and systemic institutional inequalities.[23] Although the right to continuous improvement of living conditions is not part of this list, there are many ways in which reproductive health impacts on the living conditions of women and their families. As a start, access to contraception has been key to women's ability to improve their own and their families' living conditions. Yet there are still large deficits in its availability. It is well-documented that large numbers of children impact on the standard of living of women and the family as a whole. Women with more children face more barriers in combining their unpaid care work with paid work in the market, often leaving few real choices in the quality of employment. Women form the majority of precarious workers and are concentrated among the lowest paid workers. For adolescent girls, pregnancy almost invariably ends their time at school, and makes it difficult to progress in the paid labour force. Yet the global rate for adolescent births remains high. Although the adolescent birth rate declined slightly from 45 births in 2015 to 41 births in 2020, the level of adolescent fertility in sub-Saharan Africa, was still as high as 101 births annually per 1,000 adolescent women.[24]

Even more seriously, rates of maternal mortality remain unpardonably high. Every day in 2017, a shocking 810 women around the world died due to complications of pregnancy and childbirth. Sub-Saharan Africa and Southern Asia account for about 86% of maternal deaths globally.[25] Moreover, these figures conceal vast inequalities. In 2017, the Maternal Mortality Rate (MMR) in the world's least developed countries (LDCs) was as high as 415 maternal deaths per 100 000 live births.[26] This is more than 40 times higher than the MMR in Europe and almost 60 times higher than that in Australia and New Zealand. In Sub-Saharan Africa the MMR was appallingly high, with a MMR of 542 deaths per 100,000 live births. This means that the lifetime risk of maternal death in Sub-Saharan Africa was as much as 1 in 37, by contrast with 1 in 7800 in Australia and New Zealand.[27] Yet it is well-known that the vast majority of maternal deaths can be prevented, and in most cases, with relatively low cost implications.

[22] ibid paras 9 and 10.

[23] ibid para 8.

[24] UN, 'The Sustainable Development Goals Report 2020' (2020) <https://unstats.un.org/sdgs/report/2020/> 29.

[25] ibid 28.

[26] World Health Organization (WHO), UN Children's Fund, UN Population Fund, World Bank Group, and UN Population Division, 'Trends in Maternal Mortality 2000–2017' (2017) 2 <https://apps.who.int/iris/bitstream/handle/10665/327596/WHO-RHR-19.23-eng.pdf?ua=1>.

[27] ibid 2.

As well as differences between countries, there are vast distinctions between the wealthiest and the poorest within countries, reflecting the importance of access to high quality health services.[28] Nor is this only an issue for developing countries. The US has the highest maternal mortality ratio in the developed world. Unlike most countries, maternal mortality in the US is in fact on the rise. Even worse, it is concentrated among poor women and Black women. Black women in the US are three to four times more likely to die from pregnancy complications than white women.[29] In all countries, the scourge of maternal mortality particularly affects adolescent girls. Complications in pregnancy are the leading cause of death among adolescent girls in developing countries; and this is also the second leading cause of death among adolescent girls globally. Adolescent girls are more likely to undergo unsafe abortions than adults: statistics show that as many as three million unsafe abortions occur annually among girls aged 15 to 19.[30]

By adding the right to continuous improvement of living conditions to the cluster of rights identified in GC22, it is possible to capture the centrality of a dynamic approach to sexual and reproductive health rights (SRHR), which must be continually improved to ensure that living conditions can likewise progress. This has been recognised since the 1990s by women's groups, encapsulated in the 1994 programme of action adopted at the International Conference on Population and Development (ICPD) which declared that 'advancing gender equality and equity and the empowerment of women, the elimination of all kinds of violence against women, and ensuring women's ability to control their own fertility, are cornerstones of population and development-related programmes.'[31] The ICPD report emphasised that it was crucial to any population strategy that existing inequities and barriers to women in the workforce should be eliminated. In addition, women's participation in all policy-making and implementation, their access to productive resources and right to inherit property should be strengthened, and governments should invest in education and skill development of women and girls.[32]

The challenge of setting goals, establishing correlative obligations, and measuring progress is therefore acute. However, the experience of measuring

[28] A Chapman, 'Evaluating the health-related targesin the Sustainable Development Goals from a human rights perspective' (2017) 21 *International Journal of Human Rights* 1098, 1103.

[29] WHO and others above (n 26) 70–77; Centers for Disease Control and Prevention, 'Pregnancy Mortality Surveillance System' <https://www.cdc.gov/reproductivehealth/maternalinfanthealth/pmss.html>; A Creanga and others, 'Racial and Ethnic Disparities in Severe Maternal Morbidity: A Multistate Analysis, 2008-2010' (2014) 210(5) *American Journal of Obstetrics and Gynaecology* 435, 437.

[30] High Level Political Forum on Sustainable Development, '2017 HLPF Thematic Review of SDG3: Ensure healthy lives and promote well-being for all at all ages' (2017) 2–3 <https://sustainabledevelopment.un.org/content/documents/14367SDG3format-rev_MD_OD.pdf>.

[31] UN Population Fund, 'International Conference on Population and Development (ICPD)' (adopted 30 June 1999) <https://www.unfpa.org/publications/international-conference-population-and-development-programme-action> principle 6.

[32] ibid para 3.18.

progress through the development goals is salutary, both in relation to the SDGs and their predecessor MDGs. The ICPD report called for fundamental changes in gender relations and underlying social structures which were not easily reduced to quantifiable outcome measures.[33] However, the MDGs' exclusive concentration on maternal mortality obscured the systemic issues related to gender and social inequalities which continue to sustain the appallingly high levels of maternal deaths in childbirth. In their trenchant critique of the reductionism of this approach, Yamin and Boulanger point out that issues crucial to the advancement of sexual and reproductive health rights, such as comprehensive sex education, were left out of funding priorities.[34] Moreover, the estimated 13% of maternal mortality due to unsafe abortions was often explicitly excluded from the data indicating maternal mortality ratios.[35] Instead, a much more holistic approach was required, including the provision of comprehensive sexuality education for both boys and girls; access to contraception and health services; reducing child marriage; and supporting young women to remain in school.

These insights were powerfully advanced by women's groups in the drafting process of the SDGs, leading to some important advances.[36] Thus, the SDGs situate maternal mortality as part of a more general commitment to gender equality and the empowerment of women and girls, as well as making a specific commitment to SRHR. SDG 3, which promises to ensure healthy lives and promote well-being for all, has two targets relating to SHRH. Target 3.1 commits the world to reducing maternal mortality to less than 70 per 100,000 live births by 2030 on maternal mortality. In Sub-Saharan Africa, this entails a dramatic drop, from 542 in 2017. Target 3.7 is equally ambitious. It pledges to ensure 'universal access to sexual and reproductive health-care services,

[33] ibid.

[34] A Yamin and V Boulanger, 'Why Global Goals and Indicators Matter: The Experience of Sexual and Reproductive Health and Rights in the Millennium Development Goals' (2014) 15 *Journal of Human Development and Capabilities* 218.

[35] ibid 225. See also Committee on the Elimination of Discrimination Against Women, 'Views of the Committee on the Elimination of Discrimination against Women under article 7, paragraph 3, of the Optional Protocol to the Convention on the Elimination of All Forms of Discrimination against Women concerning Communication No. 17/2008' (11 to 29 July 2011) UN Doc CEDAW/C/49/D/17/2008.

[36] See A Yamin, 'Power, Politics and Knowledge Claims: Sexual and Reproductive Health and Rights in the SDG era' (2019) 10 *Global Policy* 52; A Galati, 'Onward to 2030: Sexual and Reproductive Health and Rights in the context of the Sustainable Development Goals' (2015) 18(4) *Guttmacher Policy Review* <https://www.guttmacher.org/gpr/2015/10/onward-2030-sexual-and-reproductive-health-and-rights-context-sustainable-development>; A Starrs, 'How SRHR has become central to achieving the SDGs' (Devex, 30 November 2015) <https://www.devex.com/news/how-srhr-has-become-central-to-achieving-the-sdgs-87337>.
For the process leading up to the SDGs see K Donald and S Way, 'Accountability for the Sustainable Development Goals: A Lost Opportunity' (2016) 30 *Ethics and International Affairs* 201; M Langford, 'Lost in Transformation? The Politics of the Sustainable Development Goals' (2016) 30 *Ethics & International Affairs* 167.

including for family planning, information and education, and the integration of reproductive health into national strategies and programmes', again by 2030. Also crucial is Target 3.8 which promises to achieve universal health coverage, including access to quality essential health-care services. To support these changes, Target 3.C undertakes to substantially increase health financing and the recruitment, training and development of the health workforce in developing countries. This is complemented by further targets in SDG5, which aims to achieve gender equality and empower all women and girls. A result of sustained and well-developed campaigning by women's groups,[37] SDG5 includes targets on ending discrimination against women and girls everywhere, eliminating all forms of violence against all women and girls, eliminating all harmful practices, such as child marriage, early and forced marriage and female genital mutilation, and recognising and valuing unpaid care and domestic work through the provision of public service, infrastructure and social protection policies and the promotion of shared responsibility within the household. Most pertinent for SRHR is the commitment to ensure universal access to sexual and reproductive health and reproductive rights as agreed in accordance with the Programme of Action of the ICPD and the Beijing Platform for Action (5.6).

This on the face of it is an impressive set of targets. However, when these potentially transformative goals are reduced to specific tools of measurement, much of their energy drains away. Particularly disappointing are the indicators for maternal mortality, where the two main indicators, the maternal mortality ratio (3.1.1), and the proportion of births attended by skilled health personnel (3.2.2) simply replicate the MDG indicators. This means that the risk remains that inequalities and rights violations will be obscured.[38] Obstetric violence will not feature in the statistics showing an increase in skilled birth attendance. Emergency obstetric care, also seen as key to decreasing women's mortality and morbidity in childbirth, is not mentioned. Particularly glaring is the absence of any mention of abortion, which is a key contributor to maternal death in childbirth. Moreover, as the WHO points out, accurate measurement of maternal mortality is challenging, and many deaths still go uncounted. Many countries lack well-functioning registration systems, and where they do exist, there are still many unregistered deaths, and misclassification of the cause of death.[39]

The same could be said in relation to universal access to sexual and reproductive health care services, including family planning and education. Here there are two indicators: the proportion of women of reproductive age who have their need for family planning satisfied with modern methods (3.7.1); and the

[37] Yamin (n 36).
[38] Chapman (n 28).
[39] WHO and others (n 26).

adolescent birth rate per 1,000 women within the age range 10–14 and 15–19 (3.7.2). Target 5.6, which promises universal access to SRHR in accordance with ICPD and the Beijing Programme for Action, is measured by two indicators: the proportion of women aged 15–49 years who make their own informed decisions regarding sexual relations, contraceptive use and reproductive health care (5.6.1) and the number of countries with laws and regulations that guarantee full and equal access to women and men aged 15 years and older to sexual and reproductive health care, information and education (5.6.2). However, here too the SDG indicators' focus on outcomes rather than the means to achieve those outcomes and do not grapple with some of the deep-seated obstacles to full reproductive rights for women. In particular, the SDGs are not able to identify or address the role of religion in undermining gender equality in this respect.[40]

Equally problematically, the SDGs do not put in place specific obligations or steps which States must take to achieve these goals. This in turn ignores the need to address the interactions between disadvantage, stigma and stereotyping, lack of participation and structural obstacles, all elements of the right to substantive equality.[41] The closest it gets is indicator 3.8.1, which measures the average coverage of essential health services, including reproductive and maternal health. However, progress on this target is not auspicious. According to the 2019 SDG report, based on available data from 2013 to- 2018, almost 40% of countries had fewer than 10 medical doctors per 10,000 people. Equally problematic was the fact that more than 55% had fewer than 40 nursing and midwifery personnel per 10,000 people. The picture was particularly stark in least developed countries, all of which had fewer than 10 medical doctors per 10,000 people, and almost all (98%) had fewer than 40 nursing and midwifery personnel per 10,000 people.[42]

The result is that progress has been painfully slow, and the WHO predicts that the world will fall short of ending preventable maternal deaths by over one million lives by 2030 at the current pace of progress. The WHO points specifically to the need to work much harder to achieve the underlying structural changes, and specifically primary health care, as the most cost effective and

[40] See Committee on the Elimination of Discrimination against Women, 'Summary of the inquiry concerning the Philippines under art 8 of the Optional Protocol to the Convention on the Elimination of All Forms of Discrimination against Women' (22 April 2015) <https://tbinternet.ohchr.org/_layouts/15/treatybodyexternal/Download.aspx?symbolno=CEDAW/C/OP.8/PHL/1&Lang=en>.

[41] S Fredman, 'Substantive Equality Revisited' (2016) 14 *International Journal of Constitutional Law* 712; S Fredman and B Goldblatt, 'Gender Equality and Human Rights Discussion Paper' (2015) Discussion Paper No. 4 For Progress of the World's Women 2015–2016 <https://www.unwomen.org/-/media/headquarters/attachments/sections/library/publications/2015/goldblatt-fin.pdf?la=en&vs=1627>.

[42] UN Economic and Social Council, 'Special edition: Progress towards the Sustainable Development Goals Report of the Secretary-General' (2019) UN Doc E/2019/68 <https://undocs.org/E/2019/68> para 24.

inclusive means of delivering health services, and the cornerstone for achieving universal health coverage. As it emphasises,

> health services that are unavailable/inaccessible or of poor quality, however, will not support the achievement of UHC, as envisioned. Ultimately, we need to expand horizons beyond a sole focus on mortality, to look at the broader aspects – country and regional situations and trends including health systems, UHC, quality of care, morbidity levels and socioeconomic determinants of women's empowerment and education – and ensure that appropriate action is taken to support family planning.[43]

The current focus on quantifiable indicators does not, however, allow such a qualitative view of the interaction between different factors leading to poor quality health care. The 'apparent hegemonic acceptance of indicators as a technology of global governance', Yamin argues, 'is … troubling'.[44] This elevation of technical measures to give the impression of progress disguises the lack of a robust accountability structure and reliance on the private sector for financing. This, in Yamin's view, has meant 'that these noble aspirations would merely add window dressing to the steady march of neoliberal globalization and the inexorably gendered effects of macroeconomic policies'.[45]

Therefore, while the SDGs substantively represent an unquestionable triumph of some of the key aspirations relating to SRHR, the tools to measure progress have waylaid the achievement of these aspirations. Measuring the right to continuous improvement of living conditions should take care to avoid these traps. In particular, the normative commitments inherent in a human rights based approach should expressly guide choices as to determine whether improvements have been instituted and from whose perspective improvements are judged. Positive freedom, substantive equality and social solidarity in the arena of SRHR require a clear focus on redressing the gendered stereotypes which continue to fuel breaches of SHRH, a commitment to providing feasible options for women in relation to reproduction, and a commitment to public services available to all. Without these normative commitments, the rights risk falling into the same traps as the SDGs.

B. Care and Work: A Gendered Perspective

A second way of considering the challenges of measuring the right to continuous improvement of living conditions is through the lens of care and caring work. The Covid-19 pandemic has cast a harsh spotlight on the discord between the foundational role of caring work in society and its undervaluation and

[43] WHO (n 26).
[44] Yamin (n 38) 56.
[45] ibid 55.

invisibility. As schools, playgrounds, nurseries and other public provision for children were forced to close their doors to help slow the spread of the pandemic, parents and family members have had to add multiple caring roles to their existing responsibilities. At the same time, workers in health and elderly care have been in more demand than ever. This has added personal risk to their low pay, their precarious work status, and stressful position. Whether paid or unpaid, caring work has become more visible but not necessarily more valued.

The pandemic has stridently revealed deep-seated fault lines which were already familiar. Women still spend, on average, three times as much time on unpaid domestic and care work than men, according to survey data from 90 countries and areas.[46] This inevitably limits their ability to engage in paid work, leisure and education. Research from high-income countries demonstrates that for women, motherhood brings with it a significant penalty in terms of wages. This contrasts with fatherhood: for most men, fatherhood comes with a wage 'bonus',[47] or higher pay. Moreover, recent cuts to public services in some parts of the world due to austerity have increased women's unpaid work, particularly for low-income women, as well as removing important opportunities for paid caring work for women. The unequal burden of caring work is of particular concern for women living in poverty. It has been shown that the amount, intensity and drudgery of unpaid care work increases with poverty. Poor women often live in inadequate housing, where basic cleanliness and hygiene require great and unremitting exertion. They do not have the resources to invest in labour-saving technology, and might not even have access to electricity or running water to operate washing machines, vacuum cleaners or cookers. Because of lack of access to contraception and family planning services, women in poverty are also likely to have more children.[48] This is exacerbated for women in rural areas, who additionally have the gruelling tasks of collecting fuel and water. Unpaid caring work is a lifetime responsibility for women, from girls taking care of younger siblings, to grandmothers with primary responsibility for grandchildren.[49] This section considers how the SDGs have addressed caring and caring work in their vision of progress. Again, it will be shown that the ambition of the targets is undermined by the narrowness of the measurement processes.

The need for recognition of unpaid care and domestic work was one of the central demands in the negotiations over the SDGs.[50] This campaign

[46] UN Women, 'Families in a Changing World: Global Factsheet' (2019–2020) Report For Progress of the World's Women 2019–2020 <https://www.unwomen.org/en/digital-library/progress-of-the-worlds-women> 6.

[47] ibid 6.

[48] M Carmona and K Donald, 'What does care have to do with human rights? Analysing the impact on women's rights and gender equality' (2014) 22 *Gender & Development* 441.

[49] ibid 444.

[50] For a seminal intervention, see UNGA, 'Report of the Special Rapporteur on Extreme Poverty and Human Rights' (2013) UN Doc A/68/293 <https://ssrn.com/abstract=2437791>.

yielded some important successes. Target 5.4 calls on States to 'recognise and value unpaid care and domestic work through the provision of public services, infrastructure and social protection policies and the promotion of shared responsibility within the household and the family as nationally appropriate'. There is much promise in this formulation. Importantly, it brings together the need to provide public services, infrastructure and social protection, with the promotion of shared responsibility. SDG 5's emphasis on participation is a further and integral part of the drive to address caring work. Target 5.5 requires States to ensure women's full and effective participation and equal opportunities for leadership at all levels of decision-making in political, economic and public life.

The emphasis on unpaid care and domestic work in SDG 5 leaves out of account the crucial interaction between unpaid and paid work, whether through the undervaluation of caring work or through the difficulty in reconciling unpaid care and domestic work with full participation of women in the paid workforce. SDG 8, on growth and prosperity, contains several targets specifically referring to decent work.[51] Most important is target 8.5 which aims to achieve full and productive employment and decent work for all women and men, including for young people and persons with disabilities and equal pay for work of equal value. This is complemented by Target 8.8, which aims to protect labour rights and promote safe and secure working environments for all workers. It makes specific reference to migrant workers, particularly women migrants, and those in precarious employment. Target 8.3 aims to promote development-oriented policies that support, inter alia, decent job creation and the formalisation and growth of micro-, small-, and medium-sized enterprises. Given the very high prevalence of women in informal and precarious employment as well as among migrants, especially in Sub-Saharan Africa, these two targets are potentially of great importance for women. Finally, Target 8.7 aims to eradicate forced labour, end modern slavery and human trafficking, and secure the prohibition and elimination of the worst forms of child labour.

Targets on unpaid work and decent work are further augmented by other SDG goals and targets. Although there is no specific reference to gender, SDG 6 (water and sanitation) and SDG 7 (access to affordable energy) are particularly important for women who are subject daily to the drudgery of carrying water and finding fuel. Target 6.1 sets the goal of achieving universal and equitable access to safe and affordable drinking water for all by 2030; and Target 7.1 aims to ensure universal access to affordable, reliable and modern energy services by then. The same is true for SDG11 (sustainable cities). Target 11.1, by ensuring access for all to adequate, safe and affordable housing and basic services, will have a particular benefit for women, whose primary responsibility for domestic work means that they are especially heavily burdened by poor housing conditions.

[51] S Rai, B Brown and K Ruwanpura, 'SDG 8: Decent work and economic growth – A gendered analysis' (2019) 113 *World Development* 368.

These are constructive and ambitious ways to define progress and could certainly be a major component in determining the content of the continuous improvement of living conditions. Once again, however, these visionary possibilities are emptied of some of their energy by the measurement tools. This is particularly true for Target 5.4, on recognising and valuing unpaid care and domestic work. Here, the only indicator is the proportion of time spent on unpaid domestic and care work, by sex, age and location. However, this indicator is, at best, too bland. As a start, time-use surveys are not available in many countries. In any event, it is difficult to distinguish between unpaid domestic work and care work, as they often overlap.[52] More fundamentally, it does not measure the provision of public services, or infrastructure, or the promotion of shared responsibility.

Similarly disappointing are the indicators for Target 6.1, which, it will be recalled, aims at universal and equitable access to safe and affordable drinking water for all. However, the indicator looks only at the proportion of the population using safely managed drinking water services, without taking into account distance from water services, or investigating who is responsible for fetching water. The same can be said for Target 6.2. which aims to achieve access to adequate and equitable sanitation and hygiene for all, paying special attention to the needs of women and girls. The indicator here is even blander, measuring the proportion of the population using safely managed sanitation services, including a hand-washing facility with soap and water. Since it leaves the gender dimension entirely out of the picture, it will not be able to detect key requirements for women and girls. Most urgent is the need for girls to have access to safe and clean toilets at schools. Otherwise, menstruating girls will continue to choose not to go to school, or, if they do go, risk the discomfort and potential humiliation of dealing with menstruation without proper sanitation.

Similarly deflating are the targets in SDG 8 on decent work. The indicator for Target 8.3 on decent job creation simply counts the proportion of informal employment in non-agricultural employment, disaggregated by sex. Informal employment in agriculture is clearly a key source of informality, and without considering decent job creation in the agricultural sector, many workers will be left out. For Target 8.5 on full employment and decent work, there are only two indicators. The first measures the unemployment rate by sex, age and persons with disabilities. The second measures average hourly earnings of female and male employees by occupation, age and persons with disabilities. Although average hourly earnings are an important measure, this indicator will not on its own capture the different ingredients of hourly earnings discrepancies, which include job segregation, lack of seniority, undervaluation of work and lack of access

[52] UN Women, 'Spotlight on Sustainable Development Goal 5: Achieve gender equality and empower all women and girls' (5 July 2017) <http://www.unwomen.org/en/digital-library/multimedia/2017/7/infographic-spotlight-on-sdg-5>.

to lucrative overtime and bonus opportunities. This makes it difficult to create effective pathways to change. Moreover, by focusing on employees, it entirely leaves out of account workers who fall outside of the formal sector and are precarious. Particularly glaring is the absence of any other criteria for decent work, such as maximum working hours, holiday leave, parental leave and sickness leave. The need for paid sickness leave has become a crucial issue in the time of the pandemic. When workers cannot afford to stay at home despite being potentially infected with the virus, it becomes obvious that paid sickness leave is a community issue. Similarly disappointing are the indicators for Target 8.8 on the protection of labour rights, which chart only frequency rates of occupational injuries, and increase in national compliance of labour rights (freedom of association and collective bargaining).

Decent work is part of the wider exhortation to progress in SDG 8 which commits the world to 'promote sustained, inclusive and sustainable economic growth, full and productive employment and decent work for all.' Here too, the targets are rich and wide-ranging but the indicators measuring progress squeeze out most of their substance. Thus the first set of SDG 8 targets commit the world to sustain per capita growth and to achieve higher levels of economic productivity through diversification, including a focus on high value added and labour-intensive sectors. However, both refer only to annual growth rate of real GDP, per capita for the first, and per employed person for the second. It is well known that GDP is not a comprehensive measure of progress. It does not capture economic inequality, environmental impacts, health, education or life expectancy, and perhaps most importantly, the value of all activities, such as unpaid care work.[53] This will become particularly problematic with the dramatic reversals in progress caused by Covid-19, where steep declines in the real GDP per capita will not reflect the acute inequalities in the cost imposed on those who are well-off compared to those who are already poor and marginalised.

A more nuanced and revealing measurement framework has been developed by the International Trade Union Congress (ITUC), which uses a composite SDG 8 indicator on the basis of four sub-domains, namely, economic well-being, employment quality, labour vulnerability and labour rights.[54] The first sub-domain, economic well-being, specifically demonstrates that income per capita is a poor measure of the well-being of people. Once inequality is included, some higher income countries (measured by GDP) slip down behind some upper middle and even some lower middle income countries.

Similarly, the correlation between GNI per capita and the second sub-domain, employment quality, is weak, with high income countries scoring behind low, lower middle and upper middle income countries in many instances. Recognising that employment and unemployment rates and productivity

[53] Rai and others (n 51).

[54] International Trade Union Confederation, 'SDG decade of action – trade union policy responses' (2020) 27 <https://www.ituc-csi.org/sdg-decade-of-action-trade-union-policy-responses>.

performances cannot be a reliable proxy for quality employment, this index also covers some proxies for quality, including whether jobs are able to fairly maintain purchasing power of salaries and distribute productivity gains, as well as, importantly, whether salaries are able to keep wage-earners far from poverty.

The third sub-domain, labour vulnerability, includes the additional indicator of time-related underemployment and whether the worker will be vulnerable at the end of her career, captured by whether the worker will accrue the right to receive a pension income. For this domain, the majority of countries are below 100 which means that the vulnerability of workers is present all over the world.

The above discussion has shown that, as in the case of SRHR, the question of measurement of paid and unpaid care-work can hide ideological choices behind technical data. Once care is brought within the domain of the right to continuous improvement of living conditions, human rights-based values need to expressly guide choices of measurement criteria. It has been argued above that these values should encompass positive freedom, substantive equality and social solidarity. For care work, to incorporate the objective of positive freedom in the measurement of continuous improvement of living conditions means that data should measure the extent to which such work can enhance the quality of life and feasible options available to carers, for example, through quality public child-care and decent pay and conditions. The objective of substantive equality requires qualitative measurement to include the extent to which care work is properly valued, free of gender stereotypes, and shared between men and women and others in society. The objective of social solidarity requires data to measure the role of the State in providing public services and ensuring decent pay, countering the neo-liberal ideology of privatisation and insisting on transparency and an absence of cronyism in the use of public funds.

III. FROM QUANTITY TO QUALITY: THE SDGS AND THE RIGHT TO CONTINUOUS IMPROVEMENT OF LIVING CONDITIONS

What then is the relevance of this experience for the task of measuring the fulfilment of the right to continuous improvement of living conditions and how can the right inform improvement of the SDGs? Human rights differ crucially from development goals in their focus on the individual, rather than on aggregate outcomes. Human rights are premised on the intrinsic value of each human being, insisting that humans cannot be regarded as a means to an end. Correspondingly, human rights are individual entitlements. Development goals, by contrast, measure success through the improvement of aggregate welfare. In this sense, they are more concerned with how much of the goal has been achieved than the welfare of each individual.

This raises the question of how the aggregate approach to monitoring the SDGs can be reconciled with the individual nature of human rights. On the one hand, the SDGs have the potential to take a systemic approach to key social and economic rights, such as health, food and housing. They can also bring powerful rhetoric towards the mobilisation of resources. On the other hand, the aggregate approach could conceal inequalities, discrimination and exclusion of the most disadvantaged.[55] In their important critical evaluation of the MDG targets, entitled *the Power of Numbers*, Fukuda-Parr, Yamin and Greenstein argue that 'while quantification is the key strength of global goals, it also involves simplification, reification and abstraction, which have far-reaching implications for redefining priorities'.[56] This reductionism of the MDGs, they argue, risks reversing the progress made in the 1990s to see development, not just as economic performance, but as improving human well-being, with human rights at their centre. Instead, they suggest, the methodology of setting targets and selecting indicators needs to go beyond numerical criteria. They also need to give information on equity, participation, transparency and accountability. This requires both quantitative and qualitative targets and indicators. Since the values of equity, participation, transparency and accountability are central to a human rights approach, this suggests that any process of measuring progress under the right to continuous improvement of living conditions cannot rest entirely on numerical criteria.

It is clear therefore that a human rights approach to the conception of continuous improvement of living conditions requires the use of qualitative criteria, which depart from the utilitarian assumptions behind the measurement of development goals. However, a human rights approach is itself contested. The traditional view of human rights as restraining the State from interfering in individual freedom is clearly insufficient, as the reference to 'the ideal of free human beings enjoying freedom from fear and want' in the ICESCR preamble itself attests. It is argued here that the conception must be infused with the values of positive freedom, social solidarity, and substantive equality.[57] Drawing on Sen's capabilities approach the first principle, positive freedom, requires attention to be paid, not just to the existence of rights, but to the extent to which individuals can exercise their rights. The second principle, social solidarity, moves beyond the liberal ideal of an abstract individual and recognises that individuals are interdependent and embedded in society. Continuous improvement of living conditions is only possible through co-operation and ultimately through

[55] Donald and Way (n 36) 203–04.

[56] S Fukuda-Parr, A Yamin and J Greenstein, 'The Power of Numbers: A Critical Review of the Millennium Development Goal Targets for Human Development and Human Rights' (2014) 15 *Journal of Human Development and Capabilities* 105, 105.

[57] This section draws heavily on Fredman (n 6).

social institutions and the State. The third principle, substantive equality, means that progress cannot favour the privileged, and inequalities should be reduced. In particular, substantive equality means that the right to continuous improvement of living conditions should aim to achieve equality in a multi-dimensional way which simultaneously includes redressing disadvantage, overcoming stigma and stereotyping, facilitating voice for the under-represented, and accommodating difference and transforming the underlying structures which perpetuate inequality.

It is notable that Sen developed his positive notion of freedom as agency in the context of defining the goals and measurement of development. His capabilities approach stresses the importance of considering the extent to which people are able to exercise their choices, rather than having the formal right to do so.[58] He also centres his approach in a version of social solidarity. For him, 'individual freedom is quintessentially a social product, and there is a two-way relation between (1) social arrangements to expand individual freedoms and (2) the use of individual freedoms not only to improve the respective lives but also to make the social arrangements more appropriate and effective'.[59] This led him to reject measurement of progress in terms of GDP, and instead to propose the Human Development Index (HDI), which is now widely used. The HDI aims to give a richer measurement of progress by measuring three key dimensions of human development: a long and healthy life; access to education; and a decent standard of living.

However, even these laudable aims are thinned out in the process of measurement. The first dimension, a long and healthy life, is measured by life expectancy; access to education is measured by expected years of schooling of children at school-entry age and mean years of schooling of the adult population; and a decent standard of living is measured by GNI per capita adjusted for the price level of the country. This suggests that while quantitative methods have a role, the human rights value-based approach requires that the focus of attention should be on values and qualitative measurement. In this way, some of the challenges of an individual right, which must be embedded in a wider social context, can begin to be addressed. It should be stressed of course that measuring continuous improvement should not be regarded as the only or even the prime action to be taken in fulfilling the right. As many have pointed out, the SDG indicator framework has taken on its own life, obscuring the need to take targeted and effective action. Measurement should only be seen as a reflection of change, not as change itself.

There is already some commitment to such a qualitative approach to giving content to State's obligations to fulfil human rights, which can be linked to the right to continuous improvement of living conditions. Of the two issues dealt

[58] Sen (n 8) 5.
[59] ibid 31.

with here, reproductive rights has been better developed in recent years. The Convention on the Elimination of All Forms of Discrimination against Women (CEDAW) gives the most detailed attention to reproductive rights. Article 12 requires States Parties to eliminate discrimination against women in the field of health care and to ensure equal access to health care services including family planning. States Parties have an obligation to ensure appropriate services to women in connection with pregnancy, confinement and the post-natal period. This includes granting free services where necessary, as well as adequate nutrition during pregnancy and breast-feeding.[60] This right extends specifically to rural women.[61] In addition, the Committee on Elimination of Discrimination against Women in its General Recommendation 24 (GR24) on the right to health expressly situates its approach to women's reproductive rights in the ICPD programme and the follow-up Beijing programme of action.[62] As mentioned above, the ICESCR does not refer specifically to reproductive rights. However in its General Comment 22 (GC22) on reproductive health in 2016, the CESR locates sexual and reproductive health in a cluster of rights, which include the rights to health, life, education, just and favourable working conditions and the right to be free from violence and discrimination. It also expressly includes civil and political rights, specifically, privacy; security of the person; freedom from torture and other cruel, inhuman or degrading treatment.

Both CEDAW and the ICESCR go some way to countering the SDGs' exclusive focus on outcome measures by paying attention to the means to achieve those outcomes. For example, under CEDAW, it is not sufficient to report solely on outcome data. In addition, States must report on how they supply free services where necessary to ensure safe pregnancy, childbirth and post-partum periods for women. The CEDAW Committee also re-emphasises the duty on States to allocate resources to the maximum available extent.[63] Furthermore, the CESCR Committee recognises that aggregate data outcomes will not be achieved unless appropriate means are put in place. This means at the very least that sexual and reproductive health services should be affordable for all. Essential goods and services should be provided at no cost or ensure that people without sufficient means are given the support to cover the costs, and this includes essential goods and services relating to the underlying determinant of sexual and reproductive health.[64] To this it adds the right to information on sexual and reproductive

[60] Convention on the Elimination of All Forms of Discrimination Against Women (adopted 18 December 1979, entered into force 3 September 1981) UN Doc A/RES/34/180 (CEDAW) Art 12(1).

[61] ibid Art 14(2)(g).

[62] CEDAW Committee, 'General Recommendation No. 24: Article 12 of the Convention (Women and Health)' (1999) UN Doc A/54/38/Rev.1, para 3.

[63] ibid para 27.

[64] CESCR, 'General comment No. 22 (2016) on the right to sexual and reproductive health (article 12 of the International Covenant on Economic, Social and Cultural Rights)' (2016) UN Doc E/C.12/GC/22, para 17.

health. All of this must be of good quality, by which it means that they are evidence-based and up-to-date.[65]

The more in-depth approach to redressing disadvantage in the human rights framework is particularly notable in relation to the right to emergency obstetric services, which, as we have seen, was not included expressly in the SDGs. CEDAW's GR24 emphasises that the duty of States Parties to ensure women's right to safe motherhood includes the right to emergency obstetric services. It also re-emphasises the duty on States to allocate resources to the maximum available extent.[66] The CESCR General Comment goes even further. Far from simply ignoring the importance of emergency obstetric services, as the SDGs do, it declares that lack of emergency obstetric care services constitutes a violation of the right to life and can amount to cruel, inhuman or degrading treatment.[67]

There is less specific attention paid to caring work, whether paid or unpaid, in either CEDAW or ICESCR. Indeed, in many respects, the SDGs are ahead of the human rights framework in their explicit acknowledgement of care and domestic work, and the need both to value care for its own sake, while also reducing the drudgery associated with domestic work and redistributing care between men and women and society more generally. To add qualitative depth requires us to piece together different aspects of both ICESCR and CEDAW. The right to work is recognised by ICESCR in Article 6, 7, and 8 and the right to social security in Article 9. The right to just and favourable conditions of work in Article 7, which is elaborated on in General Comment No 23 of 2016,[68] has important potential for developing a framework for a more qualitative approach, using the concepts of fair wages, equal pay for equal work, a decent living for all, and maximum working hours and periodic holidays with pay. However, the connection with unpaid caring work is not made explicit. CEDAW makes more of a connection. Article 11 of CEDAW requires States Parties to take all appropriate measures to eliminate discrimination against women in the field of employment. Dismissal on grounds of pregnancy or maternity leave should be prohibited, and maternity leave with pay must be introduced without loss of former employment, seniority or social allowances. This is augmented by Article 11's requirement of the right to equal treatment in respect of work of equal value as well as, importantly, in the evaluation of the quality of work. This connects to some extent with unpaid caring work in Article 5, which requires States Parties to ensure that family education includes a 'proper understanding of maternity as a social function and the recognition of the common responsibility of men and women in the upbringing and development of their children'.

[65] ibid para 21.

[66] General Recommendation No 24 (n 62) para 27.

[67] General Comment No 22 (n 64) para 10.

[68] CESCR, 'General Comment No. 23 (2016) on the right to just and favourable conditions of work' E/C.12/GC/23, 27 April 2016.

CEDAW also goes some way towards structural change in its requirement, in Article 11, that States should encourage parents to combine family obligations with work responsibilities and participation in public life, especially through promoting the establishment of a network of child-care facilities.

However, a truly transformative approach would need to go much further than the sum of each of these elements. There remain some crucial aspects of caring work which are not expressly dealt with by CEDAW or ICESCR which could be recognised within a right to continuous improvement of living conditions. This in turn means that more attention needs to be paid to how to monitor continuous improvement, without falling into the reductionism of the SDG approach to monitoring. The principles of positive freedom, solidarity and substantive equality should be mobilised to ensure that a qualitative approach can be taken, focused on putting relevant structures in place rather than relying on aggregate data and utilitarian outcomes.

This raises the question of whether the human rights approach should be read back into the SDGs. There is a potential conduit to do so in that the 2030 SDG Agenda expressly links human rights and development goals. In its preamble, *Transforming our World* declares that the Agenda is grounded in the UDHR and international human rights treaties. Furthermore, it resolves to protect human rights and promote gender equality and the empowerment of women and girls.[69] However, as Yamin argues, 'inserting the language of rights into the declaration of the Agenda 2030 or the SDG targets did not guarantee either the laws, social practices or institutional structures to promote, interpret and enforce them'.[70] Most governments, global institutions and private sector actors were quite content with a weak accountability structure. In addition, there was an overwhelming reliance on the private sector for financing and implementation. The proliferation of indicators became a conveniently technical edifice to obscure these normative commitments. The CESCR has attempted to redress this deficit by pointing out that national action plans for the implementation of the SDGs should take full account of the recommendations it issues to States Parties in the context of the periodic reporting process.[71] In its statement on the ICESCR and the SDGs in 2019, the CESCR sets out what it calls a 'rights-based methodology' for States in implementing their obligations under the Covenant. According to the statement, the Covenant requires outcomes to be realised in ways that are consistent with the principles of participation, transparency, accountability, non-discrimination, empowerment of beneficiaries, and respect for the rule of law. This normative framework, the statement declares, can be applied to the implementation of all SDGs.[72] While these are all laudable, they

[69] UNGA (n 2) Preamble paras 3 and 8.

[70] Yamin (n 36) 55.

[71] Committee on Economic, Social and Cultural Rights, 'The Pledge to "Leave No One Behind": The ICESCR and the 2030 Agenda for Sustainable Development', 8 March 2019, para 19.

[72] ibid paras 11, 12.

tend to be process-oriented rather than providing a substantive content. This is especially true of the principles of participation, transparency, accountability and respect for the rule of law. Here too, to ensure a genuine commitment to continuous improvement of living conditions, the principles of positive freedom, solidarity and substantive equality should be applied to go further than a rights-based methodology, to a rights-based outcome.

IV. CONCLUSION

In this chapter I have examined the extent to which the experience of the SDGs can illuminate the challenges faced in capturing an ideal of progress through the right to continuous improvement of living conditions in ICESCR. In particular, I have demonstrated that the process of measurement, while seemingly technical, disguises key value judgements and risks giving a misleading impression of progress. I have argued that the SDG experience of measuring progress strongly suggests that, to avoid a similar obfuscation of values behind technical measures, the principles and values informing the elaboration of Article 11(1) need to be clarified. By focusing in on reproductive rights and caring and domestic work, this chapter has exposed the risks of measuring progress by means of aggregate data, which subtly denude the ideal of progress of much of its richness. Instead, I have argued that the right to continuous improvement of living conditions should be tethered to a set of substantive values, namely, in this context, positive freedom, social solidarity and substantive equality. In this way, monitoring the key concept of continuous improvement can remain firmly based on a qualitative, genuinely human rights based approach. Most importantly, attention should be paid to State obligations to put in place appropriate structures and funding, rather than regarding data-gathering as a substitute for achievement.

13

Entangled Rights and Reproductive Temporality

Legal Form, Continuous Improvement of Living Conditions, and Social Reproduction

RUTH FLETCHER

I. INTRODUCTION: ON RIGHTS-WORK AS LEGAL REPRODUCTION

In watching this collection build in response to Goldblatt and Hohmann's call,[1] I have begun to see this rights-work as a kind of collaborative legal reproduction. We contributors to this collection have taken hold of an empty legal form and turned it into a range of legal beings that might thrive if supported, or might fade away. Yet it quickly became obvious that the right to continuous improvement of living conditions[2] was not as empty as we might have first imagined it to be.[3] As we talked and wrote, wrote and talked, people and things tumbled out of the form and claimed attention. The possibility of fleshing out the right, a possibility that once seemed to take us down an open and free path, came to reveal a variety of expectations, some easier to handle than others. Chief amongst them perhaps was the concern that a commitment to continuous improvement of living conditions may buy into an extractive model of growth, one which depletes[4] rather than restores.[5] Others emerged through

[1] Hohmann and Goldblatt, introduction to this volume.

[2] The right is part of Article 11 of the UN's International Covenant on Economic, Social and Cultural Rights adopted 16 December 1966, entered force 3 January 1976) UNGA resolution 2200A (XXI) (ICESCR).

[3] Hohmann, chapter two in this volume.

[4] SM Rai, C Hoskyns and D Thomas, 'Depletion: The Cost of Social Reproduction' (2014) 16(1) *International Feminist Journal of Politics* 86.

[5] Goldblatt, chapter eleven in this volume; Skogly, chapter eight in this volume; for an account of the problem with an extractive property-based approach see M Davies, 'Can Property Be Justified in an Entangled World?' (2020) 17 *Globalizations* 1104.

thinking about different rights infrastructures[6] and their cultures, resources and likely effects in fleshing out the right. When we scholars do this work of searching out rightful paths – watching how they are used, imagining how they might be, adopting resources from elsewhere in fixing them up – we take rights as material legal forms and reproduce them anew.

We are not in full control of our reproductive labour,[7] and this work pulls us in uncomfortable directions.[8] There will be times when withdrawal from rights labour seems best because the rights have become encrusted with channels that divert resources away from those that need them. But this work of imagining and actualising[9] what rights might be is socially necessary labour. It offers a way of doing legal rights that is neither the promotion of a liberal progressive agenda nor a critical rights-scepticism, but stays attentive to both while holding on to a materialist approach to the world. Struggling over rights is socially necessary work because rights struggle is one of the life-making activities that is routinely denigrated and devalued by worldly arrangements. Feminists and other critical legal actors have come to occupy this terrain of rights labour by developing sets of practices which entail selecting in the people and things that might just push the legal form of rights in a direction that comforts and shelters.[10] As we write, and as the writing feeds into other activities, we are actively reproducing those legal worlds and making law accountable to social reproduction.

I turn to the materialist feminist thought of social reproduction theory to help me make sense of this rights work because it calls for the identification of the actual ways that life-making activities contribute to capitalist social relations, *and* promise to make the world otherwise.[11] As Ferguson[12] explains in her recent account of the development of social reproduction thought, the utopian dimensions of social reproduction theory are more evident in the autonomist Marxist feminist school,[13] while the more critical-of-the-world-as-it-is

[6] S Fredman, chapter twelve in this volume.

[7] M O'Brien, *The Politics of Reproduction* (Routledge and Kegan Paul 1989).

[8] R Chadwick, 'On the politics of discomfort' (2021) *Feminist Theory* online at doi:10.1177/1464700120987379.

[9] D Cooper, *Everyday Utopias* (Duke University Press 2013).

[10] M Enright, K McNeilly and F De Londras, 'Abortion Activism, Legal Change and Taking Feminist Law Work Seriously' (2020) 71 *Northern Ireland Legal Quarterly* OA7; G Bhattacharya, 'The Poetics of Justice: Aphorism and Chorus as Modes of Anti-Racism' (2019) 27 *Identities* 53.

[11] D Alessandrini, 'Of Value, Measurement and Social Reproduction' (2018) 27(4) *Griffith Law Review* 393; D Alessandrini, 'Immaterial Labour and Alternative Valorisation Processes in Italian Feminist Debates: (re)exploring the "commons" of re-production' (2012) *Feminists@Law* <https://journals.kent.ac.uk/index.php/feministsatlaw/article/view/32>; I Bakker, 'Social Reproduction and the Constitution of a Gendered Political Economy' (2007) 12(4) *New Political Economy* 541; T Bhattacharya (ed), *Social Reproduction Theory: Remapping Class, Recentering Oppression* (Pluto Press 2017); J Elias and SM Rai, 'Feminist everyday political economy: Space, time and violence' (2019) 45(2) *Review of International Studies* 20. P Kotiswaran, 'The laws of social reproduction: A lesson in appropriation' (2013) 64(3) *Northern Ireland Legal Quarterly* 317.

[12] S Ferguson, *Women and Work: Feminism, Labour and Social Reproduction* (Pluto 2020).

[13] S Federici, *Revolution at Point Zero: Housework, Reproduction, and Feminist Struggle* (PM Press 2012).

dimensions come through in those social reproduction theorists who continue to draw on a Marxist theory of value.[14] Social reproduction theory has shown us how the continuous time needed for suturing reproduction and production together in liveable ways is extracted from gendered and marginalised bodies with no return.[15] If social time can be filled out more slowly[16] and sustainably, this allows us to imagine that a legal norm of continuous improvement could mean something other than a commitment to a linear, progressive and extractive continuity. How the continuity of 'continuous improvement' takes legal form, and goes on to shape and be shaped by social worlds through that form, is a matter for rights labourers and their kin. Social reproduction offers the potential to think through the content and the form of the right[17] in ways which see, but distance themselves from, commodifying and extractive practices. Building on social reproduction theory's concern for the non-recognition of time spent on life-making activities,[18] and its commitment to the valuing of time spent providing care on non-capitalist terms, I turn to scholarship on law and time[19] to flesh

[14] Such as L Vogel, *Marxism and the Oppression of Women: Toward a Unitary Theory* 2nd edn (Haymarket Books 2013).

[15] A Mezzadri, 'On the value of social reproduction' (2019) *Radical Philosophy* <https://www.radicalphilosophy.com/article/on-the-value-of-social-reproduction>.

[16] On this point, social reproduction theory connects with critical race perspectives that document and critique the uneven exhaustion of differently situated racialised bodies, eg A Emejulu and F Sobande (eds), *To Exist is to Resist: Black Feminism in Europe* (Pluto 2020), including through accelerated rates of death, see R Gilmore Wilson, *Golden Gulag: Prisons, Surplus, Crisis and Opposition in Globalizing California* (University of California Press 2007), and erasure of entitlement to land through title registration, see S Keenan, 'From Historical Chains to Derivative Futures: Title Registries as Time Machines' (2019) 20(3) *Social and Cultural Geography* 283. The commitment to a political aesthetics of slowness in the university is a kind of material intervention that seeks to challenge these dynamics of exhaustion, extraction and erasure and their infection of academic labour eg A Mountz et al, 'For slow scholarship: A feminist politics of resistance through collective action in the neoliberal university' (2015) 14(4) *ACME: An International Journal for Critical Geographies* 1235 <https://www.acme-journal.org/index.php/acme/article/view/1058>; K van Marle, '"Life is not simply fact": Aesthetics, atmosphere and the neoliberal university' (2018) 29 *Law and Critique* 293.

[17] For an earlier account of how the materialist legal analysis of rights as commodity forms needs to accommodate patterns of consumption and social reproduction, see R Fletcher, 'Legal Form, Commodities and Reproduction: Reading Pashukanis' in M Drakopoulou (ed), *Feminist Encounters with Legal Philosophy* (Routledge 2013) 138.

[18] Ferguson comments: 'women do the majority – 75 per cent – of the world's unpaid care and domestic work. They spend up to three hours more per day cooking and cleaning than men do, and anywhere from two to ten hours more per day looking after children and the elderly. Whatever the hardship or rewards of such work, it remains the case that those who govern our countries and economies do not recompense or adequately recognise it as a contribution to overall social wealth'. Ferguson (n 12) 9.

[19] T Chowdhury, *Time, Temporality and Legal Judgment* (Routledge 2020); M Enright, '"No. I Won't Go Back to It": National Time, Trauma and Legacies of Symphysiotomy in Ireland' in E Grabham and S Beynon-Jones (eds), *Law and Time* (Routledge 2018); E Grabham, *Brewing Legal Times: Things, Form and the Enactment of Law* (University of Toronto Press 2016); C Greenhouse, *A Moment's Notice* (Cornell University Press 1996); J Harrington, 'Time' in *Towards a Rhetoric of Medical Law* (Routledge 2017) ch 4; S Keenan (n 16); R Mawani, 'The Times of Law' (2015) 40 *Law and Social Inquiry* 253; M Valverde, *Chronotopes of Law* (Routledge 2015).

out how a legal form of continuous improvement of living conditions (CILC) might reproduce itself anew through rights-work which selects-in less obvious sources.

Some scholarship on law and time addresses international human rights explicitly by asking questions about the *progressive* realisation of rights,[20] or the *cyclical* monitoring of human rights implementation,[21] or *delay* in addressing injustices.[22] But most of the scholarship on the relationship between law and time that I am drawing on here does not focus on international human rights in particular. Rather, I think it could be useful for thinking through the under-explored right to continuous improvement of living conditions, because it speaks to the more ephemeral, intangible dimensions of the right. Thinking about the right from a perspective which theorises law and time helps us identify the temporal particularity of the right, while also seeing its connections to other rights. Secondly, the law and time literature approaches law as a diverse field of activity comprised of statute, cases, activist lawyering, and other processes of legal reproduction that move in and out of the terrain of international human rights. These porous processes reproduce law as they take and make time by translating the apparently non-legal (eg evidence of the probability that a disease will develop in a particular time frame) into legal phenomena (eg legal standards for deciding when a claim for financial assistance or compensation is met), and back again. By drawing on the insights of scholarship on law and time, I show how rights labour might reproduce the legal form of the right to continuous improvement of living conditions so as to flesh out alternatives to an extractive, flattening version.

First, I show how the scholarship on time and human rights is concerned with an overly linear approach to law's sense of normative progress over time, and that this contributes to a critical attachment to the disruptive potential of an 'untimely' future as an alternative. I argue that one way to avoid being limited by binaries of progress and disruption, is to build on this concern about the progressive time of human rights and engage with distinctions between the normative, material and affective dimensions of law's timeliness, time, and temporality respectively. My hope is that such an engagement will facilitate future conversations between international human rights and other legal sources of rights. If we can draw on senses of legal time that operate across constitutional,[23]

[20] JN Erdman, 'Theorizing Time in Abortion Law and Human Rights' (2017) 19(1) *Health and Human Rights* 29.

[21] K McNeilly, 'Are Rights out of Time? International Human Rights Law, Temporality and Radical Social Change' (2019) 28(6) *Social and Legal Studies* 817.

[22] KG Young, 'Waiting for Rights: Progressive Realization and Lost Time' in KG Young (ed), *The Future of Economic and Social Rights* (CUP, 2019); Enright (n 19).

[23] ibid; see also F de Londras on an ecosystem of constitutional interpretation that could include judicial innovation with timely matters: 'In Defence of Judicial Innovation and Constitutional Evolution' in L Cahillane, T Hickey and J Gallen, (eds) *Judges, Politics and the Irish Constitution* (Manchester University Press 2016).

common law,[24] statutory,[25] and vernacular[26] rights, this is likely to make a dialogue of mutual interest in 'continuous improvement' more relevant across different constituencies of rights labourers. Different rights labourers will have different expertise and motivation. Making the most of a dialogue between them means imagining a multi-dimensional process which has points of connection and disconnection so that the dialogue can move things along, possibly in different but mutually supportive directions, and possibly at different paces. When I use the label 'normative' to draw attention to the parts of the scholarship which see some sense of a prescriptive timeliness at work, I am reading others reparatively[27] for my purposes. For example, I show how Harrington's work on law as rhetoric[28] provides insights which help me draw out normative dimensions of legal time, even though his main concern is with material and affective dimensions of law's persuasive and rhetorical use of time. I identify enduring, punctual and porous time as evidence of light normative commitments in the persuasive rhetoric of common law, statute and evidence-based methods of legal claim-making, respectively. The material dimensions of law's relationship with time allows me to put the older materialist attachments of social reproduction into conversation with a newer materialist approach to lively, or eager, objects.[29] The vibrant matter of Grabham's eager objects throws up concrete things, from cells to paperwork, that make a material difference to how time is counted. Eager objects are social artefacts of a world which an older materialist sees as generating value for capitalism through the sequencing and synchronising of activities that suture together productive and reproductive worlds. The third, felt, dimension of time draws our attention to the visceral sensations and knowing emotions that are felt as temporal legal arrangements

[24] Chowdhury traces a spectrum of abstract and concrete adjudicative temporalities as judges make some factual contexts more proximate than others (n 19) 13; Mawani reads Parker through Bergson's attachment to the flow of time to think about the common law as having duration and being in a state of becoming 'oriented to the past while reaching to the unforeseeable future' (n 19) 255. Ring shows how the Irish courts constructed a 'dominion-centred' approach to enable prosecutions of historical child sexual abuse cases by justifying a delay in reporting of abuse if the victim was under the dominion of the perpetrator, see S Ring, 'The Victim of Historical Child Sexual Abuse in the Irish Courts 1999–2006' (2017) 26(5) *Social & Legal Studies* 562.

[25] C Murray, 'Moving Towards Rights-based Mental Health Law: The Limits of Legislative Reform' (2013) 49 *Irish Jurist* 161.

[26] S Madhok, *Vernacular Rights Cultures: The Politics of Origins, Human Rights and Gendered Struggles for Justice* (CUP 2021). C Pierson and F Bloomer, 'Macro- and Micro-political Vernacularizations of Rights: Human Rights and Abortion Discourses in Northern Ireland' (2017) 19(1) *Health and Human Rights Journal* 173.

[27] A reparative reading is one that seeks out other contributions in the work for the purposes of enriching the 'gene pool' of critical perspectives; see E Kosofsky Sedgwick, 'Paranoid Reading and Reparative Reading; or, You're So Paranoid, You Probably Think This Introduction is About You' in E Kosofsky Sedgwick (ed), *Novel Gazing: Queer Readings in Fiction* (Duke University Press 1997).

[28] Harrington (n 19).

[29] Grabham (n 19) ch 1; J Hohmann, 'Diffuse Subjects and Dispersed Power: New Materialist Insights and Cautionary Lessons for International Law' (forthcoming 2021) *Leiden Journal of International Law*; A Perry-Kessaris, The Pop Museum of Legal Objects Project: An Experiment in Socio-Legal Design' (2017) 68(3) *Northern Ireland Legal Quarterly* 225.

send a charge through space, a charge which might calm things down, exert pressure, or express concern. If legal sources can demonstrate such diversity and multidimensionality in the experience of time, then imagining and actualising the continuous improvement of living conditions as a legal form of time which replenishes rather than depletes becomes more tangible.

Thinking about how the legal form of continuous improvement could reproduce with these different sources of legal time offers a pathway that pulls against extractive possibilities. By pressing against a legal trend of ongoing relentless 'improvement' and doing more with less, it offers the possibility of a replenishing alternative, but one which knows its own potential for co-option. This pressing seeks out a legal form of rights which refuses the flattening consequences of commensurable contractual exchange and the thinning effects of linear progression. By watching and working law's porosity, as social relations become legal and legal relations become social, we can make visible-for-use a thicker, multi-layered and circuitous series of connections between timely norms, materials and affects. Such a reproductive temporality of the continuous could animate the legal right by working its relationship with material resources and affective arrangements in generating continuous improvement of living conditions. I argue that we might best think of the legal form of this right as 'entangled' since it holds different relations together and could go in different directions depending on how it is used. In thinking through entangled rights, I'm working with one of Haraway's knots of citation as an indicator of a mixed genealogy of knowledge, a knot that is crafted by weaver and fabric.[30]

I started to think about entangled legal forms while trying to make sense of everyday rights engagements as they connect different moments of reproductive in/justice.[31] But the entangled forms of new materialists were also hovering in the air, with their feminist concern for the materiality of lively objects,[32] a concern that has had significant influence on scholarship about law and time. But my aim here is to think through the right to continuous improvement of living conditions from an 'older' materialist feminist perspective, one which sees connections with these other sources of knowledge, and imagines the right as fruitfully, if sometimes frustratingly, entangled. How is such a right a legal form of social reproduction – a kind of legal reproduction we might say – as it reproduces with legal sources of normative timeliness, material time and felt temporality?

In what follows, I show firstly how legal commitments to timeliness are not just a matter of good process, but carry normative dimensions, normative dimensions that could be light touch. Progressiveness may be the default norm

[30] D Haraway, *Staying with the Trouble: Making Kin in the* Chthulucene (Duke University Press 2016) 91.

[31] R Fletcher, '#Repealedthe8th: Translating Travesty, Global Conversation and the Irish Abortion Referendum' (2018) 26 *Feminist Legal Studies* 233, 244.

[32] Grabham (n 19); Davies (n 5); M Davies, 'Material subjects and vital objects – prefiguring property and rights for an entangled world' (2016) 22(2) *Australian Journal of Human Rights* 37.

informing a sense of legal timeliness that rights labourers could put to work in the right to continuous improvement of living conditions. But other light legal norms of timeliness – disruptive, enduring, punctual – are also available for the legal reproduction of the right. The right may indeed become entangled as the interactivity of legal relations brings these different norms to bear on it. That tangle may confuse and distract, but it could also become a kind of care infrastructure as rights labourers find sources of shelter in the different normative layers for reproducing continuity. Secondly, rights labour could reproduce continuous improvement by drawing on the material resources of care labour and lively objects. It could synchronise and sequence the different rhythms and routines involved in juggling multiple materialities for counting time sustainably. This synchronising and sequencing sometimes occurs by working with the micro-processes of time as the counting of cells or the predictions of drugs manuals provide speeds which expand or contract the pace of the sequence. Thirdly, continuity might reproduce temporality by producing feelings, emotions and affects which hold up, or support, the people, things and relations of time-making and flesh out an ephemeral legal infrastructure for social reproduction.

II. SOCIAL REPRODUCTION, MATERIALITY AND CONTINUOUS TIME

> All the care work, cleaning, and maintenance, and the work done within the health care system and in agriculture are *indispensable* infrastructure today. What are the criteria for declaring them as such? It is the fact that they express *capital's limit: what social life cannot do without in order to continue.*[33]

I turn to social reproduction theory in seeking out a materialist approach to the form as well as the content of rights, a materialist approach which sees the danger that 'continuous improvement' will be mobilised by extractive social relations whatever our good intentions, but offers a hopeful alternative to paranoid[34] critique. Social reproduction theory explains and values the life-making activities that contribute to capitalist economies by generating the people, shelter and community that labour power needs to reproduce itself. As Elias and Rai explain, social reproduction encompasses 'all of those activities involved in the production of life. This includes biological reproduction, the work of caring for and maintaining households and intimate relationships, the reproduction of labour, and the reproduction of community itself – including forms of social provisioning and voluntary work. Social reproduction also includes unpaid production in the home of goods and services and the reproduction of culture

[33] L Cavallero and V Gago, 'Feminism, the Pandemic and What Comes Next?' (*Critical Times: Interventions in Global Critical Theory*, 21 April 2020) <https://ctjournal.org/2020/04/21/feminism-the-pandemic-and-what-comes-next/>.

[34] Kosofsky Sedgwick (n 27).

and ideology that stabilises (as well as sometimes challenges) dominant social relations'.[35]

Adopting a social reproduction perspective means that we consider, and value, those life-making activities that are necessary for the 'continuous improvement of living conditions'. Social reproduction offers us resources which take us beyond binary approaches to production and reproduction.[36] By focusing on the life-making activities that are necessary for production's generation of surplus value, social reproduction has traced a relationship between reproduction and production. As care and cleaning work have been increasingly commodified in ways which generate precarious, gendered and racialised workforces, life-making activities are rendered productive, but stratified.[37] The interactions involved in practical life-making activities may become extractive innovations of capitalist relations, in much the way that the flexibility colleagues practised for each other while 'balancing' work and family life has been taken up through governance as a means for stretching the worker into constant availability.[38] But they may also be organised so as to hold racialised patriarchal capitalism to account and generate the potential for a feminist world.

When feminist strikers withhold care, they generate shelter and sustenance for each other.[39] If social reproduction offers us a materialist feminist theory which is concerned with tracing relationships between reproduction and production, and the many forms they can take, it also offers us a way to imagine engaging and valuing the work of life-making on its own terms. And the legal labour of making rights work so as to claim necessary resources, build social infrastructure and generate spaces for life, becomes a kind of social reproduction. This is why social reproduction theory offers a critical path beyond the materialist analysis of rights as commodity forms that flatten out social life.[40] If we think about the practical human activity of making rights work for the production of life, this brings rights labour into view as a contribution to social reproduction. This legal contribution is about making life liveable under, and even beyond, capitalism. It offers hope that the legal lifeline offered by rights might become a way out, even as it also might become another thread in the capitalist machine. If the right to continuous improvement is to deliver on such a potential then we need to identify how law makes time, and how legal time-making might contribute to critical rights labour.

[35] Elias and Rai (n 11).

[36] Mezzadri (n 15).

[37] S Colen, '"Like a Mother to Them": Stratified Reproduction and West Indian Childcare Workers and Employers in New York' in F Ginsburg and R Rapp (eds), *Conceiving the New World Order* (University of California Press 1995).

[38] Grabham (n 19) ch 5; E Grabham, 'Doing Things with Time: Flexibility, Adaptability, and Elasticity in UK Equality Cases (2011) 26(3) *Canadian Journal of Law and Society* 485.

[39] V Gago, '#WeStrike: Notes Towards a Political Theory of the Feminist Strike' (2018) 117(3) *South Atlantic Quarterly* 660; C Arruzza, 'From Social Reproduction Feminism to the Women's Strike' in T Bhattacharya (ed), *Social Reproduction Theory* (Pluto Press 2017) ch 10.

[40] Fletcher (n 17).

One challenge is that much of the law and time literature is informed by theoretical perspectives which are not particularly visible in valuing social reproduction. As Franklin has noted,[41] new materialism and old materialism tend not to be put in conversation with each other. I respond to Franklin's provocation and argue that the new thing-focused materialist approach to timely reproduction may be put to work with an older value-focused materialist approach towards a feminist world of valuing the things that contribute to social reproduction. If we understand the lively objects of a new materialist interest in time, as things which are made and remade, this can complement an old materialist interest in identifying the value of such re/making and organising it for non-capitalist purposes. By figuring out how different theoretical contributions speak to mutual interests in time, we make rights labour reproduce itself in a way which connects across theoretical constituencies.

A materialist perspective on the value of time, such as that provided by Elias and Rai,[42] is important because it calls for continuity to be replenished. Their work draws out the significance of invisible time spent suturing together productive and reproductive activities, and of its possible redirection. An old materialist approach to time has tended to emphasise the way that clock time organises labour power into blocks of time with deadlines that are commensurable and become the object of exchange.[43] More recently, Adkins has argued that we are seeing event time displace clock time as the key mode of post-Fordist organising of gendered labour.[44] But social reproduction theory helps us see time and continuity not just as clock time which passes us through the machinery of modern capitalism, and not just as the rhythms of the natural world, but as social time which is material in its need to be fed, nourished and sheltered while developing a world that works with natural rhythms as it lengthens the shadow of machine clocks. A new materialist approach to time such as Grabham's[45] helps us see how eager objects and artefacts contribute to this process as they also participate in the suturing together of reproduction and production.

Watching how law reproduces with time helps us imagine, and actualise, what continuous improvement might be, and how it could work in multiple ways. The term 'continuous' directly invokes time by conjuring up a normative sense of a commitment to the enduring and ongoing. The 'continuous improvement' also captures time indirectly as a material resource that is a dimension of the living conditions, which are to be continuously improved. Working with the

[41] S Franklin, 'Sexism as a means of reproduction: Some reflections on the politics of academic practice' (2015) 86 *New Formations* 15.

[42] Elias and Rai (n 11).

[43] C Everingham, 'Engendering Time: Gender Equity and Discourses of Workplace Flexibility' (2002) 11(2–3) *Time & Society* 335.

[44] L Adkins, 'Sociological Futures: From Clock Time to Event Time' (2009) 14(4) *Sociological Research Online* 88.

[45] Grabham (n 19) ch 1.

continuous improvement of living conditions can also be thought of as having an affective dimension because different feelings of exhaustion, elation, boredom and more, are conjured up as rights work reproduces this commitment. By drawing on the law and time scholarship to imagine what a right to continuous improvement might be, I consider the value of lively objects for the utopian dimensions of social reproduction theory and see the right as the kind of entangled legal form that connects and reproduces even as it holds, and is held by, a range of vibrant things. This entangled right has a role to play in building and rebuilding social infrastructure as its legal form approaches time as a legal norm, as a collection of material resources, and as a felt legal arrangement.

III. THE RIGHT TO CONTINUOUS IMPROVEMENT OF LIVING CONDITIONS AS A MULTIPLE NORMATIVE COMMITMENT TO TIMELINESS

Working with a normative sense of continuous improvement does not have to commit rights reproducers to the kind of continuity we associate with capitalist extractive or liberal progressive social arrangements. Rather, reproducing with rights means that we can search for normative commitments that may be more faded in legal backgrounds or buried in legal processes and select them into the form of continuity that comes to occupy the right. Even if rights labour works on uneven terrain, it is a labour which involves numerous processes of socio-legal translation and carries multiple normative commitments as a result. As I show here, norms of progression, disruption, endurance and punctuation are among those available for legal reproduction of continuity.

When scholars of law and time show how ideals of timeliness come to operate as commitments that drive law along, they are drawing out the more normative implications of time-in-law. Much of this work problematises an understanding of time as a passive medium through which law passes.[46] Rather, they draw out and criticise the assumption that timeliness, particularly the State's timeliness, is measured by reference to linear progression and, what we might term, a modernist will to improve.[47] The critique of linear timeliness has produced a desire for the untimely, as a 'leap into the future',[48] a move which seeks to unlock the disruptive potential of the untimely as that which is not recognisable in the terms of the present. For McNeilly untimeliness offers international human rights an orientation not just to the future, but to the radical possibilities of an unknowable future.[49] This call for untimeliness represents a yearning for disruption and a break with the here-and-now of international human rights, a here-and-now that is constantly retrieving 'the past as a source or rationalisation

[46] See Mawani (n 19); Grabham (n 19); Chowdhury (n 19).

[47] Greenhouse (n 19).

[48] E Grosz, 'The Untimeliness of Feminist Theory' (2010) 18(1) *NORA* 48, 49.

[49] McNeilly (n 21) 818.

of present obligation'.[50] The unknown untimely represents an open uncontaminated future for human rights, one which is 'inherently open to unexpected voices and directions',[51] with their promise of novelty and excitement. This is a move from criticising the flattening, thinning effects of a commitment to linear progression towards valuing the disruptive, unsettling effects of breaking away from the line. The challenge perhaps is to hold onto lines and breaks as one way of understanding the timely, and to welcome the exploratory generative possibilities that may come with turns to unknown times, while recognising the limits of the known and timely as they exist. But other ways of knowing timeliness beyond the linear and disruptive as it moves in and out of international human rights call for recognition.

Parfitt has offered a modular approach to the history of international law as an alternative to the linear, link-in-a-single-'progressive'-chain approach.[52] She suggests that the historical time of international law can be organised into items in a frame, and taking the form of a shadow box assemblage of found objects and images, which may be viewed from different angles. This sense of law's time as a matter of on-going assemblage and retrieval takes us away from the linear norm of progression and instead offers the possibility of holding multiple norms together as we flesh out what the continuous might be. If the normative timeliness of the continuous can be *multiple* then the form of the legal right can become visible less as something flattened and flattening and more as something layered, porous and entangled.

In anticipating how the legal form of the right to continuous improvement of living conditions might be worked into being, it might be fruitful to pay attention to how time multiplies across other legal sources that have an impact on rights forms. Harrington has shown us how 'rival modes of temporality' work through law even as general forms such as precedent or statute seem attached to singular modes.[53] Echoing Mawani's depiction of the common law as enduring in a Bergsonian sense,[54] Harrington notes that precedent is typically seen as producing *enduring* time, while statute produces *punctual* time as the adoption of legislation announces some significant legal change.[55] The sense in which the common law doctrine of precedent conjures up enduring legal time is important since it captures one key dimension of law's perceived contribution to social infrastructure as continuity and stability. Legal order is represented as ongoing and ever present as precedent makes law reproduce

[50] A Orford, 'On International Legal Method' (2013) 1 *London Review of International Law* 166, 175.

[51] McNeilly (n 21) 824.

[52] R Parfitt, *The Process of International Legal Reproduction: Inequality, Historiography, Resistance* (CUP 2019) ch 4.

[53] J Harrington, 'Time as a Dimension of Medical Law' (2012) 20(4) *Medical Law Review* 491, 495; see also Harrington (n 19) ch 4.

[54] Mawani (n 19).

[55] Harrington (n 19) 73–74.

by looking backwards to pick up the legal thread that it will carry forward, seamlessly. But as Chowdhury[56] has shown, the adjudicative temporality of judicial working of precedent sometimes makes the factual context disappear, and often has half-hidden modes of selecting certain factual aspects, modes whose discovery, application and reproduction become part of legal expertise. For my purposes, this shows how the legal reproduction of continuity through common law reasoning is not exclusive, but works with other registers of time. If even the legal forms of common law, with their deep attachment to duration, reproduce with diverse commitments to timeliness, then it becomes even more possible to see a right to continuous improvement of living conditions as having multiple commitments to progressive, disruptive *and* enduring time. If continuous improvement of living conditions is to endure as a legal form, the form itself will need to be sustained by selecting in timely legal knowledge in sustainable ways.

In Harrington's terms, the *punctual* legal timeliness of statute makes a different normative contribution to the relationship between law and time, because it is a legal form which is focused on facilitating legal change and a break with the past. We might think then of punctual timeliness as contributing to an ephemeral legal infrastructure for social reproduction by providing a different kind of legal support, one which builds a legal system from discrete legal pieces that are separate from each other, as they fit together. The punctual time of a statute that is normatively committed to change also operates in a non-exclusive way. The different senses of normative timeliness that operate in, around and beyond linear progression of time and its future and past disruptions, give us a different way to understand the story of rights as legal forms that contribute, unevenly, to social reproduction. Thinking about different norms of timeliness as they actually exist in legal forms may give us a way of working rights with a light normative touch, and one that recognises and selects from co-existing multiple normative commitments.

IV. THE RIGHT TO CONTINUOUS IMPROVEMENT OF LIVING CONDITIONS AS A COLLECTION OF MATERIAL RESOURCES FOR TIME

Time becomes continuous as it is made and remade with material resources. If we identify how material processes and things have the effect of re/making continuous time, then we can trace a form of rights that holds these resources together for replenishing, and makes continuous improvement of living conditions possible. While old materialists tend to draw attention to the processes that generate value for capitalism as they organise time, new materialists are more interested in the energy that circulates through the unfolding of lively objects.

[56] T Chowdhury, 'Temporality and Criminal Law Adjudication's Multiple Pasts' (2017) 38(2) *Liverpool Law Review* 187; see also Chowdhury (n 19).

Even if each school of thought tends to avoid the preoccupations of the other,[57] there is increasing interest in a dialogue between them.[58] From an older materialist perspective, scholars such as Everingham[59] have engaged with a Thompson-inflected Marxist distinction between the clock time of the factory and the rhythmic time of social and environmental life, to draw out the significance of the time spent in domestic labour. She argues that making arrangements for feeding, clothing, and cleaning, involves not just the spending of time on care, but engages a kind of managerial labour which has to juggle multiple schedules and commitments. Co-ordinating the different schedules of household members by sequencing different activities, so that the shopping gets done after work and before picking up the children, is labour which keeps capitalism going by softening the effects of work.[60] While the clock and calendar of the marketplace will often take priority in being accommodated by this domestic juggling, Everingham shows us how domestic labour contributes to social reproduction by making time for other people.

This labour, or 'conscious practical activity',[61] negotiates with the biological and communal rhythms that run through eating and other necessary activities, as well as accommodating the clock time of schedules geared towards market production. By doing the background work of sequencing and synchronising the activities which contribute to social reproduction, domestic labourers generate value by making time available for others. When the activities of domestic labour are commodified and stratified, the material process of juggling can be seen to move across reproduction and production.[62] Activities such as mood management, though once associated with a domestic sphere of unpaid, sacrificial labour, have come to be recognised as occupying a key material role in the paid work-place, even if they get characterised as 'immaterial labour'.[63] A reproductive temporality, which enables, supports and replenishes this juggling of activities, calls for a legal form of continuity that holds things together by sequencing and synchronising.

Social reproduction theory is being revitalised as the pressure on care provision, even before the Covid-19 pandemic, demands renewed engagement with theory which values the withdrawal of labour and care from capitalist arrangements and its redeployment elsewhere.[64] As feminists reinvent the strike so that it also entails more sporadic and less durational withdrawals of care, this social form makes the value of care visible as that which we cannot do without.[65]

[57] Franklin (n 41).
[58] See Hohmann (n 29).
[59] Everingham (n 43).
[60] Adkins (n 44).
[61] Ferguson (n 12) 9–19.
[62] Colen (n 37); Bakker (n 11).
[63] See further Alessandrini (n 11).
[64] C Barbagallo and S Federici, 'Introduction to Care Work and the Commons' (2012) *The Commoner* 15 <https://libcom.org/library/commoner-15-care-work-commons>.
[65] Gago (n 39); Arruzza (n 39).

One of the ongoing tensions in social reproduction theory is the degree to which it is held accountable to Marxist theories of value.[66] Ferguson claims that social reproduction feminists of the autonomist school (such as Federici) have not provided an adequate account of how social reproduction contributes to capitalism if not as commodifiable labour. But this social reproduction theory is giving value to the labour of re-arranging life-making on its own terms, and not on capitalist terms. Federici and Gago draw out the significance of soup kitchens[67] and communal gardens[68] as sites of life-making activity, but life-making activity which is not accountable to capitalist production. Other activities such as mutual aid neighbourhood groups[69] and abortion support networks[70] organise support and sustenance in ways that refuse to be accountable to capitalism. Time which is spent in making more time for others through cooking, cleaning and caring, shows us how social reproduction may generate a non-capitalist care infrastructure. The slow movement, including the version which seeks to re-organise the neo-liberal university,[71] similarly explicitly intervenes into the accelerated paces and intense rhythms of universities, farms, and kitchens in order to claim space for doing otherwise. These thinking activities forge a continuity with the material time that is given value and taken from us through capitalism, but sequence reproductive events so as to achieve a re-arrangement of material time in a way that is sustaining and supportive.

This sense of time as a material resource that is reproductive has a materialist feminist sensibility in wanting to value time spent in making life. Time may be natural but of a nature that is also always social, a social nature that is organised by the operations of the mechanistic clock, but may escape those operations. This time is part of a socio-natural world which shapes and is shaped by labour, including rights labour. Grabham's new materialist understanding of brewing time, shares this understanding of time as being re-arranged and shaped in the social world. Building on Greenhouse, she is interested in displacing the understanding of time as a vacuum through which law passes.[72] Time is not a neutral medium in which we exist, but a product of our (partial) being in the world, a product which may attach to and detach from that world and the beings in it.

For Grabham, the material aspects of temporality are co-produced through the interaction of humans and non-humans, as objects emerge and make their presence felt. She looks at how time is made out of things in interaction, and gives us a way to identify how 'small things' – cells, documents – are brewed into

[66] Ferguson (n 12); Alessandrini (n 11); Bakker (n 11); Mezzadri (n 15).

[67] V Gago, *Feminist International* (Verso 2020) 40; Cavallero and Gago (n 33).

[68] Federici (n 13).

[69] D Spade, *Mutual Aid: Building Solidarity Through This Crisis (and the Next)* (Verso 2021).

[70] D Duffy, 'From Feminist Anarchy to Decolonisation: Understanding Abortion Health Activism Before and After the Repeal of the 8th Amendment' (2020) 124(1) *Feminist Review* 69.

[71] Mountz et al (n 16); Van Marle (n 16).

[72] Grabham (n 19); Greenhouse (n 19); see also Mawani (n 19); Keenan (n 16).

legal time. Stretches of time take on a life of their own, but a life which does not begin or end just with itself. According to this understanding, continuous time can be made run differently depending on how non-human things interact with humans. Grabham is interested in drawing out the significance of the things that are the objects of labour in the co-production processes that she explores, rather than in the labour itself. While her approach foregrounds the co-producing of time that happens as cell loads are counted and drug manuals are read, Grabham pays close attention to the activist lawyering for clients living with HIV/AIDS as the legal process through which time is brewed for clients. This lawyering is socially necessary labour which facilitates the counting of cell loads and the reading of drug manuals for client-led purposes.

The new materialist desire to focus on the liveliness, vitality or eagerness of objects and the vibrancy of matter gives old materialists and social reproduction theorists a way to show how material things take on life. The legal labour of the activist lawyer goes the extra mile to work out ways of counting a client's lifetime by reference to their viral load so that a disabled future comes into legal view for the purposes of making a claim. This going the extra mile is a kind of social reproduction that is done in the site of productive labour. It is a life-making activity that takes us beyond the binary of reproduction and production.[73] The brewing of time with such eager objects could be thought of as a kind of legal reproduction, which joins with the juggling of material activities to make time for others. Both forms of working material time, and juggling lively objects, show us the importance of sequences and synchronicities to the legal labour that reproduces a right to continuous improvement of living conditions.

V. THE RIGHT TO CONTINUOUS IMPROVEMENT OF LIVING CONDITIONS AS A FELT ARRANGEMENT OF TEMPORALITY

Rights are typically figured as a kind of solution to some kinds of exhaustion as they promise a remedy for a lack of housing, or the loss of a loved one. Being made to wait for rights[74] continues the felt experience of being neglected and abandoned by law, a continuity that pulses with intensity as waiting deepens and reiterates the trauma of neglect. As Enright has shown, the delay and denial of legal remedies for historical injustices such as institutional abuse and obstetric violence deal a double blow to survivors.[75] Reproducing with rights surfaces an anticipation that the rights labour will itself be exhausting, an exhaustion which falls unevenly on racialised, gendered and classed bodies, even if moments of joy are shared along the way. Knowing that the system can speed up when matters become characterised as urgent, and the uneven way this happens, becomes

[73] See further Alessandrini (n 11); Bakker (n 11); Mezzadri (n 15).
[74] Young (n 22).
[75] Enright (n 19).

another source of frustration, if sometimes the motivating kind. As different feelings of exhaustion, joy, and urgency run through encounters with law, they generate mood and atmosphere. A sense of curiosity hovers in the legal air. Could a legal form of continuity reproduce an atmosphere of shelter through the deployment of rights' affective and emotional connections?

Scholars of affect have taught us to appreciate the visceral embodied responses which move people and things along and contribute to our sense of 'being in time'.[76] Feelings encompass a multitude. We might want to distinguish 'emotions' or those feelings that work with consciousness, and may even be rehearsed in their expression of anger, frustration and joy, from 'affects' as those feelings that are more visceral and spontaneous in their almost pre-conscious reaction to pain and pleasure. Drawing on Bakhtinian chronotopes, or space-times, Valverde shows us how temporalities are enacted through legal rhetoric as space becomes charged and time 'takes on flesh'.[77] This affective charging means that governance projects at the same spatiotemporal scale might well be distinguished by mood. For Valverde, mood means 'the ready-made combination of affective and aesthetic elements that are widely used'[78] and not idiosyncratic. She gives the example of how the documentation of the effects of climate change on infrastructure will likely have very different governance responses depending on whether the prevailing mood is one of optimistic can-do reformism, or one of apocalyptic fatalism. In thinking about how rights labour might combine different affective and emotional elements through a legal form of continuity, I turn to those who have shown us how practices of rendering likely, expressing concern, and translating travesty make a difference to the felt reproduction of temporality

Grabham's activist lawyers picked over legal technicalities and mundane bits of evidence in order to flesh out temporalities of likelihood, uncertainty, and progression through the generation or modification of affects of pressure and urgency.[79] As lawyers move clients along towards a claim for disability by finding ways to turn HIV-related cell counts and drug regimens into legal evidence of a qualifying illness, a temporality of pressure with its atmosphere of anticipated fearful affects is generated. The use of timely material resources, with their affective dimensions, generates feelings and visceral sensations, which themselves go on to manage the use of timely resources. The feeling of being rushed along, or of being uncertain about the likelihood of something happening, is a sensual arrangement of time. A temporality like likelihood meant that 'more likely than not' became the legal test for a future impairment as a result of living with HIV, a legal test which involved testing for antibodies in the here and now, and reading a likely, not certain, future from test results. Generating

[76] Valverde (n 19) 78.
[77] ibid 33.
[78] ibid 78.
[79] Grabham (n 19) ch 3.

this feeling of something being more likely than not provides a way of managing uncertainty and looking towards the future, without erasing the uncertainty or disconnecting the now from that future. If we understand continuous through the register of likelihood and continuous becomes more continuous than not, then the possibility for continuity to have different rhythms and intensities while keeping going, comes into view.

In Roele's[80] review of Valverde's *Chronotopes*, she talks about how the preambulatory practices of international law play with mood as they conjure up a community that has long existed, while fixing the expression of concern to the moment of creation through the grammatical form of the continuous present. Preambular paragraphs set the mood of the United Nations Security Council's resolutions as they express concern, condemn or, graver still, deplore[81] activities that step outside the zone of acceptability. Roele shows how this chronotope's use of time, space and mood in evoking continuity had the legal effect of providing the UK with support for the otherwise unlawful war against Iraq. Overcoming the fact of a 12-year hiatus between the UNSCR's authorisation of force against Iraq over the invasion of Kuwait in 1990, and the 2002 recognition of a material breach of Iraq's obligations was made more plausible, Roele argues, by relying on the chronotope of the continuous threat as reflected in the grammar and language of the original's preambular paragraph. If the continuity of a concerning threat in a UNSCR can draw on the time, space and mood of its chronotope to render war plausible, perhaps the continuity of an improvement in living conditions can similarly put mood to work in generating a plausible atmosphere of sustainability.

Rights movements, which have laboured long and hard to 'translate a travesty'[82] by getting a right on the legal table give us another perspective on the significance of a mood of continuous concern.[83] Such movements teach us the importance of finding ways to claim the joy of achieving a rights gain while being attentive to the solemnities of simultaneous rights failures.[84] The movement to repeal the eighth amendment and legalise abortion in Ireland was, is, an example of a campaign which achieved a momentous legal change against significant odds and through a popular vote for constitutional amendment after

[80] I Roele, 'Reading UN Security Council Resolutions Through Valverde's Chronotopes' (2015) 23(3) *Feminist Legal Studies* 369.

[81] ibid 372.

[82] Fletcher (n 31).

[83] K Browne and S Calkin, *After Repeal: Rethinking Abortion Politics* (Zed Books 2020); A Carnegie and R Roth, 'From the Grassroots to the Oireachtas: Abortion Law Reform in the Republic of Ireland' (2019) 21(2) *Health and Human Rights Journal* 109; E Drążkiewicz et al, 'Repealing Ireland's Eighth Amendment: Abortion Rights and Democracy Today' (2020) 28 *Social Anthropology* 561; Enright, McNeilly and de Londras (n 10).

[84] F de Londras, '"A Hope Raised and Then Defeated?": The Continuing Harms of Irish Abortion Law' (2020) 124 *Feminist Review* 33; P Rivetti, 'Race, Identity and the State After the Irish Abortion Referendum' (2019) 122 *Feminist Review* 181–88.

35 years of critique. But it was, is, also one moment in an ongoing and continuous struggle for reproductive justice. The moment of repeal may always be fixed to the joyful tears of the 25th May 2018. But it is also intimately connected to all the other moments of continued struggle for repair of the heartache of forced adoptions, concealed burials and bruised reproductive bodies that continue to reverberate and claim legal space.[85] If continuity can work a mood of concern into a justification for war, continuity can also conjure up felt arrangements for joyful rights-making, rights-making which provides shelter from the storm.

VI. CONCLUSION: ENTANGLED LEGAL FORMS

A right to continuous improvement of living conditions needs to stand tall against practices of continuity which extract support and deplete supporters without return. Such a right could be informed by practices of continuity which work with timely norms, materials and feelings. This means figuring out how to hold multiple normative commitments to continuity in place with a light touch, how to arrange time's material resources sustainably through sequencing and synchronising, and how to generate an atmosphere of continuous shelter through rights' felt connections. Engaging with materialist scholarship on social reproduction and legal scholarship on time brings the possibility of putting old and new versions of materialism into conversation with each other, and reproducing temporality anew. This theorising also gives us a way to pick up the critique of binary approaches to timeliness in human rights, engage with different legal senses of time, and use an appreciation for reproductive temporality to flesh out a materialist feminist approach to the legal form of rights.

If the right is to become capable of providing an alternative to the extractive processes associated with commodified forms, the legal form needs to foreground the significance of rights labour which does care work and builds indispensable social infrastructure. Current older materialist approaches to rights forms remain focused on the way that rights extract commodity value, and implement a flattening exchange of apparent commensurables. This critical work is important, and I count myself as a participant in it.[86] But we need a theoretical means of articulating the material value of all the other ways of doing rights including in their vernacular forms. When rights-work is doing sustainable social reproduction and making life liveable, it takes the material legal form beyond the commodity-form since these rights are thick with multiple normative possibilities, layered in their sequencing and synchronous dimensions, and full of felt arrangements.

[85] See M O'Rourke, K O'Donnell and J Smith (eds), 'Towards Transitional Justice in Ireland? Addressing Legacies of Harm' (2020) 55(1&2) *Eire-Ireland: A Special Issue*.

[86] Fletcher (n 17).

Moving from a legal context where time for social reproduction is extracted with little return, to one where it would be replenished, requires the transformation of the form of rights through its occupation. Such occupations could make rights hold multiple matterings of timeliness, and make movement beyond the binaries of un/timely progress possible. They would draw on material processes and things in reproducing continuity, and they would arrange affects and feelings so as to keep life moving along. The unwieldiness and multi-directionality of these rights occupations means that there is always the risk that they fail either by falling apart or by being captured and co-opted. But while they persist they throw out a lifeline which could become a thicker care infrastructure joining and supporting all those engaged in life-making activities.

These entangled legal forms carry their social relations within the right and hold out a lifeline even as they absorb the right-holder into the entangled system. Entangled legal forms of rights offer an alternative to the more conventional materialist approach to rights which sees them as commodity forms facilitating exchange and extraction. Entangled rights share the materialist understanding that such legal forms are likely to overwhelm and exhaust, as entanglements wear rights-holders out and distract from the systems holding the tangles in place. But tangled threads also offer a sheltering lifeline as they provide legal places for critical occupation and legal pathways through the violence. If we can make these faint places and pathways more visible through pulling on the entangled legal form of a right to continuous improvement of living conditions, we can expand the collective work of transforming rights protections into the building blocks of another world. Such a materialist conception of rights as legal forms that reproduce *with* time could work concretely as international human rights, but also in collaboration with constitutional rights, common law rights, statutory rights, and vernacular rights. Reproductive temporalities of entangled rights provide a hopeful but grounded alternative to the idea of rights as either instruments of progress or tools of commodification, an alternative which identifies rights-work as a kind of reproductive labour.

Index

www.ingramcontent.com/pod-product-compliance
Ingram Content Group UK Ltd.
Pitfield, Milton Keynes, MK11 3LW, UK
UKHW020248290926
15470UKWH00002B/803

9 781509 947836